IMAGE FUSION AND ITS APPLICATIONS

Edited by **Yufeng Zheng**

Image Fusion and Its Applications
Edited by Yufeng Zheng

Published by InTech

Janeza Trdine 9, 51000 Rijeka, Croatia

Publishing Process Manager Davor Vidic

Technical Editor Teodora Smiljanic

Cover Designer InTech Design Team

Additional hard copies can be obtained from orders@intechopen.com

Image Fusion and Its Applications, Edited by Yufeng Zheng
p. cm.
ISBN 978-953-307-182-4

For EU product safety concerns:
IN TECH d.o.o., Prolaz Marije Krucifikse Kozulić 3, 51000 Rijeka, Croatia,
info@intechopen.com or visit our website at intechopen.com.

Meet the editor

Yufeng Zheng received his Ph.D. degree in Optical Engineering/Image Processing from Tianjin University (Tianjin, China) in 1997. He is presently with Alcorn State University (Mississippi, USA) as an associate professor. Dr. Zheng serves as a program director of the Computer Network and Information Technology major, as well as the director of Pattern Recognition and Image Analysis Lab. He is the principle investigator on three federal research grants in night vision enhancement, thermal face recognition, and multispectral face recognition. He was the Co-PI on a breast cancer detection research grant. Dr. Zheng holds two patents on glaucoma classification and face recognition, and has published one book, six book chapters, and more than 70 peer-reviewed papers. His research interests include biomedical imaging, pattern recognition, biometrics, information fusion, colorization, bio-inspired image analysis, and computer-aided diagnosis. Dr. Zheng is a Cisco Certified Network Professional (CCNP), a senior member of SPIE, a member of IEEE & Computer Society, as well as a technical reviewer.

Contents

Preface

The purpose of this book is to provide an overview of basic image fusion techniques and an introduction to image fusion applications in variant fields. It is anticipated that this book will be useful for research scientists to capture recent developments and to spark new ideas within the image fusion domain.

Due to its wide applications in remote sensing, medical imaging, and machine vision, image fusion is an active area of research and one that combines multiple imaging modalities into one image to provide more comprehensive information. It is expected that the fused image contains more meaningful information but less distortions or artifacts.

Classical fusion methods include PCA, image pyramids, and wavelet transform. Yet, while the fused image is usually a grayscale image that is good for automatic target recognition, color image fusion, however, is sometimes useful for special applications involving human users such as surveillance applications. Most evaluation methods for image fusion are based on particular applications, and general evaluation metrics for image fusion are highly desired.

This book emphasizes both basic concepts and advanced applications of image fusion. There are 12 chapters in this book. The first chapter gives a survey of image fusion techniques. A wavelet-based image fusion is then introduced in Chapter 2, while color image fusions are presented in next two chapters. A 3D fusion is proposed in Chapter 5. The following chapters are the exhibitions of application-orientated image fusions, which cover the areas of medical applications, remote sensing and GIS, material analysis, face detection, and plant water stress analysis.

The editor would like to sincerely acknowledge the contributions from all chapter authors and their positive interactions to continuously improve the quality of this book. Special thanks are given to Davor Vidic and other InTech staff for their editorial assistance in publishing this book.

Yufeng Zheng
Alcorn State University
USA

1

Survey of Multispectral Image Fusion Techniques in Remote Sensing Applications

Dong Jiang, Dafang Zhuang, Yaohuan Huang and Jinying Fu
*Data Center for Resources and Environmental Sciences,
State Key Lab of Resources and Environmental Information System,
Institute of Geographical Sciences and Natural Resources Research,
Chinese Academy of Sciences, Beijing,
China*

1. Introduction

1.1 Definition of image fusion

With the development of multiple types of biosensors, chemical sensors, and remote sensors on board satellites, more and more data have become available for scientific researches. As the volume of data grows, so does the need to combine data gathered from different sources to extract the most useful information. Different terms such as data interpretation, combined analysis, data integrating have been used. Since early 1990's, "Data fusion" has been adopt and widely used. The definition of data fusion/image fusion varies. For example:

- *Data fusion* is a process dealing with data and information from multiple sources to achieve refined/improved information for decision making (Hall 1992)[1].
- *Image fusion is the combination of two or more different images to form a new image by using a certain algorithm (Genderen and Pohl 1994)[2].*
- *Image fusion is the process of combining information from two or more images of a scene into a single composite image that is more informative and is more suitable for visual perception or computer processing. (Guest editorial of Information Fusion, 2007)[3].*
- *Image fusion is a process of combining images, obtained by sensors of different wavelengths simultaneously viewing of the same scene, to form a composite image. The composite image is formed to improve image content and to make it easier for the user to detect, recognize, and identify targets and increase his situational awareness. 2010. (http://www.hcltech.com/aerospace-and-defense/enhanced-vision-system/).*

Generally speaking, in data fusion the information of a specific scene acquired by two or more sensors at the same time or separate times is combined to generate an interpretation of the scene not obtainable from a single sensor [4]. Image fusion is a component of data fusion when data type is strict to image format (Figure 1). Image fusion is an effective way for optimum utilization of large volumes of image from multiple sources. Multiple image fusion seeks to combine information from multiple sources to achieve inferences that are not feasible from a single sensor or source. It is the aim of image fusion to integrate different data in order to obtain more information than can be derived from each of the single sensor data alone ('1+1=3')[4].

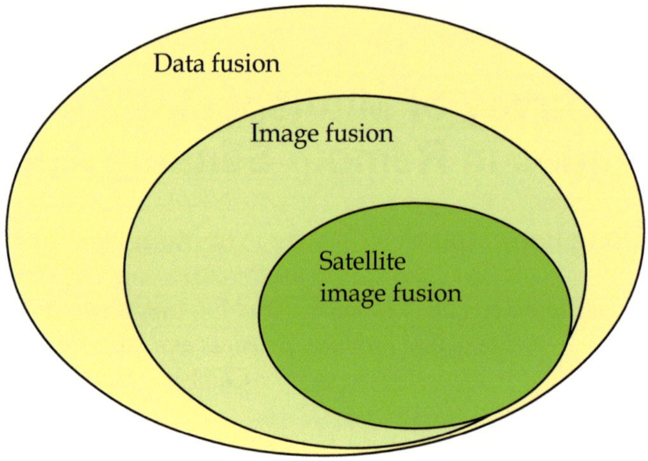

Fig. 1. Illustration of relationship of data fusion and image fusion

The literature on data fusion in computer vision, machine intelligence and medical imaging is substantial, but will not be discussed here. This chapter focused on multi-sensor data fusion in satellite remote sensing area. The fusion of information from sensors with different physical characteristics enhances the understanding of our surroundings and provides the basis for planning, decision-making, and control of autonomous and intelligent machines [1].

1.2 Advance of image fusion

In the past decades it has been applied to different fields such as pattern recognition, visual enhancement, object detection and area surveillance [4].In 1997, Hall and Llinas gave a general introduction to multi-sensor data fusion [1]. Another in-depth review paper on multiple sensors data fusion techniques was published in 1998 [4]. This paper explained the concepts, methods and applications of image fusion as a contribution to multi-sensor integration oriented data processing. Since then, image fusion has received increasing attention. Further scientific papers on image fusion have been published with an emphasis on improving fusion quality and finding more application areas. As a case in point, Simone *et al.* describe three typical applications of data fusion in remote sensing, such as obtaining elevation maps from synthetic aperture radar (SAR) interferometers, the fusion of multi-sensor and multi-temporal images, and the fusion of multi-frequency, multi-polarization and multi-resolution SAR images [5]. Vijayaraj provided the concepts of image fusion in remote sensing applications [6]. Quite a few survey papers have been published recently, providing overviews of the history, developments, and the current state of the art of image fusion in the image-based application fields [7-9], but recent development of multi-sensor data fusion in remote sensing fields has not been discussed in detail. The objectives of this paper are to present an overview of new advances in multi-sensor satellite image fusion, focused on its main application fields in remote sensing.

Data source	Objective	Authors	Time
SPOT HRV & ERS SAR	Automatic registration	Olivier Thepaut, Kidiyo Kpalma, Joseph Ronsin [10]	1994
Hyperspectral image & SAR image	Automatic target cueing	Tamar Peli, Mon Young, Robert Knox, Ken Ellis, Fredrick Bennet[11]	1999
Multifrequency, multipolarization SAR images	Land use classification	G. Simone, A. Farina, F.C. Morabito, S.B. Serpico, L. Bruzzone[5]	2001
Landsat ETM+ Pan band & CBERS-1 multiple spectral data	Methods comparison	Marcia L.S. Aguena, Nelson D.A. Mascarenhas[12]	2006
Landsat ETM+ & MODIS	Urban sprawl monitoring	Ying Lei, Dong Jiang, and Xiaohuan Yang[13]	2007
AVIRIS and LIDAR	Coastal mapping	Ahmed F. Elaksher[14]	2008

Table 1. Examples of application of image fusion

1.3 Categorization of image fusion techniques

Image fusion can be performed roughly at four different stages: signal level, pixel level, feature level, and decision level. Figure 2 illustrates of the concept of the four different fusion levels [15].

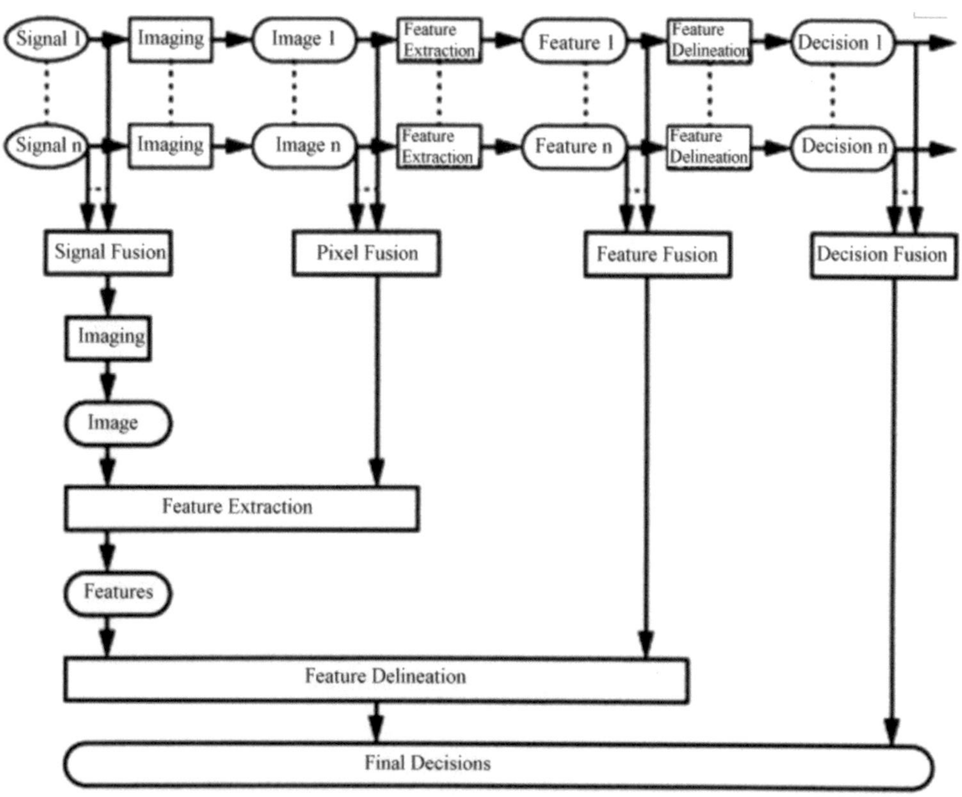

Fig. 2. An overview of categorization of the fusion algorithms [15].

1. Signal level fusion. In signal-based fusion, signals from different sensors are combined to create a new signal with a better signal-to noise ratio than the original signals.
2. Pixel level fusion. Pixel-based fusion is performed on a pixel-by-pixel basis. It generates a fused image in which information associated with each pixel is determined from a set of pixels in source images to improve the performance of image processing tasks such as segmentation
3. Feature level fusion. Feature-based fusion at feature level requires an extraction of objects recognized in the various data sources. It requires the extraction of salient features which are depending on their environment such as pixel intensities, edges or textures. These similar features from input images are fused.
4. Decision-level fusion consists of merging information at a higher level of abstraction, combines the results from multiple algorithms to yield a final fused decision. Input images are processed individually for information extraction. The obtained information is then combined applying decision rules to reinforce common interpretation.

2. Advance in image fusion techniques

During the past two decades, several fusion techniques have been proposed. Most of these techniques are based on the compromise between the desired spatial enhancement and the spectral consistency. Among the hundreds of variations of image fusion techniques, the widely used methods include, but are not limited to, intensity-hue-saturation (IHS), high-pass filtering, principal component analysis (PCA), different arithmetic combination(e.g. Brovey transform), multi-resolution analysis-based methods (e.g. pyramid algorithm, wavelet transform), and Artificial Neural Networks (ANNs), etc. The chapter will provide a general introduction to those selected methods with emphases on new advances in the remote sensing field.

2.1 Traditional fusion algorithms

The PCA transform converts inter-correlated multi-spectral (MS) bands into a new set of uncorrelated components. To do this approach first we must get the principle components of the MS image bands. After that, the first principle component which contains the most information of the image is substituted by the panchromatic image. Finally the inverse principal component transform is done to get the new RGB (Red, Green, and Blue) bands of multi-spectral image from the principle components.

The intensity-hue-saturation (HIS) fusion converts a color MS image from the RGB space into the IHS color space. The HIS components can be defined as follows:

$$I = (R + G + B)/3 \tag{1}$$

$$H = (B-R)/3(I-R),\ S = 1-R/I,\ \text{when } R = \text{Minimum}(R, G, B) \tag{2}$$

$$H = (R-G)/3(I-G),\ S = 1-G/I,\ \text{when } G = \text{Minimum}(R, G, B) \tag{3}$$

$$H = (G-B)/3(I-B),\ S = 1-B/I,\ \text{when } B = \text{Minimum}(R, G, B) \tag{4}$$

Were I,H,S stand for intensity, hue and saturation components respectively; R, G, B mean Red, Green, and Blue bands of multi-spectral image.

Because the intensity (I) band resembles a panchromatic (PAN) image, it is replaced by a high-resolution PAN image in the fusion. A reverse IHS transform is then performed on the PAN together with the hue (H) and saturation (S) bands, resulting in an IHS fused image.

Different arithmetic combinations have been developed for image fusion. The Brovey transform, Synthetic Variable Ratio (SVR), and Ratio Enhancement (RE) techniques are some successful examples [9]. The basic procedure of the Brovey transform first multiplies each MS band by the high resolution PAN band, and then divides each product by the sum of the MS bands. The algorithm is shown in equation (5) .

$$DN_{fused} = DN_{pan} \times DN_{b1} / (DN_{b1} + DN_{b2} + DN_{b3}) \quad (5)$$

Where DN_{fused} means the digital number(DN) of the resulting fused image; DN_{b1}, DN_{b2} and DN_{b3} stand for pixel values of three bands of multiple spectral image; DN_{pan} stand for pixel values of high resolution Pan band.

The SVR and RE techniques are similar, but involve more sophisticated calculations for the MS sum for better fusion quality. For example (Fig.3), Spot 5 Pan band data with spatial resolution of 2.5m of Yanqing city, Beijing China, in 2005 was fused with multiple spectral bands of Landsat TM data (spatial resolution:30m) in 2007. A simple Brovey transformation fusion method was used and the 3rd, 4th, 7th bands of TM were selected for calculation. The building areas remained unchanged from 2005-2007 were grey-purple, meanwhile, the newly established buildings were highlighted (lime color in Figure 3) in the composed image and could be easily detected.

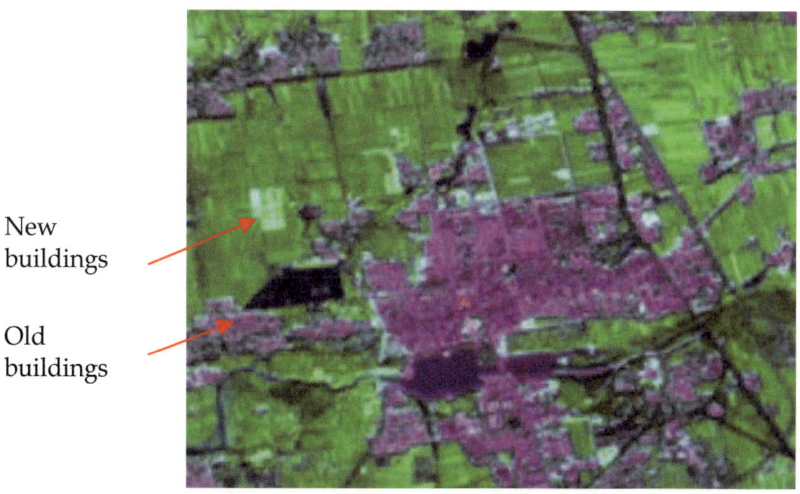

Fig. 3. An example of Brovey transform based image fusion

Traditional fusion algorithms mentioned above have been widely used for relatively simple and time efficient fusion schemes. However, several problems must be considered before their application: (1) These fusion algorithms generate a fused image from a set of pixels in the various sources. These pixel-level fusion methods are very sensitive to registration accuracy, so that co-registration of input images at sub-pixel level is required; (2) One of the main limitations of HIS and Brovey transform is that the number of input multiple spectral bands should be equal or less than three at a time; (3) These image fusion methods are often successful at improves the spatial resolution, however, they tend to distort the original spectral signatures to some extent [16,17]. More recently new techniques such as the wavelet transform seem to reduce the color distortion problem and to keep the statistical parameters invariable.

2.2 Multi-resolution analysis-based methods

Multi-resolution or multi-scale methods, such as pyramid transformation, have been adopted for data fusion since the early 1980s [18]. The Pyramid-based image fusion methods, including Laplacian pyramid transform, were all developed from Gaussian pyramid transform, have been modified and widely used [19,20].

In 1989, Mallat put all the methods of wavelet construction into the framework of functional analysis and described the fast wavelet transform algorithm and general method of constructing wavelet orthonormal basis. On the basis, wavelet transform can be really applied to image decomposition and reconstruction [21-23]. Wavelet transforms provide a framework in which an image is decomposed, with each level corresponding to a coarser resolution band. For example, in the case of fusing a MS image with a high-resolution PAN image with wavelet fusion, the Pan image is first decomposed into a set of low-resolution Pan images with corresponding wavelet coefficients (spatial details) for each level. Individual bands of the MS image then replace the low-resolution Pan at the resolution level of the original MS image. The high resolution spatial detail is injected into each MS band by performing a reverse wavelet transform on each MS band together with the corresponding wavelet coefficients (Figure 4).

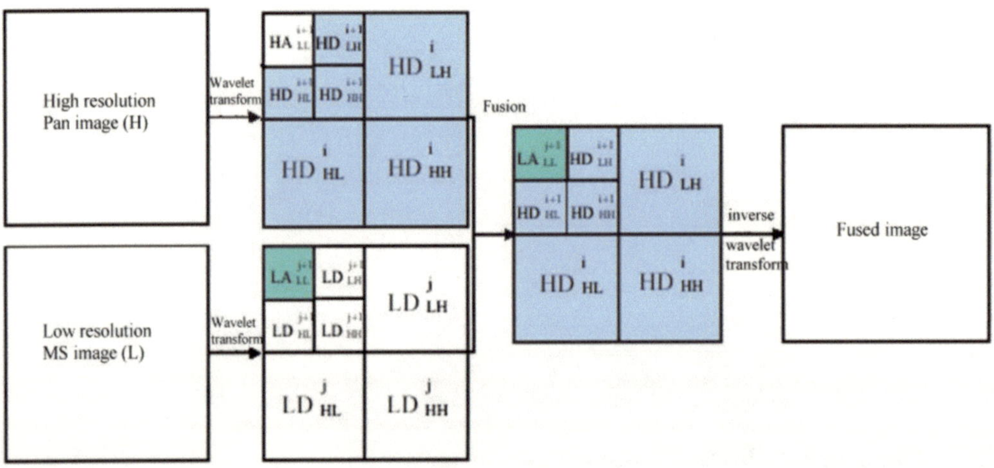

Fig. 4. Generic flowchart of wavelet-based image fusion

In the wavelet-based fusion schemes, detail information is extracted from the PAN image using wavelet transforms and injected into the MS image. Distortion of the spectral information is minimized compared to the standard methods [24]. For example, CBERS multiple spectral image (Figure 5, a) with spatial resolution of 19.2 m of Yiwu City, Zhejiang Province, China, in 2007 was fused with CBERS-HR PAN image(Figure 5, b) with spatial resolution of 2.4 m. Buildings and liner objects (roads,etc.) could be easily identified from fused images(c).

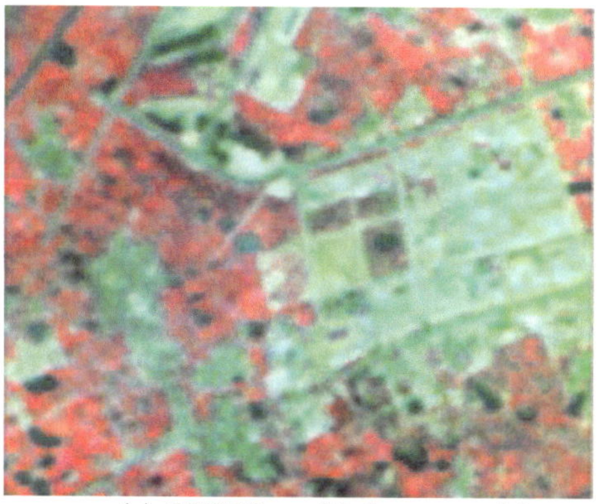

(a) CBERS multiple spectral image

(b) CBERS-HR PAN image

(c) Fused image

Fig. 5. Example of wavelet-based image fusion

In order to achieve optimum fusion results, various wavelet-based fusion schemes had been tested by many researchers. Among these schemes several new concepts/algorithms were presented and discussed. Candes provided a method for fusing SAR and visible MS images using the Curvelet transformation. The method was proven to be more efficient for detecting edge information and denoising than wavelet transformation [25]. Curvelet-based image fusion has been used to merge a Landsat ETM+ panchromatic and multiple-spectral image. The proposed method simultaneously provides richer information in the spatial and spectral domains [26]. Donoho *et al.* presented a flexible multi-resolution, local, and directional image expansion using contour segments, the Contourlet transform, to solve the problem that wavelet transform could not efficiently represent the singularity of linear/curve in image processing [27,28]. Contourlet transform provides flexible number of directions and captures the intrinsic geometrical structure of images.

In general, as a typical feature level fusion method, wavelet-based fusion could evidently perform better than convenient methods in terms of minimizing color distortion and denoising effects. It has been one of the most popular fusion methods in remote sensing in recent years, and has been standard module in many commercial image processing soft wares, such as ENVI, PCI, ERDAS. Problems and limitations associated with them include: (1) Its computational complexity compared to the standard methods; (2) Spectral content of small objects often lost in the fused images; (3) It often requires the user to determine appropriate values for certain parameters (such as thresholds). The development of more sophisticated wavelet-based fusion algorithm (such as Ridgelet, Curvelet, and Contourlet transformation) could improve the performance results, but these new schemes may cause greater complexity in the computation and setting of parameters.

2.3 Artificial neural network based fusion method

Artificial neural networks (ANNs) have proven to be a more powerful and self-adaptive method of pattern recognition as compared to traditional linear and simple nonlinear analyses [29,30]. The ANN-based method employs a nonlinear response function that iterates many times in a special network structure in order to learn the complex functional relationship between input and output training data. The general schematic diagram of the ANN-based image fusion method can be seen in Figure 6.

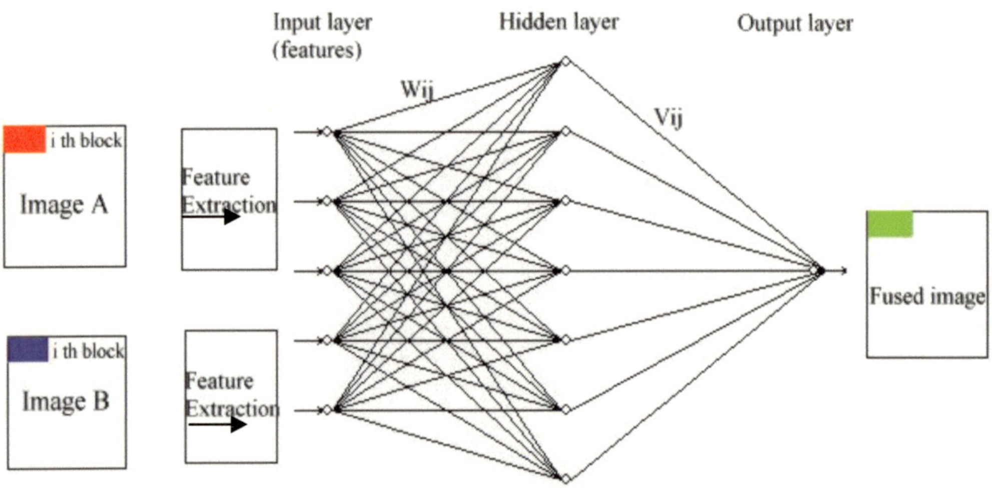

Fig. 6. General schematic diagram of the ANN-based image fusion method.

The input layer has several neurons, which represent the feature factors extracted and normalized from image A and image B. The function of each neuron is a sigmoid function given by:

$$f(x) = \frac{1}{1+e^{-x}} \tag{6}$$

In Figure 6, the hidden layer has several neurons and the output layer has one neuron (or more neuron). The *i*th neuron of the input layer connects with the *j*th neuron of the hidden layer by weight W_{ij}, and weight between the jth neuron of the hidden layer and the *t*th neuron of output layer is V_{jt} (in this case $t = 1$). The weighting function is used to simulate and recognize the response relationship between features of fused image and corresponding feature from original images (image A and image B). The ANN model is given as follows:

$$Y = \frac{1}{1 + \exp\left[-\left(\sum_{j=1}^{q} V_j H_j - \gamma\right)\right]} \tag{7}$$

In equation (7), Y=pixel value of fused image exported from the neural network model, q = number of nodes hidden (q~8 here), V_j=weight between jth hidden node and output node (in this case, there is only one output node), γ=threshold of the output node, H_j=exported values from the jth hidden node:

$$H_j = \frac{1}{1 + \exp\left[-\left(\sum_{i=1}^{n} W_{ij} a_i - \theta_j\right)\right]} \tag{8}$$

Where W_{ij}=weight between ith input node and the jth hidden node, a_i=values of the ith input factor, n=number of nodes of input (n~5 here), θ_j=threshold of the jth hidden node.

As the first step of ANN-based data fusion, two registered images are decomposed into several blocks with size of M and N (Figure 6). Then, features of the corresponding blocks in the two original images are extracted, and the normalized feature vector incident to neural networks can be constructed [31]. The features used here to evaluate the fusion effect are normally spatial frequency, visibility, and edge. The next step is to select some vector samples to train neural networks. An ANN is a universal function approximator that directly adapts to any nonlinear function defined by a representative set of training data. Once trained, the ANN model can remember a functional relationship and be used for further calculations. For these reasons, the ANN concept has been adopted to develop strongly nonlinear models for multiple sensors data fusion. Thomas *et al.* discussed the optimal fusion method of TV and infrared images using artificial neural networks [32]. After that, many neural network models have been proposed for image fusion such as BP, SOFM, and ARTMAP neural networks. BP algorithm has been mostly used. However, the convergence of BP networks is slow and the global minima of the error space may not be always achieved [33]. As an unsupervised network, SOFM network clusters input sample through competitive learning. But the number of output neurons should be set before constructing neural networks model [34]. RBF neural network can approximate objective function at any precise level if enough hidden units are provided. The advantages of RBF network training include no iteration, few training parameters, high training speed, simply process and memory functions [35]. Hong explored the way that using RBF neural networks combined with nearest neighbor clustering method to cluster, and membership weighting is used to fuse. Experiments show this method can obtain the better effect of cluster fusion with proper width parameter [36].

Gail *et al.* used Adaptive Resonance Theory (ART) neural networks to form a new framework for self-organizing information fusion. The ARTMAP neural network can act as a self-organizing expert system to derive hierarchical knowledge structures from inconsistent training data [37]. ARTMAP information fusion resolves apparent contradictions in input pixel labels by assigning output classes to levels in a knowledge hierarchy [38]. Rong *et al.* presented a feature-level image fusion method based on segmentation region and neural networks. The results indicated that this combined fusion scheme was more efficient than that of traditional methods [39].

The ANN-based fusion method exploits the pattern recognition capabilities of artificial neural networks, and meanwhile, the learning capability of neural networks makes it feasible to customize the image fusion process. Many of applications indicated that the ANN-based fusion methods had more advantages than traditional statistical methods, especially when input multiple sensor data were incomplete or with much noises. It is often served as an efficient decision level fusion tools for its self learning characters, especially in land use/land cover classification. In addition, the multiple inputs - multiple outputs framework make it to be a possible approach to fuse high dimension data, such as long-term time-series data or hyper-spectral data.

2.4 Dempster-Shafer evidence theory based fusion method

Dempster-Shafer decision theory is considered a generalized Bayesian theory, used when the data contributing to the determination of the analysis of the images is subject to uncertainty. It allows distributing support for proposition not only to a proposition itself but also to the union of propositions that include it. Huadong Wu et.al. presented a system framework that manages information overlap and resolves conflicts, and the system provides eneralizable architectural support that facilitates sensor fusion [40].
Compared with Bayesian theory, the Dempster-Shafer theory of evidence feels closer to our human perception and reasoning processes. Its capability to assign uncertainty or ignorance to propositions is a powerful tool for dealing with a large range of problems that otherwise would seem intractable [40]. The Dempster-Shafer theory of evidence has been applied on image fusion using SPOT/HRV image and NOAA/AVHRR series. The results show unambiguously the major improvement brought by such a data fusion, and the performance of the proposed method [41]. H. Borotschnig et.al. compared three frameworks for information fusion and view-planning using different uncertainty calculi: probability theory, possibility theory and Dempster-Shafer theory of evidence[42]. The results indicated that Dempster-Shafer decision theory based sensor fusion method will achieve much higher performance improvement, and it provides estimates of imprecision and uncertainty of the information derived from different sources

2.5 Multiple algorithm fusion

As a coin has two sides, each fusion method has its own set of advantages and limitations. The combination of several different fusion schemes has been approved to be the useful strategy which may achieve better quality of results [16,24]. As a case in point, quite a few researchers have focused on incorporating the traditional IHS method into wavelet transforms, since the IHS fusion method performs well spatially while the wavelet methods perform well spectrally [24,41]. However, selection and arrangement of those candidate fusion schemes are quite arbitrary and often depends upon the user's experience. Optimal combining strategy for different fusion algorithms, in another word, 'algorithm fusion' strategy, is thus urgent needed. Further investigations are necessary for the following aspects: 1)Design of a general framework for combination of different fusion approaches; 2) Development of new approaches which can combine aspects of pixel/feature/decision level image fusion; 3)Establishment of automatic quality assessment method for evaluation of fusion results.

3. Applications of image fusion

Remote sensing techniques have proven to be powerful tools for the monitoring of the Earth's surface and atmosphere on a global, regional, and even local scale, by providing important coverage, mapping and classification of land cover features such as vegetation, soil, water and forests [5] The volume of remote sensing images continues to grow at an enormous rate due to advances in sensor technology for both high spatial and temporal resolution systems. Consequently, an increasing quantity of image data from airborne/satellite sensors have been available, including multi-resolution images, multi-temporal images, multi-frequency/spectral bands images and multi-polarization image. The goal of multiple sensor data fusion is to integrate complementary and redundant information to provide a composite image which could be used to better understanding of the entire scene. It has been widely used in many fields of remote sensing, such as object identification, classification, and change detection. The following paragraphs describe the recent achievements of image fusion in more detail.

3.1 Object identification

The feature enhancement capability of image fusion is visually apparent in VIR/VIR combinations that often results in images that are superior to the original data. In order to maximize the amount of information extracted from satellite image data useful products can be found in fused images [4]. A Dempster-Shafer fusion method for urban building detection was presented in 2004. First and last pulse of LIDAR data and multi-spectral aerial imagery were used. Apart from buildings, the classes 'tree', 'grass land', and 'bare soil' are also distinguished by a classification method based on the Dempster-Shafer theory of data fusion. Identification of linear objects such as roads could also benefit from image fusion techniques. An integrated system for automatic road mapping from high-resolution multi-spectral satellite imagery by information fusion was discussed by Xiaoying *et al.* in 2005 [43]. Andrea presents a solution to enhance the spatial resolution of MS images with high-resolution PAN data. The proposed method exploits the undecimated discrete wavelet transform, and the vector multi-scale Kalman filter, which is used to model the injection process of wavelet details. Fusion simulations on spatially degraded data and fusion tests at

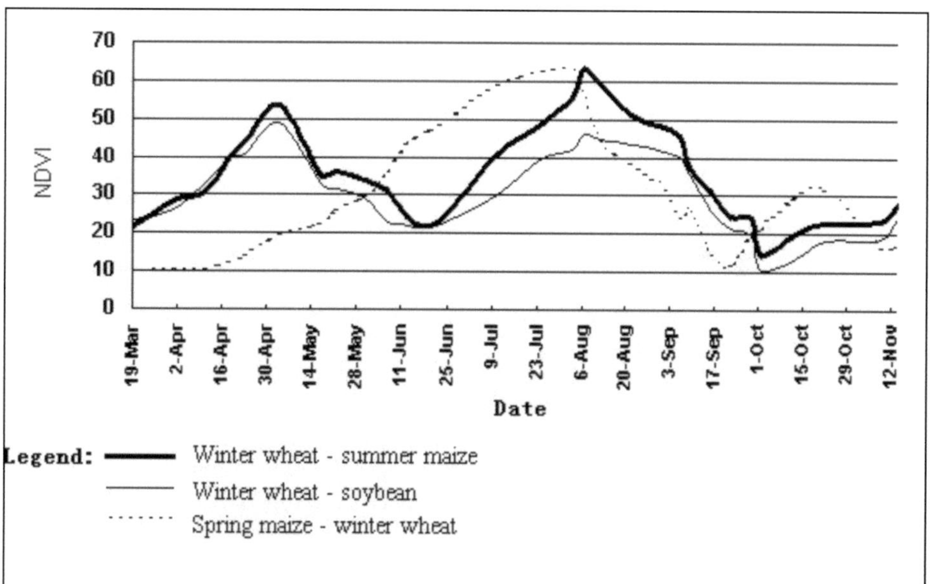

Fig. 7. NDVI profile for different crop types.

the full scale reveal that an accurate and reliable PAN-sharpening is achieved by the proposed method [44]. A case study, which extract crop field using high spatial resolution image and images with high time repetitiveness, was shown as follows.

Identification of crop types from satellite imagery is a challenging task. Here we present an automatic approach for planting areas extracting in mixed planting regions around Beijing city using MODIS data and Landsat TM data. Firstly, planting areas were distinguished with non-crop areas from Landsat TM image using traditional supervised classifier. Then, time series NDVI derived from MODIS data were used for indentifying different types of crops. Because different crop has different growth stage, maximum or minimum value of crop's NDVI is not same and it appears in different date.

After investigating the planting structure of main crops and analyzing the NDVI value of different crop from the middle of March to the middle of November 2002 in Beijing, planting area of winter wheat, spring maize, summer maize and bean in Beijing has been extracted.

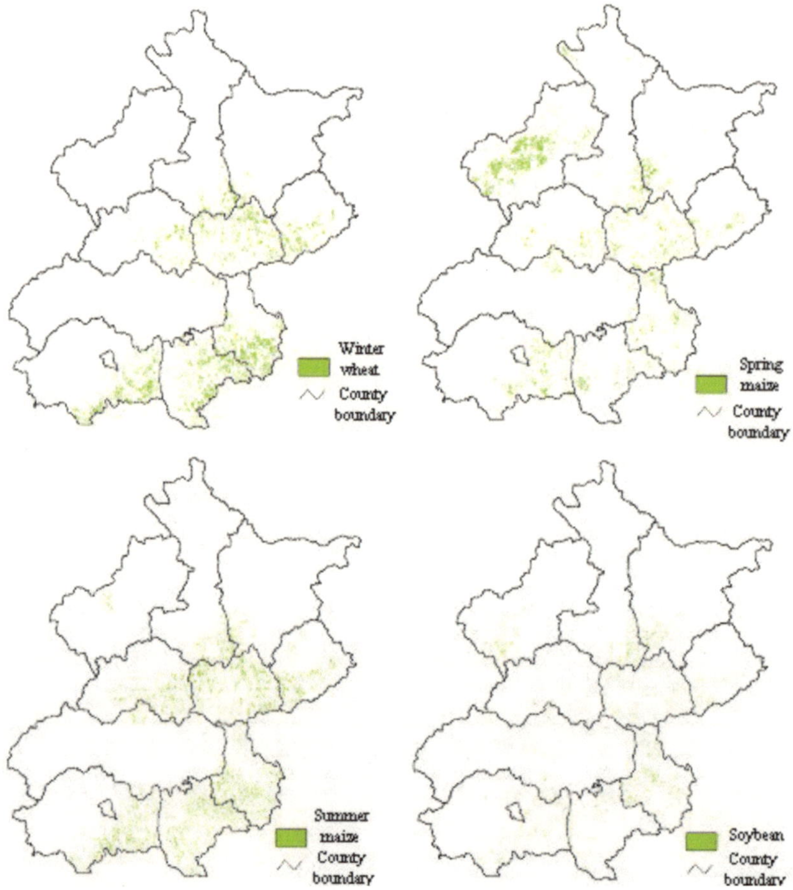

Fig. 8. Spatial distribution of main crops of Beijing in 2002

3.2 Classification

Classification is one of the key tasks of remote sensing applications. The classification accuracy of remote sensing images is improved when multiple source image data are introduced to the processing [4]. Images from microwave and optical sensors offer complementary information that helps in discriminating the different classes. As discussed in the work of Wang *et al.*, a multi-sensor decision level image fusion algorithm based on fuzzy theory are used for classification of each sensor image, and the classification results are fused by the fusion rule. Interesting result was achieved mainly for the high speed classification and efficient fusion of complementary information [45]. Land-use/land-cover classification had been improved using data fusion techniques such as ANN and the Dempster-Shafer theory of evidence. The experimental results show that the excellent performance of classification as compared to existing classification techniques [46, 47]. Image fusion methods will lead to strong advances in land use/land cover classifications by use of the complementary of the data presenting either high spatial resolution or high time repetitiveness.

For example, Indian P5 Panchromatic image(Figure 9 b) with spatial resolution of 2.18 m of Yiwu City, Southeast China, in 2007 was fused with multiple spectral bands of China-Brazil CBERS data (spatial resolution: 19.2m) (Figure 9 a)in 2007. Brovey transformation fusion method was used.

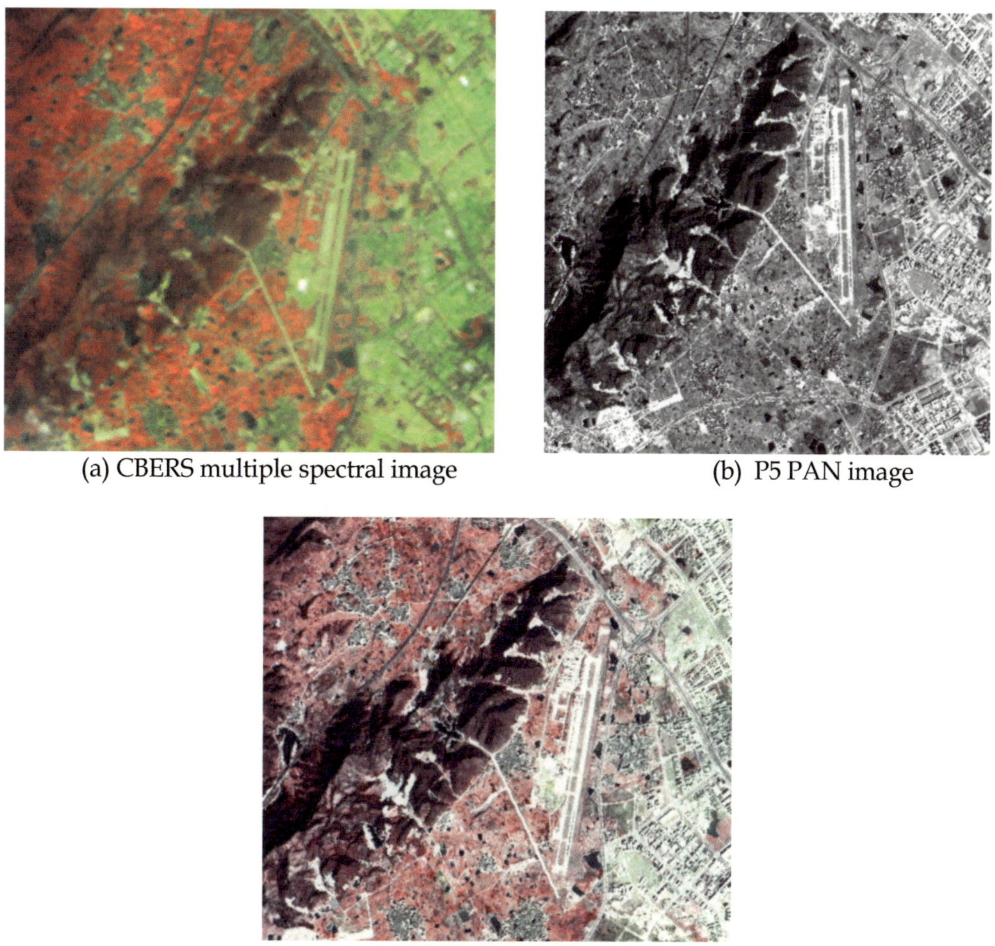

(a) CBERS multiple spectral image

(b) P5 PAN image

(c) Fused image

Fig. 9. Result of image fusion: CBERS MS and P5 PAN

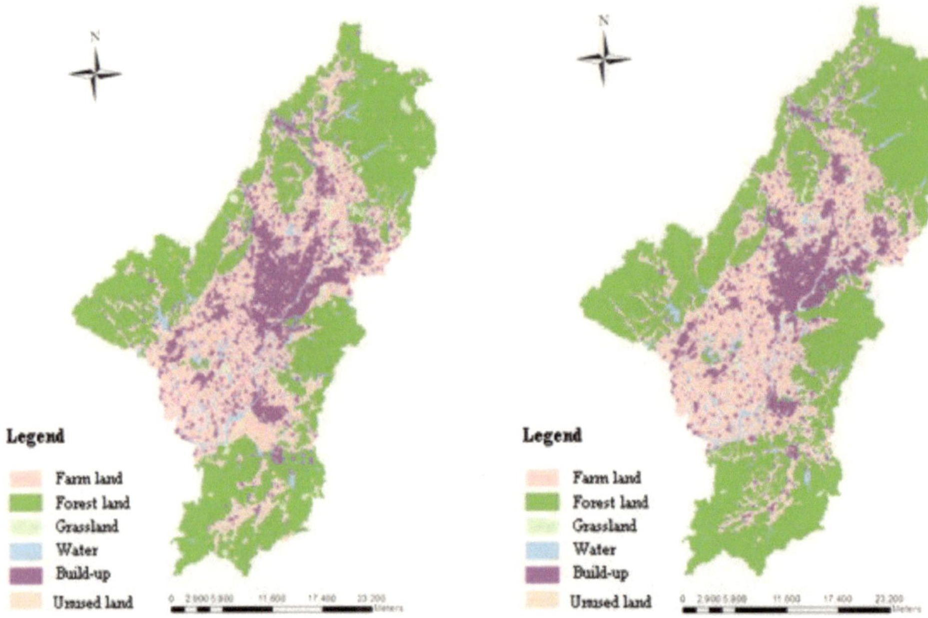

(a) Land use classification based on CBERS multiple spectral image

(b) Land use classification based on fused image

Fig. 10. Land use classification of Yiwu city,2007

Results indicated that the accuracy of residential areas of Yiwu city derived from fused image is much higher than result derived from CBERS multiple spectral image(Table 2).

Data sources	Residential and build-up areas (km^2)	Accuracy (%)
CBERS	86	82
P5 + CBERS	67	92
Statistical data	73	-

Table 2. Comparison of land use classification results

3.3 Change detection

Change detection is the process of identifying differences in the state of an object or phenomenon by observing it at different times [48]. Change detection is an important process in monitoring and managing natural resources and urban development because it provides quantitative analysis of the spatial distribution of the population of interest [49]. Image fusion for change detection takes advantage of the different configurations of the platforms carrying the sensors. The combination of these temporal images in same place enhances information on changes that might have occurred in the area observed. Sensor image data with low temporal resolution and high spatial resolution can be fused with high temporal resolution data to enhance the changing information of certain ground objects. Madhavan *et al.* presented a decision level fusion system that automatically performs fusion of information from multi-spectral, multi-resolution, and multi-temporal high-resolution airborne data for a change-detection analysis. Changes are automatically detected in buildings, building structures, roofs, roof color, industrial structures, smaller vehicles, and vegetation [50]. Two examples of Change detection using image fusion method are shown as follows.

1. Change detection using Landsat ETM+ and MODIS data

Recent study indicated that urban expansion could be efficiently monitored using satellite images with multi-temporal and multi-spatial resolution. For example, Landsat ETM+ Panchromatic image(Figure 4 a) with spatial resolution of 10 m of Chongqing City, Southwest China, in 2000 was fused with daily-received multiple spectral bands of MODIS data (spatial resolution: 250m) (Figure 4 b)in 2006. Brovey transformation fusion method was used. The building areas remained unchanged from 2000 to 2006 were in grey-pink. Meanwhile, the newly established buildings were in dark red color in the composed image (Figure 5) and could be easily identified.

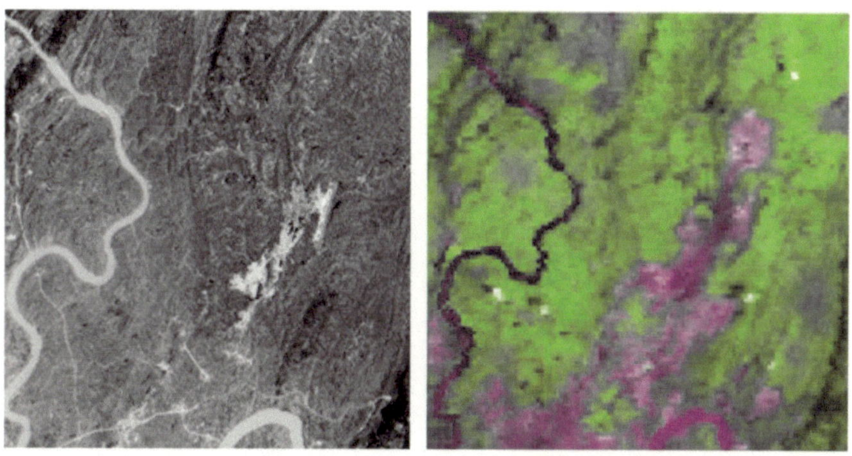

a) ETM image, 2000 b) MODIS image, 2006

Fig. 4. Satellite images of Chongqing City

Fig. 5. Fusion result of multiple sources images of Chongqing City

2. Change detection using former land-cover map and multiple spectral images

In the study area, Qingpu district of Shanghai City,China, two kinds of data were fused for automatic urban sprawl monitoring, which include land cover map, multiple spectral image of Environment Satellites1(HJ-1). The land cover map of 2005 was used as prior knowledge for hyperspace analysis and segment. HJ-1 image of September 22, 2009 were geometric and radiometric corrected. HJ-1 images consisted of four spectral bands, which are three visible bands and a near infra-red (NIR) band.

Two data layers were overlapped and spectral DN value of the five kinds of land cover types were extracted. The results in Figure 3 show that spectral DN value of the five land cover types most clusters in relevant three-dimensional ellipsoid spaces. Outliers were considered pixels with higher probability of changed area. Based on three-dimensional feature space analysis, the map of urban expansion could be achieved.

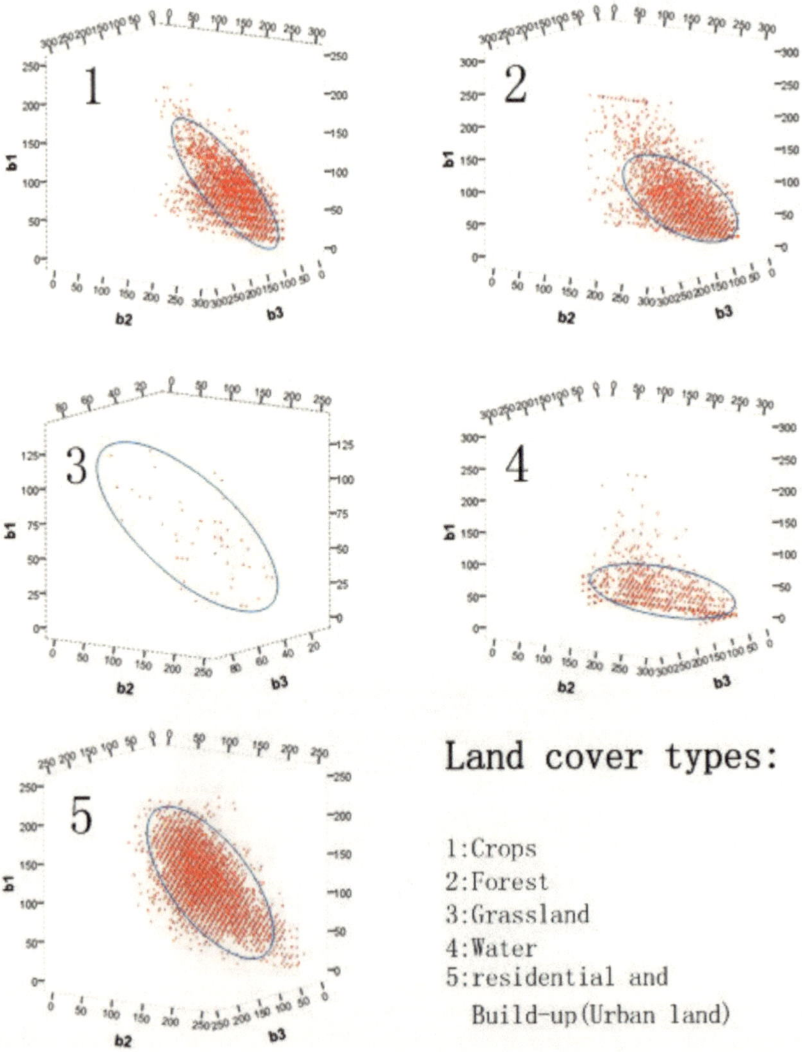

Fig. 6. Three-dimensional scatter plots and feature space of five kinds of land cover types

In recent years, object-oriented processing techniques are becoming more popular, compared to traditional pixel-based image analysis, object-oriented change information is necessary in decision support systems and uncertainty management strategies. An in-depth paper presented by Ruvimbo *et al.* introduced the concept and applications of object-oriented change detection for urban areas [49]. In general, due to the extensive statistical and derived information available with the object-oriented approach, a number of change images can be presented depending on research objectives. In land use and land cover analysis; this level of precision is valuable as analysis at the object level enables linkage with other GIS databases or derived socio-economic attributes.

3.4 Maneuvering target tracking

Maneuvering target tracking is a fundamental task in intelligent vehicle research. With the development of sensor techniques and signal/image processing methods, automatic maneuvering targets tracking can be conducted operationally. Meanwhile, multi-sensor fusion is found to be a powerful tool to improve tracking efficiency. The tracking of objects using distributed multiple sensors is an important field of work in the application areas of autonomous robotics, military applications, and mobile systems [51].

The numbers of the papers focused on the problem of fusion between radar and image sensors in targets tracking have appeared in recent years [52,53]. Fusion of radar data and infrared images could improve the positioning accuracy and narrow down the image working area [54]. Vahdati-khajeh addressed the multi-target tracking problem for maneuvering targets in cluttered environments. The multiple scan joint probabilistic data association (MJPDA) algorithm was used for the sake of overcoming the problem of clutter points and targets which have joint observation [55]. In order to overcome the defects of the current statistical model on non-maneuvering target tracking, Chen *et al.* presented a novel multi-sensor data fusion algorithm for tracking the large-scale maneuvering target. The fuzzy adaptive Kalman filtering algorithm with maneuvering detection was used for large-scale maneuvering target which extracts feature data from Kalman filtering processes to estimate the magnitude and time of maneuvering. The simulation results showed that the tracking system with active and passive radar has higher precision than those with a single sensor for large-scale problems [52].

4. Discussion and conclusions

Multi-sensor image fusion seeks to combine information from different images to obtain more inferences than can be derived from a single sensor. It is widely recognized as an efficient tool for improving overall performance in image based application. The chapter provides a state-of-art of multi-sensor image fusion in the field of remote sensing. Below are some emerging challenges and recommendations.

1. Improvements of fusion algorithms.

Among the hundreds of variations of image fusion techniques, methods which had be widely used including IHS, PCA, Brovey transform, wavelet transform, and Artificial Neural Network (ANN). For methods like HIS, PCA and Brovey transform, which have lower complexity and faster processing time, the most significant problem is color distortion [16]. Wavelet-based schemes perform better than those methods in terms of minimizing color distortion. The development of more sophisticated wavelet-based fusion algorithm (such as Ridgelet, Curvelet, and Contourlet transformation) could evidently improve performance result, but they often cause greater complexity in computation and parameters setting. Another challenge on existing fusion techniques will be the ability for processing hyper-spectral satellite sensor data. Artificial neural network seem to be one possible approach to handle the high dimension nature of hyper-spectral satellite sensor data.

2. Establishment of an automatic quality assessment scheme.

Automatic quality assessment is highly desirable to evaluate the possible benefits of fusion, to determine an optimal setting of parameters for a certain fusion scheme, as well as to compare results obtained with different algorithms [34]. Mathematical methods were used to judge the quality of merged imagery in respect to their improvement of spatial resolution while preserving the spectral content of the data. Statistical indices, such as cross entropy, mean square error, signal-to-noise ratio, have been used for evaluation purpose. While recently a few image fusion quality measures have been proposed, analytical studies of these measures have been lacking. The work of Yin *et al.* focused on one popular mutual information-based quality measure and weighted averaging image fusion [56]. Jiying presented a new metric based on image phase congruency to assess the performance of the image fusion algorithm [57]. However, in general, no automatic solution has been achieved to consistently produce high quality fusion for different data sets [58]. It is expected that the result of fusing data from multiple independent sensors will offer the potential for better performance than can be achieved by either sensor, and will reduce vulnerability to sensor specific countermeasures and deployment factors. We expect that future research will address new performance assessment criteria and automatic quality assessment methods [59].

5. References

Hall, L.; Llinas, J. (1997).An introduction to multisensor data fusion. *Proc. IEEE.* Vol.85,pp. 6-23,ISSN 0018-9219

Genderen, J. L. van, and Pohl, C. Image fusion: Issues, techniques and applications. Intelligent Image Fusion, Proceedings EARSeL Workshop, Strasbourg, France, 11 September 1994, edited by J. L. van Genderen and V. Cappellini (Enschede: ITC), 18- 26.

Guest editorial. (2007). Image fusion: Advances in the state of the art. *Information Fusion.* Vol.8,pp.114-118, ISSN 1566-2535

Pohl, C.; Van Genderen, J.L. (1998). Multisensor image fusion in remote sensing: concepts, methods and applications. *Int. J. Remote Sens.Vol.* 19,pp.823-854, ISSN 0143-1161

Simone, G.; Farina, A.; Morabito, F.C.; Serpico, S.B.; Bruzzone, L. (2002). Image fusion techniques for remote sensing applications. *Information Fusion.* Vol.3,pp.3-15, ISSN 1566-2535

Vijayaraj, V.; Younan, N.; O'Hara, C.(2006). Concepts of image fusion in remote sensing applications. *In Proceedings of IEEE International Conference on Geoscience and Remote Sensing Symposium, Denver, CO, USA, July 31–August 4, 2006,* pp.3798-3801,

Dasarathy, B.V. (2007). A special issue on image fusion: advances in the state of the art. *Information Fusion.* Vol.8,pp.113, ISSN 1566-2535

Smith, M.I.; Heather, J.P. (2005). Review of image fusion technology in 2005. *In Proceedings of Defense and Security Symposium, Orlando, FL, USA, 2005.*

Blum, R.S.; Liu, Z. (2006). Multi-Sensor Image Fusion and Its Applications; special series on Signal Processing and Communications; *CRC Press: Boca Raton, FL, USA*, 2006.

Olivier TheÂpaut, Kidiyo Kpalma, Joseph Ronsin. (2000). Automatic registration of ERS and SPOT multisensory images in a data fusion context. *Forest Ecology and Management* . Vol.123,pp.93-100, ISSN 0378-1127

Tamar Peli, Mon Young, Robert Knox, Kenneth K. Ellis and Frederick Bennett, Feature-level sensor fusion, Proc. SPIE 3719, 1999,332, ISSN 0277-786X

Marcia L.S. Aguena, Nelson D.A. Mascarenhas.(2006). Multispectral image data fusion using POCS and super-resolution. *Computer Vision and Image Understanding* Vol.102,pp.178-187, ISSN 1077-3142

Ying Lei, Dong Jiang, and Xiaohuan Yang .(2007). Appllcation of image fusion in urban expanding detection. *Journal of Geomatics*,vol.32,No.3,pp.4-5,ISSN 1007-3817

Ahmed F. Elaksher. (2008). Fusion of hyperspectral images and lidar-based dems for coastal mapping. *Optics and Lasers in Engineering* Vol.46,pp.493-498,ISSN 0143-8166

Dai, X.; Khorram, S. (1999). Data fusion using artificial neural networks: a case study on multitemporal change analysis. *Comput. Environ. Urban Syst.*Vol.23,pp.19-31,ISSN 0198-9715

Yun, Z. (2004). Understanding image fusion. *Photogram. Eng. Remote Sens.*Vol.6, pp.657-661,ISSN 2702-4292

Pouran, B.(2005). Comparison between four methods for data fusion of ETM+ multispectral and pan images. *Geo-spat. Inf. Sci.*Vol.8,pp.112-122,ISSN

Adelson, C.H.; Bergen, J.R.(1984). Pyramid methods in image processing. *RCA Eng.* Vol.29,pp.33-41,

Miao, Q.G.; Wang, B.S. (2007). Multi-sensor image fusion based on improved laplacian pyramid transform. *Acta Opti. Sin.* Vol.27,pp.1605-1610,ISSN 1424-8220

Xiang, J.; Su, X. (2009). A pyramid transform of image denoising algorithm based on morphology. *Acta Photon. Sin.*Vol.38,pp.89-103,ISSN 1000-7032

Mallat, S.G. (1989). A theory for multiresolution signal decomposition: the wavelet representation. *IEEE Trans. Pattern Anal. Mach. Intell.*Vol.11,pp.674-693,ISSN 0162-8828

Ganzalo, P.; Jesus, M.A. (2004). Wavelet-based image fusion tutorial. *Pattern Recognit.* Vol.37,pp.1855-1872, ISSN 0031-3203

Ma, H.; Jia, C.Y.; Liu, S. (2005).Multisource image fusion based on wavelet transform. *Int. J. Inf. Technol.* Vol. 11,pp 81-91,

Krista, A.; Yun, Z.; Peter, D. (2007).Wavelet based image fusion techniques — An introduction, review and comparison. *ISPRS J. Photogram. Remote Sens.* Vol. 62, pp.249-263.

Candes, E.J.; Donoho, D.L.(2000). Curvelets-A Surprisingly Effective Nonadaptive Representation for Objects with Edges.Curves and Surfcaces; *Vanderbilt University Press: Nashville, TN, USA,* pp.105-120,

Choi, M.; Kim, RY.; Nam, MR. Fusion of multi-spectral and panchromatic satellite images using the Curvelet transform. *IEEE Geosci. Remote Sens. Lett.* Vol.2,pp. 136-140,ISSN 0196-2892

Donoho, M.N.; Vetterli, M. (2002).Contourlets; *Academic Press: New York, NY, USA*, ISSN 0890-5401

Minh, N.; Martin, V.(2005). The contourlet transform: an efficient directional multiresolution image representation. Available online: http://lcavwww.epfl.ch/~vetterli/IP-4-2005.pdf (accessed June 29, 2009).

Louis, E.K.; Yan, X.H. (1998).A neural network model for estimating sea surface chlorophyll and sediments from thematic mapper imagery. *Remote Sens. Environ.Vol.*,66, pp.153-165,ISSN 0034-4257

Dong. J.; Yang, X.; Clinton, N.; Wang, N. (2004).An artificial neural network model for estimating crop yields using remotely sensed information. *Int. J. Remote Sens.* Vol. 25,pp. 1723-1732,ISSN 0143-1161

Shutao, L.; Kwok, J.T.; Yaonan W.(2002). Multifocus image fusion using artificial neural networks. *Pattern Recognit. Lett.* Vol. 23,pp. 985-997.,ISSN 0167-8655

Thomas, F.; Grzegorz, G. (1995).Optimal fusion of TV and infrared images using artificial neural networks. *In Proceedings of Applications and Science of Artificial Neural Networks, Orlando, FL, USA, April 21, 1995*;Vol. 2492, pp.919-925,

Huang, W.; Jing, Z.(2007). Multi-focus image fusion using pulse coupled neural network. *Pattern Recognit. Lett.* Vol. 28,pp.1123-1132, ,ISSN 0167-8655

Wu, Y.; Yang, W. (2003).Image fusion based on wavelet decomposition and evolutionary strategy. *Acta Opt. Sin.* Vol. 23,pp. 671-676, ISSN 0253-2239

Sun, Z.Z.; Fu, K.; Wu, Y.R. (2003).The high-resolution SAR image terrain classification algorithm based on mixed double hint layers RBFN model. *Acta Electron. Sin. Vol.*, 31,pp. 2040-2044,

Zhang, H.; Sun, X.N.; Zhao, L.; Liu, L. (2008).Image fusion algorithm using RBF neural networks. *Lect. Notes Comput. Sci.* Vol. 9,pp. 417-424,

Gail, A.; Siegfried, M.; Ogas, J.(2005). Self-organizing information fusion and hierarchical knowledge discovery- a new framework using ARTMAP neural networks. *Neural Netw.* Vol. 18, pp.287-295,

Gail, A.; Siegfried, M.; Ogas, J.(2004). Self-organizing hierarchical knowledge discovery by an ARTMAP image fusion system. *In Proceedings of the 7th International Conference on Information Fusion, Stockholm, Sweden, 2004*; pp. 235-242, ISSN 1210-0552

Wang, R.; Bu, F.L.; Jin, H.; Li, L.H.(2007). A feature-level image fusion algorithm based on neural networks. *Bioinf. Biomed. Eng.* Vol. 7,pp. 821-824,

Huadong Wu;Mel Siegel; Rainer Stiefelhagen;Jie Yang.(2002).Sensor Fusion Using Dempster-Shafer Theory ，*IEEE Instrumentation and Measurement Technology Conference Anchorage, AK, USA, 21-23 May 2002,*

S. Le Hégarat-Mascle, D. Richard, C. (2003).Ottlé, Multi-scale data fusion using Dempster-Shafer evidence theory, *Integrated Computer-Aided Engineering*, Vol.10,No.1,pp.9-22, ISSN：1875-8835

H. Borotschnig, L. Paletta, M. Prantl, and A. Pinz, Graz. (1999).A Comparison of Probabilistic, Possibilistic and Evidence Theoretic Fusion Schemes for Active Object Recognition. *Computing*. Vol.62,pp. 293–319,

Jin, X.Y.; Davis, C.H. (2005).An integrated system for automatic road mapping from high-resolution multi-spectral satellite imagery by information fusion. *Information Fusion. Vol.* 6, pp.257-273, ISSN 1566-2535

Garzelli, A.; Nencini, F. (2007).Panchromatic sharpening of remote sensing images using a multiscale Kalman filter. *Pattern Recognit.*Vol. 40,pp. 3568-3577, ISSN: 0167-8655

Wu, Y.; Yang, W.(2003). Image fusion based on wavelet decomposition and evolutionary strategy. *Acta Opt. Sin.*Vol. 23,pp.671-676, ISSN 0253-2239

Sarkar, A.; Banerjee, A.; Banerjee, N.; Brahma, S.; Kartikeyan, B.; Chakraborty, M.; Majumder, K.L.(2005). Landcover classification in MRF context using Dempster-Shafer fusion for multisensor imagery. IEEE Trans. *Image Processing* , Vol.14,pp. 634-645, ISSN : 1057-7149

Liu, C.P.; Ma, X.H.; Cui, Z.M.(2007). Multi-source remote sensing image fusion classification based on DS evidence theory. *In Proceedings of Conference on Remote Sensing and GIS Data Processing and Applications; and Innovative Multispectral Technology and Applications, Wuhan, China, November 15–17, 2007;* Vol. 6790, part 2.

Rottensteiner, F.; Trinder, J.; Clode, S.; Kubik, K.; Lovell, B.(2004) .Building detection by Dempster-Shafer fusion of LIDAR data and multispectral aerial imagery. *In Proceedings of the 17th International Conference on Pattern Recognition, Cambridge, UK, August 23–26,2004;* Vol. 2, pp. 339-342, ISSN: 1001-0920

Ruvimbo, G.;Philippe, D.; Morgan, D.(2009). Object-oriented change detection for the city of Harare, Zimbabwe. *Exp. Syst. Appl.*Vol. 36, pp.571-588, ISSN 0013-8703

Madhavan, B.B.; Sasagawa, T.; Tachibana, K.; Mishra, K.(2005). A decision level fusion of ADS-40, TABI and AISA data. *Nippon Shashin Sokuryo Gakkai Gakujutsu Koenkai Happyo Ronbunshu* , Vol.2005, 163-166,

Duncan, S.; Sameer, S. (2006).Approaches to multisensor data fusion in target tracking: a survey. *IEEE Trans. Knowl. Data Eng.* Vol. 18,pp. 1696-1710,ISSN 1041-4347

Chen, Y.; Han, C. (2005).Maneuvering vehicle tracking based on multi-sensor fusion. *Acta Autom. Sin.*Vol. 31, pp.625-630,

Liu, C.; Feng, X.(2006). An algorithm of tracking a maneuvering target based on ir sensor and radar in dense environment. *J. Air Force Eng. Univ.* Vol. 7,pp. 25-28,ISSN 1009-3516

Zheng, M.; Zhao, Y.; Tian, H.(2006). Maneuvering target tracking based on fusion of multi-sensor. *J. Detect. Control,* Vol. 28,pp. 43-45,

Vahdati-khajeh, E. (2004).Tracking the maneuvering targets using multiple scan joint probabilistic data association algorithm. In Proceedings of the Target Tracking 2004: Algorithms and Applications, IEE, Sussex University, Brighton, UK, January 1, 2004. ISSN : 0537-9989

Chen, Y.; Xue, Z.Y.; Blum, R.S. (2008).Theoretical analysis of an information-based quality measure for image fusion. *Information Fusion* ,Vol. 9,pp. 161-175, ISSN 0018-9251

Zhao, J.Y.; Laganiere, R.; Liu, Z.(2006). Image fusion algorithm assessment based on feature measurement. In Proceedings of the 1st International Conference on Innovative Computing, Information and Control, Beijing, China, August 30 – September 1, Vol. 2,pp. 701-704,

Goshtasby, A.; Nikolov, S.(2007). Image fusion: advances in the state of the art. *Information Fusion*. Vol. 8, pp.114-118,ISSN 1566-2535

Dong Jiang;Dafang Zhuang,; Yaohuan Huang; Jingying Fu.(2009). Advances in multi-sensor data fusion: algorithms and applications. *Sensors*, Vol.9,No.10,pp. 7771- 7784,ISSN 1424-8220

2

Image Fusion Based on Integer Lifting Wavelet Transform

Gang Hu[1], Yufeng Zheng[2] and Xin-qiang Qin[1]
[1]*School of Science, Xi'an University of Technology,*
[2]*Dept. of Advanced Technologies, Alcorn State University, Alcorn State, MS*
[1]*China,*
[2]*USA*

1. Introduction

Image fusion can synthesize many images from different sensors into a picture which can meet specific application by using a mathematical model. It can effectively combine the advantages from different images and improve the analysis ability (Blum et al., 2005). In recent years, the image fusion in automatic target recognition, computer vision, remote sensing, robots, medical image processing and military fields has a very wide range of applications.

In many of the image fusion technology, image fusion based on multi-resolution analysis has become the focus of research and hotspot now. At present, the image fusion base on multi-resolution method can be divided into three kinds(Hu et al., 2008): the first kind is based on the pyramid decomposition (such as Laplace pyramid, ratio low-pass pyramid, contrast pyramid, gradient pyramid, etc.). The second type is based on wavelet decomposition, such as discrete wavelet transform(Li &Wu, 2003), wavelet and wavelet packet framework(Wang, 2004), multi-wavelet transform(Zhang et al., 2005), integer wavelet transform(Wang et al., 2008), FILWT (Li&Zhu, 2007), the dual tree complex wavelet transform(Yang et al., 2007), etc. The third type is new multiresolution methods, such as image fusion based on finite ridgelet transform(Liu et al., 2007), curvelet transform(Filippo et al., 2007) and contourlet transform(Li et al., 2008; Yang & Jiao, 2008) .

In the multi-resolution fusion process, the choices of rules and operators is crucial and it will affects the quality of fusion image. However, the existing multiresolution image fusion research and experiment are basically only for two images and the model is only suitable for 2 image fusion. It cannot be generalized to many images (two above) fusion. Although in the multiresolution image fusion methods, the existing simple fusion rules model can be extended to the fusion which has more than two image. Such as average accurate measurement, pixel absolute value choose big quasi measurement and based on region characteristics (such as regional energy, entropy, variance, average gradient, contrast and markov distance etc) choice of large prospective measurement, etc, but the result is very limited.

Therefore, this paper, a novel fusion algorithm of multiple images based on fast integer lifting wavelet transform is proposed. The algorithm may consider both of the result and speed of the fusion with tools of lifting wavelet. Also, according to the image promotion wavelet transformation different sub-bands characteristics, two kinds of new high and low frequency fusion strategy are proposed respectively. The result of experiment shows that this algorithm is not only suitable for rebalanced source image fusion, and can achieve good fusion result and faster fusion speed.

2. Integer lifting wavelet transform

Sweldens from Bell Labs proposed a method which does not depend on the Fourier transform of ascension wavelet construction in the mid 1990's, it not only inherited the time-frequency localization features of traditional wavelet but also has some other advantages(Li&Zhu, 2007; Lin, 2005)

2.1 The basic principle of integer lifting wavelet transform

In spatial domain, the realization process of lifting wavelet transform mainly divided into three steps:

Step 1. Split. Which produce a simple lazy wavelet and it make a original signal $s_{0,n}$ into two smaller each intersection Wavelet subset $s^0_{l,k}$ and $d^0_{l,k}$ according to the parity of split,

$$split(s_{0,n}) = (s^0_{l,k}, d^0_{l,k}) \tag{1}$$

Where the " $split(\cdot)$ "means Split operator.

Step 2. Calculate. The process of calculation mainly means dual lifting. The adjacent even number sequence can be used to predict the odd sequence because of the dependence between the data,

$$d^i_{l,k} = d^{i-1}_{l,k} - predict(s^{i-1}_{l,k}) \tag{2}$$

Step 3. Update. The update is further improving properties of original process of ascension. The basic idea is to find a better son data $s^i_{l,k}$. Make it retain some of the scale character of original subsets $s^0_{l,k}$. The expression of the process of update is:

$$d^i_{l,k} = d^{i-1}_{l,k} - predict(s^{i-1}_{l,k}) \tag{3}$$

Where the " $update(\cdot)$ "means Update operators.

After the finite layer of ascension, even sequences represent wavelet decomposition of low-frequency even after the ascending sequence represents wavelet decomposition low-frequency and odd sequence represents the high coefficients of low-frequency do the same operation can be get to the next level transformation. Ascension wavelet transform inverter change just put the above steps in turn.

2.2 Biorthogonal symmetric 9/7 wavelet decomposition of integer ascension

Any limited long wavelet filters can be decomposed by factor its corresponding mechanism of promoting realization. This paper used for image fusion of ascension wavelet transforms using image processing use most (9/7) filter. If the input signal recorded as $s = \{s_k | k \in Z\}$ .Then the corresponding implementation method for ascension(Lin, 2005):

$$
\begin{aligned}
& s_l^{(0)} = s_{2k},\ d_l^{(0)} = s_{2k+1} \\
& d_l^{(1)} = d_l^{(0)} + [\alpha(s_l^{(0)} + s_{l+1}^{(0)}) + 1/2] \\
& s_l^{(1)} = s_l^{(0)} + [\beta(d_l^{(1)} + d_{l-1}^{(1)}) + 1/2] \\
& d_l^{(2)} = d_l^{(1)} + [\gamma(s_l^{(1)} + s_{l+1}^{(1)}) + 1/2] \\
& s_l^{(2)} = s_l^{(1)} + [\delta(d_l^{(2)} + d_{l-1}^{(2)}) + 1/2] \\
& s_l = s_l^{(2)} / K,\ d_l = K d_l^{(2)}
\end{aligned}
\quad (4)
$$

Where

$$\alpha = -1.586134342,\ \beta = -0.0529801185$$

$$\gamma = 0.8829110762,\ \delta = 0.4435068522$$

$$K = 1.149604398$$

s_l and d_l respectively means the low frequency and high frequency components of the wavelet decomposition. Wavelet decomposition of the low and high component inverter change just pour push back.

For image promotion wavelet transform method usually adopts the ranks of image is hierarchically, first did them ascension decomposition of matrix transformation, again to results obtained by columns are ascending decomposition transform, after a layer decomposes available source image smooth characteristics respectively reflect the low-frequency sub image and reflect brightness mutation and details of the three characteristics in horizontal and vertical direction (in) and diagonal high-frequency sub image. Compared with the traditional based on convolution computation of wavelet transform compared, adopting lifting scheme can wavelet transform the calculation average halved, in two-dimensional image data processing, can reduce about 3/4 computation (Li&Zhu, 2007; Lin, 2005). Figure 1 (Top) shows a two dimensional example of visible light image for integer lifting wavelet decomposition with depth 2 and with depth 3.

3. Image fusion based on integer lifting wavelet transform

Assume $I_1, I_2, \cdots, I_n$ are already registration source image, F is fusion image, J is ascension wavelet decomposition layers; Suppose $C_{J,I1}, C_{J,I2}, \cdots, C_{J,In}$ and $C_{J,F}$ respectively are source image $I_1, I_2, \cdots, I_n$ and the low-frequency sub-image in J of F,Soppose $D_{j,I1}^{\varepsilon}, D_{j,I2}^{\varepsilon}, \cdots, D_{j,In}^{\varepsilon}$ and $D_{j,F}^{\varepsilon}$ respectively are $I_1, I_2, \cdots, I_n$ and F In decomposed scale j $(1 \le j \le J)$ on the direction of high-frequency sub image of ε , $\varepsilon = 1,2,3$ respectively denote vertical, HPOS and diagonal position.

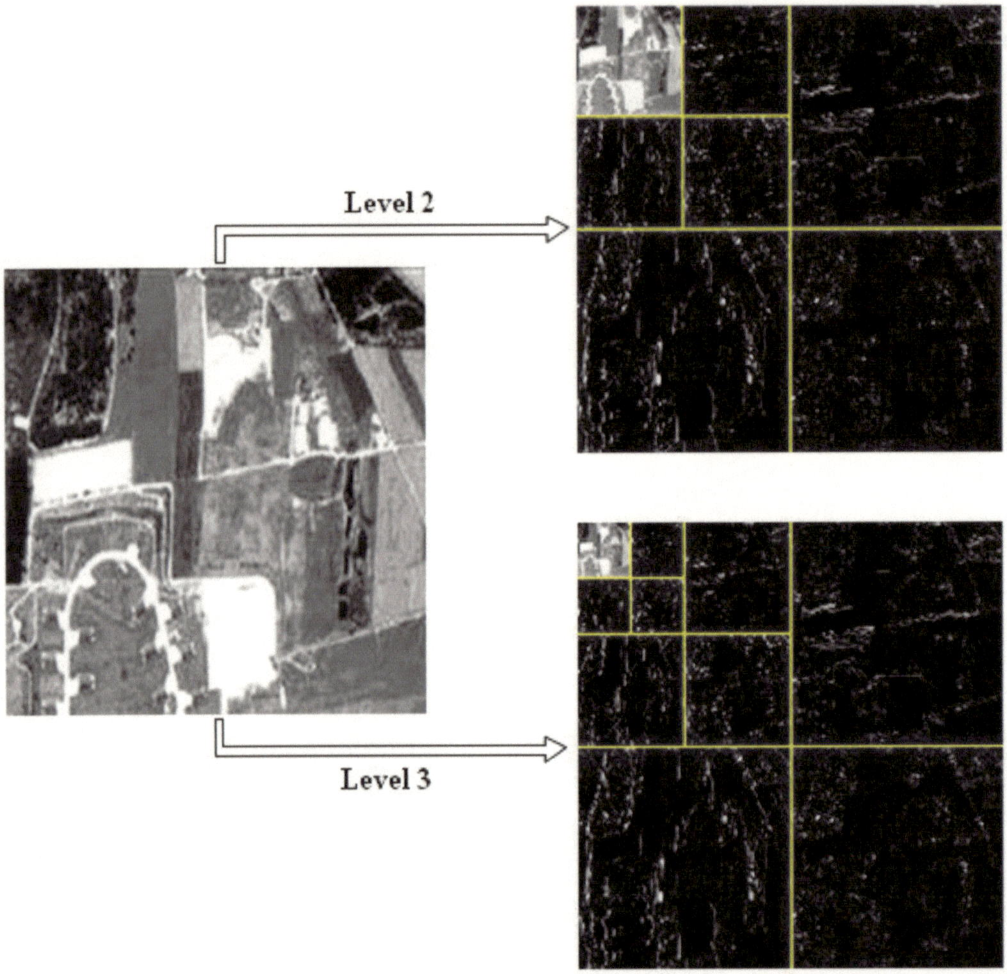

Fig. 1. (Top) Two-dimensional integer lifting wavelet decomposition of visible light image with depth 2. (Bottom) Two-dimensional integer lifting wavelet decomposition of visible light image with depth 3.

3.1 The fusion rules of the low frequency area

First, suppose the ABS of the Low-frequency coefficients of $I_1, I_2, \cdots, I_n$ are $|C_{J,I1}|, |C_{J,I2}|, \cdots, |C_{J,In}|$, normalize for:

$$NC_{J,Ii}(x,y) = |C_{J,Ii}(x,y)| \Big/ \sum_{i=1}^{n} |C_{J,Ii}(x,y)| \quad (i = 1,2,\cdots,n) \tag{5}$$

Then defining a matching degree $MNC_J(x,y)$:

$$\begin{aligned} &MNC_J(x,y) \\ &= \max_{i\in\{1,2,\cdots,n\}} \{NC_{J,Ii}(x,y)\} - \min_{i\in\{1,2,\cdots,n\}} \{NC_{J,Ii}(x,y)\} \end{aligned} \tag{6}$$

Finaly, determine fusion operators. Defining a threshold T (Usually in $0.5 \sim 1$), if $MNC_J(x,y) \geq T$, then

$$C_{J,F}(x,y) = \sum_{i=1}^{n} p_{I_i} C_{J,I_i}(x,y) \tag{7}$$

Where, the complete computational algorithm of weighting coefficient $p_{I_i} (i = 1,2,\cdots,n)$ is detailed in Table 1.

If there have a C_{J,I_k} satisfy:

$$\left|C_{J,I_k}(x,y)\right| = \max_{i \in \{1,2,\cdots,n\}} \left\{ \left|C_{J,I_i}(x,y)\right| \right\}$$

then $p_{I_k} = 1$.

Else

Let $p_{I_i} = 0 \ (i = 1,2,\cdots,n \text{ and } i \neq k)$.

Table 1. The algorithm of computation on weighting coefficient p_{I_i}

If $MNC_J(x,y) < T$, then

$$C_{J,F}(x,y) = \sum_{i=1}^{n} q_{I_i} C_{J,I_i}(x,y) \tag{8}$$

Where, q_{I_i} is the new weighting coefficient defined as:

$$q_{I_i}(x,y) = NC_{J,I_i}(x,y), \quad (i = 1,2,\cdots,n) \tag{9}$$

By above knowable, while the ABS of the low-frequency coefficients have large differences, then choose the coefficient absolute value larger as the fusion of pixels; while the ABS of the low-frequency coefficients have rarely differences, adopt WA-Weighted Average determine fusion of low-frequency coefficients. So the low-frequency fusion rules may, according to the characteristics of the image itself dynamically select the weighted average method and the pixel of absolute value chosen 51, thus namely suitable for low frequence part complementary stronger image, and suitable for low frequence part more similar, complementary poor image.

3.2 The fusion rules of the high frequency area

First, we can compute respectively the local average value variance $MSE^{\varepsilon}_{j,I_i} (i = 1,2,\cdots,n; \varepsilon = 1,2,3; 1 \leq j \leq J)$ of image $I_i \ (i = 1,2,\cdots,n)$ in decomposition scale j and in direction ε :

$$MSE^{\varepsilon}_{j,I_i}(x,y) = \frac{1}{M \times N} \sum_{m=1}^{M} \sum_{n=1}^{N} [D^{\varepsilon}_{j,I_i}(x + m - \frac{M+1}{2}, y + n - \frac{N+1}{2}) - \bar{m}^{\varepsilon}_{j,I_i}(x,y)]^2 \tag{10}$$

Where, M 、N indicate the local area respectively the rows and columns number (General took for odd); $\overline{m}^{\varepsilon}_{j,Ii}(x,y)$ indicate I_i local area to should the average value of a pixel,

$$\overline{m}^{\varepsilon}_{j,Ii}(x,y) = \frac{1}{M\times N}\sum_{m=1}^{M}\sum_{n=1}^{N} D^{\varepsilon}_{j,Ii}(x+m-\frac{M+1}{2}, y+n-\frac{N+1}{2}) \quad (11)$$

By the reason of $MSE^{\varepsilon}_{j,Ii}$ can describe the local area grayscale value variations and dispersion degree. It fully represented parties upward of local significant, and it can reflect the detail of the image and the peripheral information. Mean variance is bigger, the local area grayscale value more change, grey value more scattered. So, this image of local area chooses mean variance as active measure for high frequency components of the fusion.

Then, we can normalize the mean variance $MSE^{\varepsilon}_{j,Ii}$ of the source image in decomposition scale j and in direction ε to be:

$$NMSE^{\varepsilon}_{j,Ii}(x,y) = \frac{MSE^{\varepsilon}_{j,Ii}(x,y)}{\sum_{i=1}^{n} MSE^{\varepsilon}_{j,Ii}(x,y)}, \quad 1\le j\le J;\ \varepsilon=1,2,3;\ i=1,2,\cdots,n \quad (12)$$

Then, a matching degrees is defined as given below.

$$MNMSE^{\varepsilon}_{j}(x,y) = \max_{i\in\{1,2,\cdots,n\}}\left\{NMSE^{\varepsilon}_{j,Ii}(x,y)\right\} - \min_{i\in\{1,2,\cdots,n\}}\left\{NMSE^{\varepsilon}_{j,Ii}(x,y)\right\} \quad (13)$$

At last, a matching degree threshold α is defined that its value usually from 0.5 to 12. If $MNMSE^{\varepsilon}_{j}(x,y)\ge\alpha$, then

$$D^{\varepsilon}_{j,F}(x,y) = \sum_{i=1}^{n} p'_{Ii} D^{\varepsilon}_{j,Ii}(x,y) \quad (14)$$

Where, the complete computational algorithm of weighting coefficient $p'_{Ii}\ (i=1,2,\cdots,n)$ is detailed in Table 2.

If the corresponding mean variance $MSE^{\varepsilon}_{j,Ik}$ of a high coefficients $D^{\varepsilon}_{j,Ik}$ is satisfied with:

$$MSE^{\varepsilon}_{j,Ik}(x,y) = \max_{i\in\{1,2,\cdots,n\}}\left\{MSE^{\varepsilon}_{j,Ii}(x,y)\right\}$$

then $p'_{Ik}=1$.

Else

Let $p'_{Ii}=0\ (i=1,2,\cdots,n \text{ and } i\ne k)$.

Table 2. The algorithm of computation on weighting coefficient p'_{Ii}

Namely select with current processing pixels (x, y) as the center of local area the mean variance biggest image of wavelet coefficients as fusion image and the corresponding wavelet coefficients.

If $MNMSE_j^{\varepsilon}(x,y) < \alpha$, then

$$D_{j,F}^{\varepsilon}(x,y) = \sum_{i=1}^{n} q'_{I_i} D_{j,I_i}^{\varepsilon}(x,y) \quad (15)$$

Where, q'_{I_i} is the new weighting coefficient defined as:

$$q'_{I_i}(x,y) = NMSE_{j,Ii}^{\varepsilon}(x,y) \;\; (i = 1,2,\cdots,n) \quad (16)$$

Above fusion rules indicate, while the high frequency component of source image have large difference in local mean variance in the corresponding decomposition layers and the corresponding on the direction, the corresponding decomposition layers and the corresponding on the direction of local mean variance large difference, that one of the source image contains rich details information, and other source image containing less detailed information, then use local mean variance choose big fusion rules. And in other hands, while the high frequency component of source image have less difference in local mean variance in the corresponding decomposition layers and the corresponding on the direction, it explained that the high coefficients contain rich details information, when using the weighted average fusion operators determine after fusion of wavelet coefficients. This can be clearly retention of image significantly signal details, can avoid again missing information, reduce the noise again at the same time ensure the consistency of the fused image.

3.3 The image fusion scheme

The fusion framework using integer lifting wavelet transform is shown in Fig.2. The approach to image fusion in ILWT (integer lifting wavelet transform) domain is as follows.

Step 1. First, separately two-dimensional integer lifting wavelet decomposition to the source image $I_1, I_2, \cdots, I_n$ which have registration already.

Step 2. Adopt the rules of selection and weighted average low-frequency fusion in section 3.1 for the low-frequency decomposition coefficient; the corresponding low-frequency fused images are obtained by using (7) and (9).

Step 3. For the vertical and horizontal and diagonal three orientations of high-frequency decomposition coefficient, go for high frequency component by using (14) and (15) in section 3.2.

Step 4. Finally, determine the Scale coefficients $C_{J,F}$ and the coefficients $D_{j,F}^{\varepsilon}$ $(1 \le j \le J;\, \varepsilon = 1,2,3)$ for each wavelet of the fused image. By IILWT (inverter integer lifting wavelet transform), we can get the ultimate fusion image.

4. Experimental study and analysis

In order to verify the algorithm the effect and the performance, we focus more on three pieces of the image fusion simulation experiment. At the same time, also with the other two traditional wavelet images fusion algorithms of results were compared. In this algorithm, the source image on three-layer integer ascension wavelet decomposition, take a Form with

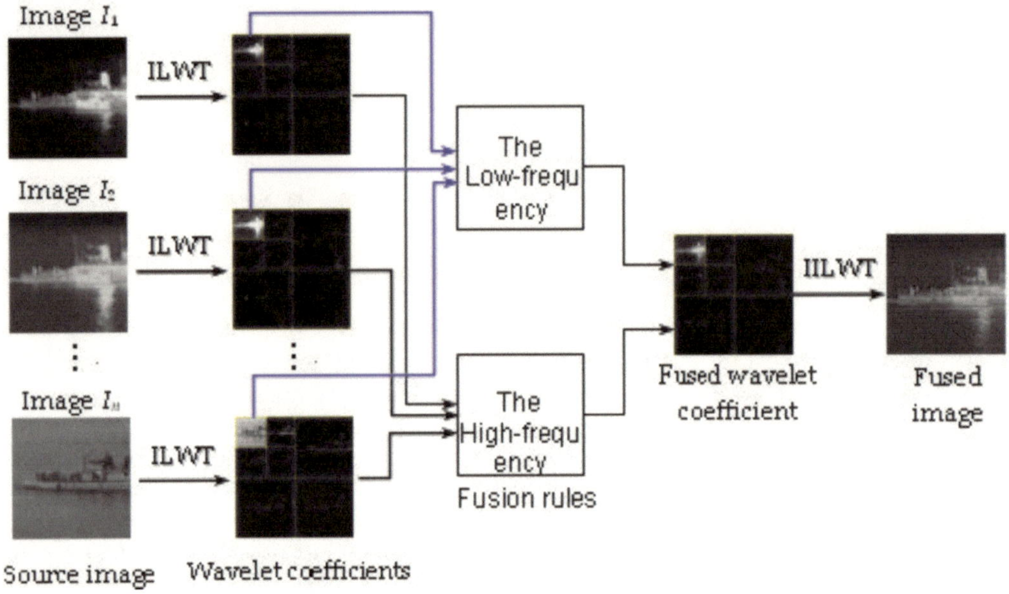

Fig. 2. The fusion framework using integer lifting wavelet transform

size of 3×3 in local region; the fusion when matching degree threshold of high frequency part and the low frequency part are separately took to be 0.75 and 0.65. In order to facilitate comparison, here the other two traditional wavelet image fusion algorithms are recorded as: wavelet fusion algorithm I and wavelet fusion algorithm II. Including, wavelet fusion algorithm of I high and low frequency component used respectively to local variance choose big norms and weighted average of low-frequency fusion rule, and the wavelet fusion algorithm of high and low frequency component II respectively by means of absolute value choose big norms and take an average of low-frequency fusion rules。In addition, the fusion algorithm of wavelet II and algorithm II, choose sym type 4 as multi-scale wavelet image decomposition and reconstruction tool, but wavelet decomposition layers and the local window size of the region and the algorithm are consistent.

Figure 3 gives more focused on three pictures of image fusion result. Figure 3 (a) and (b), (c) respectively, focusing on the left, middle and the right target for fusion source image, its image size are 512 x 512, and with precise registration. Figure 3 (a) from left of target clearer, figure 3 (b) closer to the middle goal on the relatively clear, figure 3 (c) on the right target clearer. Fusion purpose is to get a picture on the left, and right among both imaging of fused image is very clear. Figure 3 (d) and (e), (f) in order to take advantage of this paper fusion algorithm, wavelet and wavelet I fusion algorithm fusion algorithm II income of fused image. From the fusion results can see, three algorithms can get quite satisfactory visual effect, as far as possible to eliminate the source image focusing of the difference, raises the fused image of overall clarity. But by comparing it was evident that this algorithm can income of fused image is best effect, the fused images in all goals are the most clearly. In order to better compare three algorithm is superior, figure 2 shows three algorithm of fused image left, income from middle and right to local area of large PIC。Among them, the figure 4 (a) and (d), (g) respectively derived from the algorithm income of fused image left, and right among local regions; Figure 4 (b), (e), (h) respectively from fusion algorithm I income fused images, left, and right among the local area; Figure 4 (c), (f), (I) respectively from fusion algorithm respectively from II income fused images, left, and right among the local area. By figure 4 can see, this algorithm can income of fused image left, center and local area are very clear right and other details are well reserve. For example, figure 4 (a) the rings and the cord (dotted line box labeled part) was obviously reservation; Figure 4 (d) of saw tooth and background passage clearly visible; Figure 4 (g) the edge of the ball was the most obvious, the most clear, the details to double eliminate the most clean。Relative to character, the algorithm of wavelet fusion algorithm I income of fusion result commercial and wavelet fusion algorithm II income of fusion result worst, such as figure 4 (c) of the rings and the cord almost invisible, figure 4 (f) the zigzag and background line and figure 4 (I), the ball is not too clear.

Subjective visual evaluation can be given fusion result intuitive contrast, but are susceptible to personal experience and visual psychology factors, so need and objective evaluation standard combining comprehensive evaluation. Here we use the information entropy (IE), average gradient (AG) and SD as objective performance evaluation standard(Blum et al., 2005), is presented in table 3 the above image fusion result the objective performance evaluation results. From table 3 shows an objective evaluation index data can see: relative wavelet fusion algorithm, this algorithm can I and II obtained relatively good objective evaluation index and faster fusion. From figure 1 of the fusion results can see, relative to other two kinds of wavelet fusion method, this chapter algorithm of fused image edge details of income is more significant. In order to more intuitive to assess the algorithm can well reserve the detail information source image edge, Laplace operator selects the edge extraction of fused image in figure 3, and the edge extraction of fused image is shown in Fig.5. Obviously the algorithm fusion image edges detail information richer, more conducive to image segmentation, identification further treatment.

5. Conclusion

Based on the analysis of the existing multi-resolution fusion method, based on most current fusion effect good multi-resolution fusion model is only suitable for two images fusion, unable to better suit many images fusion of the problem, this paper proposes an integer ascension based on wavelet transform many images fusion algorithm. For many, blurring the amplitude image fusion experimental simulation and the experimental results were compared and analyzed. Experimental results show that the algorithm not only suitable for real-time rebalanced source image fusion, and can obtain rapid visual effect is better, details, and more abundant of fused image. In addition, can put the image fusion effect the objective evaluation index is introduced to this paper matching degree of the threshold of adaptive selection process, the matching degree of the threshold of optimal choice problem is transformed into an optimal problem, so using intelligent optimization algorithm (such as immune genetic algorithm, cloning algorithm and the particle swarm optimization algorithm, etc) to realize the matching degree of the threshold of optimal choice, it needs to be further research.

(a)The image focused on the left

(b)The image focused on the center

(c)The image focused on the right

(d)Fused image using the proposed menthod

(e) Fused image using algorithm I based on wavelet transform

(f) Fused image using algorithm II based on wavelet transform

Fig. 3. Multi-focus Source image and fusion results

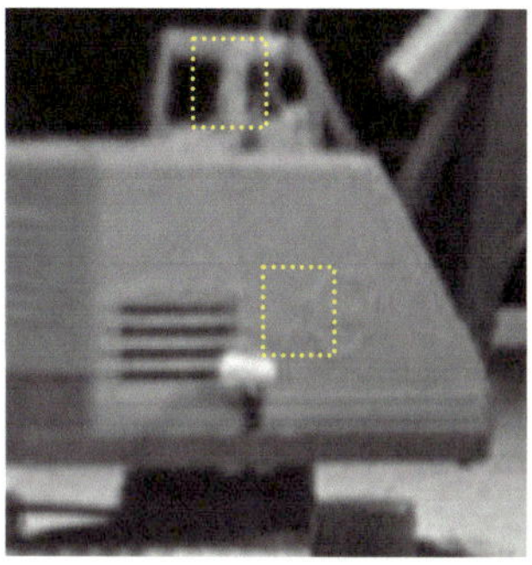

(a)The image taken from the left of Fig.3(d)

(b)The image taken from the left of Fig.3(e)

(c) The image taken from the left of Fig.3(f)

(d) The image taken from the center of Fig.3(d)

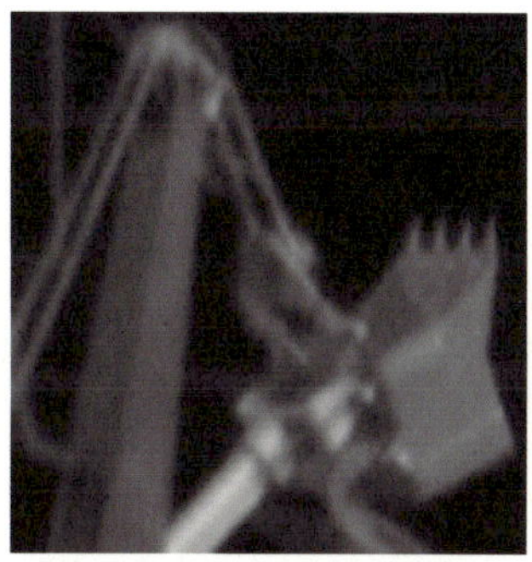

(e) The image taken from the center of Fig.3 (e)

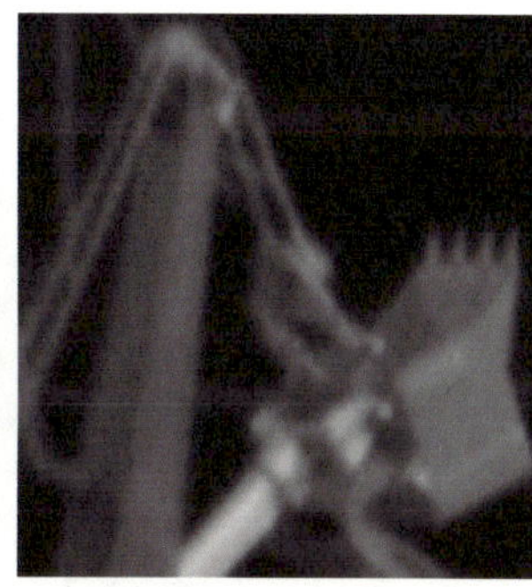

(f) The image taken from the center of Fig.3(f)

(g) The image taken from the right of Fig.3(d)

(h) The image taken from the righ of Fig.3(e)

(i) The image taken from the right of Fig.3(f)

Fig. 4. Zoom-in of image fusion results

Fused image	Objective evaluation index			Fusion time consuming /S
	Entropy	Average gradient	Standard deviation	
Fig.3(d)	7.1869	22.9037	58.1062	1.819
Fig.3(e)	7.1043	20.4479	56.8517	2.358
Fig.3(f)	7.0795	19.0536	55.9841	2.137

Table 3. Performance comparison of difference fusion schemes Multi-focus image

(g) The image taken from the right of Fig.3(d)

(h) The image taken from the righ of Fig.3(e)

(i) The image taken from the right of Fig.3(f)

Fig. 5. Edge extraction from image fusion results

6. References

Blum R S, Xue Z&Z Zhang, M. (2005). *Multi-sensor image fusion and its applications*, InTech, ISBN 0-8493-3417-9, Boca Raton, USA

Hu G, Liu Z&Xu X. (2008). Research and Recent Revelopment of ImageFusion at Pixel Level. *Application Research of Computers*, Vol.25, No.3, (March 2008), pp. 650-655, (in Chinese)

Li M&Wu S, J. (2003).A New Image Fusion Algorithm Based on Wavelet Transform, *Proceedings of International Conference on Computational Intelligence and Multimedia Applications*, pp. 154-159 , Phoenix, Arizona, USA, May 17-22, 2003

Wang H. (2004).A New Multiwavelet-based Approach to Image Fusion. *Journal of Mathematical Imaging and Vision*, Vol.21, No.3, (March 2004), pp. 177-192.

Zhang X, Pan Q&Zhao Y.(2005). Image Fusion Method Based on Stationary Multi-wavelet Transform . *Journal of Optoelectronics Laser*, Vol.16, No.5, (May 2005), pp. 605-609.

Li W&Zhu X.(2007).An Image Fusion Algorithm Based on Second Generation Wavelet Transform and Its Performance Evaluation. *Acta Aotomatica Sinica*, Vol.33, No.8, (August 2007), pp. 817-822.

Yang X, Jin H& Jiao L. (2007). Adaptive Image Fusion Algorithm for Infrared and Visible Light Images Based on DT-CWT. *Journal of InfraredMillim.Waves*, Vol.26, No.6, (June 2007), pp. 419-424.

Wang Z, Yu X&Zhang L.B. (2008).A Remote Sensing Image Fusion Algorithm Based on Integer Wavelet Transform[J]. *Journal of Optoelectronics Laser*, Vol.19, No.11, (November 2008), pp. 1542-1545.

Filippo N, Andrea G&Stefano B. (2007). Remote Sensing Image Fusion Using the Curvelet Transform. *Information Fusion*, Vol.8, 2007, pp. 143-156.

Liu K, Guo L&Li H.H. (2007). Image Fusion Based on Finite Ridgelet Transform [J]. *Journal of Optoelectronics Laser* , Vol.18, No.11, (November 2008), pp. 1382-1385.

Yang L, Guo B.L.& Ni W.(2008).Multimodality Medical Image Fusion Based on Multiscale Geometric Analysis of Contourlet Transform[J]. *Neurocomputing*, Vol.72, 2008, pp. 203-211.

Yang X.H. &Jiao L.C.(2008).Fusion Algorithm for Remote Sensing Images Based on Nonsubsampled Contourlet Transform[J]. *Acta Automatica Sinica*, Vol.34, No.3, (March 2008), pp. 274-281.

Lin Z.X, D. (2005). Study on Algorithms of Wavelet Transform for Image Processing Via Lifting Scheme, In: *wavelet technology*, 47-68, S.D. Xidian University, Xi'an, China

3

An Exploration of Color Fusion with Multispectral Images for Night Vision Enhancement

Yufeng Zheng
Alcorn State University
USA

1. Introduction

Multispectral images usually present complimentary information such as visual-band imagery and infrared imagery (near infrared or long wave infrared). There are strong evidences that the fused multispectral imagery (in gray scales) increases the reliability of interpretation (Rogers & Wood, 1990; Essock et al., 2001) and thus good for machine analysis (computer vision); whereas the colorized multispectral imagery improves observer performance and reaction times (Toet et al. 1997; Varga, 1999; Waxman et al., 1996) and thus good for visual analysis (human vision).

Imagine a nighttime navigation task that may be executed by an aircraft equipped with a multispectral imaging system. Analyzing the synthesized (fused or colorized) multisensory image will be more informative and more efficient than simultaneously monitoring multispectral images such as visual-band imagery (e.g., image intensified, II), near infrared (NIR) imagery, and infrared (IR) imagery, which may be displayed either on several split panels on a big screen or on several small screens. The focus of this chapter is how to synthesize a color presentation of multispectral images in order to enhance night vision. It is anticipated that the successful applications of night vision colorization techniques will lead to improved performance of remote sensing, nighttime navigation, target detection, and situational awareness. This colorization approaches mentioned here involve two main techniques, image fusion and colorization, which are briefly reviewed as follows, respectively.

Image fusion combines multiple-source imagery by integrating complementary data in order to enhance the information apparent in the respective source images, as well as to increase the reliability of interpretation. This results in more accurate data (Keys et al., 1990) and increased utility (Rogers & Wood, 1990; Essock et al., 1999). In addition, it has been reported that fused data provides far more robust aspects of operational performance such as increased confidence, reduced ambiguity, improved reliability and improved classification (Rogers & Wood, 1990; Essock et al., 2001). A general framework of image fusion can be found in Reference (Pohl & Genderen, 1998). The discussions of image fusion here are limited to *pixel-level fusion*.

Two commonly used fusion methods are the discrete wavelet transform (DWT) (Pu & Ni, 2000; Nunez et al., 1999) and various pyramids (such as Laplacian, contrast, gradient, and morphological pyramids) (Jahard et al., 1997; Ajazzi et al., 1998), which both are *multiscale fusion* methods. Recently, an advanced wavelet transform (*a*DWT) method (Zheng et al., 2004) has been proposed, which incorporates principal component analysis (PCA) and morphological processing into a regular DWT fusion algorithm. The *a*DWT method can produce a better fused image in comparison with pyramid methods and regular DWT methods. Image fusion is a necessary step for the following color fusion and colorization methods.

On the other hand, a *night vision colorization* technique can produce colorized imagery with a naturalistic and stable color appearance by processing multispectral night-vision imagery. Although appropriately false-colored imagery is often helpful for human observers in improving their performance on scene classification, and reaction time tasks (Essock et al., 1999; Waxman et al., 1996), inappropriate color mappings can also be detrimental to human performance (Toet & IJspeert, 2001; Varga, 1999). A possible reason is lack of physical color constancy (Varga, 1999). Another drawback with false coloring is that observers need specific training with each of the unnatural false color schemes so that they can correctly and quickly recognize objects; whereas with colorized nighttime imagery rendered with natural colors, users should be able to readily recognize and identify objects.

Toet (2003) proposed a night vision (NV) colorization method that transfers the natural color characteristics of daylight imagery into multispectral NV images. Essentially, Toet's natural color-mapping method matches the statistical properties (i.e., mean and standard deviation) of the NV imagery to that of a natural daylight color image (manually selected as the "target" color distribution). However, this color-mapping method colorizes the image regardless of scene content, and thus the accuracy of the coloring is very much dependent on how well the target and source images are matched. Specifically, Toet's method weights the local regions of the source image by the "global" color statistics of the target image, and thus will yield less naturalistic results (e.g., biased colors) for images containing regions that differ significantly in their colored content. Another concern of Toet's "*global-coloring*" method is that the scene matching between the source and target is performed manually. To address the aforementioned bias problem in global coloring, Zheng et al. (2005; 2008) presented a "*local coloring*" method that can colorize the NV images more like daylight imagery. The local-coloring method will render the multispectral images with natural colors segment by segment (i.e., "segmentation-based"), and also provide automatic association between the source and target images (i.e., avoiding the manual scene-matching in global coloring). This local coloring method is also referred to as "segmentation-based" colorization in contrast with "channel-based" color fusion introduced later.

In this chapter, we will discuss and explore how to enhance human night vision by presenting a color image with a set of multispectral images. Certainly, a color presentation of multispectral night vision images can provide a better visual result for human users. We would prefer the color images resembling natural daylight pictures that we are used to; meanwhile the coloring process shall be efficient enough ideally for real time applications. A segmentation-based colorization procedure is first reviewed, and a channel-based color fusion is then introduced. The remainder of this chapter is organized as follows. The multispectral image preprocessing, registration and fusion are described in Section 2. Next, the *segmentation-based colorization* method is completely discussed in Section 3. Then, a new *channel-based color fusion* method is introduced in Section 4. The experiments and discussions are given in Section 5. Conclusions are finally drawn in Section 6.

2. Multispectral image preprocessing

The multispectral images that we acquired include visible (RGB color) images, image intensified (II, enhanced visible) images, near infrared (NIR; spectral range: 0.9~1.7 μm) images, and long-wave infrared (LWIR; spectral range: 7.5~13 μm) images. Before performing multispectral colorization, image preprocessing, image registration, and image fusion are required.

2.1 Standard preprocessing

Standard image preprocessing such as *denoising*, *normalization* and *enhancement* can favorite the following processes, i.e., image registration, fusion, and colorization. The noise in digital images may be caused by imperfection of imaging sensors, scene contents in FOV (field of view, extremely cold or hot objects for infrared imaging), environment (atmosphere) disturbance, or poor illumination (for visible band imaging). Noise can be reduced according to the nature of the noise sources that depends on a particular application. For example, pepper-and-salt noise can be removed by a median filter; periodic noise may be reduced by a designed frequency filter in Fourier transformed domain; and a random noise can be suppressed by a Gaussian filter or a nonlinear diffusion filter.

Night-vision images (NIR and LWIR) were acquired under different background and conditions, which may cause images to have different background (brightness) and contrast (dynamic range). We employed a general *image normalization* (also called *contrast stretching*) to standardize all multispectral images.

$$\mathbf{I}_N = (\mathbf{I}_0 - I_{\mathrm{Min}})\frac{L_{\mathrm{Max}} - L_{\mathrm{Min}}}{I_{\mathrm{Max}} - I_{\mathrm{Min}}} + L_{\mathrm{Min}} \tag{1}$$

where $\mathbf{I}_N$ is the normalized image, $\mathbf{I}_0$ is the original image; I_{Min} and I_{Max} are the maximum and minimum pixel values in $\mathbf{I}_0$, respectively; L_{Min} and L_{Max} are the expected maximum and minimum pixel values in $\mathbf{I}_N$, which normally equal 0 and 1, respectively. After image normalization, $\mathbf{I}_N \in [0, 1]$.

The image contrasts of near infrared (NIR) images are significantly affected by illumination conditions. Nonlinear enhancement like histogram equalization or histogram matching usually increases noises while enhancing a NIR image. A linear enhancement such as *piecewise contrast stretching* is preferred. Eq. (1) is still applicable but just applied within each piece of intensity interval. For example, given $[I_{Min}, I_{Max}] = [0, 0.8]$, and $[L_{Min}, L_{Max}] = [0, 1.0]$, after piecewise contrast stretching, the pixels within [0, 0.8] will be linearly scaled to [0, 1.0], while those pixels originally within (0.8, 1.0] are unchanged. To simply writing, this transform can be notated as $\mathrm{S}_{[0,0.8]}^{[0,1.0]}$ thereafter.

2.2 Image registration

Image registration is a required preprocess by image fusion and image colorization. In general, image registration aligns multiple images by performing *affine transformations* that allows *translation*, *rotation*, and *scaling*. Similarity metrics are used to decide the optimized transformation parameters. *Normalized mutual information* (NMI) turns out to be the robust metric for noisy and multi-modality image registration (Hill & Batchelor, 2001). The computation complexity increases with the number of degrees of freedom. For 2D image registration, Fourier-Mellin transform (FMT, Chen et al., 1994) is much faster than NMI-based registration, but FMT is sensitive to noise. For multispectral night-vision image registration, we utilize two registration algorithms, i.e., use the FMT method for translation registration, and then use the NMI-based method for scaling and rotation registration.

We used the FMT method only accounting for translation alignment although it can be alternated for scaling and rotation (but not reliable). The image alignment by scaling and rotation is accomplished with affine transforms using NMI metric. The image transforming parameters can be estimated by maximizing the NMI value. Calculation of NMI and interpolation of transforming (e.g., fractional scaling) are quite time consuming. However, the searching spaces of parameters (for scaling and rotation) are small because two cameras are sitting on the same fixture by turns and aiming at the same target. This expedites the registration process on the other hand.

Different FOV of multispectral images is another challenge for image registration. For example, FLIR SC620 camera (used in our experiments) is a two-band imaging device with a LWIR camera (640×480 pixels; FOV: 24°) and a built-in visible camera (2048×1536 pixels; FOV: 32°). Before registration with LWIR image cropping the visible image is desired. To find the *matched block* (region) of LWIR on the visible image, (i) scan the visible image block by block with step movement 5~10 pixels (Left to Right, Top to Bottom), where the block image is of size (960×720, estimated according to view angles); (ii) compute the NMI between the scanning block (on the visible image) and LWIR; (iii) select the scanning block (region) with maximal NMI as the matched block for the following registration. The framework of general image registration was documented elsewhere (Brown, 1992), and the details of our proposed course-to-fine registration method will be discussed in a separate paper.

2.3 Image fusion

Image fusion is a necessary step for the color fusion discussed in this chapter. Image fusion serves to combine multiple-source imagery using advanced image processing techniques. Laplacian pyramid and DWT-based fusion methods are briefly reviewed, while the details of image fusion were documented elsewhere (Zheng et al., 2005).

The Laplacian pyramid was first introduced as a model for binocular fusion in human stereo vision (Burt & Adelson, 1985), where the implementation used a Laplacian pyramid and a maximum selection rule at each point of the pyramid transform. Essentially, the procedure involves a set of band-pass copies of an image is referred to as the Laplacian pyramid due to its similarity to a Laplacian operator. Each level of the Laplacian pyramid is recursively constructed from its lower level by applying the following four basic steps: blurring (low-pass filtering); sub-sampling (reduce size); interpolation (expand); and differencing (to subtract two images pixel by pixel) (Burt & Adelson, 1983). In the Laplacian pyramid, the lowest level of the pyramid is constructed from the original image.

The regular DWT method is a multi-scale analysis method. In a regular DWT fusion process, DWT coefficients from two input images are fused pixel-by-pixel by choosing the average of the *approximation* coefficients (i.e., the low-pass filtered image) at the highest transform scale; and the larger absolute value of the *detail* coefficients (i.e., the high-pass filtered images) at each transform scale. Then, an inverse DWT is performed to obtain a fused image. At each DWT scale of a particular image, the DWT coefficients of a 2D image consist of four parts: approximation, horizontal detail, vertical detail, and diagonal detail. In the *advanced DWT* (*a*DWT) method (Zheng et al., 2004), we apply PCA (principle component analysis) to the two input images' approximation coefficients at the highest transform scale. That is, we fuse them using the principal eigenvector (corresponding to the larger eigenvalue) derived from the two original images, as described in Eq. (2) below:

$$C_F = (a_1 \cdot C_A + a_2 \cdot C_B) / (a_1 + a_2) \tag{2}$$

where C_A and C_B are approximation coefficients (image matrices) transformed from input images A and B. C_F represents the fused coefficients; a_1 and a_2 are the elements (scalars) of the principal eigenvector, which are computed by analyzing the original input images. Note that the denominator in Eq. (2) is used for normalization so that the fused image has the same energy distribution as the original input images.

For the detail coefficients (the other three quarters of the coefficients) at each transform scale, the larger absolute values are selected, followed by neighborhood morphological processing, which serves to verify the selected pixels using a "filling" and "cleaning" operation (i.e., the operation fills or removes isolated pixels locally). Such an operation (similar to smoothing) can increase the consistency of coefficient selection thereby reducing the distortion in the fused image.

3. Segmentation-based colorization

In segmentation-based colorization (i.e., local coloring) method, multispectral night vision imagery is rendered segment-by-segment with the statistical color properties of natural scenes by using the color mapping technique. Eventually, the colorized images resemble daylight pictures. The main steps of segmentation-based colorization are given below: (1) A false-color image (source image) is first formed by assigning multispectral (two or three band) images to three RGB channels. The false-colored images usually have an unnatural color appearance. (2) Then, the false-colored image is segmented using the features of color properties, the techniques of nonlinear diffusion, clustering, and region merging. A set of "clusters" are formed by analyzing the histograms of the three components of the diffused image in *lαβ* color space. Those clusters are merged to "segments" if their similarity values in *lαβ* space are greater than a preset threshold. (3) The averaged mean, standard deviation, and histogram of a large sample of natural color images are used as the target color properties for each color scheme. The target color schemes are grouped by their contents and colors such as plants, mountain, roads, sky, water, buildings, people, etc. (4) The association between the source region segments and target color schemes is carried out automatically utilizing a classification algorithm such as the nearest neighbor paradigm. (5) The color mapping procedures (statistic-matching and histogram-matching) are carried out to render natural colors onto the false-colored image segment by segment. (6) The mapped image is then transformed back to the RGB space. (7) Finally, the mapped image is transformed into HSV (Hue-Saturation-Value) space and the "value" component of the mapped image is replaced with the "fused NV image" (a grayscale image). Note that this fused image replacement is necessary to allow the colorized image to have a proper and consistent contrast.

3.1 Color space transform

In this subsection, the RGB to *LMS* (long-wave, medium-wave and short-wave) transform is discussed first. Then, an *lαβ* space is introduced from which the resulting data representation is compact and *symmetrical*, and provides a higher *decorrelation* than the second order. The reason for the color space transform is to decorrelate three color components (i.e., l, α and β) so that the manipulation (such as statistic matching and

histogram matching) on each color component can be performed independently. Inverse transforms (*lαβ* space to the ***LMS*** and *LMS* to RGB) are needed to complete the proposed segmentation-based colorization, which are given elsewhere (Zheng & Essock, 2008).
The actual conversion (matrix) from RGB tristimulus to device-independent XYZ tristimulus values depends on the characteristics of the display being used. Fairchild (1998) suggested a "general" device-independent conversion (while non-priori knowledge about the display device) that maps white in the chromaticity diagram to white in the RGB space and vice versa.

$$\begin{bmatrix} X \\ Y \\ Z \end{bmatrix} = \begin{bmatrix} 0.5141 & 0.3239 & 0.1604 \\ 0.2651 & 0.6702 & 0.0641 \\ 0.0241 & 0.1228 & 0.8444 \end{bmatrix} \begin{bmatrix} R \\ G \\ B \end{bmatrix} \tag{3}$$

The XYZ values can be converted to the *LMS* space using the following equation

$$\begin{bmatrix} L \\ M \\ S \end{bmatrix} = \begin{bmatrix} 0.3897 & 0.6890 & -0.0787 \\ -0.2298 & 1.1834 & 0.0464 \\ 0.0000 & 0.0000 & 1.0000 \end{bmatrix} \begin{bmatrix} X \\ Y \\ Z \end{bmatrix} \tag{4}$$

A logarithmic transform is employed here to reduce the data skew that existed in the above color space:

$$\boldsymbol{L} = \log L, \quad \boldsymbol{M} = \log M, \quad \boldsymbol{S} = \log S. \tag{5}$$

Ruderman et al. (1998) presented a color space, named *lαβ* (Luminance-Alpha-Beta), which can decorrelate the three axes in the ***LMS*** space:

$$\begin{bmatrix} l \\ \alpha \\ \beta \end{bmatrix} = \begin{bmatrix} 0.5774 & 0.5774 & 0.5774 \\ 0.4082 & 0.4082 & -0.8165 \\ 1.4142 & -1.4142 & 0 \end{bmatrix} \begin{bmatrix} \mathbf{L} \\ \mathbf{M} \\ \mathbf{S} \end{bmatrix} \tag{6}$$

The three axes can be considered as an achromatic direction (*l*), a yellow-blue opponent direction (*α*), and a red-green opponent direction (*β*). The *lαβ* space has the characteristics of compact, symmetrical and decorrelation, which highly facilitate the subsequent process of color-mapping (see Section 3.4).

3.2 Image segmentation

The nonlinear diffusion procedure has proven to be equivalent to an adaptive smoothing process (Barash & Comaniciu, 2004). The diffusion is applied to the false-colored NV image here to obtain a smooth image, which significantly facilitates the subsequent segmentation process. The clustering process is performed separately on each color component in the *lαβ* color space to form a set of "clusters". The region merging process is used to merge the fragmental clusters into meaningful "segments" (based on a similarity metric defined in 3D *lαβ* color space) that will be used for the color-mapping process.

3.2.1 Adaptive smoothing with nonlinear diffusion

Nonlinear diffusion methods have been proven as powerful methods in the denoising and smoothing of image intensities while retaining and enhancing edges. Barash and Comaniciu (2004) have proven that nonlinear diffusion is equivalent to adaptive smoothing and bilateral filtering is obtained from an extended nonlinear diffusion. Nonlinear diffusion filtering was first introduced by Perona and Malik (1990). Basically, diffusion is a PDE (partial differential equation) method that involves two operators, smoothing and gradient, in 2D image space. The diffusion process smoothes the regions with lower gradients and stops the smoothing at region boundaries with higher gradients. Nonlinear diffusion means the smoothing operation depends on the region gradient distribution. For color image diffusion, three RGB components of a false-colored NV image are filtered separately (one by one). The number of colors in the diffused image will be significantly reduced and will benefit the subsequent image segmentation procedures - clustering and merging.

3.2.2 Image segmentation with clustering and region merging

The diffused false-colored image is transformed into the $l\alpha\beta$ color space. Each component (l, α or β) of the diffused image is *clustered* in the $l\alpha\beta$ space by individually analyzing its histogram. Specifically, for each intensity component (image) l, α or β, (i) normalize the intensity onto [0,1]; (ii) bin the normalized intensity to a certain number of levels N_{Bin} and perform the histogram analysis; (iii) with the histogram, locate local extreme values (i.e., peaks and valleys) and form a stepwise mapping function using the peaks and valleys; (iv) complete the clustering utilizing the stepwise mapping function.

The local extremes (peaks or valleys) are easily located by examining the crossover points of the first derivatives of histograms. Furthermore, "peaks" and "valleys" are expected to be interleaved (e.g., valley-peak-valley-…-peak-valley); otherwise, a new valley value can be calculated with the midpoint of two neighboring peaks. In addition, two-end boundaries are considered two special valleys. In summary, all intensities between two valleys in a histogram are squeezed in their peak intensity and the two end points in the histogram are treated as valleys (rather than peaks). If there are n peaks in a histogram, then an n-step mapping function is formed. If there are two or more valley values (including the special valley at the left end) at the left side of the leftmost peak, then use the special (extreme) valley intensity.

Clustering is done by separately analyzing three components (l, α & β) of the false-colored image, which may result in inconsistent clusters in the sense of colors. *Region merging* is necessary to incorporate the fragmental "clusters" into meaningful "segments" in the sense of colors, which will improve the color consistency in a colorized image. If two clusters are similar (i.e., $Q_{\mathrm{w}}(x,y) > T_{\mathrm{Q}}$ (a predefined threshold)), these two clusters will be merged. $Q_{\mathrm{w}}(x,y)$ is a similarity metric between two clusters, x and y, which is defined in the $l\alpha\beta$ color space as follows:

$$Q_w(x,y) = \sum_{k=\{l,\alpha,\beta\}} [w_k \cdot Q_k(x,y)] \tag{7a}$$

where w_{k} is a given weight for each color component. $Q_{\mathrm{k}}(x,y)$ is formulated below:

$$Q_k(x,y) = \frac{2\overline{xy}}{(\overline{x}^2 + \overline{y}^2)} \cdot \frac{2\sigma_x \sigma_y}{(\sigma_x^2 + \sigma_y^2)} \tag{7b}$$

where $\overline{x}$ and σ_x are the mean and the standard deviation of cluster x in a particular component, respectively. Similar definitions are applied to cluster y. The sizes (i.e., areas) of two clusters (x and y) are usually unequal. Notice that $Q_{\mathrm{k}}(x,y)$ is computed with regard to the diffused false-color image.

3.3 Automatic segment recognition

A *nearest neighbor* (NN) paradigm (Keysers et al., 2002) is demonstrated to classify the segments obtained from the preceding procedure (described in Section 3.2). To use the NN algorithm, a distance measure between two segments is needed. The similarity metric $Q_w(x,y)$ (as defined in Eqs. (7)) between two segments, x and y, is used as the distance measure. Thus, the closer two segments in *lαβ* space, the larger their similarity.

Similar to a training process, a look up table (LUT) has to be built under supervision to classify a given segment ($\mathbf{s}_j$) into a known color group (C_i), i.e., $C_i = T(\mathbf{s}_j)$, ($i \le j$), where $\mathbf{s}_j$ is a feature vector that distinguishingly describes each segment; C_i stands for a known color scheme (e.g., sky, clouds, plants, water, ground, roads, etc.); and T is a classification function (i.e., a trained classifier). We use segment color statistics (e.g., mean and deviation of each channel) as features (of six statistical variables). The statistical features ($\mathbf{s}_j$) are computed using the diffused false-color images and the color mapping process is carried out between a false-color segment and a daylight color scheme. The reason for using the diffused false-color images here is because the diffused images are less sensitive to noise. In a training stage, a set of multispectral NV images are analyzed and segmented such that a sequence of feature vectors, $\{\mathbf{s}_j\}$ can be computed and the LUT (mapping) between $\{\mathbf{s}_j\}$ and $\{C_i\}$ can be manually set up upon the experimental results. In a classifying (testing) stage, all $Q_w(\mathbf{x}_k, \mathbf{s}_j)$ values (for j = 1, 2, 3, …) are calculated, where $\mathbf{x}_k$ means the current classified segment and $\mathbf{s}_j$ represents one of the existing segments from the training stage. Certainly, $\mathbf{x}_k$ is automatically classified into the color group of the largest Q_w (similarity). For example, if $Q_w(\mathbf{x}_1, \mathbf{s}_5)$ is the maximum, then the segment of $\mathbf{x}_1$ will be colorized using the color scheme $T(\mathbf{s}_5)$ that is the color used to render the segment of $\mathbf{s}_5$ in the training stage.

3.4 Color mapping

3.4.1 Statistic matching

A "*statistic matching*" is used to transfer the color characteristics from natural daylight imagery to false color night-vision imagery, which is formulated as:

$$I_C^k = (I_S^k - \mu_S^k) \times \frac{\sigma_T^k}{\sigma_S^k} + \mu_T^k, \qquad \text{for } k = \{\, l, \alpha, \beta \,\}, \tag{8}$$

where $\mathbf{I}_C$ is the colored image, $\mathbf{I}_S$ is the source (false-color) image in *lαβ* space; $\boldsymbol{\mu}$ denotes the mean and $\boldsymbol{\sigma}$ denotes the standard deviation; the subscripts 'S' and 'T' refer to the source and target images, respectively; and the superscript 'k' is one of the color components: $\{\, l, \alpha, \beta\}$.

After this transformation, the pixels comprising the multispectral source image have means and standard deviations that conform to the target daylight color image in *lαβ* space. The color-mapped image is transformed back to the RGB space through the inverse transforms (*lαβ* space to the ***LMS***, exponential transform from ***LMS*** to *LMS*, and *LMS* to RGB, refer to Eqs. (3-6)) (Zheng & Essock, 2008).

3.4.2 Histogram matching

Histogram matching (also referred to as histogram specification) is usually used to enhance an image when histogram equalization fails (Gonzalez & Woods, 2002). Given the shape of the histogram that we want the enhanced image to have, histogram matching can generate a processed image that has the specified histogram. In particular, by specifying the histogram of a target image (with daylight natural colors), a source image (with false colors) resembles the target image in terms of histogram distribution after histogram matching. Similar to statistic matching, histogram matching also serves for color mapping and is performed component-by-component in *lαβ* space. Histogram matching and statistic matching can be applied separately or jointly.

4. Channel-based color fusion

The segmentation-based colorization described in Section 3 can usually produce colorized night-vision images closely resembling natural daylight pictures. However, this segmentation-based coloring procedure involves many processes and heavy computations such as histogram analysis, color space transform, image segmentation, and pattern classification. It will be a grand challenge for real time applications. Therefore, we propose a fast color fusion method, termed as *channel-based color fusion*, which is efficient enough ideally for real time applications. Notice that the term of "color fusion" means combing multispectral images into a color-version image with the purpose of resembling natural scenes. Relative to "night vision colorization", color fusion trades the realism of colors with speed. On the other hand, false coloring techniques have no intention of resembling natural color scenery.

The general framework of channel-based color fusion is as follows, (i) prepare for color fusion, preprocessing (denoising, normalization and enhancement) and image registration; (ii) form a color fusion image by properly assigning multispectral images to red, green, and blue channels; (iii) then fuse multispectral images (gray fusion) using *a*DWT algorithm (see Section 2.3); and (iv) replace the *value* component of color fusion in HSV color space with the gray-fusion image, and finally transform back to RGB space.

In night vision imaging, there may be two or several bands of images available, for example, visible (RGB), image intensified (II), near infrared (NIR), medium wave infrared (MWIR), long wave infrared (LWIR, also called thermal). The discussions of following subsections focus on how to form a channel-wise color fusion with the available multispectral images.

4.1 Color fusion with two-band images

Upon the available images and common applications, we will discuss two-band color fusion of (II $\oplus$ LWIR), (NIR $\oplus$ LWIR), (RGB $\oplus$ LWIR), and (RGB $\oplus$ NIR), although other combinations of two bands may be possible in some applications. The symbol '$\oplus$' denotes the fusion of multiband images.

4.1.1 Color fusion of (II $\oplus$ LWIR)

Suppose a color fusion image (F_C) consists of three color planes, F_R, F_G, F_B, the color fusion of II and LWIR images are formed by using the following expressions,

$$F_R = S_{[0,1.0]}^{[0,0.7]}(I_{LWIR}), \tag{9a}$$

$$F_G = S_{[0.1,I\_Gmax]}^{[0.2,1]}(I_{II}), \tag{9b}$$

$$F_B = S_{[0,1.0]}^{[0.1,0.75]}([1.0- I_{LWIR}] \bullet I_{II}), \tag{9c}$$

$$V_F = Fus(I_{II}, I_{LWIR}); \tag{9d}$$

where $S^{[0.2,1]}_{[0.1,I\_Gmax]}$ denotes *piecewise contrast stretching* defined in Eq. (1) and $I_{\_Gmax}$ = $min([\mu_{II} + 3\sigma_{II}], 0.8)$, μ and σ are the mean and standard deviation of an II image; $[1.0- I_{LWIR}]$ is to invert LWIR image; symbol '•' means element-by-element multiplication; V_F is the *value* component of F_C in HSV space, *Fus*() means image fusion operation using *a*DWT algorithm. Although the limits given in contrast stretching are obtained empirically according to the night vision images that we had, it is viable to formulate the expressions and automate the fusion based upon a set of conditions (imaging devices, imaging time, and application location). Notice the transform parameters in Eqs. (9) were applied to all color fusions in our experiments.

4.1.2 Color fusion of (NIR ⊕ LWIR)

A color fusion of NIR and LWIR is formulated by,

$$F_R = S^{[0.2,0.9]}_{[0,1.0]}(I_{LWIR}), \tag{10a}$$

$$F_G = S^{[0.2,1]}_{[0.1,I\_Gmax]}(I_{NIR}), \tag{10b}$$

$$F_B = S^{[0.1,0.7]}_{[0,1.0]}([1.0- I_{LWIR}] \bullet I_{NIR}); \tag{10c}$$

$$V_F = Fus(I_{NIR}, I_{LWIR}); \tag{10d}$$

where $I_{\_Gmax} = min([\mu_{NIR} + 2\sigma_{NIR}], 0.8)$, *min*() is an operation to get the minimal number. Other notes are the same as that in Eqs. (9).

4.1.3 Color fusion of (RGB ⊕ LWIR)

Two-band color fusion of RGB and LWIR is described as follows,

$$F_R = S^{[0,I\_Rmax]}_{[0,1.0]}(max[I_{LWIR}, I_{Red}]), \tag{11a}$$

$$F_G = I_{Green}, \tag{11b}$$

$$F_B = I_{Blue}; \tag{11c}$$

where I_{Red}, I_{Green} and I_{Blue} are the three channel images of a RGB image; $I_{\_Rmax}$ = $min([\mu_{Red} + 8\sigma_{Red}], 0.6)$, *min*() is an operation to get the minimal number; $max[I_{LWIR}, I_{Red}]$ is to take the maximal pixel values between I_{LWIR} and I_{Red}. In fact, this color fusion only modifies the red channel in a RGB image, where the piecewise contrast stretching in Eq. (11a) is to keep a good color balance and contrast. No image fusion is used because the RGB images captured at night time are usually very noisy. Of course, no HSV transform is performed.

4.1.4 Color fusion of (RGB ⊕ NIR)

The color fusion of RGB and NIR is defined as,

$$F_R = I_{Red}, \tag{12a}$$

$$F_G = S_{[0,1.0]}^{[0,I\_Gmax]}(max[I_{NIR}, I_{Green}]), \quad (12b)$$

$$F_B = I_{Blue}; \quad (12c)$$

where $I\_{Gmax} = min([\mu_{Green} + 6\sigma_{Green}], 0.6)$. Other notes are the same as that in Eqs. (11). This color fusion actually modifies the green channel in a RGB image. No image fusion and no HSV transform are performed. The color fusion of (RGB $\oplus$ NIR) is not used as often as the fusion of (RGB $\oplus$ LWIR).

4.2 Color fusion with three-band images

Due to the available image databases, we only discuss one application of three-band color fusions, (RGB $\oplus$ NIR $\oplus$ LWIR). A color fusion of RGB, NIR and LWIR can be described as,

$$F_R = S_{[0,1.0]}^{[0,0.6]}(I_{LWIR}), \quad (13a)$$

$$F_G = S_{[0.1,I\_Gmax]}^{[0.1,0.9]}(I_{NIR}), \quad (13b)$$

$$F_B = S_{[0,I\_Bmax]}^{[0.2,1]}(I_{Blue}); \quad (13c)$$

$$V_F = Fus(I_{NIR}, I_{LWIR}); \quad (13d)$$

where $I\_{Gmax} = min([\mu_{NIR} + 2.5\sigma_{NIR}], 0.8)$, $I\_{Bmax} = min([\mu_{Blue} + 3\sigma_{Blue}], 0.85)$, I_{Blue} is the *blue* channel image of a RGB image. The other two channels (red and green) are not used for the color fusion.

5. Experimental results and discussions

Two sets of multispectral images were used in our experiments, which were taken at night time and referred as to "NV-set 1" and "NV-set 2". In NV-set 1, three pairs of multispectral images (as shown Figs. 1-3), image intensified (II) and long wave infrared (LWIR), were analyzed by using the *a*DWT fusion algorithm and segmentation-based colorization (also referred as to "local coloring") algorithm as described in Section 3. The results of segmentation-based colorization are illustrated in Figs. 1-3. Note that there was no post-processing imposed on the resulted fusion and colorization images.

The two input images and the fused images used in the coloring process are shown in Figs. 1-3a, Figs. 1-3b and Figs. 1-3c, respectively. The image resolutions are given in figure captions. Two input images in NV-set 1 were preregistered. The false colored images (not shown in Figs. 1-3) were obtained by assigning image intensified (II) images to blue channels, infrared (IR) images to red channels, and providing averaged II and IR images to green channels. The rationale of forming a false-color image is to assign a long-wavelength NV image to the red channel and to assign a short-wavelength NV image to the blue channel. The number of false colors were reduced with the nonlinear diffusion algorithm with AOS (additive operator splitting for fast computation) implementation that facilitated the subsequent segmentation. The segmentation was done in *lαβ* space through clustering and

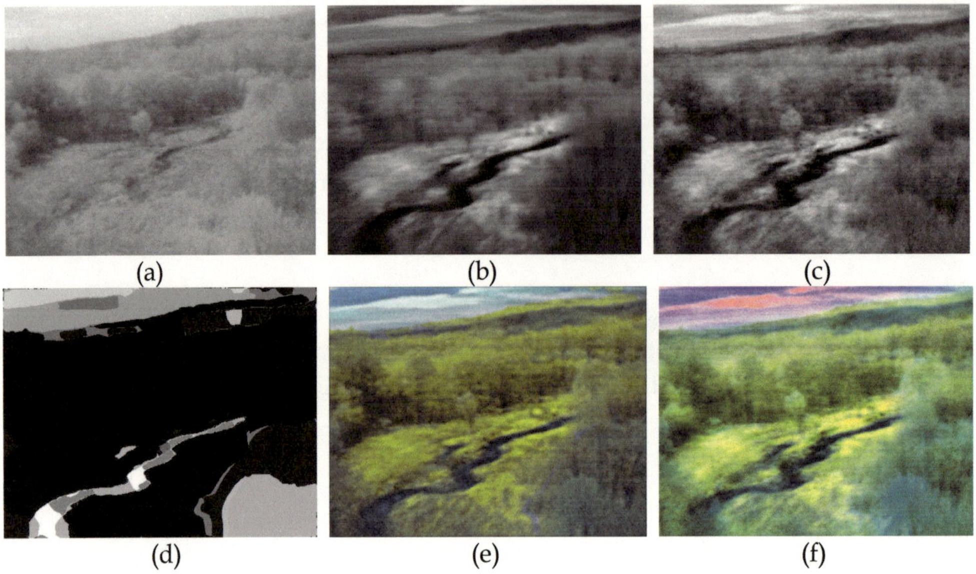

Fig. 1. Segmentation-based colorization with Sample #1 (531×401 pixels) in NV-set 1: (a) and (b) are II and LWIR images; (c) Fused image by *a*DWT; (d) is the segmented image from a false-colored image (not shown), where 16 segments were merged from 36 clusters; (e) is the colored image, where six auto-classified color schemes (sky, clouds, plants, water, ground and others) were mapped by jointly using histogram-matching and statistic-matching; (f) Channel-based color fusion of (II $\oplus$ LWIR).

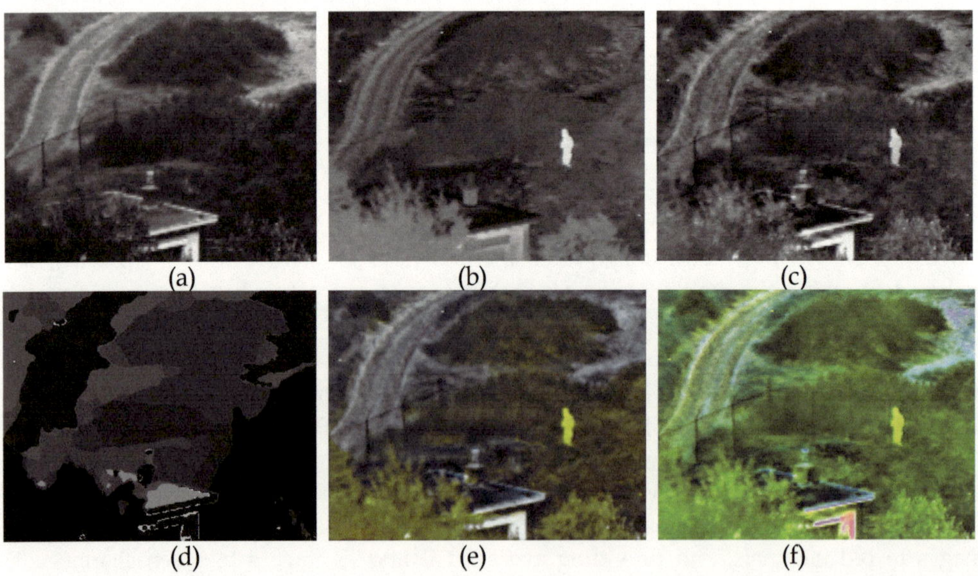

Fig. 2. Segmentation-based colorization with Sample #2 (360×270 pixels) in NV-set 1: (a) and (b) are II and LWIR images; (c) Fused image by *a*DWT; (d) is the segmented image of 12 segments merged from 21 clusters; (e) is the colored image with five auto-classified color schemes (plants, roads, ground, building and others); (f) Channel-based color fusion of (II $\oplus$ LWIR).

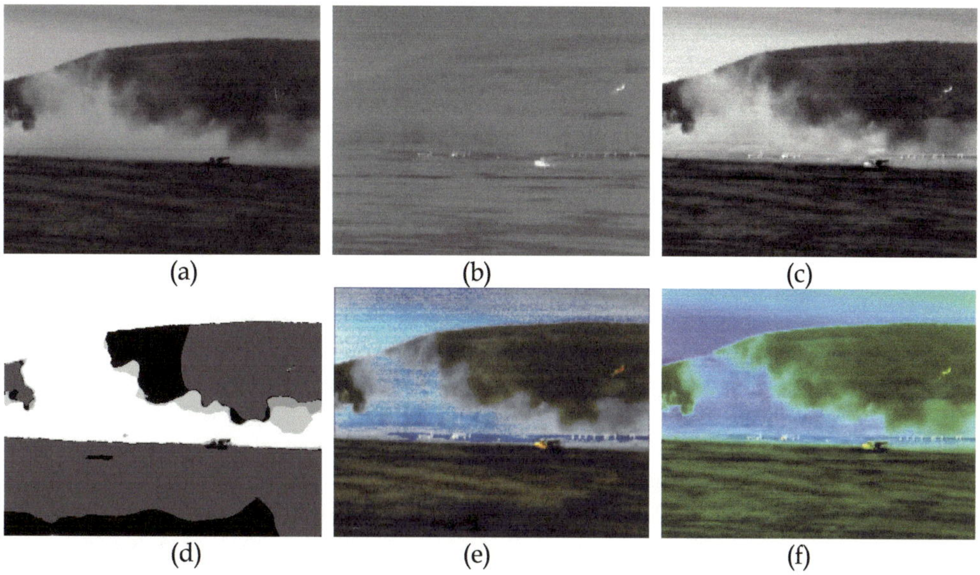

Fig. 3. Segmentation-based colorization with Sample #3 (360×270 pixels) in NV-set 1: (a) and (b) are II and LWIR images; (c) Fused image by *a*DWT; (d) is the segmented image of 14 segments merged from 28 clusters; (e) is the colored image with three auto-classified color schemes (plants, smoke and others); (f) Channel-based color fusion of (II $\oplus$ LWIR).

merging operations (the clustered images are not shown in Figs. 1-3). The parameter values used in clustering and merging are N_{Bin} = [24 24 24], w_k = [0.25 0.35 0.40] and T_Q = 0.90. To emphasize two chromatic channels (due to more distinguishable among segments) in $l\alpha\beta$ space, relatively larger weights were assigned in w_k. With the segment map as shown in Figs. 1-3d, the histogram-matching and statistic-matching were performed segment by segment in $l\alpha\beta$ space. The source region segments were automatically recognized and associated with proper target color schemes (after the training process is done). The finally colored images by segmentation-based colorization are shown in Figs. 1-3e. From a visual examination, the colored images appear very natural, realistic, and colorful. The comparable colorization results by using *global coloring* algorithm are presented in Reference (Zheng & Essock, 2008). This segmentation-based coloring process is fully automatic and well adaptive to different types of multispectral images.

Two-band channel-based color fusion (described in Eqs. (9)) was applied to the II and LWIR images (shown in Figs. 1-3a, b), and the results are illustrated in Figs. 1-3f. The color fusion results are very good especially in representing vegetation. Compared to the segmentation-based colorization results, the channel-based color fusion seems less realistic such as the sky and roads shown in Figs. 1-2f. However, the processes of channel-based color fusion eliminate the needs of segmentation and classification, and also reduced the color transforms. The processing speed of is much faster than that of segmentation-based colorization.

In NV-set 2, four pairs of multispectral images (as shown Figs. 4-7), color RGB, near infrared (NIR) and long wave infrared (LWIR), were analyzed by using the channel-based color fusion algorithm as described in Section 4. The results of channel-based color fusion are presented in Figs. 4-8.

The three-band input images used in the color fusion process are shown in Figs. 4-7a, b and c, respectively. The image resolutions are given in figure captions. The RGB images and LWIR images were taken by a FLIR SC620 two-in-one camera, which has LWIR camera (of 640×480 pixel original resolution and 7.5~13 μm spectral range) and an integrated visible-band digital camera (2048×1536 pixel original resolution). The NIR images were taken by a FLIR SC6000 camera (640×512 pixel original resolution and 0.9~1.7 μm spectral range). Two cameras (SC620 and SC6000) were sat on the same fixture by turns and aimed at the same direction. The images were captured during sunset time and dusk time in fall season. Of course, image registration as described in Section 2.2 was applied to the three band images shown in Figs. 4-7, where manual alignments were employed to the RGB images shown in Figs. 6-7a since those visible images are so dark and noisy. To better present the RGB images, contrast and brightness adjustments (as described in figure captions) were applied. Notice that piecewise contrast stretching (Eq. (1)) was used for NIR enhancements. The fused images using *a*DWT algorithm was shown in Figs. 4-7d. Two-band channel-based color fusion (Eqs. (10)) was applied to the NIR and LWIR images (shown in Figs. 4-7b, c), and the results are illustrated in Figs. 4-7e; while three-band color fusion (Eqs. (13)) of (RGB $\oplus$ NIR $\oplus$ LWIR) are shown in Figs. 4-7f. Relative to gray-fusion (Figs. 4-7d), the images shown in two-band color fusion (Figs. 4-7e) resemble natural colors, which makes scene classification much easier. In the color-fusion images, the trees and grasses can be easily distinguished from grounds (parking lots) and sky. The car and person are easily identified in Figs. 6-7e. In Fig. 6e, the water area (between ground and trees, shown in cyan color) is clearly noticeable, but it is hard to realize the water area in the gray-fusion image (Fig. 6d). There is some improvement in three-band color fusion of (RGB $\oplus$ NIR $\oplus$ LWIR) in Figs. 4-5f when the light condition is good. For example, the tree, sky and ground shown in Figs. 4-5f are represented in more realistic colors than that in Figs. 4-5e. However, there is no significant difference between two-band and three-band color fusions as shown in Figs. 6-7 because the RGB images were taken at poor lighting condition.

The two-band channel-based color fusion of (RGB $\oplus$ LWIR) as defined in Eq. (11) is demonstrated in Fig. 8a-c; while the color fusion of (RGB $\oplus$ NIR) as defined in Eq. (12) is illustrated in Fig. 8d-f. No additional brightness or contrast adjustments were applied to these color-fusion images. In Fig. 8, the top-row images appear reddish, while the bottom-row images show greenish. These color-fusion images (under poor illumination) are not very realistic but have better representations and visibilities than the original RGB images (Figs. 4-6a). No color fusions of (RGB $\oplus$ LWIR) or (RGB $\oplus$ NIR) using the images shown in Fig. 7 are presented here due to the poor quality of RGB image (Fig. 7a).

The segmentation-based colorization demonstrated here took two-band multispectral images (II and LWIR) as inputs. Actually, this segmentation-based colorization procedure can accept two or three input images (e.g., II, NIR, LWIR). If there are more than three bands of images available (e.g., II, NIR, MWIR, LWIR), we may choose the low-light intensified (visual band) image and two bands of IR images. As far how to choose two bands of IR images, we may use the image fusion algorithm as a screening process. The two selected IR images for colorization should be the two images that can produce the most (maximum) informative fused image among all possible fusions. For example, given three IR images, IR_1, IR_2, IR_3, the two chosen images for colorization, I_{C1}, I_{C2}, should satisfy the following equation: $Fus(I_{C1}, I_{C2}) = max\{Fus(IR_1, IR_2), Fus(IR_1, IR_3), Fus(IR_2, IR_3)\}$, where *Fus* stands for the fusion process and *max* means selecting the fusion of maximum information.

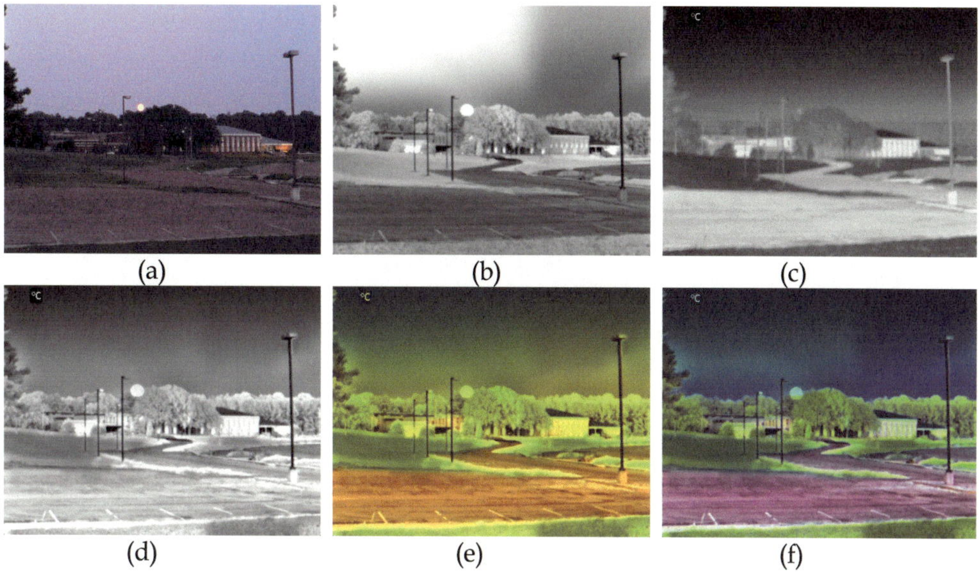

Fig. 4. Channel-based color fusion with Sample #1 (Case# AT008 - sunset time; 640×480 pixels) in NV-set 2: (a) Color RGB image (contrast increased by 10%); (b) NIR image; (c) LWIR image; (d) Fused image of (b) & (c) by *a*DWT algorithm; (e) Channel-based color fusion of (NIR $\oplus$ LWIR); (f) Channel-based color fusion of (RGB $\oplus$ NIR $\oplus$ LWIR).

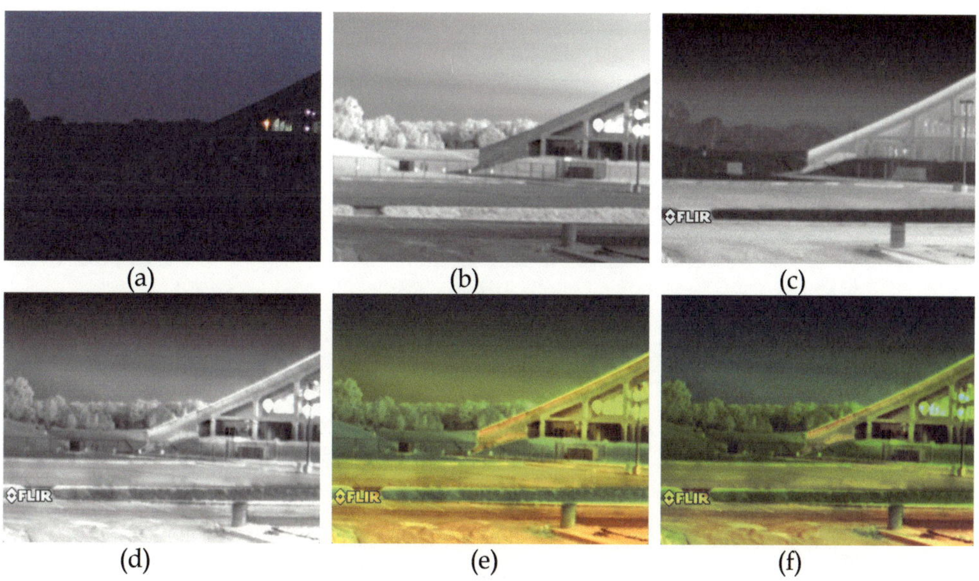

Fig. 5. Channel-based color fusion with Sample #2 (Case# AT010 - after sunset; 640×480 pixels) in NV-set 2: (a) Color RGB image (brightness and contrast both increased by 10%); (b) NIR image; (c) LWIR image; (d) Fused image of (b) & (c) by *a*DWT algorithm; (e) Channel-based color fusion of (NIR $\oplus$ LWIR); (f) Channel-based color fusion of (RGB $\oplus$ NIR $\oplus$ LWIR).

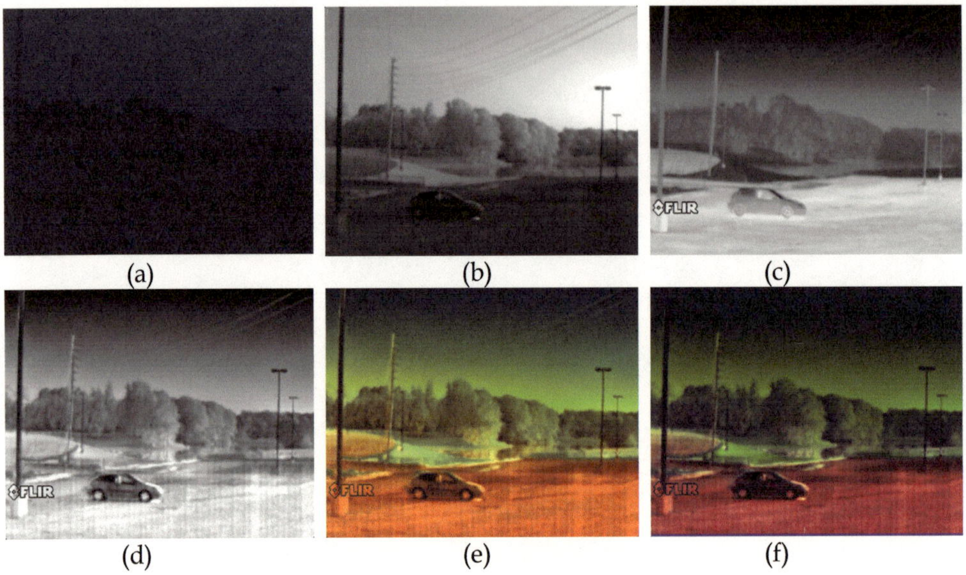

Fig. 6. Channel-based color fusion with Sample #3 (Case# AT012 – dusk time; 640×480 pixels) in NV-set 2: (a) Color RGB image (brightness and contrast both increased by 10%); (b) NIR image; (c) LWIR image; (d) Fused image of (b) & (c) by *a*DWT algorithm; (e) Channel-based color fusion of (NIR $\oplus$ LWIR); (f) Channel-based color fusion of (RGB $\oplus$ NIR $\oplus$ LWIR).

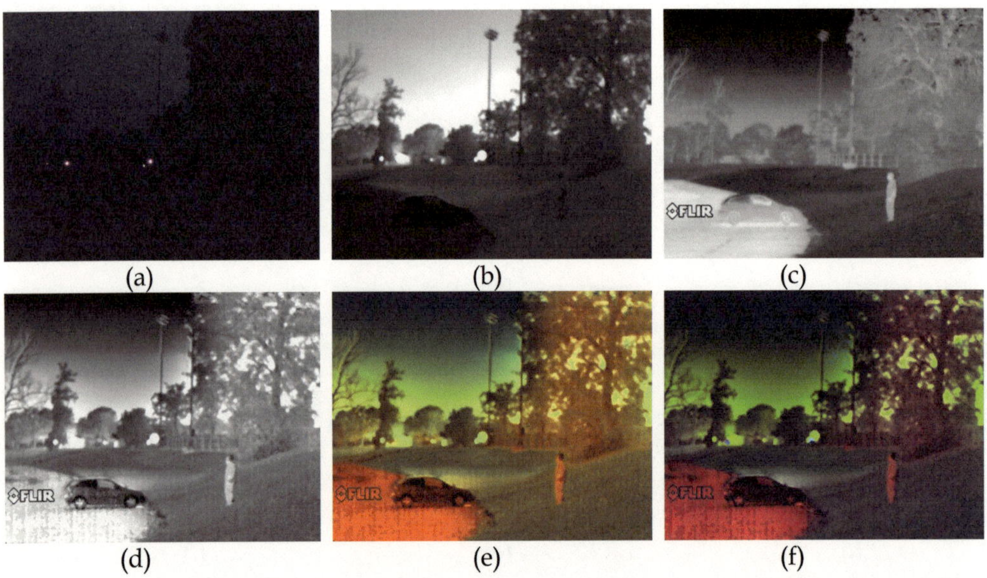

Fig. 7. Channel-based color fusion with Sample #4 (Case# AT013 – dusk time; 640×480 pixels) in NV-set 2: (a) Color RGB image (brightness and contrast both increased by 10%); (b) NIR image; (c) LWIR image; (d) Fused image of (b) & (c) by *a*DWT algorithm; (e) Channel-based color fusion of (NIR $\oplus$ LWIR); (f) Channel-based color fusion of (RGB $\oplus$ NIR $\oplus$ LWIR).

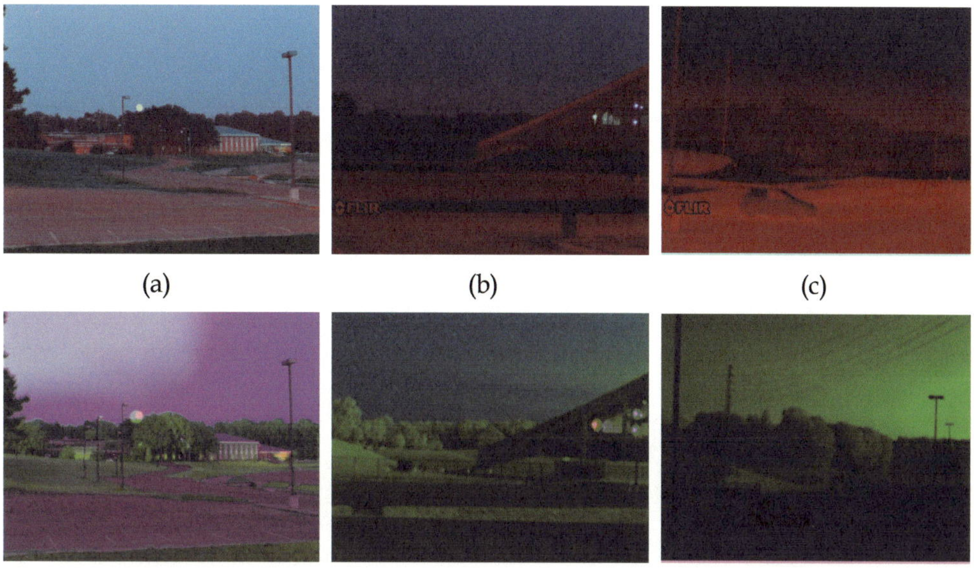

(a) (b) (c)

(d) (e) (f)

Fig. 8. Two-band channel-based color fusion: (a-c) Color fusion of (RGB ⊕ LWIR); (d-f) Color fusion of (RGB ⊕ NIR). Original images are shown in Figs. 4-6a, b, and c.

We exhibited the channel-based color fusion with possible combinations of two-band and three-band multispectral images. The processing speed of channel-based fusion is much faster than segmentation-based colorization, while the colors in channel-based fusion are less natural than the colors in segmentation-based colorization. Parameter settings in channel-based color fusion (Eqs. (9-13)) may be varied with different bands of images and with image capturing time and season, which can be conducted and stored before a field application.

6. Conclusions

In this chapter, a set of color fusion and colorization approaches are presented to enhance night vision for human users, which can be performed automatically and adaptively regardless of the image contents. Experimental results with multispectral imagery showed that the colored images contain clear information, and realistic colors. Specifically, the segmentation-based colorization (local-coloring) procedure is based on image segmentation, pattern recognition, and color mapping, which produces more colorful and more realistic colorized night-vision images. On the other hand, the channel-based color fusion procedure generates very impressive color-fusion images using linear transforms and channel assignments, which can be implemented very efficiently for real-time applications. The synthesized multispectral imagery with proposed colorizing approaches will eventually lead to improved performance of remote sensing, nighttime navigation, and situational awareness.

7. Acknowledgements

This research is supported by the U. S. Army Research Office under grant number W911NF-08-1-0404.

8. References

Ajazzi, B.; Alparone, L.; Baronti, S.; & Carla, R.; (1998). Assessment of pyramid-based multisensor image data fusion, in *Proc. SPIE 3500*, 237–248.

Barash, D. & Comaniciu, D. (2004). A common framework for nonlinear diffusion, adaptive smoothing, bilateral filtering and mean shift, *Image Vision Computing* 22(1), 73-81.

Brown, L. (1992). A survey of image registration techniques, ACM Comput. Surv., vol. 24, pp. 325–376.

Burt, P. J. & Adelson, E. H. (1983). The Laplacian pyramid as a compact image code, *IEEE Trans. Commun.* Com-31 (4), 532–540.

Burt, P. J. & Adelson, E. H. (1985). Merging images through pattern decomposition, *Proc. SPIE* 575, 173–182.

Chen, Q.; Defrise, M.; Deconinck, F. (1994). Symmetric Phase-Only Matched Filtering of Fourier-Mellin Transforms for Image Registration and Recognition, IEEE Transactions on Pattern Analysis and Machine Intelligence, vol. 16, no. 12, pp. 1156-1168.

Essock, E. A.; McCarley, J. S.; Sinai, M. J. & DeFord, J. K. (2001). Human perception of sensor-fused imagery, in *Interpreting Remote Sensing Imagery: Human Factors*, R. R. Hoffman and A. B. Markman, Eds., Lewis Publishers, Boca Raton, Florida.

Essock, E. A.; Sinai, M. J. & et al. (1999). Perceptual ability with real-world nighttime scenes: imageintensified, infrared, and fused-color imagery, *Hum. Factors* 41(3), 438–452.

Fairchild, M. D. (1998). *Color Appearance Models*, Addison Wesley Longman Inc., ISBN: 0-201-63464-3, Reading, MA.

Gonzalez, R. C. & Woods, R. E. (2002). *Digital Image Processing* (Second Edition), Prentice Hall, ISBN: 0201180758, Upper Saddle River, NJ.

Hill, D. L. G. & Batchelor P. (2001). Registration methodology: concepts and algorithms, in Medical Image Registration, Hajnal, J. V.; Hill, D. L. G.; & Hawkes, D. J. Eds, Boca Raton, FL.

Jahard, F.; Fish, D. A.; Rio, A. A. & Thompson C. P. (1997). Far/near infrared adapted pyramid-based fusion for automotive night vision, in *IEEE Proc. 6th Int. Conf. on Image Processing and its Applications* (IPA97), pp. 886–890.

Keys, L. D.; Schmidt, N. J.; & Phillips, B. E. (1990). A prototype example of sensor fusion used for a siting analysis, in Technical Papers 1990, ACSM-ASPRS Annual Conf. *Image Processing and Remote Sensing* 4, pp. 238–249.

Keysers, D.; Paredes, R.; Ney, H. & Vidal, E. (2002). Combination of tangent vectors and local representations for handwritten digit recognition, Int. Workshop on Statistical Pattern Recognition, Lecture Notes in Computer Science, Vol. 2396, pp. 538-547, Windsor, Ontario, Canada.

Nunez, J.; Otazu, X.; & et al. (1999). Image fusion with additive multiresolution wavelet decomposition; applications to spotllandsat images, *J. Opt. Soc. Am. A* 16, 467–474.

Perona, P. & Malik, J. (1990). Scale space and edge detection using anisotropic diffusion, *IEEE Transactions on Pattern Analysis and Machine Intelligence* 12, 629–639.

Pohl C. & Genderen J. L. V. (1998). Review article: multisensor image fusion in remote sensing: concepts, methods and applications, *Int. J. Remote Sens.* 19(5), 823–854.

Pu T. & Ni, G. (2000). Contrast-based image fusion using the discrete wavelet transform, *Opt. Eng.* 39(8), 2075–2082.

Rogers, R. H. & Wood, L (1990). The history and status of merging multiple sensor data: an overview, in Technical Papers 1990, ACSMASPRS Annual Conf. *Image Processing and Remote Sensing* 4, pp. 352–360.

Toet, A. (2003). Natural colour mapping for multiband nightvision imagery, *Information Fusion* 4, 155-166.

Toet, A. & IJspeert, J. K. (2001). Perceptual evaluation of different image fusion schemes, in: I. Kadar (Ed.), *Signal Processing, Sensor Fusion, and Target Recognition X*, The International Society for Optical Engineering, Bellingham, WA, pp.436–441.

Toet, A.; IJspeert, J.K.; Waxman, A. M. & Aguilar, M. (1997). Fusion of visible and thermal imagery improves situational awareness, in: J.G. Verly (Ed.), *Enhanced and Synthetic Vision 1997*, International Society for Optical Engineering, Bellingham, WA, pp.177–188.

Varga, J. T. (1999). Evaluation of operator performance using true color and artificial color in natural scene perception (Report ADA363036), Naval Postgraduate School, Monterey, CA.

Waxman, A.M.; Gove, A. N. & et al. (1996). Progress on color night vision: visible/IR fusion, perception and search, and low-light CCD imaging, *Proc. SPIE Vol. 2736*, pp. 96-107, Enhanced and Synthetic Vision 1996, Jacques G. Verly; Ed.

Zheng, Y. & Essock, E. A. (2008). A local-coloring method for night-vision colorization utilizing image analysis and image fusion, *Information Fusion* 9, 186-199.

Zheng, Y.; Essock, E. A. & Hansen, B. C. (2005). An advanced DWT fusion algorithm and its optimization by using the metric of image quality index, *Optical Engineering* 44 (3), 037003-1-12.

Zheng, Y.; Essock, E. A. & Hansen, B. C. (2004). An advanced image fusion algorithm based on wavelet transform—incorporation with PCA and morphological processing, *Proc. SPIE 5298*, 177–187.

Zheng, Y.; Hansen, B. C. & Haun, A. M. & Essock, E. A. (2005). Coloring Night-vision Imagery with Statistical Properties of Natural Colors by Using Image Segmentation and Histogram Matching, *Proceedings of the SPIE*, Vol. 5667, pp. 107-117.

4

Image Fusion Based on Color Transfer Technique

Guangxin Li
Changchun Institute of Optics, Fine Mechanics and Physics, Chinese Academy of Sciences
P.R. China

1. Introduction

In 2001, with the nonlinear lαβ space (Ruderman et al., 1998), Reinhard et al. (Reinhard et al., 2001) introduced a method to transfer colors between two color images. The goal of their work was to make a synthetic image take on another image's look and feel. Applying Reinhard's statistical color transfer strategy, Toet (Toet, 2003) subsequently developed a color-transfer-based image fusion algorithm. With an appropriate daylight color image as the target image, the method can produce a natural appearing "daytime-like" color fused image and significantly improve observer performance. Therefore, the Toet's approach has received considerable attention in recent years (Li & Wang, 2007b; Li et al., 2010a; Li et al., 2010b; Li et al., 2005; Tsagaris & Anastassopoulos, 2005; Toet & Hogervorst, 2008; Toet & Hogervorst, 2009; Wang et al., 2007; Zheng & Essock, 2008).

Although Toet's work implies that Reinhard's lαβ color transfer method can be successfully applied to image fusion, it is difficult to develop a fast color image fusion algorithm based on this color transfer technique. The main reason is that it is restricted to the nonlinear lαβ space (See Appendix A). This color space is logarithmic, the transformation between RGB and lαβ spaces must be transmitted through *LMS* and log*LMS* spaces. This therefore increases the system's storage requirements and computational time. On the other hand, since the dynamic range of the achromatic component in lαβ space is very different from that of a normal grayscale image, it becomes inconvenient to enhance the luminance contrast of the final color fused image in lαβ space by using conventional methods, such as directly using a high contrast grayscale fused image to replace the luminance component of the color fused image.

To eliminate the limitations mentioned above, we (Li et al., 2010a) employed YC_BC_R space to implement Reinhard's color transfer scheme and applied the YC_BC_R color transfer technique to the fusion of infrared and visible images. Through a series of mathematical derivation and proof, we (Li et al., 2010b) further presented a fast color-transfer-based image fusion algorithm. Our experiments demonstrate the performance of the fast color-transfer-based image fusion method is superior to other related color image fusion methods, including the Toet's approach.

The rest of this chapter is organized as follows. Section 2 reviews Reinhard's lαβ color transfer method. Section 3 outlines our YC_BC_R color transfer method. Section 4 describes two basic image fusion methods based on the YC_BC_R color transfer technique. Section 5 introduces our fast color-transfer-based image fusion method. Experimental results and associated discussions are provided in Section 6. Finally, in Section 7, conclusions are drawn and future works are suggested.

2. lαβ color transfer method

Studies by Reinhard et al. (Reinhard et al., 2001) have found that straightforward color statistics can capture some important subjective notions of style and appearance in images. Their work shows how to transfer them from one image to another to copy some of the atmosphere and mood of a good picture. With the pixel data represented in lαβ space, Reinhard et al. transfer color statistics from the target image to the source image by applying a linear map to each axis separately:

$$\theta_s^* = (\sigma_t^\theta / \sigma_s^\theta)(\theta_s - \mu_s^\theta) + \mu_t^\theta, \quad \text{for } \theta = l, \alpha, \beta \tag{1}$$

where the indexes 's' and 't' refer to the source and target images respectively. θ denotes an individual color component of an image in lαβ space. $(\mu_s^\theta, \sigma_s^\theta)$ and $(\mu_t^\theta, \sigma_t^\theta)$ are the means and standard deviations of the source and target images, respectively, both over the channel θ. Following this step, the resulting source image data is converted back to RGB space for display. After the transform described in (1), the first and second order statistics of color distribution of the source image conform to those of the target color image. This color statistics match procedure is quite simple but can successfully transfer one image's color characteristics to anther.

3. YC_BC_R color transfer method

Instead of using the nonlinear lαβ space, our proposed YC_BC_R color transfer method (Li et al., 2010a) transfers the color distribution of the target image to the source image in the linear YC_BC_R color space. The forward and backward YC_BC_R transformations (Neelamani et al., 2006; Skodras et al., 2001) are achieved by means of (2) and (3), respectively.

$$\begin{bmatrix} Y \\ C_B \\ C_R \end{bmatrix} = \begin{bmatrix} 0.2990 & 0.5870 & 0.1140 \\ -0.1687 & -0.3313 & 0.5000 \\ 0.5000 & -0.4187 & -0.0813 \end{bmatrix} \begin{bmatrix} R \\ G \\ B \end{bmatrix} \tag{2}$$

$$\begin{bmatrix} R \\ G \\ B \end{bmatrix} = \begin{bmatrix} 1.0000 & 0.0000 & 1.4020 \\ 1.0000 & -0.3441 & -0.7141 \\ 1.0000 & 1.7720 & 0.0000 \end{bmatrix} \begin{bmatrix} Y \\ C_B \\ C_R \end{bmatrix} \tag{3}$$

where Y denote the luminance, C_B and C_R are two chromatic channels, which correspond to the color difference model (Poynton, 2003; Jack, 2001). As shown in (4), C_B and C_R stand for blue and red color difference channels, respectively.

$$\begin{aligned} C_B &= \frac{0.5}{0.886}(B - Y) \\ C_R &= \frac{0.5}{0.701}(R - Y) \end{aligned} \tag{4}$$

Since the YC_BC_R transformation is linear, its computational complexity is far lower than that of the lαβ conversion. Let N be the number of the columns and rows of the input RGB image. The lαβ transformation requires a total of $22N^2$ additions, $34N^2$ multiplications, $3N^2$ logarithm and $3N^2$ exponential computations. In contrast, the YC_BC_R transformation avoids the logarithm and exponential operations. From (2) and (3), we can observe that only $10N^2$ additions and $13N^2$ multiplications are required for its implementation. Obviously, the simplicity of the YC_BC_R transformation enables a more efficient implementation of color transfer between images. Like the Reinhard's scheme, the result's quality of the YC_BC_R color transfer method also depends on the images' similarity in composition.

The YC_BC_R transformation can be extended into a general formalism defined in (5) and (6). For color transfer, using color spaces conforming to this general YC_BC_R space framework, such as YUV space (Pratt, 2001), can produce same recoloring results as using YC_BC_R space.

$$\begin{bmatrix} \tilde{Y} \\ \tilde{C}_B \\ \tilde{C}_R \end{bmatrix} = \begin{bmatrix} 0.2990x & 0.5870x & 0.1140x \\ -0.1687y & -0.3313y & 0.5000y \\ 0.5000z & -0.4187z & -0.0813z \end{bmatrix} \begin{bmatrix} R \\ G \\ B \end{bmatrix} + \begin{bmatrix} c_1 \\ c_2 \\ c_3 \end{bmatrix} \tag{5}$$

$$\begin{bmatrix} R \\ G \\ B \end{bmatrix} = \begin{bmatrix} 1.0000x^{-1} & 0.0000 & 1.4020z^{-1} \\ 1.0000x^{-1} & -0.3441y^{-1} & -0.7141z^{-1} \\ 1.0000x^{-1} & 1.7720y^{-1} & 0.0000 \end{bmatrix} \left(\begin{bmatrix} \tilde{Y} \\ \tilde{C}_B \\ \tilde{C}_R \end{bmatrix} - \begin{bmatrix} c_1 \\ c_2 \\ c_3 \end{bmatrix} \right) \tag{6}$$

where x, y, z, c_1, c_2 and c_3 are constants, and x, y and z are nonzero. This fact can be proved by the following proposition.

Proposition 1: Let $[\tilde{R}_s^*, \tilde{G}_s^*, \tilde{B}_s^*]^T$ and $[R_s^*, G_s^*, B_s^*]^T$ be the recolored source images obtained by the $\tilde{Y}\tilde{C}_B\tilde{C}_R$ and YC_BC_R based color transfer methods, respectively. Suppose the two cases use the same target image, then for a fixed source image,

$$[\tilde{R}_s^*, \tilde{G}_s^*, \tilde{B}_s^*]^T = [R_s^*, G_s^*, B_s^*]^T \tag{7}$$

Proof: See Appendix B.

The $\tilde{Y}\tilde{C}_B\tilde{C}_R$ transformation specified in (5) and (6) can be regarded as an extension of the YC_BC_R transformation. If x = y = z = 1, and $c_1 = c_2 = c_3 = 0$, then the $\tilde{Y}\tilde{C}_B\tilde{C}_R$ transformation becomes equivalent to the YC_BC_R transformation. If x = 1, y =0.872, z = 1.23, and $c1 = c_2 = c_3 = 0$, then the $\tilde{Y}\tilde{C}_B\tilde{C}_R$ transformation is equivalent to the YUV transformation as follows.

$$\begin{bmatrix} Y \\ U \\ V \end{bmatrix} = \begin{bmatrix} 0.2990 & 0.5870 & 0.1140 \\ -0.1471 & -0.2888 & 0.4359 \\ 0.6148 & -0.5148 & -0.1000 \end{bmatrix} \begin{bmatrix} R \\ G \\ B \end{bmatrix} \tag{8}$$

$$\begin{bmatrix} R \\ G \\ B \end{bmatrix} = \begin{bmatrix} 1.0000 & 0.0000 & 1.1403 \\ 1.0000 & -0.3947 & -0.5808 \\ 1.0000 & 2.0325 & 0.0000 \end{bmatrix} \begin{bmatrix} Y \\ U \\ V \end{bmatrix} \tag{9}$$

4. Basic fusion method based on YC_BC_R color transfer technique

With the YC_BC_R color transfer method, it is very easy to develop color image fusion methods for merging infrared and visible images. We introduced two basic fusion approaches, one named StaCT (Standard Color-Transfer-Based Fusion Method), the other called CECT (Contrast Enhanced Version of Color-Transfer-Based Fusion Method) (Li et al., 2010b). These two basic fusion methods have to produce a source false color fused image, we employed the NRL (Naval Research Laboratory) scheme (Scribner et al., 1998; McDanie et al., 1998) to generate the source color fused image. The NRL algorithm is very simple and fast, and greatly useful for developing fast image fusion method.

4.1 StaCT method

The StaCT method uses the YC_BC_R color transfer method to directly recolor the source false color fused image, its whole steps are as follows.

1. Construct the source false color fused image $[R_f, G_f, B_f]^T$ by using the NRL scheme:

$$[R_f, G_f, B_f]^T = [IR, Vis, Vis]^T \tag{10}$$

where IR and Vis represent the input infrared and visible images, respectively.

2. Convert the image $[R_f, G_f, B_f]^T$ to YC_BC_R space and produce the source YC_BC_R components $[Y_s, C_{B,s}, C_{R,s}]^T$:

$$\begin{bmatrix} Y_s \\ C_{B,s} \\ C_{R,s} \end{bmatrix} = \begin{bmatrix} Y_f \\ C_{B,f} \\ C_{R,f} \end{bmatrix} = \begin{bmatrix} 0.2990 & 0.5870 & 0.1140 \\ -0.1687 & -0.3313 & 0.5000 \\ 0.5000 & -0.4187 & -0.0813 \end{bmatrix} \begin{bmatrix} R_f \\ G_f \\ B_f \end{bmatrix} \tag{11}$$

3. Stretch the source YC_BC_R components to make their statistics match the color statistics of the target daylight color image:

$$\begin{aligned} Y_c &= \frac{\sigma_t^Y}{\sigma_s^Y}(Y_s - \mu_s^Y) + \mu_t^Y \\ C_{B,c} &= \frac{\sigma_t^{C_B}}{\sigma_s^{C_B}}(C_{B,s} - \mu_s^{C_B}) + \mu_t^{C_B} \\ C_{R,c} &= \frac{\sigma_t^{C_R}}{\sigma_s^{C_R}}(C_{R,s} - \mu_s^{C_R}) + \mu_t^{C_R} \end{aligned} \tag{12}$$

where Y_c, $C_{B,c}$ and $C_{R,c}$ are the three color components of the final color fused image $[R_c, G_c, B_c]^T$ in YC_BC_R space. The indexes 's' and 't' stand for the source and target images, respectively. $(\mu_s^\theta, \sigma_s^\theta)$ and $(\mu_t^\theta, \sigma_t^\theta)$, where $\theta = Y, C_B, C_R$, are the means and standard deviations of the source and target images, respectively, both over the channel θ.

4. Transform the result back into RGB representation and get the final color fused image $[R_c, G_c, B_c]^T$:

$$\begin{bmatrix} R_c \\ G_c \\ B_c \end{bmatrix} = \begin{bmatrix} 1.0000 & 0.0000 & 1.4020 \\ 1.0000 & -0.3441 & -0.7141 \\ 1.0000 & 1.7720 & 0.0000 \end{bmatrix} \begin{bmatrix} Y_c \\ C_{B,c} \\ C_{R,c} \end{bmatrix} \tag{13}$$

The Toet's algorithm (Toet, 2003) produces the color fused imagery by using lαβ space. The main difference between the StaCT method and the Toet's method lies in the color space conversion of images. As explained above, the linear YC_BC_R transformation has lower computational complexity in comparison with the nonlinear lαβ transformation. Hence, the StaCT method offers a more efficient and simpler way to produce a color fused image compared to the Toet's method.

4.2 CECT method

The luminance contrast reduction issue, as described by Toet (Toet, 2003), may arise when the contrast of an image detail varies strongly among the different bands. In some conditions a detail may be represented with opposite contrast in different spectral bands. The combination of the individual image bands into a single color image may therefore significantly reduce the luminance contrast of an image detail. As a result, a detail that is noticeable in the individual image bands may be much less visible in the final color representation, due to the lack of luminance contrast. An appropriate grayscale fused image obtained by combining the individual sensor images can preserve all relevant contrast details of the individual bands. Hence, we can enhance the luminance contrast of the final color fused image by replacing the luminance component of the source false color fused image with the grayscale fused image. Based on this strategy, we proposed the CECT method (Li et al., 2010b). Its whole steps to perform are the following.

1. Construct the source false color fused image $[R_f, G_f, B_f]^T$ by using the NRL scheme given in (10).
2. Convert the image $[R_f, G_f, B_f]^T$ to YC_BC_R space as in (11).
3. Replace the luminance component Y_f by the grayscale fused image F, which as well as the $C_{B,f}$ and $C_{R,f}$ components are directly used as the source YC_BC_R components:

$$[Y_s, C_{B,s}, C_{R,s}]^T = [F, C_{B,f}, C_{R,f}]^T \tag{14}$$

4. Stretch the source YC_BC_R components to make their statistics match the color statistics of the target daylight color image as shown in (12).
5. Transform the result back into RGB representation as in (13).

The color spaces conforming to the $\tilde{Y}\tilde{C}_B\tilde{C}_R$ framework defined in (5) and (6) can also be used in the CECT method. When the constant x is positive, using any form of $\tilde{Y}\tilde{C}_B\tilde{C}_R$ space can yield the same color fused image as in YC_BC_R space. This result can be proved by the following proposition.

Proposition 2: Let $[\tilde{R}_c, \tilde{G}_c, \tilde{B}_c]^T$ and $[R_c, G_c, B_c]^T$ be the color fused images obtained by the $\tilde{Y}\tilde{C}_B\tilde{C}_R$ and YC_BC_R based CECT methods, respectively. Suppose the two cases use the same grayscale fusion method and target image. In addition, assume x defined in the $\tilde{Y}\tilde{C}_B\tilde{C}_R$ transform is positive, then for a fixed pair of input images,

$$[\tilde{R}_c, \tilde{G}_c, \tilde{B}_c]^T = [R_c, G_c, B_c]^T \tag{15}$$

The proof of this proposition is similar to the one of Proposition 1. Hence, we do not prove it here.

The achromatic component in lαβ space cannot be used directly for the luminance replacement process because its dynamic range is very different from that of the grayscale fused image. Therefore, Toet (Toet, 2003) suggested using HSV (Hue, Saturation, and Value) color space, in which the value component (V) has the same amplitude range as the grayscale fused image, to address this problem. The final high contrast color fused image is constructed by converting the recolored fused image into HSV space, replacing the value component by the high contrast grayscale fused image and then transforming back to RGB space. One can see that three color spaces (RGB, lαβ and HSV) are employed and four color space transformations (RGB to lαβ, lαβ to RGB, RGB to HSV, and HSV to RGB) are needed in the above manner. This is not an efficient way relative to the CECT method. Taking advantage of the linear YC_BC_R space, the CECT method only uses two color spaces (RGB and YC_BC_R) and requires two color space conversions (RGB to YC_BC_R and YC_BC_R to RGB) during the whole procedure to obtain the high contrast output image.

5. Fast fusion method based on YC_BC_R color transfer technique

For real-time image fusion system, faster methods are always desirable. We proposed a fast algorithm by mathematically optimizing the CECT approach's architecture, which is named AOCT (Architecture-Optimized Version of Color-Transfer-Based Fusion Method) (Li et al., 2010b). Fig. 1 illustrates the fusion architecture of the AOCT approach, and its whole steps are as follows.

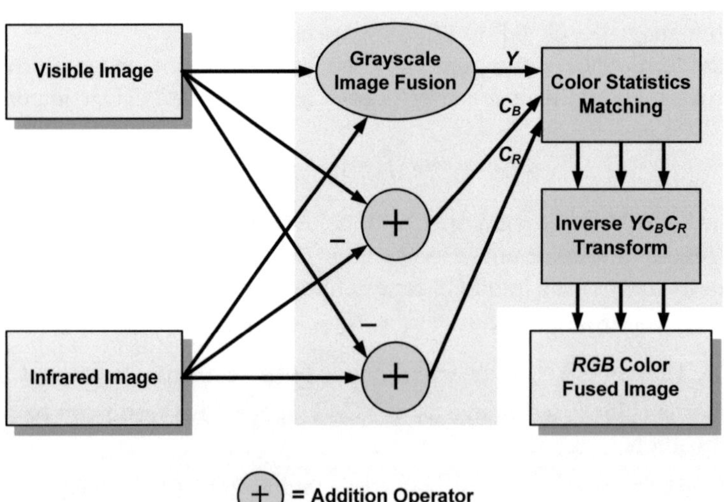

Fig. 1. Fusion architecture of the AOCT method

1. Use $[F, Vis-IR, IR-Vis]^T$ to form the source YC_BC_R components:

$$\begin{bmatrix} Y_s \\ C_{B,s} \\ C_{R,s} \end{bmatrix} = \begin{bmatrix} F \\ Vis-IR \\ IR-Vis \end{bmatrix} \tag{16}$$

Steps 2 and 3 are the same as the steps 4 and 5 of the CECT method. Thus,

2. Perform color statistics matching as in (12).
3. Perform the inverse YC_BC_R transform to obtain the final color fused image as in (13).

We have demonstrated that the AOCT method has the same performance as the CECT method (Li et al., 2010b). The PA (Pixel Averaging) and MR (Multiresolution) fusion schemes are adopted to produce the grayscale fused image in the AOCT method. The AOCT approach using the PA grayscale fusion algorithm is named P-AOCT. The AOCT approach using the MR grayscale fusion algorithm is called M-AOCT.

Similar to the CECT approach, the AOCT method also allows us to choose other color spaces conforming to the $\tilde{Y}\tilde{C}_B\tilde{C}_R$ framework in (5) and (6). When the constants x, y and z are positive, using any form of $\tilde{Y}\tilde{C}_B\tilde{C}_R$ space can produce the same color fusion result as in YC_BC_R space. This conclusion can be proved by the following proposition.

Proposition 3: Let $[\tilde{R}_c, \tilde{G}_c, \tilde{B}_c]^T$ and $[R_c, G_c, B_c]^T$ be the color fused images obtained by the $\tilde{Y}\tilde{C}_B\tilde{C}_R$ based and YC_BC_R based AOCT methods, respectively. Suppose the two cases use the same grayscale fusion method and target image. In addition, assume the constants x, y and z defined in the $\tilde{Y}\tilde{C}_B\tilde{C}_R$ transformation are positive, then for a fixed pair of input images,

$$[\tilde{R}_c, \tilde{G}_c, \tilde{B}_c]^T = [R_c, G_c, B_c]^T \tag{17}$$

Proof: See Appendix C.

In contrast, the construction process of the source chromatic components ($C_{B,s}$ and $C_{R,s}$) in the AOCT method is quite simpler than that in the CECT method. After performing the YC_BC_R transform and replacing the luminance component in the CECT method (by inserting (10) and (11) in (14)), we arrive at

$$\begin{bmatrix} Y_s \\ C_{B,s} \\ C_{R,s} \end{bmatrix} = \begin{bmatrix} F \\ C_{B,f} \\ C_{R,f} \end{bmatrix} = \begin{bmatrix} F \\ -0.1687IR - 0.3313Vis + 0.5Vis \\ 0.5IR - 0.4187Vis - 0.0813Vis \end{bmatrix} \tag{18}$$

Let N be the number of the columns and rows of the input images. According to (18), the CECT method requires $4N^2$ additions and $6N^2$ multiplications to obtain the source chromatic components. The AOCT method skips the YC_BC_R forward transformation and directly uses the simple difference signals of the input images (that is, Vis−IR and IR−Vis) to form the source chromatic components. Equation (16) states that the AOCT method only requires $2N^2$ additions in the construction process. Therefore, the AOCT method is faster and easier to implement compared to the CECT method.

The following strategies can help the AOCT method to be implemented in an extremely fast and memory efficient way.

1. The PA fusion method can be expressed as

$$F = 0.5(IR + Vis) \tag{19}$$

We have proved that the source luminance component Y_s can be directly achieved by the following solution when the P-AOCT method is adopted (Li et al., 2010b).

$$Y_s = IR + Vis \tag{20}$$

2. From (16), we deduce

$$C_{R,s} = -C_{B,s} = -(Vis - IR) \tag{21}$$

From this by applying the mean and standard deviation properties, we can derive that

$$\begin{aligned} \mu_s^{C_R} &= -\mu_s^{C_B} \\ \sigma_s^{C_R} &= \sigma_s^{C_B} \end{aligned} \tag{22}$$

Equations (21) and (22) imply that, after computing $C_{B,s}$, $\mu_s^{C_B}$, and $\sigma_s^{C_B}$, there is no need to recalculate $C_{R,s}$, $\mu_s^{C_R}$, and $\sigma_s^{C_R}$. A more efficient way is to obtain them directly from the negative polarity $C_{B,s}$, the negative polarity $\mu_s^{C_B}$, and $\sigma_s^{C_B}$, respectively.

3. From (12), we can see that only six target color statistical parameters (μ_t^Y, $\mu_t^{C_B}$, $\mu_t^{C_R}$, σ_t^Y, $\sigma_t^{C_B}$ and $\sigma_t^{C_R}$) are required in color statistics matching process. Hence, in practice, there is no real need to store target images. A system that is equipped with a look-up table of color statistical parameters for different types of backgrounds is sufficient to enable users to adjust the color to their specific needs.

6. Experimental results

6.1 Color transfer between landscape photographs

Fig. 2. Color transfer between landscape photographs. Left: the different source images. Second column: the corresponding target images. Third column: the results of the lαβ color transfer method. Right: the results of the YC_BC_R color transfer method. Top to bottom: trees, sunset, and mountains image pairs. (All the source and target images courtesy of © Ian Britton - FreeFoto.com.)

To demonstrate the potential of the YC_BC_R color transfer method, we applied it to some landscape photographs of scenes, including trees, sunset, and mountains. The lαβ color transfer scheme (Reinhard et al., 2001) was selected to serve as a comparison. The source image of each scene is shown in the left column of Fig. 2. The second left column represents their respective target images. Note that each source image contains similar composition as the corresponding target image. The third and right columns illustrate the results of applying the lαβ and YC_BC_R color transfer methods respectively to the source image at the left column with the corresponding image in the second column as the target. lαβ space works very well on the task of recoloring these natural color photographs. This provides some validation for Reinhard et al.'s work (Reinhard et al., 2001). The images produced by using YC_BC_R space look a little lighter than in lαβ space, but the results are also pleasing and reasonable. This indicates that the YC_BC_R color transfer method can be applied to many image types.

6.2 Comparison among different color image fusion methods

Fig. 3. show some examples of color image fusion methods related to color transfer technique, inculding the NRL (Scribner et al., 1998; McDanie et al., 1998), Toet's (Toet, 2003), improved Toet's, StaCT, P-AOCT, M-AOCT schemes. The CECT approach has the same fusion performance as the AOCT method (Li et al., 2010b), thus, we do not discuss the CECT approach in our experiments.

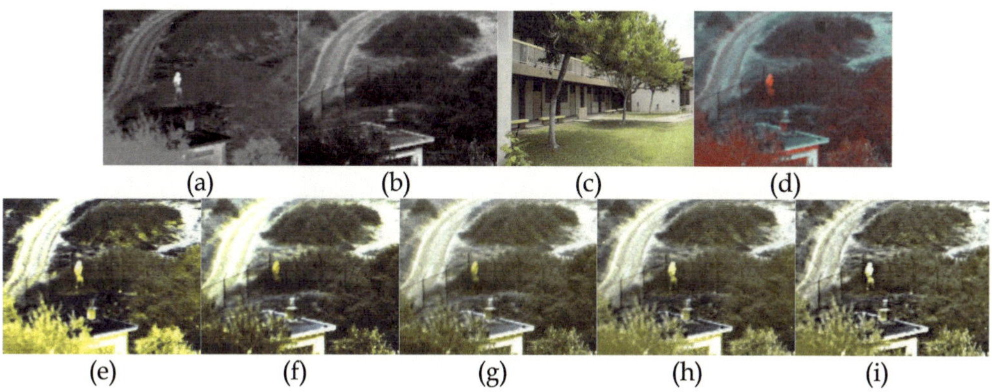

Fig. 3. Fusion results of applying different color image fusion methods to the UN Camp images of a nighttime scene representing a building, a path, heather, and a person walking along the fence. (a) The input 3-5 μ m midwave infrared image. (b) The input visible image. (c) The target image. (d) The result of the NRL method. (e)-(i) are the results of the Toet's method, the improved Toet's method, the StaCT method, the P-AOCT method and the M-AOCT method respectively, all with (c) as the target image. (The target image courtesy of Alexander Toet.)

As described above, the Toet's method (Toet, 2003) produces a color fused image by using the lαβ color transfer approach to recolor a source false color fused image. In his study, the source false color fused image is generated by mapping the infrared image and the visible image respectively to the green and blue channels of an RGB image, the red channel is set to zero or black. Similar to the Toet approach, the improved Toet's method also employs lαβ space to perform color transfer, the difference is that the improved Toet's method uses the NRL scheme to yield the source false color fused image.

In this study, we employ a discrete wavelet transform based fusion scheme (Li et al., 2007a) to achieve the grayscale fused image in the M-AOCT method, and use a 4-level wavelet transform with '5-3' biorthogonal filters (Cohen et al., 1992; Daubechies, 1992) to implement the MR decompositions of the input images. The approximation images at the highest level (low resolution) are combined by taking the average of them. The detail images at each high frequency band of each decomposition level are fused by a weighted average fusion rule based on the local amplitude ratio. This weighted average fusion rule can achieve a fused image with less 'ringing' artifacts compared to the widely used maximum selection fusion rule (Zhang & Blum, 1999; Piella, 2003).

The original registered infrared (3-5 μm) and visible test images are supplied by Toet at TNO Human Factors and available online at www.imagefusion.org. Since the corresponding daylight color photographs are not available for these images, we adopt an arbitrary color image as target.

Fig. 3 corresponds to a nighttime scene, which represents a building, a path, heather, and a person walking along the fence. The input infrared (3-5 μm) and visible images are shown in Fig. 3(a) and (b), respectively. Fig. 3(c) shows an arbitrary daytime color image with similar color distribution as the source scene. Fig. 3(d) shows the false color fused image constructed by the NRL method. Most salient features from the inputs are clearly visible in this image, but the color appearance is rather unnatural. Fig. 3(e) shows the fusion result obtained by the Toet's method with Fig. 3(c) as target. The image has a comparatively natural color appearance. But the color characteristics are just roughly close to those of the target image. It doesn't preserve the trees' green colors in the target image very well. Note that some heather appears yellow. Moreover, there emerges excessive saturation phenomenon in the resulting color fused image, and thus produces a glaring white, which severely hides some salient detail information contained in the input images, such as the textures of the road. In addition, some image details, such as the poles of the fence and the outlines of the building, are represented with low contrast in Fig. 3(e). Fig. 3(f) shows the fused image produced by the improved Toet's method with Fig. 3(c) as target. The image takes the target image's color characteristics and has high contrast, but the excessive saturation phenomenon doesn't disappear, some salient details, such as the textures of the road, are hiden by the glaring white. Fig. 3(g) shows the fused image generated by the StaCT method with Fig. 3(c) as target. The image does not only gain the natural color appearance of the target image, but contains most salient information from the input images, moreover, avoids the excessive saturation phenomenon. Fig. 3(h) shows the fused image produced by the P-AOCT method with Fig. 3(c) as target. The image has better visual quality in comparison with the result obtained by the StaCT scheme as shown in Fig. 3(g). The visibility of image details in Fig. 3(h), such as the poles of the fence and the outlines of the person, is evidently higher than in the StaCT algorithm. Fig. 3(i) illustrates the fused image achieved by the M-AOCT method with Fig. 3(c) as target. Clearly, the M-AOCT approach has the best overall performance.

The M-AOCT method employs the MR fusion scheme, the Toet's and improved Toet's methods utilize the lαβ color transfer strategy. Therefore, the computational complexities of these three methods are all higher than that of the P-AOCT method. In fact, the StaCT method has the same complexity as the P-CECT method (the CECT approach using the PA fusion algorithm to implement grayscale fusion). Thus, according to the algorithm analysis in Section 5, we can confirm that the computational cost of the P-AOCT method is lower than that of the StaCT method. Hence, in the five color-transfer-based image fusion algorithms (the Toet's, improved Toet's, StaCT, P-AOCT, and M-AOCT methods), the P-AOCT method has the lowest implementation complexity.

Although it can be seen from Fig. 3 that the salient information from the input images is represented with higher contrast in the fused image obtained by the M-AOCT method than those produced by other approaches, this superior performance of the M-AOCT method comes at a cost of increased computational complexity of the fusion process. In contrast, the P-AOCT method is much faster and easier to implement. Moreover, this algorithm can provide a visually pleasing color fused image with available contrast, and the salient information contained in the input images is also represented quite well. Hence, if there is no special requirement, in practice, it is not necessary to utilize the M-AOCT method to merge images, the low computational-cost P-AOCT method is generally sufficient to fulfill user needs.

6.3 Choice of target image

For the AOCT method, the actual choice of the target image is not critical. The method can provide a natural looking color fused image as long as the color distribution of the target image is to some extent similar to that of the source scene.

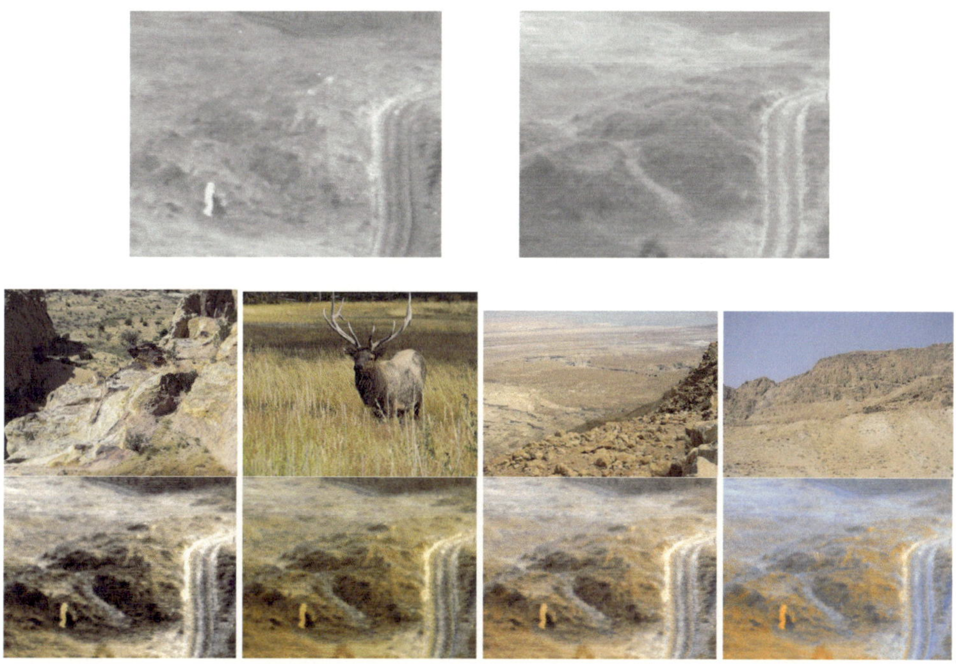

Fig. 4. Fusion results of applying the P-AOCT method with different target images to the Dune images of a nighttime scene representing a person walking over a dune area covered with semi-shrubs and sandy paths. Top left: the input 3-5 μm midwave infrared image. Top right: the input visible image. Middle: four different target images. Bottom: the corresponding fusion results corresponding to each target image. (The two left target images courtesy of www.pics4learning.com, and the two right target images courtesy of www.bigfoto.com.)

To demonstrate this fact, we applied the P-AOCT method to merging the Dune images with different target images. The original registered infrared (3-5 μm) and visible test images are shown at the top left and right of Fig. 4 respectively. In this scene, a person is walking over a dune area covered with semi-shrubs and sandy paths. These images are also supplied by Toet at TNO Human Factors and available online at www.imagefusion.org. The second row of Fig. 4 represents the different target images. The third row illustrates the results of applying the P-AOCT approach respectively to the input images at the top row with the corresponding image in the second row as the target. The second left column of Fig. 4 shows an interesting example where a color photograph representing a grassland area with an elk in it was adopted as the target image. The content of the target image in this case is quite dissimilar to that of the source scene, but the target image has similar color distribution as the source scene. As a result, the corresponding color fused images still have a fairly natural appearance. Another special example depicted in the right column of Fig. 4 shows that the P-AOCT method fails when the color compositions of the target image and the source scene are too dissimilar. In this case, the target image also displays a dune like scene, but has more bright blue sky in the background. Consequently, the appearance of the resulting fused images is quite unnatural and the sandy paths are represented in unreasonable blue.

From the above examples, we can see that the depicted scenes of the target and source images don't have to be identical, as long as their color distributions resemble each other to some extent. In practice, surveillance systems usually register a fixed scene, a daylight color image of the same scene that is being monitored could be used as an optimal target image.

7. Conclusion

In this chapter, we introduced color transfer techniques and some typical image fusion methods based on color transfer technique. More importantly, we presented a fast image fusion algorithm based on YC_BC_R color transfer technique, named AOCT. Depending on the PA and MR grayscale image fusion schemes, we developed two solutions, namely the P-AOCT and M-AOCT methods, to fulfill different user needs. The P-AOCT method answers to a need of easy implementation and speed of use. The M-AOCT method answers to the high quality need of the fused products. Experimental results demonstrate that the AOCT method can effectively produce a natural appearing "daytime-like" color fused image with good contrast. Even the low-complexity P-AOCT method can provide a satisfactory result.

Another important contribution of this chapter is that we have mathematically proved some useful propositions about color-transfer-based image fusion. These theories clarify that other color spaces, which are founded on the basis of luminance, blue and red color difference components, such as YUV space, can be used as an alternative to YC_BC_R space in the image fusion approaches based on YC_BC_R color transfer technique, including the StaCT, CECT, and AOCT methods.

Currently, the AOCT method only supports the fusion of imagery from two sensors. Future research effort will be the extension of the AOCT method to accept imagery from three or four spectral bands, e.g. visible, short-wave infrared, middle-wave infrared, and long-wave infrared bands. In addition, designing quantitative measure for color image fusion performance is another worthwhile and challenging research topic.

8. Appendix

A. RGB to lαβ transform

In this Appendix we present the RGB to lαβ transform (Ruderman et al., 1998). This transform is derived from a principal component transform of a large ensemble of hyperspectral images that represents a good cross-section of natural scenes. The resulting data representation is compact and symmetrical, and provides automatic decorrelation to higher than second order. The actual transform is as follows. First the RGB tristimulus values are converted to *LMS* space by

$$\begin{bmatrix} L \\ M \\ S \end{bmatrix} = \begin{bmatrix} 0.3811 & 0.5783 & 0.0402 \\ 0.1967 & 0.7244 & 0.0782 \\ 0.0241 & 0.1288 & 0.8444 \end{bmatrix} \begin{bmatrix} R \\ G \\ B \end{bmatrix} \tag{23}$$

The data in this color space shows a great deal of skew, which is largely eliminated by taking a logarithmic transform:

$$\begin{bmatrix} \mathbf{L} \\ \mathbf{M} \\ \mathbf{S} \end{bmatrix} = \begin{bmatrix} \log L \\ \log M \\ \log S \end{bmatrix} \tag{24}$$

The inverse transform from **LMS** cone space back to RGB space is as follows. First, the **LMS** pixel values are raised to the power ten to go back to linear *LMS* space.

$$\begin{bmatrix} L \\ M \\ S \end{bmatrix} = \begin{bmatrix} 10^{\mathbf{L}} \\ 10^{\mathbf{M}} \\ 10^{\mathbf{S}} \end{bmatrix} \tag{25}$$

Then, the data can be converted from *LMS* to RGB using the inverse transform of (23):

$$\begin{bmatrix} R \\ G \\ B \end{bmatrix} = \begin{bmatrix} 4.4679 & -3.5873 & 0.1193 \\ -1.2186 & 2.3809 & -0.1624 \\ 0.0497 & -0.2439 & 1.2045 \end{bmatrix} \begin{bmatrix} L \\ M \\ S \end{bmatrix} \tag{26}$$

Ruderman et al. (Ruderman et al., 1998) presented the following simple transform to decorrelate the axes in the **LMS** space:

$$\begin{bmatrix} l \\ \alpha \\ \beta \end{bmatrix} = \begin{bmatrix} 1/\sqrt{3} & 0 & 0 \\ 0 & 1/\sqrt{6} & 0 \\ 0 & 0 & 1/\sqrt{2} \end{bmatrix} \begin{bmatrix} 1 & 1 & 1 \\ 1 & 1 & -2 \\ 1 & -1 & 0 \end{bmatrix} \begin{bmatrix} \mathbf{L} \\ \mathbf{M} \\ \mathbf{S} \end{bmatrix} \tag{27}$$

If we think of the **L** channel as red, the **M** as green, and **S** as blue, we see that this is a variant of a color opponent model:

$$\begin{aligned} &\text{Achromatic} \propto R + G + B \\ &\text{Yellow-blue} \propto R + G - B \\ &\text{Red-green} \propto R - G \end{aligned} \tag{28}$$

After processing the color signals in the lαβ space the inverse transform of (27) can be used to return to the **LMS** space:

$$\begin{bmatrix}\mathbf{L}\\\mathbf{M}\\\mathbf{S}\end{bmatrix}=\begin{bmatrix}1&1&1\\1&1&-1\\1&-2&0\end{bmatrix}\begin{bmatrix}1/\sqrt{3}&0&0\\0&1/\sqrt{6}&0\\0&0&1/\sqrt{2}\end{bmatrix}\begin{bmatrix}l\\\alpha\\\beta\end{bmatrix}\tag{29}$$

B. Proof of Proposition 1

From (5) we derive that

$$\begin{bmatrix}\tilde{Y}\\\tilde{C}_B\\\tilde{C}_R\end{bmatrix}=\begin{bmatrix}x&0&0\\0&y&0\\0&0&z\end{bmatrix}\begin{bmatrix}0.2990&0.5870&0.1140\\-0.1687&-0.3313&0.5000\\0.5000&-0.4187&-0.0813\end{bmatrix}\begin{bmatrix}R\\G\\B\end{bmatrix}+\begin{bmatrix}c_1\\c_2\\c_3\end{bmatrix}$$

$$=\begin{bmatrix}x&0&0\\0&y&0\\0&0&z\end{bmatrix}\begin{bmatrix}Y\\C_B\\C_R\end{bmatrix}+\begin{bmatrix}c_1\\c_2\\c_3\end{bmatrix}=\begin{bmatrix}xY\\yC_B\\zC_R\end{bmatrix}+\begin{bmatrix}c_1\\c_2\\c_3\end{bmatrix}\tag{30}$$

Hence, we can prove that the original source and target images respectively satisfy

$$\begin{bmatrix}\tilde{Y}_s\\\tilde{C}_{B,s}\\\tilde{C}_{R,s}\end{bmatrix}=\begin{bmatrix}xY_s\\yC_{B,s}\\zC_{R,s}\end{bmatrix}+\begin{bmatrix}c_1\\c_2\\c_3\end{bmatrix}\text{ and }\begin{bmatrix}\tilde{Y}_t\\\tilde{C}_{B,t}\\\tilde{C}_{R,t}\end{bmatrix}=\begin{bmatrix}xY_t\\yC_{B,t}\\zC_{R,t}\end{bmatrix}+\begin{bmatrix}c_1\\c_2\\c_3\end{bmatrix}\tag{31}$$

where $[\tilde{Y}_s,\tilde{C}_{B,s},\tilde{C}_{R,s}]^T$ and $[Y_s,C_{B,s},C_{R,s}]^T$ are the three components of the source image in $\tilde{Y}\tilde{C}_B\tilde{C}_R$ and YC_BC_R spaces, respectively. $[\tilde{Y}_t,\tilde{C}_{B,t},\tilde{C}_{R,t}]^T$ and $[Y_t,C_{B,t},C_{R,t}]^T$ represent the three components of the target image in $\tilde{Y}\tilde{C}_B\tilde{C}_R$ and YC_BC_R spaces, respectively. We know that the mean and standard deviation respectively have the following properties:

$$\mu(\lambda X+c)=\lambda\mu(X)+c\text{ and }\sigma(\lambda X+c)=|\lambda|\sigma(X)\tag{32}$$

where λ and c are constants, $\lambda,c\in\mathbb{R}$, X is a random variable. Thus for the original source and target images, the means of their achromatic components in $\tilde{Y}\tilde{C}_B\tilde{C}_R$ and YC_BC_R spaces respectively satisfy

$$\mu_s^{\tilde{Y}}=x\mu_s^Y+c_1\text{ and }\mu_t^{\tilde{Y}}=x\mu_t^Y+c_1\tag{33}$$

The corresponding standard deviations respectively satisfy

$$\sigma_s^{\tilde{Y}}=|x|\sigma_s^Y\text{ and }\sigma_t^{\tilde{Y}}=|x|\sigma_t^Y\tag{34}$$

Let $[\tilde{Y}_s^*,\tilde{C}_{B,s}^*,\tilde{C}_{R,s}^*]^T$ be the three components of $[\tilde{R}_s^*,\tilde{G}_s^*,\tilde{B}_s^*]^T$ in $\tilde{Y}\tilde{C}_B\tilde{C}_R$ space, $[Y_s^*,C_{B,s}^*,C_{R,s}^*]^T$ be the three components of $[R_s^*,G_s^*,B_s^*]^T$ in YC_BC_R space. By inserting (33), (34) and $\tilde{Y}_s=xY_s+c_1$ in

$$\tilde{Y}_s^* = (\sigma_t^{\tilde{Y}} / \sigma_s^{\tilde{Y}})(\tilde{Y}_s - \mu_s^{\tilde{Y}}) + \mu_t^{\tilde{Y}} \tag{35}$$

we can derive the relationship between $\tilde{Y}_s^*$ and Y_s^*:

$$\tilde{Y}_s^* = xY_s^* + c_1 \tag{36}$$

In a similar way, we can obtain

$$\tilde{C}_{B,s}^* = yC_{B,s}^* + c_2 \text{ and } \tilde{C}_{R,s}^* = zC_{R,s}^* + c_3 \tag{37}$$

From (6) we have

$$\begin{bmatrix} \tilde{R}_s^* \\ \tilde{G}_s^* \\ \tilde{B}_s^* \end{bmatrix} = \begin{bmatrix} 1.0000x^{-1} & 0.0000 & 1.4020z^{-1} \\ 1.0000x^{-1} & -0.3441y^{-1} & -0.7141z^{-1} \\ 1.0000x^{-1} & 1.7720y^{-1} & 0.0000 \end{bmatrix} \left(\begin{bmatrix} \tilde{Y}_s^* \\ \tilde{C}_{B,s}^* \\ \tilde{C}_{R,s}^* \end{bmatrix} - \begin{bmatrix} c_1 \\ c_2 \\ c_3 \end{bmatrix} \right) \tag{38}$$

By inserting (36) and (37) in (38), we derive that

$$\begin{aligned} \begin{bmatrix} \tilde{R}_s^* \\ \tilde{G}_s^* \\ \tilde{B}_s^* \end{bmatrix} &= \begin{bmatrix} 1.0000 & 0.0000 & 1.4020 \\ 1.0000 & -0.3441 & -0.7141 \\ 1.0000 & 1.7720 & 0.0000 \end{bmatrix} \begin{bmatrix} x^{-1} & 0 & 0 \\ 0 & y^{-1} & 0 \\ 0 & 0 & z^{-1} \end{bmatrix} \left(\begin{bmatrix} xY_s^* + c_1 \\ yC_{B,s}^* + c_2 \\ zC_{R,s}^* + c_3 \end{bmatrix} - \begin{bmatrix} c_1 \\ c_2 \\ c_3 \end{bmatrix} \right) \\ &= \begin{bmatrix} 1.0000 & 0.0000 & 1.4020 \\ 1.0000 & -0.3441 & -0.7141 \\ 1.0000 & 1.7720 & 0.0000 \end{bmatrix} \begin{bmatrix} x^{-1} & 0 & 0 \\ 0 & y^{-1} & 0 \\ 0 & 0 & z^{-1} \end{bmatrix} \begin{bmatrix} xY_s^* \\ yC_{B,s}^* \\ zC_{R,s}^* \end{bmatrix} \\ &= \begin{bmatrix} 1.0000 & 0.0000 & 1.4020 \\ 1.0000 & -0.3441 & -0.7141 \\ 1.0000 & 1.7720 & 0.0000 \end{bmatrix} \begin{bmatrix} Y_s^* \\ C_{B,s}^* \\ C_{R,s}^* \end{bmatrix} = \begin{bmatrix} R_s^* \\ G_s^* \\ B_s^* \end{bmatrix} \end{aligned} \tag{39}$$

This completes the proof.

C. Proof of Proposition 3

Let $[\tilde{Y}_s, \tilde{C}_{B,s}, \tilde{C}_{R,s}]^T$ and $[Y_s, C_{B,s}, C_{R,s}]^T$ be the source color components in the $\tilde{Y}\tilde{C}_B\tilde{C}_R$ based and YC_BC_R based AOCT methods, respectively. Thus, from the given condition we have

$$\begin{bmatrix} \tilde{Y}_s \\ \tilde{C}_{B,s} \\ \tilde{C}_{R,s} \end{bmatrix} = \begin{bmatrix} Y_s \\ C_{B,s} \\ C_{R,s} \end{bmatrix} = \begin{bmatrix} F \\ Vis - IR \\ IR - Vis \end{bmatrix} \tag{40}$$

Let $[\tilde{Y}_t, \tilde{C}_{B,t}, \tilde{C}_{R,t}]^T$ and $[Y_t, C_{B,t}, C_{R,t}]^T$ be the three components of the target image in $\tilde{Y}\tilde{C}_B\tilde{C}_R$ and YC_BC_R spaces, respectively. We know from (30) that the target image satisfies

$$\begin{bmatrix} \tilde{Y}_t \\ \tilde{C}_{B,t} \\ \tilde{C}_{R,t} \end{bmatrix} = \begin{bmatrix} xY_t \\ yC_{B,t} \\ zC_{R,t} \end{bmatrix} + \begin{bmatrix} c_1 \\ c_2 \\ c_3 \end{bmatrix} \tag{41}$$

Then, under the given assumption that x, y and z > 0, using the mean and standard deviation properties, from (40) and (41) we can derive

$$\begin{bmatrix} \mu_s^{\tilde{Y}} \\ \mu_s^{\tilde{C}_B} \\ \mu_s^{\tilde{C}_R} \end{bmatrix} = \begin{bmatrix} \mu_s^{Y} \\ \mu_s^{C_B} \\ \mu_s^{C_R} \end{bmatrix}, \begin{bmatrix} \sigma_s^{\tilde{Y}} \\ \sigma_s^{\tilde{C}_B} \\ \sigma_s^{\tilde{C}_R} \end{bmatrix} = \begin{bmatrix} \sigma_s^{Y} \\ \sigma_s^{C_B} \\ \sigma_s^{C_R} \end{bmatrix}, \begin{bmatrix} \mu_t^{\tilde{Y}} \\ \mu_t^{\tilde{C}_B} \\ \mu_t^{\tilde{C}_R} \end{bmatrix} = \begin{bmatrix} x\mu_t^{Y} \\ y\mu_t^{C_B} \\ z\mu_t^{C_R} \end{bmatrix} + \begin{bmatrix} c_1 \\ c_2 \\ c_3 \end{bmatrix}, \begin{bmatrix} \sigma_t^{\tilde{Y}} \\ \sigma_t^{\tilde{C}_B} \\ \sigma_t^{\tilde{C}_R} \end{bmatrix} = \begin{bmatrix} x\sigma_t^{Y} \\ y\sigma_t^{C_B} \\ z\sigma_t^{C_R} \end{bmatrix} \tag{42}$$

Let $[\tilde{Y}_c, \tilde{C}_{B,c}, \tilde{C}_{R,c}]^T$ be the three components of $[\tilde{R}_c, \tilde{G}_c, \tilde{B}_c]^T$ in $\tilde{Y}\tilde{C}_B\tilde{C}_R$ space, $[Y_c, C_{B,c}, C_{R,c}]^T$ be the three components of $[R_c, G_c, B_c]^T$ in YC_BC_R space, respectively. By inserting (40), (41) and (42) in (12), we deduce that

$$\begin{bmatrix} \tilde{Y}_c \\ \tilde{C}_{B,c} \\ \tilde{C}_{R,c} \end{bmatrix} = \begin{bmatrix} xY_c \\ yC_{B,c} \\ zC_{R,c} \end{bmatrix} + \begin{bmatrix} c_1 \\ c_2 \\ c_3 \end{bmatrix} \tag{43}$$

From (6) we have

$$\begin{bmatrix} \tilde{R}_c \\ \tilde{G}_c \\ \tilde{B}_c \end{bmatrix} = \begin{bmatrix} 1.0000x^{-1} & 0.0000y^{-1} & 1.4020z^{-1} \\ 1.0000x^{-1} & -0.3441y^{-1} & -0.7141z^{-1} \\ 1.0000x^{-1} & 1.7720y^{-1} & 0.0000z^{-1} \end{bmatrix} \left(\begin{bmatrix} \tilde{Y}_c \\ \tilde{C}_{B,c} \\ \tilde{C}_{R,c} \end{bmatrix} - \begin{bmatrix} c_1 \\ c_2 \\ c_3 \end{bmatrix} \right) \tag{44}$$

Thus, by inserting (43) in (44), we can derive that

$$\begin{bmatrix} \tilde{R}_c \\ \tilde{G}_c \\ \tilde{B}_c \end{bmatrix} = \begin{bmatrix} 1.0000 & 0.0000 & 1.4020 \\ 1.0000 & -0.3441 & -0.7141 \\ 1.0000 & 1.7720 & 0.0000 \end{bmatrix} \begin{bmatrix} x^{-1} & 0 & 0 \\ 0 & y^{-1} & 0 \\ 0 & 0 & z^{-1} \end{bmatrix} \left(\begin{bmatrix} xY_c + c_1 \\ yC_{B,c} + c_2 \\ zC_{R,c} + c_3 \end{bmatrix} - \begin{bmatrix} c_1 \\ c_2 \\ c_3 \end{bmatrix} \right)$$

$$= \begin{bmatrix} 1.0000 & 0.0000 & 1.4020 \\ 1.0000 & -0.3441 & -0.7141 \\ 1.0000 & 1.7720 & 0.0000 \end{bmatrix} \begin{bmatrix} x^{-1} & 0 & 0 \\ 0 & y^{-1} & 0 \\ 0 & 0 & z^{-1} \end{bmatrix} \begin{bmatrix} xY_c \\ yC_{B,c} \\ zC_{R,c} \end{bmatrix}$$

$$= \begin{bmatrix} 1.0000 & 0.0000 & 1.4020 \\ 1.0000 & -0.3441 & -0.7141 \\ 1.0000 & 1.7720 & 0.0000 \end{bmatrix} \begin{bmatrix} Y_c \\ C_{B,c} \\ C_{R,c} \end{bmatrix} = \begin{bmatrix} R_c \\ G_c \\ B_c \end{bmatrix} \tag{45}$$

This finishes the proof.

9. Acknowledgment

The author thanks everyone who contributed images to this chapter. The author also thanks TNO Human Factors, ImageFusion.org, Pics4Learning.com, BigFoto.com, and FreeFoto.com for test images acquisition.

10. References

Cohen, A., Daubechies, I. & Feauveau, J. -C. (1992). Biorthogonal Bases of Compactly Supported Wavelets. *Commun. Pure Appl. Math.*, Vol. 45, pp. 485-560

Daubechies, I. (1992). *Ten Lectures on Wavelets*, SIAM, Philadelphia, PA

Jack, K. (2001). *Video Demystified, 3rd ed.*, LLH Technology Publishing, Eagle Rock, VA

Li, G., & Wang, K. (2007a). Merging Infrared and Color Visible Images with a Contrast Enhanced Fusion Method. *Proc. SPIE*, Vol. 6571, pp. 657108-1-657108-12

Li, G. & Wang, K. (2007b). Applying Daytime Colors to Nighttime Imagery with an Efficient Color Transfer Method. *Proc. SPIE*, Vol. 6559, pp. 65590L-1-65590L-12

Li, G., Xu, S. & Zhao, X. (2010a). An Efficient Color Transfer Algorithm for Recoloring Multiband Night Vision Imagery. *Proc. SPIE*, Vol. 7689, pp. 76890A-1-76890A-12

Li, G., Xu, S. & Zhao, X. (2010b). Fast Color-Transfer-Based Image Fusion Method for Merging Infrared and Visible Images. *Proc. SPIE*, Vol. 7710, pp. 77100S-1-77100S-12

Li, Z., Jing, Z., Yang, X., et al., (2005). Color Transfer Based Remote Sensing Image Fusion Using Non-separable Wavelet Frame Transform. *Pattern Recognition Letters*, Vol. 26, No. 13, pp. 2006-2014

McDanie, R. V., Scribner, D. A., Krebs, W. K., et al. (1998). Image Fusion for Tactical Applications. *Proc. SPIE*, Vol. 3436, pp. 685-695

Neelamani, R., Queiroz, R. de., Fan, Z., et al. (2006). JPEG Compression History Estimation for Color Images. *IEEE Trans. Image Process.*,Vol. 15, No. 6, pp. 1365-1378

Poynton, C. (2003). *Digital Video and HDTV, Algorithms and Interfaces*, Morgan Kaufmann, San Francisco, CA

Pratt, W. K. (2001). *Digital Image Processing, 3rd ed.*, Wiley, New York

Piella, G. (2003). A General Framework for Multiresolution Image Fusion: From Pixels to Regions. *Inf. Fusion*, Vol. 4, pp. 259-280

Ruderman, D. L.; Cronin, T. W. & Chiao, C. C. (1998). Statistics of Cone Responses to Natural Images: Implications for Visual Coding. *J. Optical Soc. of America*, Vol. 15, No. 8, pp. 2036-2045

Reinhard, E., Ashikhmin, M., Gooch, B., et al. (2001). Color Transfer between Images. *IEEE Comput. Graph. Appl.*, Vol. 21, No. 5, pp. 34-41

Scribner, D. A., Schuler, J. M., Warren, P. R., et al. (1998). Infrared Color Vision: Separating Objects from Backgrounds. *Proc. SPIE*, Vol. 3379, pp. 2-13

Skodras, A., Christopoulos, C. & Ebrahimi, T. (2001). The JPEG 2000 Still Image Compression Standard. *IEEE Signal Processing Mag.*, Vol. 18, No. 5, pp. 36-58

Toet, A. (2003). Natural Colour Mapping for Multiband Nightvision Imagery. *Inf. Fusion*, Vol. 4, pp. 155-166

Tsagaris, V. & Anastassopoulos, V. (2005). Fusion of Visible and Infrared Imagery for Night Color Vision. Displays, Vol. 26, No. 4-5, pp. 191-196

Toet, A. & Hogervorst, M. A. (2008). Portable Real-time Color Night Vision. *Proc. SPIE*, Vol. 6974, pp. 697402-1-697402-12

Toet, A. & Hogervorst, M.A. (2009). The TRICLOBS Portable Triband Lowlight Color Observation System. *Proc. SPIE*, Vol. 7345, pp. 734503-1–734503-11

Wang, L., Zhao, Y., Jin, W., et al. (2007). Real-time Color Transfer System for Low-light Level Visible and Infrared Images in YUV Color Space. *Proc. SPIE*, Vol. 6567, pp. 65671G-1–65671G-8

Zhang, Z. & Blum, R. S. (1999). A Categorization and Study of Multiscale-Decomposition-Based Image Fusion Schemes with a Performance Study for a Digital Camera Application. *Proc. IEEE*, Vol. 87, No. 8, pp. 1315–1326

Zheng, Y. & Essock, E. A. (2008). A Local-coloring Method for Night-vision Colorization Utilizing Image Analysis and Fusion. *Inf. Fusion*, Vol. 9, No. 2, pp. 186–199

5

3D Fusion of Stereo and Spectral Series Acquired With Camera Arrays

Ioana Gheţa[1], Michael Heizmann[2] and Jürgen Beyerer[3]
[1,3]*Karlsruhe Institute of Technology KIT*
[2,3]*Fraunhofer Institute of Optronics, System Technologies and Image Exploitation IOSB*
Germany

1. Introduction

One of the main requirements of industrial visual inspection is that the information acquisition is accomplished in real-time. Camera arrays are a promising solution since they offer the possibility of simultaneous image acquisition. Moreover, the acquisition parameters of the different cameras can be varied. Due to dropping prices of industrial cameras, a large number of cameras can be employed in a camera array for automated visual inspection.
The advantages offered by camera arrays come with a price. Simultaneously triggering the cameras results in obtaining image series that contain a stereo effect. If more acquisition parameters (e. g., focus, different spectral filters) are varied, the obtained image series are combined image series, i. e., the images differ in more than one effect. For example, if the cameras are equipped with spectral filters, the obtained image series are combined stereo and spectral series, i. e., the images differ due to both the stereo effect and the acquisition in different parts of the spectrum. However, the main advantage of such image series is that they contain different types of information gained simultaneously: in this case, it is spatial information due to the stereo effect and spectral information due to the use of spectral filters. The challenge consists in fusing the image series, since the different types of information in the combined image series cannot be evaluated separately.
The present chapter deals with different methods of fusing combined stereo and spectral images in order to obtain both spatial and spectral information. For obtaining the spatial information, region based image registration methods for the exploitation of the stereo effect are presented. The problem is modeled with energy functionals, which are minimized by state-of-the-art methods, e. g., dynamic programming or graph cuts. With the help of the obtained spatial information (in form of depth maps), the spectral information can be extracted and further employed, e. g., for material classification or an improved object detection.

1.1 State of the art

For a general theory of image registration techniques, the reader is referred to Modersitzki (2004). Practical examples for fusing image series acquired with camera arrays by means of energy functionals are given in Frese & Gheţa (2006); Gheţa et al. (2006); Gheţa, Frese, Heizmann & Beyerer (2007); Gheţa, Frese, Krüger, Saur, Heinze, Heizmann & Beyerer (2007).

The topic of fusing combined stereo and spectral series for obtaining depth information has not yet been approached in the literature. However, the registration of similar image series can be found in the domains of remote sensing (Lillesand et al. (2008)) and medical image processing (Bankman (2000)). The registration for satellite images usually means finding similar image structures in order to build image carpets. The registration of images for medical purposes generally means finding an elastic transformation between possibly multimodal images in order to determine how tissue or organs change in time. These registration methods for satellite images or for medical purposes are not applicable for industrial imaging, since they do not provide registration for each pixel.

One paper though deals with the problem of registering two stereo images having different gray values for corresponding pixels (Fookes et al. (2004)), without an explicit practical application. The images are not real spectral images, but have been obtained by uniformly modifying one image, e. g., through negation. The authors use entropy based registration. Entropy based methods are not successful for scene areas with little structure, and can therefore not be employed for industrial vision like in our case.

For the analysis of spectral series, various approaches are presented in the literature (Chang (2003)). An example for the fusion of spectral images with the purpose of false color representation is given in Tyo et al. (2003).

1.2 Camera array

For the acquisition of the images, a camera array with nine cameras is employed; see Fig. 1. The cameras are of the same type and have the same geometrical properties. For acquiring the spectral properties of the scene, the cameras are equipped with 50 nm wide spectral filters covering the visual and the near-infrared spectra (400-850 nm). The positions of the filters in the array are unimportant for the image evaluation, since the proposed approaches process all images in the same way; see Section 2. It is though to be mentioned that images of neighboring spectral intervals are more likely to have similar features than images taken at very different spectral wavelengths; see, e. g., Fig. 2. Previous to acquisition, the camera array is calibrated using an improved calibration method, which is based on Weng et al. (1992).

Fig. 1. Camera array used for the acquisition of combined image series. The cameras are equipped with spectral filters.

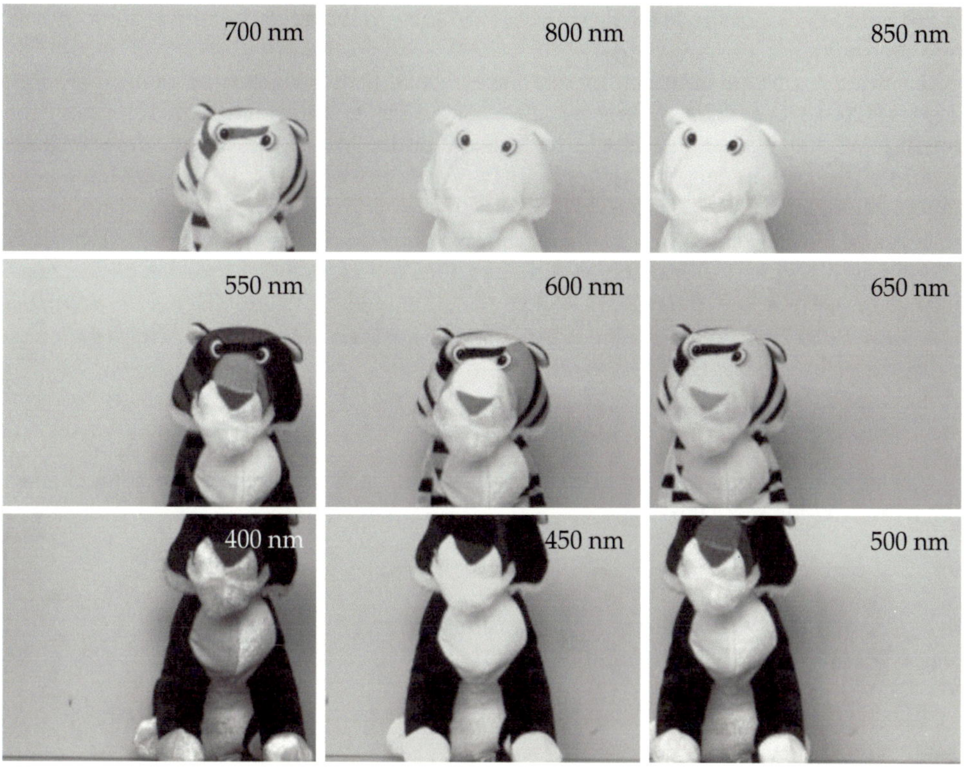

Fig. 2. Combined stereo and spectral series acquired with a camera array. The center wavelength of the filters used for acquisition is written in the upper right corner of each image. The observed scene is displayed in Fig. 3.

Fig. 3. Exemplary scene: an orange tiger with black and white stripes.

1.3 Notations and concepts

The acquired data, i. e., the image series, is denoted by $B := \{B_i,\ i = 1, \ldots, n\}$, where n is the number of images in the series. The images are interpreted as functions $B_i : \mathbb{R}^2 \rightarrow \mathbb{R}$, with the gray value $B_i(\boldsymbol{u}_i)$ of the pixel $\boldsymbol{u}_i = (u_i, v_i)^{\mathrm{T}}$ in the i-th image of the series; u and v are the image coordinates.

The registration process requires in this case rectified and segmented images (Faugeras & Luong (2004); Gonzalez & Woods (2008); Hartley & Zisserman (2003)). For image segmentation, the watershed transform is used under consideration of some additional constraints: the parameters of the operation are chosen such that the images have similar numbers of regions and the sizes of the regions lie within a given range, thus too few segments and oversegmentation are avoided. The watershed transform yields that the images are completely segmented and the obtained regions are compact and disjoint (Gonzalez & Woods (2008)). Therefore, the regions build a partition of each image. The result of the image segmentation can be described using a function $R(\cdot)$, which assigns each pixel $\boldsymbol{u}$ to a region $\mathcal{R}^{\varpi}$ (described by the respective label ϖ):

$$R : \mathbb{R}^2 \to \mathcal{Q}, \quad R(\boldsymbol{u}) = \varpi, \tag{1}$$

where $\mathcal{Q}$ is the set of labels for the regions in an image. A *region* can thus be defined as a set of points having the same label:

$$\mathcal{R}^{\varpi} := \{\boldsymbol{u} | R(\boldsymbol{u}) = \varpi\} \tag{2}$$

with $\varpi \in \mathcal{Q}$ and $|\mathcal{Q}|$ the number of regions of a given image.

A region $\mathcal{R}$ consists of its interior and its boundary:

$$\mathcal{R} := \mathcal{K}_{\mathcal{R}} \cup \mathcal{R}^{\circ}, \tag{3}$$

where the boundary $\mathcal{K}_{\mathcal{R}}$ is defined as the set of pixels located on the border. The boundary $\mathcal{K}_{\mathcal{R}}$ is thus a subset of the region $\mathcal{R}$ and the intersection of the boundaries of two different regions is the empty set. The boundaries of the regions in an image can be determined using standard edge detection operators (Gonzalez & Woods (2008)). In this case morphological operators are used. Like pixels, regions belonging to the image i are marked with $\mathcal{R}_i$.

For the registration we also employ (image) *areas* $\mathcal{B}$. They are defined as a subset of the partition of the image and consist of neighboring regions:

$$\mathcal{B} := \bigcup_{r \in \mathcal{J}} \mathcal{R}^r = \bigcup_{r \in \mathcal{J}} \mathcal{K}_{\mathcal{R}^r} \cup \bigcup_{r \in \mathcal{J}} \mathcal{R}^{r\circ}. \tag{4}$$

$\mathcal{J}$ is the set of all indices of those neighboring regions $\mathcal{R}^r$ (of the same image) belonging to the area $\mathcal{B}$. The set of all areas of an image is equivalent to the power set of the set of all regions. The main difference between regions and areas is that regions build a partition of the image, while areas do not, since areas may overlap.

A common concept used for marking corresponding pixels when registering images is *disparity*. The disparity is the distance in coordinates of corresponding pixels in stereo images (Faugeras & Luong (2004); Hartley & Zisserman (2003)). Considering that the image series acquired with the camera array contain more than two images to be registered, a more generic concept than disparity must be used, which allows the labeling of correspondences between regions and areas in all images of the series (Boykov & Kolmogorov (2004)). To this purpose, a *labeling function* $s(\cdot)$ is defined, which assigns the same label α to all pixels of corresponding regions and areas:

$$s(\boldsymbol{u}_i) : \mathbb{R}^2 \to \mathcal{L}, \quad s(\boldsymbol{u}_i) = \alpha \; \forall \, \boldsymbol{u}_i \in \mathcal{R}_i, \quad \text{if}$$
$$\mathcal{R}_i \leftrightarrow \mathcal{R}_1 \wedge \mathcal{R}_1 \leftrightarrow \mathcal{R}_2 \left(\Leftrightarrow (\bar{u}_2, \bar{v}_2)^{\mathrm{T}} = (\bar{u}_1 + \alpha, \bar{v}_1)^{\mathrm{T}} \right), \quad (5)$$

where $\bar{\boldsymbol{u}} = (\bar{u}, \bar{v})^{\mathrm{T}}$ is a characteristic point of a region, e. g., in this case, the center of gravity. The last equivalence is only valid for horizontally rectified images; the definition for vertically rectified images is similar. The labels are defined using the disparity relation between any two images of the series. The labeling function $s(\cdot)$ for areas is used similarly.

2. Region based stereo fusion

The main challenges to deal with when registering stereo and spectral series are clearly displayed in Fig. 2:

- Corresponding points (points mapping the same 3D scene point in different images) have different gray values. For example, the stripes of the tiger are not visible in near infrared (NIR, 800 nm and above).
- Neighboring regions have different contrasts in different images of the series. For example, the regions forming the nose of the tiger have similar gray values in the image at 400 nm, but considerably different values at 600 nm.

Considering these challenges, a pixel based registration (Scharstein & Szeliski (2002); Seitz et al. (2006)) of the images is not appropriate. The methods for the region based registration can be divided into three categories:

- The straightforward way is to search for 1:1 region correspondences (or 1:0, if a region does not have a correspondent) in two segmented images using features of the regions, e. g., size or shape (Wang & Zheng (2008)).
- The second possible way is to determine 1:N ($N > 0$) correspondences, i. e., allowing a region in one image to correspond to more than one region in another image. It is reasonable that these regions must be connected.
- The third way uses the images without the need of segmentation. The registration is done, e. g., by means of entropy methods, which compare image areas without using gray values, but by analyzing the information content.

We propose two different region based registration methods for evaluating the stereo effect and determining spatial information (Gheţa et al. (2010; 2008)), according to the first two possibilities. The use of entropy based methods is not appropriate in this case, due to the fact that the scenes may not be entirely structured. As already mentioned, the images of the combined series are rectified and segmented prior to evaluation (Faugeras & Luong (2004); Gonzalez & Woods (2008)). A segmentation example of the image series of Fig. 2 is given in Fig. 4.

2.1 Registration based only on regions

In this case, 1:1 (i. e., two regions correspond) or 1:0 (a region has no correspondent) correspondences are determined. Therefore, an energy functional comprising two terms is defined and minimized:

$$E(s, B) := E_{\mathrm{d}}(s, B) + E_{\mathrm{n}}(s, B) \to \min . \quad (6)$$

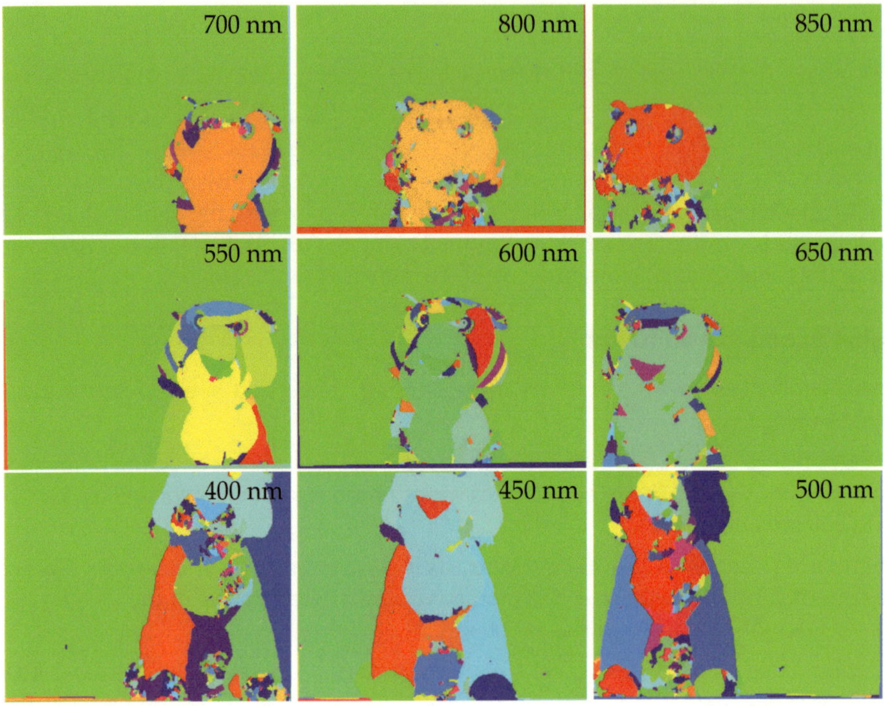

Fig. 4. False color representation of segmented images of the series in Fig. 2. The colors are just labels for the pixel assignment to regions, without marking corresponding regions.

The purpose of the minimization is to find an optimal function $s(\cdot)$ as defined in Eq. (5). The first term in Eq. (6) is the data term, which ensures the consistency of the result with the measured data, i. e., the difference between features of corresponding regions should be small. The second term defines additional constraints, e. g., neighboring constraints.
Since the images are rectified, the search for correspondences can take place without loss of generalization in an epipolar area, which is defined through two epipolar lines; see the example in Fig. 5. That way, the optimization is less time consuming.

Data term

The data term $E_{\mathrm{d}}(s, B)$ of this approach evaluates the similarities between pairs of regions according to certain features, e. g., size, shape and position with regard to epipolar lines. It is defined as a sum over all image pairs in the series and all corresponding region pairs:

$$E_{\mathrm{d}}(s, B) := \sum_{\substack{(B_i, B_j) \\ i \neq j}} \sum_{\mathcal{R}_i \leftrightarrow \mathcal{R}_j} d_{\mathrm{M}}(\boldsymbol{m}_{\mathcal{R}_i}, \boldsymbol{m}_{\mathcal{R}_j}) \tag{7}$$

with $\boldsymbol{m}_{\mathcal{R}}$ as a feature vector characterizing the region $\mathcal{R}$ and $d_{\mathrm{M}}(\cdot, \cdot)$ as a function to measure the dissimilarity between two regions. The correspondences are defined over the function $s(\cdot)$; see Section 1.3.

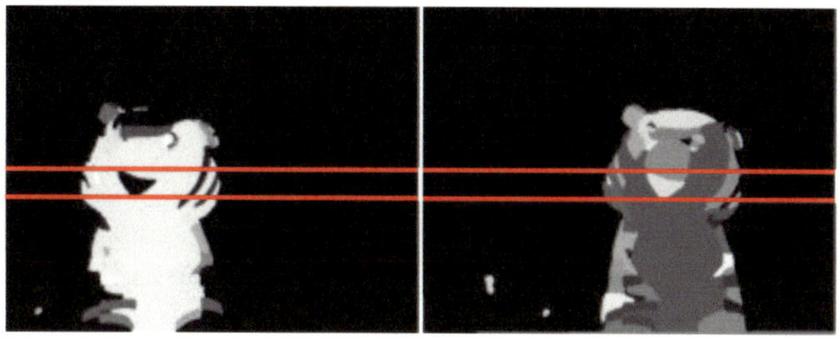

(a) Two images of a combined stereo and spectral series;

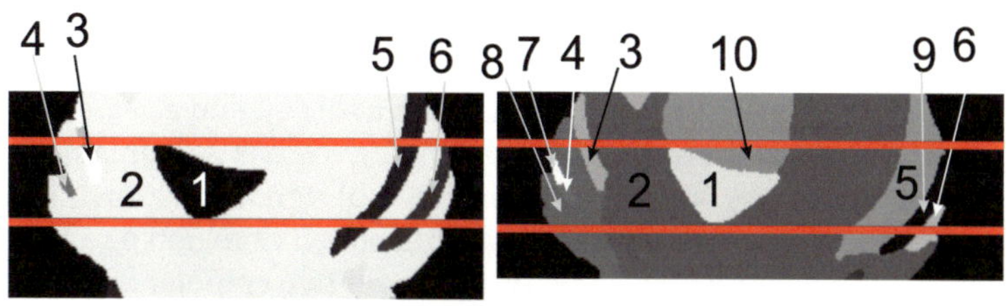

(b) Example of epipolar areas defined by two epipolar lines.

Fig. 5. Search for correspondences in an epipolar area.

$\boldsymbol{m}_{\mathcal{R}}$ contains three features of the region $\mathcal{R}$ which are invariant to gray values: size $g_{\mathcal{R}}$, shape ${\boldsymbol{k}_{\mathcal{R}}}^{\mathrm{T}}$ (defined by the boundaries of the region) and position $p_{\mathcal{R},\bar{\boldsymbol{u}}_{\mathcal{R}}}$ on the epipolar line given by $\bar{\boldsymbol{u}}_{\mathcal{R}}$:

$$\boldsymbol{m}_{\mathcal{R}} := (g_{\mathcal{R}}, {\boldsymbol{k}_{\mathcal{R}}}^{\mathrm{T}}, p_{\mathcal{R},\bar{\boldsymbol{u}}_{\mathcal{R}}})^{\mathrm{T}}. \tag{8}$$

The size of a region is given by its number of pixels:

$$g_{\mathcal{R}} := |\mathcal{R}|\,. \tag{9}$$

The shape of a region is determined by analyzing its boundaries. Considering an affiliation function

$$I_{\mathcal{R}}(\boldsymbol{u}) := \begin{cases} 1, & \boldsymbol{u} \in \mathcal{R} \\ 0, & \text{otherwise} \end{cases} \tag{10}$$

segments of the boundaries are determined according to their angular orientation: $\zeta_i := i \cdot \Delta\zeta$, $i \in \{0, 1, \ldots, N-1\}$, $N \cdot \Delta\zeta = 360°$. The boundary of a region can then be written as the union of its segments $\mathcal{K}_{\mathcal{R},\zeta_i}$, which are also interpreted as sets of pixels:

$$\mathcal{K}_{\mathcal{R}} := \bigcup_i \mathcal{K}_{\mathcal{R},\zeta_i}\,. \tag{11}$$

The feature vector ${\boldsymbol{k}_{\mathcal{R}}}^{\mathrm{T}}$ characterizing the boundary of a region $\mathcal{R}$ has the standardized number of points in each segment of the boundary as components:

$$\boldsymbol{k}_{\mathcal{R}} := (k_{\mathcal{R},0°}, \ldots, k_{\mathcal{R},\zeta_i}, \ldots)^{\mathrm{T}} = (|\mathcal{K}_{\mathcal{R},0°}|/|\mathcal{K}_{\mathcal{R}}|, \ldots, |\mathcal{K}_{\mathcal{R},\zeta_i}|/|\mathcal{K}_{\mathcal{R}}|, \ldots)^{\mathrm{T}}. \tag{12}$$

The position of the region with respect to the epipolar line is defined as the proportion of the number of points situated above $g_{\mathrm{A}\mathcal{R},\bar{\boldsymbol{u}}_{\mathcal{R}}}$ and the number of points of the region situated below

$g_{B\mathcal{R},\bar{u}_\mathcal{R}}$ the epipolar line given by the reference pixel $\bar{u}_\mathcal{R}$ (e. g., the epipolar line on which the center of gravity $\bar{u}_\mathcal{R}$ is situated):

$$p_{\mathcal{R},\bar{u}_\mathcal{R}} := \frac{g_{A\mathcal{R},\bar{u}_\mathcal{R}}}{g_{B\mathcal{R},\bar{u}_\mathcal{R}}}. \tag{13}$$

The dissimilarity between two feature vectors is measured by means of the Manhattan metric, due to its capability of dealing with different scales (Marques de Sá (2001)):

$$d_\mathrm{M}(\boldsymbol{m}_{\mathcal{R}_i}, \boldsymbol{m}_{\mathcal{R}_j}) := |g_{\mathcal{R}_i} - g_{\mathcal{R}_j}| + \sum_q |k_{\mathcal{R}_i,\zeta_q} - k_{\mathcal{R}_j,\zeta_q}| + |p_{\mathcal{R}_i,\bar{u}_{\mathcal{R}_i}} - p_{\mathcal{R}_j,\bar{u}_{\mathcal{R}_j}}|. \tag{14}$$

Neighboring term

As regularization, a neighboring term is defined using a set $\mathcal{U}_{1ij}$ and a sequence $\mathcal{U}_{2ij}$. The role of the neighboring term is that the order of corresponding regions is maintained in the images. For example, if regions 6 in Fig. 5(b) left and 9 in Fig. 5(b) right correspond, then, region 6 in Fig. 5(b) right is not allowed to correspond to any region left of region 6 in Fig. 5(b) left. The set $\mathcal{U}_{1ij}$ comprises all correspondences between regions of two epipolar areas E_i and E_j in two images, found on basis of the data term:

$$\mathcal{U}_{1ij} = \{(\mathcal{R}_i^k, \mathcal{R}_j^l) | (\mathcal{R}_i^k, \mathcal{R}_j^l) \in E_i \times E_j \wedge \mathcal{R}_i^k \leftrightarrow \mathcal{R}_j^l\}. \tag{15}$$

The sequence $\mathcal{U}_{2ij}$ comprises all correspondences out of the set $\mathcal{U}_{1ij}$, i. e., $(\mathcal{R}_i^k, \mathcal{R}_j^l)$ and $(\mathcal{R}_i^m, \mathcal{R}_j^n) \in \mathcal{U}_{1ij}$, that satisfy the neighboring constraint: the indices $k > 0$ and $m > 0$ of regions in image i must be in the same order, i. e., $k < m$, as the indices l and n, i. e., $l < n$, of their corresponding regions in image j:

$$\mathcal{U}_{2ij} = \{\ldots, (\mathcal{R}_i^k, \mathcal{R}_j^l), (\mathcal{R}_i^m, \mathcal{R}_j^n), \ldots | (\mathcal{R}_i^k, \mathcal{R}_j^l), (\mathcal{R}_i^m, \mathcal{R}_j^n) \in \mathcal{U}_{1ij} \wedge k < m \wedge l < n\}. \tag{16}$$

The neighboring term is therefore defined as a sum over all image pairs in the series and over pairs of epipolar areas:

$$E_\mathrm{n}(s, B) = \sum_{(B_i,B_j)\in\mathcal{I}} \sum_{(E_i,E_j)} \lambda\, |\mathcal{U}_{1ij} \setminus \mathcal{U}_{2ij}|, \tag{17}$$

where $\lambda > 0$ is a constant, assuring that the energy increases, if the neighboring constraint is not satisfied.

Energy minimization using dynamic programming

In the case of registration based only on regions, the minimization of the energy functional is performed by means of dynamic programming (Bellman (1957); Bertsekas (2005)). Since the problem of finding region correspondences based on their features is deterministic and finite, and the costs for each step are additive, the employment of dynamic programming assures the optimal result. Moreover, the neighboring constraint is implicitly guaranteed through the employment of the forward dynamic programming algorithm.

The results of the registration based only on regions for the example of Fig. 2 are presented in Fig. 6 in form of a depth map and a textured $2\frac{1}{2}$D reconstruction. Their quality is high, though, the obtained depth maps might not be dense. This is due to the fact that depth values can only be computed for those regions for which correspondences have been found. Due to the spectral component of the image series, the segmentation results are different within the images (i. e., the regions have different shapes and sizes), such that correspondences might not be found for all regions. In these cases, gaps may occur in depth maps.

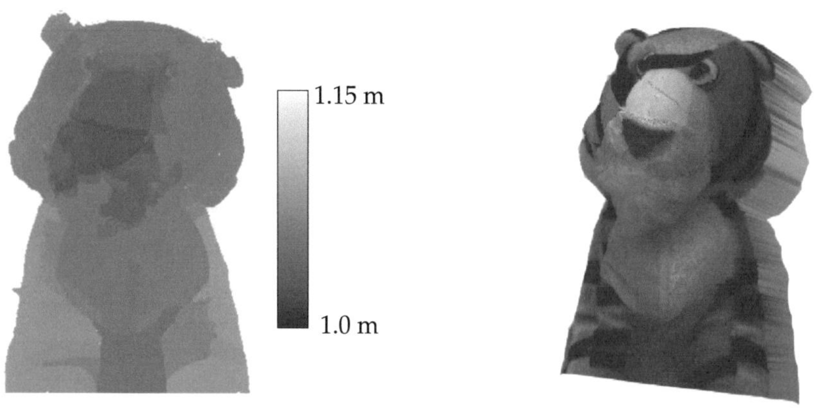

(a) Depth map; (b) Textured $2\frac{1}{2}$D reconstruction.

Fig. 6. Depth map and reconstruction resulting from the registration based only on regions of the image series shown in Fig. 2.

2.2 Registration based on regions and areas

In this context, an (image) area is defined as a union of several regions. The registration based on regions and areas considers that a region may correspond to a union of regions, i. e., an area; see Section 1.3. This way, segmentation differences are accounted for. The registration problem is then modeled by the minimization of the following energy functional:

$$E(s, B) := E_{\mathrm{d}}(s, B) + \gamma_{\mathrm{s}} E_{\mathrm{s}}(s, B) \rightarrow \min . \tag{18}$$

The data term $E_{\mathrm{d}}(s, B)$ measures the dissimilarity between a region and an area mainly based on their contours. For regularization, a smoothness term $E_{\mathrm{s}}(s, B)$ with an appropriate weighting factor γ_{s} is employed (Bleyer & Gelautz (2007)). The assumption modeled by the smoothness term is similar to the one usually made by pixel based registration: neighboring regions having similar gray values are likely to be mappings of the same 3D plane in space, and thus, they should have similar depth values.

Data term

For each region $\mathcal{R}_i$ in image i, a feature $m_{\mathcal{R}_i,j}(s)$ is computed with respect to an area $\mathcal{B}_j$ in image j and a certain label s. The feature compares mainly the conformity of the boundaries of the region $\mathcal{R}_i$ and the area $\mathcal{B}_j$. Therefore, it can be interpreted as a distance measure for the correspondence between the region $\mathcal{R}_i$ and the respective area $\mathcal{B}_j$.
Following, the computation of the feature $m_{\mathcal{R}_i,j}(s)$ is explained based on an example. The first step consists in the definition and evaluation of four sets containing the pixels of the region $\mathcal{R}_i$ and their correspondences on the boundaries or in the interior of $\mathcal{B}_j$. As an example, two segmented images are shown in Figs. 7(a) and 7(b). The exemplary region $\mathcal{R}_i$ and area $\mathcal{B}_j$ are displayed in Figs. 7(c) and 7(d), respectively. Their boundaries are shown in Figs. 7(e) and 7(f).

(a) Segmented image $B_i(\boldsymbol{u}_i)$;

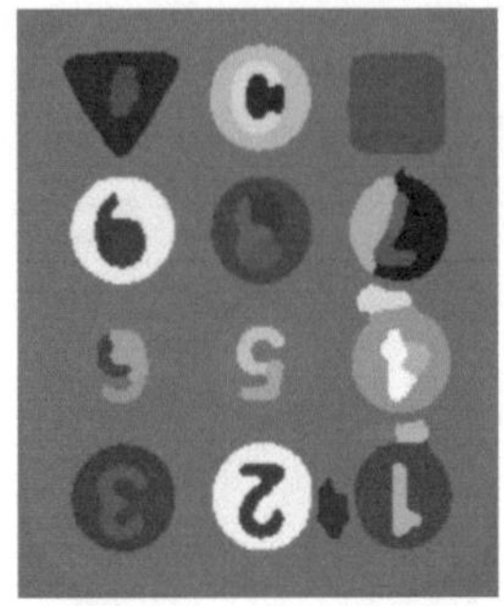

(b) Segmented image $B_j(\boldsymbol{u}_j)$;

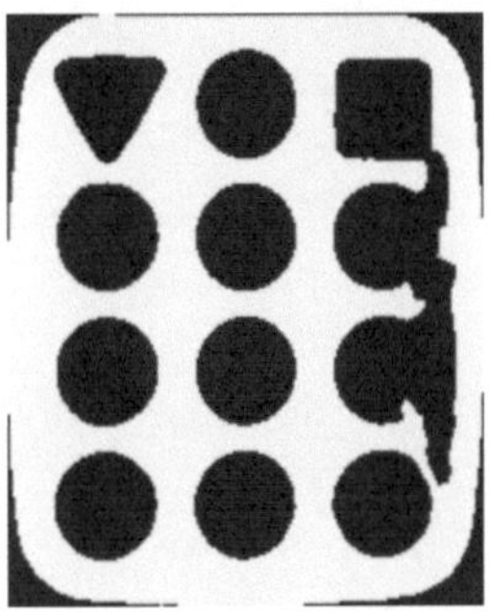

(c) Selected region $\mathcal{R}_i$ in image $B_i(\boldsymbol{u}_i)$;

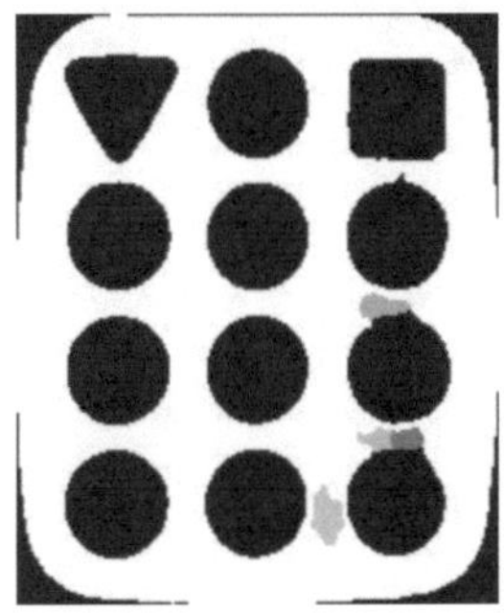

(d) Selected area $\mathcal{B}_j$ in image $B_j(\boldsymbol{u}_j)$, different regions have different gray values (except black);

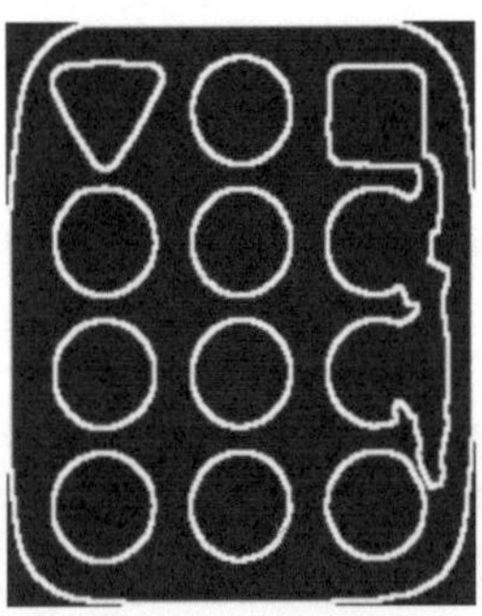

(e) $\mathcal{K}_{\mathcal{R}_i}$: Boundary of the region $\mathcal{R}_i$;

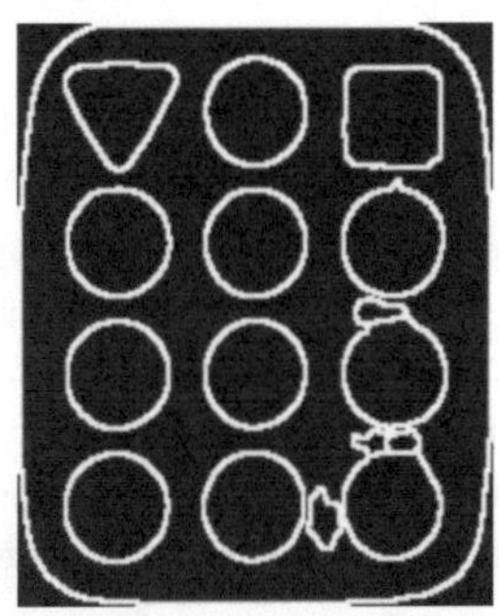

(f) $\bigcup_r \mathcal{K}_{\mathcal{R}_j^r}$: Boundaries of the area $\mathcal{B}_j$.

Fig. 7. Example of regions, areas and their boundaries for computing the sets of Eqs. (19) through (22).

The four sets used for the computation of the feature $m_{\mathcal{R}_i,j}(s)$ are defined as follows:

(a) The corresponding pixels $\boldsymbol{u}_i$ and $\boldsymbol{u}_j$ are situated both on boundaries of regions; see Fig. 8(a):

$$\mathcal{M}_{\mathrm{a},\mathcal{R}_i,j}(s) = \{\boldsymbol{u}_i | \boldsymbol{u}_i \in \mathcal{K}_{\mathcal{R}_i} \wedge \exists r \in \mathcal{J} : \boldsymbol{u}_j \in \mathcal{K}_{\mathcal{R}_j^r} \wedge s(\boldsymbol{u}_i) = s(\boldsymbol{u}_j)\} . \tag{19}$$

(b) The pixel $\boldsymbol{u}_i$ is situated on the boundary of $\mathcal{R}_i$, while its corresponding pixel $\boldsymbol{u}_j$ is situated in the interior of the area $\mathcal{B}_j$ in image j; see Fig. 8(b):

$$\mathcal{M}_{\mathrm{b},\mathcal{R}_i,j}(s) = \{\boldsymbol{u}_i | \boldsymbol{u}_i \in \mathcal{K}_{\mathcal{R}_i} \wedge \exists r \in \mathcal{J} : \boldsymbol{u}_j \in \mathcal{R}_j^{r\circ} \wedge s(\boldsymbol{u}_i) = s(\boldsymbol{u}_j)\}\,. \qquad (20)$$

(c) The pixel $\boldsymbol{u}_i$ is situated in the interior of the region $\mathcal{R}_i$, while its corresponding pixel $\boldsymbol{u}_j$ is situated on a boundary; see Fig. 8(c):

$$\mathcal{M}_{\mathrm{c},\mathcal{R}_i,j}(s) = \{\boldsymbol{u}_i | \boldsymbol{u}_i \in \mathcal{R}_i^{\circ} \wedge \exists r \in \mathcal{J} : \boldsymbol{u}_j \in \mathcal{K}_{\mathcal{R}_j^r} \wedge s(\boldsymbol{u}_i) = s(\boldsymbol{u}_j)\}\,. \qquad (21)$$

(d) Both corresponding pixels $\boldsymbol{u}_i$ and $\boldsymbol{u}_j$ are situated in the interior of the region $\mathcal{R}_i$ and the area $\mathcal{B}_j$, respectively; see Fig. 8(d):

$$\mathcal{M}_{\mathrm{d},\mathcal{R}_i,j}(s) = \{\boldsymbol{u}_i | \boldsymbol{u}_i \in \mathcal{R}_i^{\circ} \wedge \exists r \in \mathcal{J} : \boldsymbol{u}_j \in \mathcal{R}_j^{r\circ} \wedge s(\boldsymbol{u}_i) = s(\boldsymbol{u}_j)\}\,. \qquad (22)$$

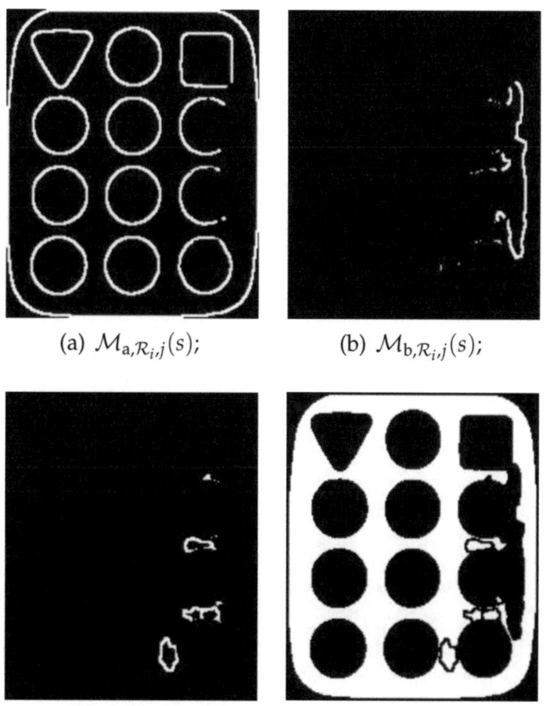

(a) $\mathcal{M}_{\mathrm{a},\mathcal{R}_i,j}(s)$; (b) $\mathcal{M}_{\mathrm{b},\mathcal{R}_i,j}(s)$;

(c) $\mathcal{M}_{\mathrm{c},\mathcal{R}_i,j}(s)$; (d) $\mathcal{M}_{\mathrm{d},\mathcal{R}_i,j}(s)$.

Fig. 8. Sets according to Eqs. (19) through (22) for the example shown in Fig. 7.

The four sets defined in Eqs. (19) through (22) are shown in Figs. 8(a) through 8(d). The first set $\mathcal{M}_{\mathrm{a},\mathcal{R}_i,j}(s)$ in Eq. (19) (see Fig. 8(a)) can be interpreted as the intersection of the boundary of the region $\mathcal{R}_i$ (see Fig. 7(e)) and those of the area $\mathcal{B}_j$ (see Fig. 7(f)).
The second set $\mathcal{M}_{\mathrm{b},\mathcal{R}_i,j}(s)$ of Eq. (20), shown in Fig. 8(b), corresponds to the intersection of the boundary of the region $\mathcal{R}_i$ (see Fig. 7(e)) and the interior of the area $\mathcal{B}_j$ (see Fig. 7(d)).
The third set $\mathcal{M}_{\mathrm{c},\mathcal{R}_i,j}(s)$ of Eq. (21), shown in Fig. 8(c), is equivalent to the intersection of the interior of the region $\mathcal{R}_i$ (see Fig. 7(c)) with the boundaries of the area $\mathcal{B}_j$ (see Fig. 7(f)).

Fig. 8(d) displays the fourth set $\mathcal{M}_{\mathrm{d},\mathcal{R}_i,j}(s)$ (see Eq. (22)), which is the intersection of the interior of the region $\mathcal{R}_i$ (see Fig. 7(c)) and the interior of the area $\mathcal{B}_j$ (see Fig. 7(d)).
The cardinal numbers of the four sets are used to build the feature $m_{\mathcal{R}_i,j}(s)$ characterizing the region $\mathcal{R}_i$ with regard to the area $\mathcal{B}_j$:

$$\begin{aligned} m_{\mathcal{R}_i,j}(s) &:= \frac{|\mathcal{M}_{\mathrm{b},\mathcal{R}_i,j}(s)|}{|\mathcal{M}_{\mathrm{a},\mathcal{R}_i,j}(s)| + |\mathcal{M}_{\mathrm{b},\mathcal{R}_i,j}(s)|} + \gamma \frac{|\mathcal{M}_{\mathrm{c},\mathcal{R}_i,j}(s)|}{|\mathcal{M}_{\mathrm{c},\mathcal{R}_i,j}(s)| + |\mathcal{M}_{\mathrm{d},\mathcal{R}_i,j}(s)|} \\ &= \frac{|\mathcal{M}_{\mathrm{b},\mathcal{R}_i,j}(s)|}{|\mathcal{K}_{\mathcal{R}_i}|} + \gamma \frac{|\mathcal{M}_{\mathrm{c},\mathcal{R}_i,j}(s)|}{|\mathcal{R}_i^{\circ}|} \end{aligned} \tag{23}$$

with $\gamma > 0$ as a weighting factor.
The first term of Eq. (23) evaluates the share of pixels on the boundary of region $\mathcal{R}_i$ having no correspondences on any boundary of the area $\mathcal{B}_j$. The term models the preference for correspondences that match the boundaries of the region $\mathcal{R}_i$ and the area $\mathcal{B}_j$.
The second term evaluates the share of pixels situated in the interior of the region $\mathcal{R}_i$ with correspondences on any boundary of the area $\mathcal{B}_j$. In this way, the possibility of a 1:N assignment is modeled, i. e., correspondences between the region $\mathcal{R}_i$ and more than one region $\mathcal{R}_j^r$ in the image j (forming the area $\mathcal{B}_j$). However, the value of the term is higher, if such 1:N correspondences occur, compared to the case of 1:1 correspondences. Therefore, 1:N correspondences are admitted, but 1:1 correspondences are favored.
The first term of Eq. (23) reaches its minimum (equal to zero), if $\mathcal{M}_{\mathrm{b},\mathcal{R}_i,j}(s) = \emptyset$. In such a case, the boundaries of the region $\mathcal{R}_i$ and those of the area $\mathcal{B}_j$ match perfectly. In any other case, the value of the term varies between zero and one. The second term has its minimum (equal to zero), when the area $\mathcal{B}_j$ consists of only one region, i. e., all pixels in the interior of the region $\mathcal{R}_i$ have correspondences in the interior of the area $\mathcal{B}_j$ (a 1:1 correspondence exists between the region $\mathcal{R}_i$ and the area $\mathcal{B}_j$).
To conclude, it can be said that the smaller the value of feature $m_{\mathcal{R}_i,j}(s)$ in Eq. (23) is, the more similar the region $\mathcal{R}_i$ and the area $\mathcal{B}_j$ are. Modeling the data term is straightforward by summing the values of the feature $m_{\mathcal{R}_i,j}(s)$ over all regions in the images of the series:

$$E_{\mathrm{d}}(s, B) := \sum_{(B_i,B_j)\in\mathcal{I}} \sum_{\mathcal{R}_i} m_{\mathcal{R}_i,j}(s) \tag{24}$$

with $\mathcal{I} := \{(B_i, B_j)|i \neq j\}$ being the set of image pairs.
For regions $\mathcal{R}_i$ with the feature $m_{\mathcal{R}_i,j}(s)$ taking the constant value one for almost all labels s (e. g., small regions), it is hard to determine the corresponding area $\mathcal{B}_j$. Such regions have no distinct minimum for the feature $m_{\mathcal{R}_i,j}(s)$ over the value range of s (see Fig. 9). To solve this problem, a second energy term is proposed, which takes the role of a smoothness term regularizing the problem.

Smoothness term

For regularization, an energy term $E_{\mathrm{s}}(s, B)$ evaluating the neighborhood relations between pairs of corresponding regions is defined. The idea is that neighboring regions with similar gray values are assumed to be part of the same 3D plane, i. e., they should be assign similar labels s. This assumption is like the smoothness assumption made in the case of pixel based registration: pixels having similar gray values are likely to belong to the same plane and should therefore be labeled similarly. Moreover, by means of the smoothness term, regions for which the data term is approximately one over the entire value range of the label s (e. g., small

(a) Segmented image pair;

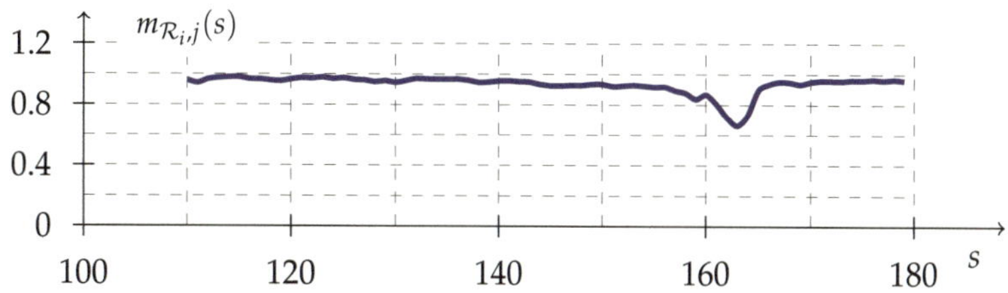

(b) Values of the feature $m_{\mathcal{R}_i,j}(s)$ for the horizontally striped region in the image of Fig. 9(a) right over the value range of the label s;

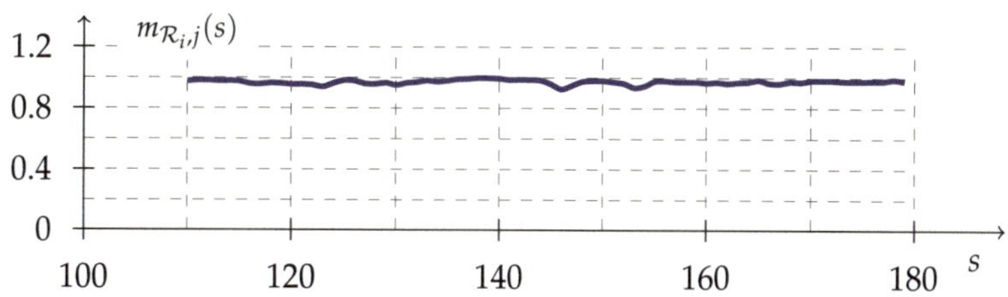

(c) Value of the feature $m_{\mathcal{R}_i,j}(s)$ for the vertically striped region in the image of Fig. 9(a) right over the value range of the label s.

Fig. 9. Value of the feature $m_{\mathcal{R}_i,j}(s)$ for regions in the image of Fig. 9(a) right over the value range of the label s, i. e., for different areas of the image in Fig. 9(a) left.

regions) receive the label of one of their neighbors. In order to determine which neighbor is appropriate, the mean gray values of the regions are computed and compared.
The smoothness term thus penalizes neighboring regions that have similar mean gray values and different labels s. The proposed model is similar to that in (Bleyer & Gelautz (2007)):

$$E_s(s,B) := \sum_{B_i}\sum_{\mathcal{R}_i^k}\sum_{\mathcal{R}_i^l \in \mathcal{N}_R(\mathcal{R}_i^k)} \left(1 - \delta_{s(\mathcal{R}_i^k)}^{s(\mathcal{R}_i^l)}\right) \cdot f_1(\mathcal{R}_i^k, \mathcal{R}_i^l) \cdot f_2(\mathcal{R}_i^k, \mathcal{R}_i^l), \tag{25}$$

where $\mathcal{N}_R(\mathcal{R}_i^k)$ is the set of neighboring regions $\mathcal{R}_i^l$ of the region $\mathcal{R}_i^k$.
Function $f_1(\mathcal{R}_i^k, \mathcal{R}_i^l)$ computes the length of the common boundary of two directly neighboring regions $\mathcal{R}_i^k$ and $\mathcal{R}_i^l$ with regard to the length of the boundary of the smaller

region:

$$f_1(\mathcal{R}_i^k, \mathcal{R}_i^l) := \frac{\left|\{\boldsymbol{u}_i^k \in \mathcal{K}_{\mathcal{R}_i^k} \,|\, \exists \boldsymbol{u}_i^l \in \mathcal{K}_{\mathcal{R}_i^l} \wedge \boldsymbol{u}_i^l \in \mathcal{N}_{\mathrm{P}}(\boldsymbol{u}_i^k)\}\right|}{\min(|\mathcal{K}_{\mathcal{R}_i^k}|, |\mathcal{K}_{\mathcal{R}_i^l}|)}, \tag{26}$$

where $\mathcal{N}_{\mathrm{P}}(\boldsymbol{u}_i^k)$ is the set of neighboring pixels $\boldsymbol{u}_i^l$ of pixel $\boldsymbol{u}_i^k$. $f_1(\mathcal{R}_i^k, \mathcal{R}_i^l)$ takes high values for small regions, which consequently increases the value of the smoothness term $E_{\mathrm{s}}(s, B)$.
Function $f_2(\mathcal{R}_i^k, \mathcal{R}_i^l)$ evaluates the differences in the mean gray values of the two neighboring regions $\mathcal{R}_i^k$ and $\mathcal{R}_i^l$:

$$f_2(\mathcal{R}_i^k, \mathcal{R}_i^l) := \left(1 - \frac{\min(|\bar{g}_{\mathcal{R}_i^k} - \bar{g}_{\mathcal{R}_i^l}|, K)}{K}\right) \cdot \gamma + (1 - \gamma) \tag{27}$$

with $0 < \gamma < 1$. $\bar{g}_{\mathcal{R}_i^k}$ is the mean gray value of the region $\mathcal{R}_i^k$:

$$\bar{g}_{\mathcal{R}_i^k} := \frac{1}{|\mathcal{R}_i^k|} \sum_{\boldsymbol{u}_i^k \in \mathcal{R}_i^k} B_i(\boldsymbol{u}_i^k). \tag{28}$$

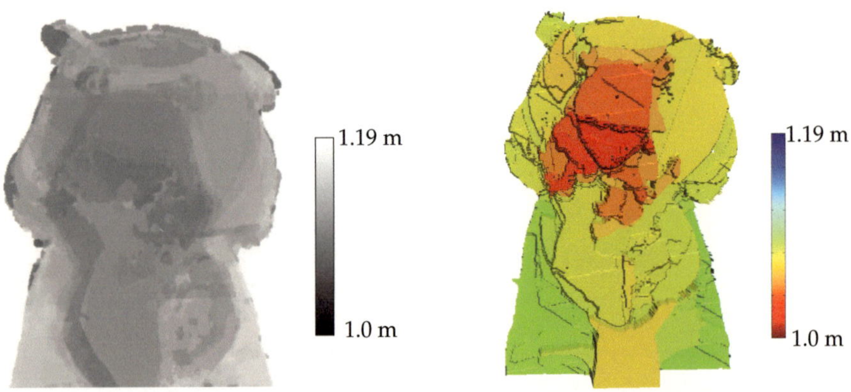

(a) Depth map; (b) $2\frac{1}{2}$D reconstruction.

Fig. 10. Results of the registration based on regions and areas.

Energy minimization using graph cuts
For the minimization of the energy functional in the case of the registration based on regions and areas, a state-of-the-art graph-cuts algorithm (Boykov et al. (2001)) is employed with minor adaptations. For example, the construction of the graph is modified such that the nodes of the graph are not pixels, but regions. The results of the registration based on regions and areas of the image series in Fig. 2 are presented in Fig. 10. The resulting depth maps using this registration approach not only have a high quality, but they are also dense, since the smoothness term insures that for each region, a depth value is determined.
The depth maps obtained by evaluating the stereo information of combined stereo and spectral series can be further used for spectral fusion.

Fig. 11. Scene of an orange model robot holding an orange log of wood and an orange background.

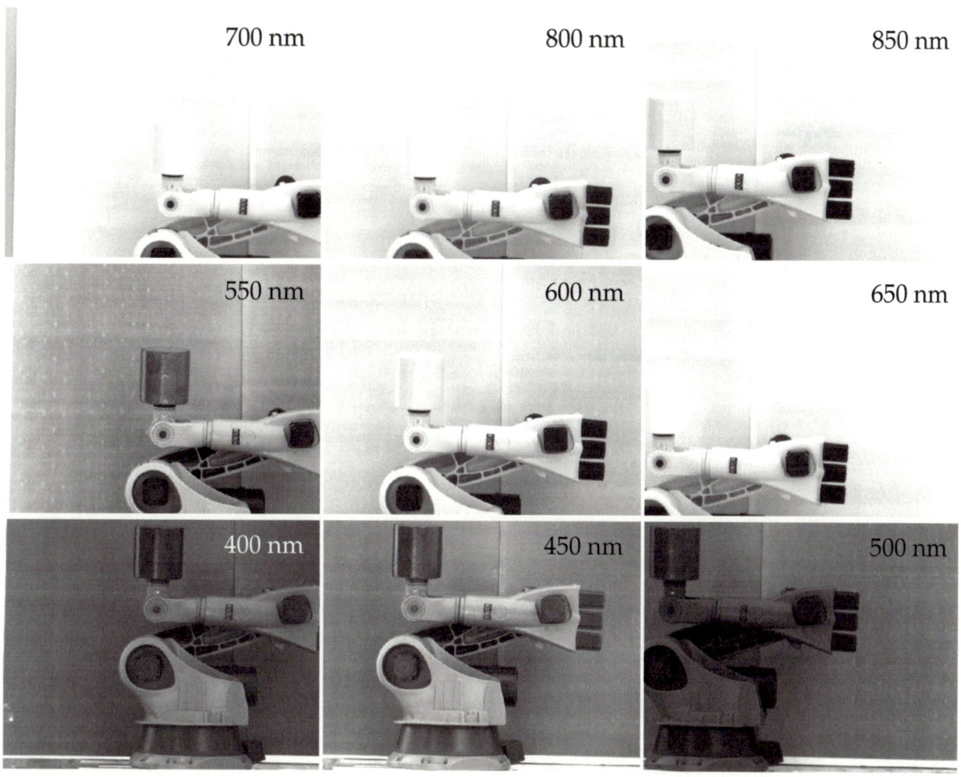

Fig. 12. Combined stereo and spectral series of the scene depicted in Fig.11.

3. Spectral fusion

For determining the spectral properties of a scene on the basis of the combined image series, the depth map obtained with the previously described registration methods is employed. An exemplary scene contains an orange model robot holding an orange log of wood and an orange background; see Fig. 11. From this scene, an image series has been acquired with a camera array equipped with spectral filters; see Fig. 12.

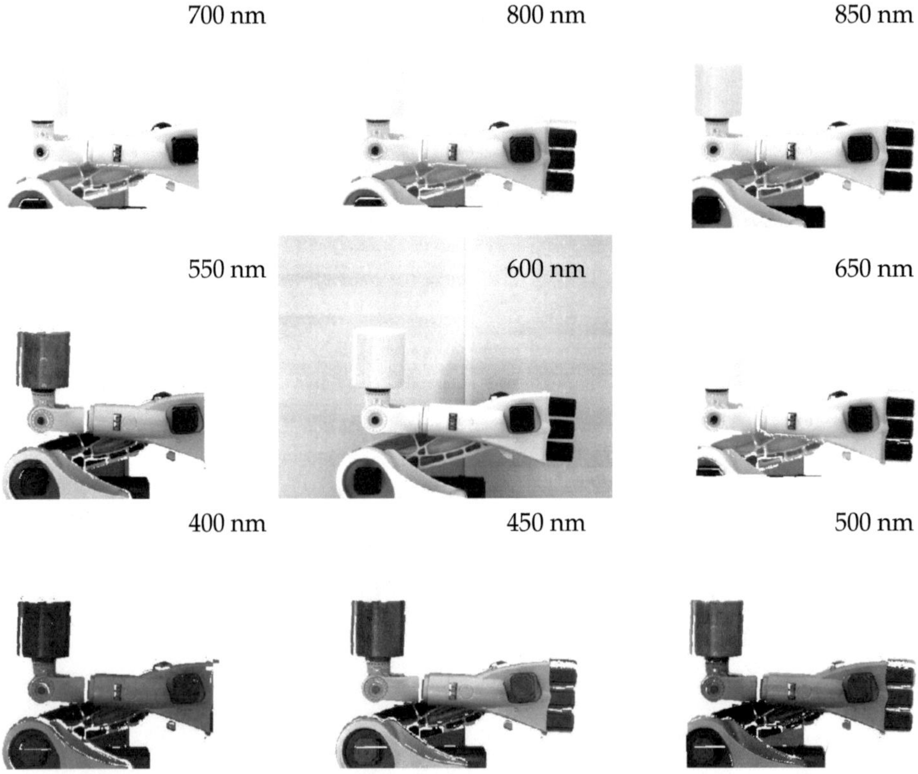

Fig. 13. Warped images of the series of Fig. 12 into the coordinate system of the middle camera of the array.

By means of image warping, all images are transferred into a common coordinate system, e. g., of one of the cameras (here we chose the middle camera of the array); see Fig. 13. In the case of stereo and spectral series, this leads to a pure spectral series, i. e., the stereo effect is eliminated. The spectral series contains the spectral characteristics for each mapped 3D scene point according to the employed spectral filters. The obtained intensity values can be interpreted as spectral features and can be further used, e. g., for material classification or for improving object detection. As an example, a common approach for analyzing spectral features is given in Tyo et al. (2003). The first step of this analysis consists in a dimension reduction for the spectral feature vectors, followed by a false color representation. The dimension reduction is done by employing the Principal Component Analysis (PCA, Gonzalez & Woods (2008)); the transformed images ($P_1, \dots, P_n$) are presented in Fig. 14. The components with the highest information content, i. e., corresponding to the highest eigenvalues, are chosen for the next step consisting in a false color representation (Tyo et al. (2003)). For a meaningful representation, the first three components are chosen according to their information content.

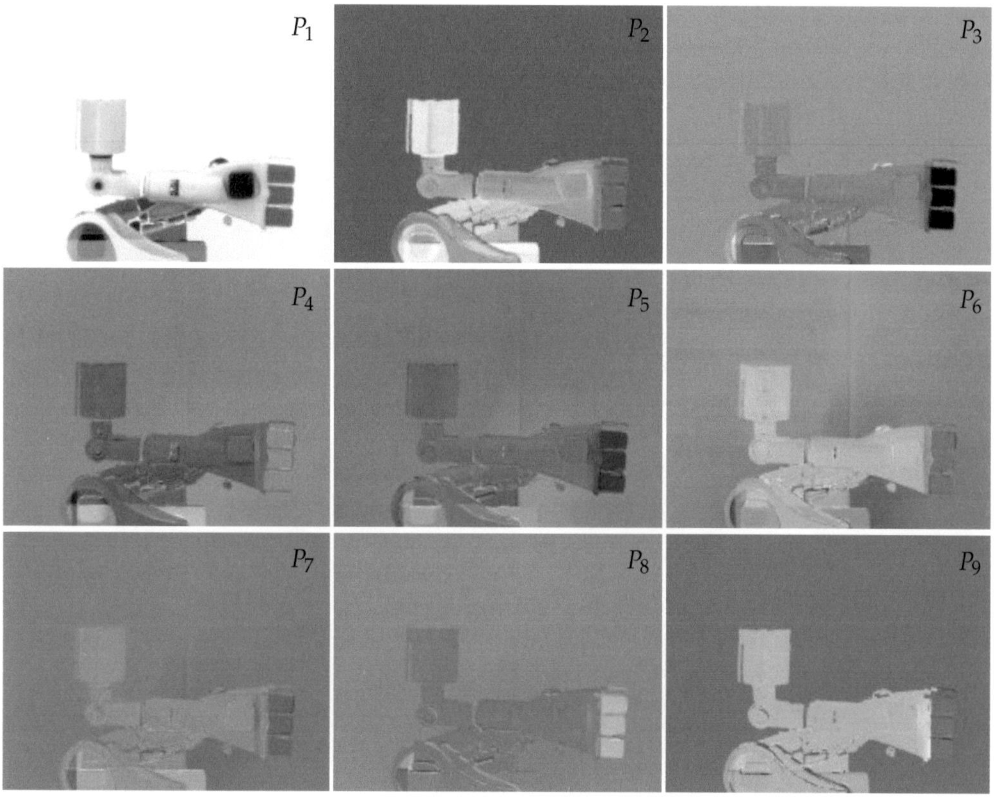

Fig. 14. Standardized principal components of the images of Fig. 13.

These images can be interpreted as RGB (red, green, blue) channels, but they can also be preferably transformed into the HSV (hue, saturation,value) color space:

$$\begin{aligned} H &: \mathbb{R}^2 \to \mathbb{R}, \quad H(\boldsymbol{u}) := \arctan\left(\frac{P_3(\boldsymbol{u})}{P_2(\boldsymbol{u})}\right), \\ S &: \mathbb{R}^2 \to \mathbb{R}, \quad S(\boldsymbol{u}) := \frac{\sqrt{P_2(\boldsymbol{u})^2 + P_3(\boldsymbol{u})^2}}{P_1(\boldsymbol{u})}, \\ V &: \mathbb{R}^2 \to \mathbb{R}, \quad V(\boldsymbol{u}) := P_1(\boldsymbol{u}). \end{aligned} \tag{29}$$

The advantages of using the HSV color space for false color representation are:

- The color representation is very similar to the way humans perceive color, i. e., three channels are considered: the achromatic channel and two orthogonal color channels. The achromatic channel, i. e., V in the HSV space, represents the intensity. The color channels are represented in the HSV color space by the components H and S.
- Data analysis in the HSV color space is simplified through the intuitively understandable meaning of its components.

The connection between the two color spaces is visually shown in Fig. 15. Figure 16 displays the H, S and V components obtained for the given example. The computed false color representation of the model robot scene is presented in Fig. 17.

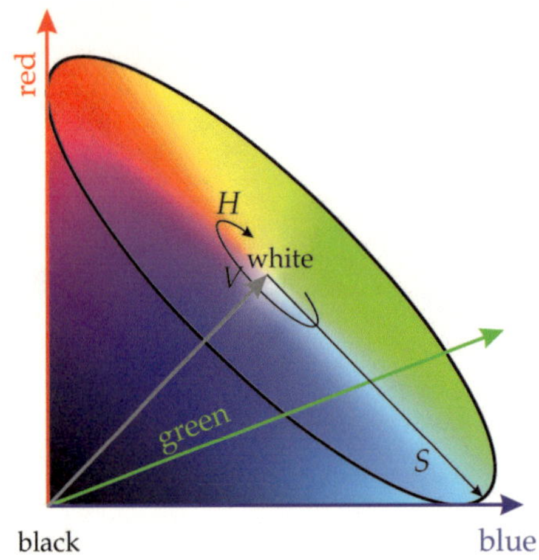

Fig. 15. Connection between RGB and HSV color spaces.

Fig. 16. H, S and V components as a result of the transformation of the first three principal components.

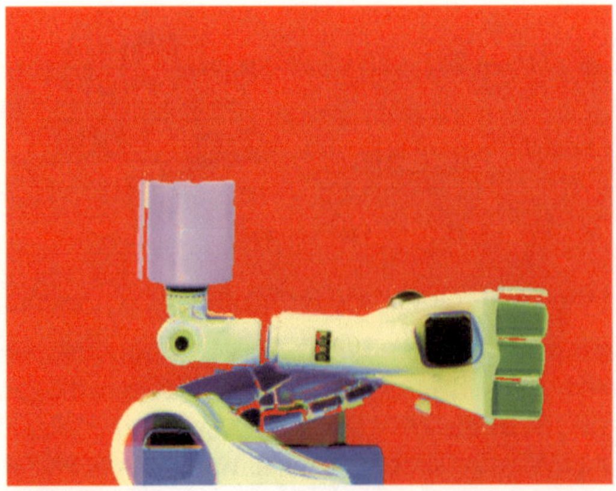

Fig. 17. False color representation for the scene of Fig. 11.

4. Conclusions

The challenges when fusing combined stereo and spectral image series are that corresponding pixels have different gray values and that neighboring image regions have different contrasts in different images. Therefore, common pixel and gray value based registration techniques cannot be applied. This chapter proposes two novel region based image registration approaches for combined stereo and spectral series. Prior to registration, the images are rectified and segmented by means of the watershed transform. The first approach, based only on regions, determines 1:1 region correspondences by measuring the dissimilarity between the feature vectors characterizing the regions. Thus, a gray value invariance is achieved. For regularization, a neighboring constraint is imposed. The second approach, based on regions and areas, searches for 1:N correspondences in images by mainly comparing the boundaries of the regions. The main advantage of this approach is that it can handle differences in the segmentation of the images, e. g., due to the use of spectral filters. As regularization, a smoothness constraint is enforced in the case of the registration based on regions and areas. In both cases, the registration problem is modeled by energy functionals. The solutions are obtained through the minimization of the functionals by dynamic programming or graph cuts algorithms. The registration results are directly employed for computing depth maps.
By means of image warping based on the obtained depth information, the originally combined image series can be transformed into a pure spectral series. In this chapter, an example of the analysis of the spectral information is given in form of a false color representation. Further work will concentrate on the evaluation of the results and on finding an appropriate method for the fusion and analysis of the spectral information.

5. Acknowledgments

We acknowledge support by Deutsche Forschungsgemeinschaft and Open Access Publishing Fund of Karlsruhe Institute of Technology.

6. References

Bankman, J. N. (ed.) (2000). *Handbook of Medical Imaging Processing and Analysis*, Academic Press.

Bellman, R. (1957). *Dynamic Programming*, Princeton University Press.

Bertsekas, D. P. (2005). *Dynamic Programming and Optimal Control*, Athena Scientific.

Bleyer, M. & Gelautz, M. (2007). Graph-cut-based stereo matching using image segmentation with symmetrical treatment of occlusions, *Signal Processing: Image Communication* 22(2): 127–143.

Boykov, Y. & Kolmogorov, V. (2004). An experimental comparison of min-cut/max-flow algorithms for energy minimization in vision, *IEEE Transactions on Pattern Analysis and Machine Intelligence* 26(9): 1124–1137.

Boykov, Y., Veksler, O. & Zabih, R. (2001). Fast approximate energy minimization via graph cuts, *IEEE Transactions on Pattern Analysis and Machine Intelligence* 23(11): 1222–1239.

Chang, C.-I. (2003). *Hyperspectral imaging: techniques for spectral detection and classification*, Kluwer Academic.

Faugeras, O. & Luong, Q.-T. (2004). *The Geometry of Multiple Images*, MIT Press.

Fookes, C., Maeder, A., Sridharan, S. & Cook, J. (2004). Multi-spectral stereo image matching using mutual information, *Proceedings of the 2nd International Symposium on 3D Data Processing, Visualization, and Transmission (3DPVT'04)*.

Frese, C. & Gheţa, I. (2006). Robust depth estimation by fusion of stereo and focus series gained with a camera array, *Proceedings of the IEEE Conference on Multisensor Fusion and Integration for Intelligent Systems*, pp. 243–248.

Gheţa, I., Frese, C. & Heizmann, M. (2006). Fusion of combined stereo and focus series for depth estimation, *Informatik 2006 – Informatik für Menschen*, Vol. 1, pp. 359–363.

Gheţa, I., Frese, C., Heizmann, M. & Beyerer, J. (2007). A new approach for estimating depth by fusing stereo and defocus information, *Informatik 2007 – Informatik trifft Logistik*, pp. 26–31.

Gheţa, I., Frese, C., Krüger, W., Saur, G., Heinze, N., Heizmann, M. & Beyerer, J. (2007). Depth estimation from flight image series using multi-view along-track stereo, *Optical 3D Measurement Techniques, Zürich*, pp. 119–125.

Gheţa, I., Höfer, S., Heizmann, M. & Beyerer, J. (2010). A novel approach for the fusion of combined stereo and spectral series, *in* D. Fofi & K. Niel (eds), *Image Processing: Machine Vision Applications III, IS&T/SPIE Electronic Imaging, Proceedings of SPIE 7538*, Vol. 7538, San Jose, California.

Gheţa, I., Mathias, M., Heizmann, M. & Beyerer, J. (2008). Fusion of combined stereo and spectral series for obtaining 3d information, *Multisensor, Multisource Information Fusion: Architectures, Algorithms, and Applications, Proceedings of SPIE 6974*, Orlando, Florida.

Gonzalez, R. C. & Woods, R. E. (2008). *Digital Image Processing*, Prentice Hall.

Hartley, R. & Zisserman, A. (2003). *Multiple View Geometry in Computer Vision*, 2 edn, Cambridge University Press.

Lillesand, T. M., Kiefer, R. W. & Chipman, J. W. (2008). *Remote Sensing and Image Interpretation*, John Wiley & Sons, Inc.

Marques de Sá, J. P. (2001). *Pattern Recognition: Concepts, Methods and Applications*, Springer Verlag.

Modersitzki, J. (2004). *Numerical Methods for Image Registration*, 1 edn, Oxford University Press.

Scharstein, D. & Szeliski, R. (2002). A taxonomy and evaluation of dense two-frame stereo correspondence algorithms, *International Journal of Computer Vision* 47(1–3): 7–42.

Seitz, S., Curless, B., Diebel, J., Scharstein, D. & Szeliski, R. (2006). A comparison and evaluation of multi-view stereo reconstruction algorithms, *2006 IEEE Computer Society Conference on Computer Vision and Pattern Recognition*, IEEE Computer Society, New York, pp. 519–528.

Tyo, J. S., Konsolakis, A., Diersen, D. I. & Olsen, R. C. (2003). Principal-components-based display strategy for spectral imagery, *IEEE Transactions on Geoscience and Remote Sensing* 41(3): 708–718.

Wang, Z.-F. & Zheng, Z.-G. (2008). A region based stereo matching algorithm using cooperative optimization, *IEEE Conference on Computer Vision and Pattern Recognition, 2008*, pp. 1–8.

Weng, J., Cohen, P. & Herniou, M. (1992). Camera calibration with distortion models and accuracy evaluation, *IEEE Transactions on Pattern Analysis and Machine Intelligence* 14(10): 965–980.

6

Medical Image Fusion Schemes Using Contourlet Transform and PCA Bases

Nemir Al-Azzawi and Wan Ahmed K. Wan Abdullah
Biomedical Electronics group, Universiti Sains Malaysia
Penang,
Malaysia

1. Introduction

Fusion imaging is one of the most modern, accurate and useful diagnostic techniques in medical imaging today. The new technology has made a clear difference in patient care by compressing the time between diagnosis and treatment. Although image fusion can have different purposes, the main aim of fusion is spatial resolution enhancement or image sharpening. Also known as integrated imaging, it provides a computer link that allows for the combination of multimodal medical images into a single image with more complete and accurate description of the same object. The benefits are even more profound in combining anatomical imaging modalities with functional ones. For example, PET-CT in lung cancer, MRI-PET in brain tumors, SPECT-CT in abdominal studies and ultrasound images-MRI for vascular blood flow (Patias, 2002). Outcome of MRI-CT image fusion has been shown to be able to assist in planning surgical procedure. Mainly, medical image fusion try to solve the issue of where there is no single modality provides both anatomical and functional information. Further more information provided by different modalities may be in agreement or in complementary nature.

An important research issue in medical image processing, specifically in information computation, is fusion of multimodal information (Daneshvar and Ghassemian, 2007; Hong *et al.*, 2007; Zhongfei *et al.*, 2003). Existing algorithms generally use discrete wavelet transform (DWT) (Anna *et al.*, 2007; Pajares and Manuel de la Cruz, 2004; Singh *et al.*, 2009) for multimodal medical image fusion because DWT preserves different frequency information in stable form and allows good localization both in time and spatial frequency domain. However, one of the major drawbacks of DWT is that the transformation does not provide shift invariance.

This causes a major change in the wavelet coefficients of the image even for minor shifts in the input image. In medical imaging, it is important to know and preserve the exact location of this information, but shift variance may lead to inaccuracies. As an alternative (Kingsbury, 1999), proposed dual-tree complex wavelet transform (DT-CWT) which provides approximate shift invariance. DT-CWT has the drawback of limited directional information. Hence, contourlet transform was proposed to capture the most important salient information in images by incorporating the DT-CWT and DFB (Chen and Li, 2005).

Extensive researches have been conducted on image fusion techniques, and various fusion algorithms for medical image have been developed depending on the merging stage (Aguilar and New, 2002; Yong *et al.*, 2008). The most well-known algorithms are image fusion with additive wavelet decomposition (Gonzalez and Woods, 2002; Nunez *et al.*, 1999; Pajares and Manuel de la Cruz, 2004) and image fusion with DT-CWT (Hill *et al.*, 2002). (Yang *et al.*, 2008) proposed a medical image fusion method that is based on multiscale geometric analysis of contourlet transform. Multiscale geometric analysis was introduced by (Toet et al., 1989) as contrast decomposition scheme that used to relate the luminance processing in the early stages of the human visual system. In this method the local energy was adopted for coefficient selection in the lowpass and region based contourlet contrast was adopted for highpass subband, which can preserve more details in source images and further improve the quality of fused image. The actual fusion process can take place at different levels of information representation. A common categorization is to distinguish between pixel, feature and decision level (Pohl and Van Genderen, 1998). Medical image fusion usually employs the pixel level fusion techniques. The advantage of pixel fusion is that the images use to contain the original information. Furthermore, the algorithms are rather easy to implement and time efficient.

Medical image fusion has been used to derive useful information from multimodality medical image data. This chapter presents a dual-tree complex contourlet transform (DT-CCT) based approach for the fusion of magnetic resonance image (MRI) and computed tomography (CT) images. The objective of the fusion of an MRI image and a CT image of the same organ is to obtain a single image containing as much information as possible about that organ for diagnosis. The limitation of directional information of dual-tree complex wavelet (DT-CWT) is rectified in DT-CCT by incorporating directional filter banks (DFB) into the DT-CWT. To improve the fused image quality, new methods for fusion rules which depend on frequency component of DT-CCT coefficients (contourlet domain) have been presented in this chapter.

For low frequency coefficients PCA and local energy weighted selection are incorporated as the fusion rules in a contourlet domain and for high frequency coefficients, the salient features are picked up based on local energy. The final fusion image is obtained by directly applying inverse dual tree complex contourlet transform (IDT-CCT) to the fused low and high frequency coefficients.

As the clinical is used of different medical imaging systems extends, the multimodality imaging acting an increasingly important part in a medical imaging field. Different medical imaging techniques may provide scans with complementary and occasionally unnecessary information. The combination of medical images can often lead to additional clinical information not noticeable in the separate images. MRI-CT image fusion presents an accurate tool for planning the correct surgical procedure and is a benefit for the operational results in computer assisted navigated neurosurgery of temporal bone tumors (Nemec *et al.*, 2007).

2. Overview of image fusion

The goal of image fusion is to integrate complementary information from multimodality images so that the new images are more suitable for the purpose of human visual perception and computer processing. Therefore, the task of image fusion is to make many salient features in the new image such as regions and their boundaries.

Image fusion consists of putting together information coming from different modality of medical images, whereas registration consists of computing the geometrical transformation between two data sets. This geometrical transformation is used to resample one image data set to match other. An excellent registration is set for an excellent fusion. The process of information fusion can be seen as an information transfer problem in which two or more information sets are combined into a new one that should contain all the information from the original sets. During the process of fusion, input images *A* and *B* are combined into a new fused image *F* by transferring, ideally all of their information into *F*. This is illustrated graphically using a simple Venn diagram (Carroll *et al.*, 2007) in Figure 1.

Fig. 1. Graphical representation of the image information fusion process.

The combination of images from different modalities leads to additional clinical information which is not apparent in the separate imaging modality. For this reason radiologists prefer multiple imaging modalities to obtain more details. Image fusion is performed to extract all the useful information from the individual modality and integrate them into one image. In general, a successful fusion should extract complete information from source images into the result, without introducing any artifacts or inconsistencies.

Medical image fusion usually employs the pixel level fusion techniques. The purpose of pixel-level image fusion is to represent the visual information present in input images, in a single fused image without the introduction of distortion or loss of information. The advantage of pixel level fusion is that the images used the contained the original information. Furthermore, the algorithms are rather easy to implement and time efficient. The classification of pixel-to-pixel based image fusion methods is illustrated in Figure 2. The aim of this classification was to identify, with different degrees of detail, complexity and accuracy. The main component is the domain of implemented the image fusion which however are not always strictly separable (Chen and Li, 2005). Many algorithms developed so far can be classified into four primary categories:

1. Substitution methods such as principal component analysis (PCA) (Ghassemian, 2001), averaging weighted, color mixed RGB (Baum *et al.*, 2008) and intensity hue saturation (IHS) (Ghassemian, 2001).
2. Mathematical combination which normalizes multispectral bands used for an RGB display such as Brovey Transform (Pohl and Van Genderen, 1998).
3. Optimization approach such as Bayesian and neural network (Lai and Fang, 2000).
4. Transform domain such as multiresolution decomposition which introduces spatial features from the high-resolution images into the multispectral images. For example, Laplacian pyramid (Burt, 1984), wavelets (Zhang and Hong, 2005), curvelet (Ali *et al.*, 2008), contourlet transform (Zheng *et al.*, 2007) and Nonsubsampled contourlet transform (Cunha *et al.*, 2006; Zhang and Guo, 2009).

Primitive fusion schemes based on substitution methods, such as averaging, weighted averaging and PCA, are performed solely in the substitution domain. In spite of easy implementation, these methods pay the expenses of reducing the contrast and distorting the spectral characteristics (Piella, 2003). Image fusion based on multiresolution decomposition (MRD) can handle the contrast and overall intensity. It decomposes images at a different scale to several components, which account for important salient features of images (Piella, 2003). Therefore, it enables a better performance than those performed in the substitution methods. The transform domain or multiresolution fusion have been discussed widely in recent studies because of their advantages over the other fusion techniques (Ali *et al.*, 2008; Mandal *et al.*, 2009; Nemec *et al.*, 2007; Piella, 2003; Zheng *et al.*, 2007). On the other hand, methods utilized Bayesian optimization, neural network or Brovey transform to find the fused image are suffered from a significant increase of computational complexity (Pohl and Van Genderen, 1998; Byeungwoo and Landgrebe, 1999). Bayesian fusion method has been proposed, allowing to adaptively estimating the relationships between the multiple image sensors in order to generate a single enhanced display (Lai and Fang, 2000).

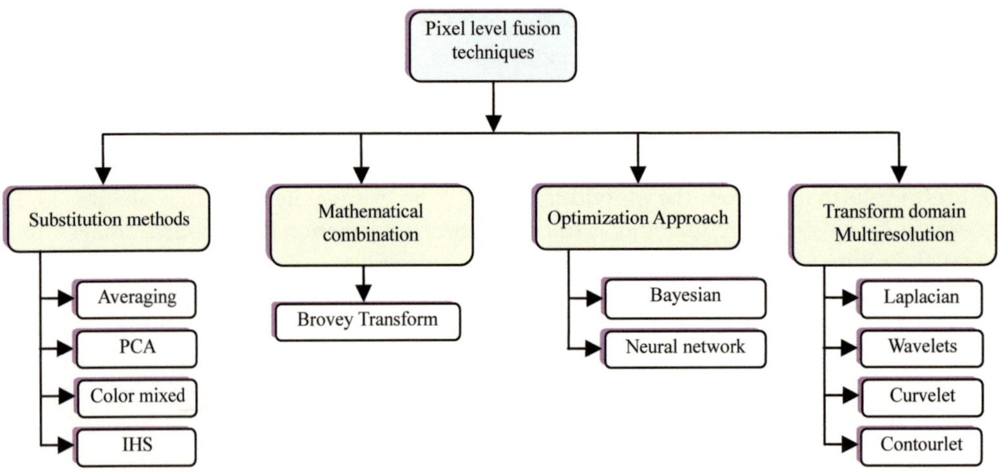

Fig. 2. The classification of pixel-to-pixel based image fusion methods.

The first multiresolution image fusion approach proposed in the literature is due to (Burt, 1984). His implementation used the Laplacian pyramid and the sample-based maximum selection rule. In (Toet, 1989) presented a similar algorithm but using the ratio of low pass pyramid. His approach is motivated by the fact that the human visual system is based on contrast, and therefore, a fusion technique which selects the highest local luminance contrast is likely to provide better details to a human observer. Several transforms have been proposed for image signals, which have incorporated directionality and multiresolution and hence, could capture edges in natural images more efficiently (Ali *et al.*, 2008; Mandal *et al.*, 2009; Nemec *et al.*, 2007; Zheng *et al.*, 2007).

3. Dual tree complex contourlet transform

A complex contourlet transform (CCT) method is proposed by (Chen and Li, 2005), which incorporates the DT-CWT (Hill *et al.*, 2002) and DFB to provide a flexible and robust scale-direction representation for source images. The DT-CWT decomposition details space W_J at the *J-th* scale, gives six subbands at each scale capturing distinct directions. Traditionally, we obtain the three highpass bands corresponding to the LH, HL, and HH subbands, indexed by $i \in \{1, 2, 3\}$. Each of them has two wavelets as real and complex part. By averaging the outputs of dual tree, we get an approximate of shift invariant (Kingsbury, 1999). In second stage for each subband applied (l_J) levels DFB (Bamberger and Smith, 1992) as shown in Figure 3. W_J of DT-CWT is nearly shift invariant and this property can be still established in the subspace $W_{J,k}^{(l_J)}$, even after applying directional filter banks on a detail subspace W_J. The mathematical form is defined as:

$$\eta_{J,k,n}^{i,(l_J)} = \sum_{m \in \mathbb{Z}^2} g_k^{l_J}[m - S_k^{(l_J)} n]\psi_{J,m}^{i} \quad i = 1,2,3 \tag{1}$$

where $g_k^{(l)}$ is the impulse response of the synthesis filter, $S_k^{(l)}$ is overall downsampling matrices of DFB and ψ is a wavelet functions. The family $\left\{\eta_{J,k,n}^{HL,(l_J)}, \eta_{J,k,n}^{LH,(l_J)}, \eta_{J,k,n}^{HH,(l_J)}\right\}_{n \in \mathbb{Z}^2}$ is a basis for the subspace $W_{J,k}^{(l_J)}$ and each consists of a complex dual tree. The location shift is denoted as m.

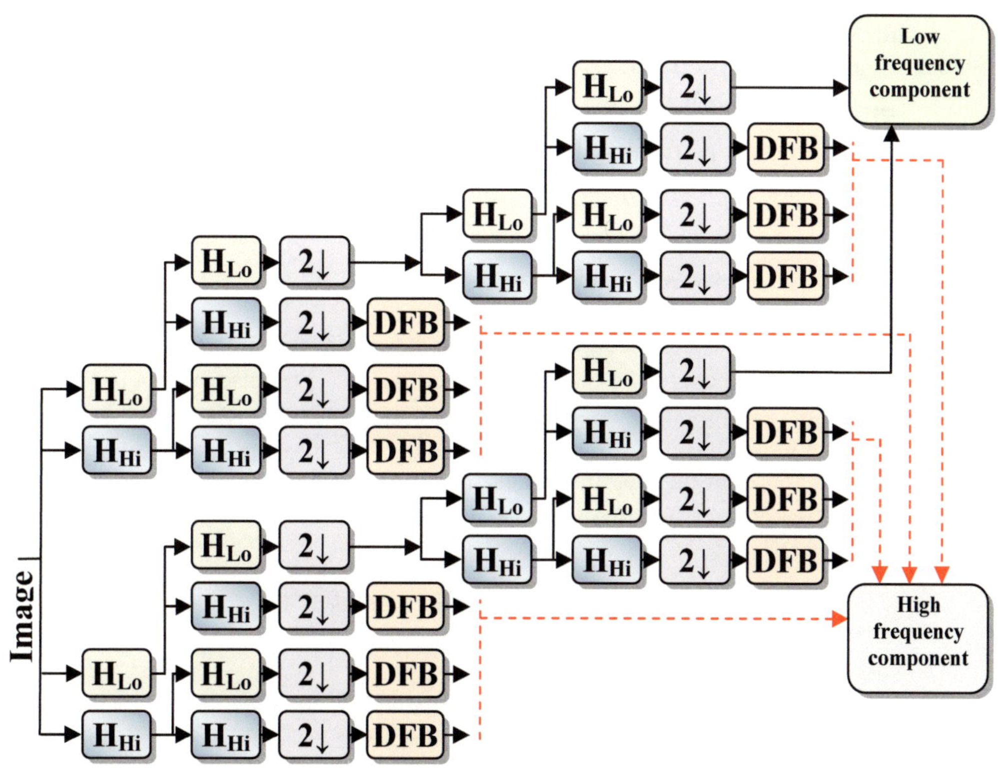

Fig. 3. The proposed of DT-CCT based on Fusion Rules.

3.1 Requirements and challenges of image fusion

The reason of image fusion is to integrate complementary and redundant information from multiple images to produce a combined that contains a superior description of the scene than any of the individual source images. Considering the objectives of image fusion and its potential advantages, some generic requirements can be imposed on the fusion algorithm (Rockinger, 1996):

- It should not discard any salient information contained in any of the input images.
- It should not introduce any artifacts which can distract or mislead a human observer or any subsequent image processing steps.
- It must be reliable, robust and, as much as possible, tolerant of imperfections such as noise or misregistrations.

However, a fusion approach which is independent of the modalities of the inputs and produces a combined image which appears accepted to a human interpreter is highly wanted.

3.2 Image fusion approach (DT-CCT-PCA and DT-CCT-PCA/LE)

The proposed image fusion approach consists of the following steps:

Step 1. Perform a DT-CCT on source images A and B, respectively, and obtain the corresponding coefficients $\{\mathrm{Coff}^{(L,A)}, \mathrm{Coff}_{J,l}^{(H,A)}\}$ and $\{\mathrm{Coff}^{(L,B)}, \mathrm{Coff}_{J,l}^{(H,B)}\}$, where $\mathrm{Coff}^{(L,A)}$ and $\mathrm{Coff}^{(L,B)}$ represent low frequency coefficients of image A and B respectively at the coarsest scale. $\mathrm{Coff}_{J,l}^{(H,A)}$ and $\mathrm{Coff}_{J,l}^{(H,B)}$ denotes the high frequency coefficients of image A and B respectively at the J-*th* scale and the l-*th* direction of DFP.

Step 2. Employ some fusion rules to reconstruct the DT-CCT coefficients of the fused image F as shown $\{\mathrm{Coff}^{(L,F)}, \mathrm{Coff}_{J,l}^{(H,F)}\}$.

Step 3. By successively performing inverse dual tree complex contourlet transform to the modified coefficients at all decomposition, the final fused image F can be reconstructed.

3.2.1 Fusion rules for low frequency coefficients

The following are the methods proposed for fusion rules:

Method 1: Complex contourlet transform based on maximum selection (CCT-Max)

As the coefficients in the coarsest scale subband $\{\mathrm{Coff}_{J0}^{(L,A\ or\ B)}\}$ represents the approximation component of the source image, the simplest way is to use the conventional maximum selection method to produce the composite coefficients. The maximum selection method is a popular choice to pick out the salient features of an image, e.g. edges and boundaries.

The normalized weight $D^{(L,A)} \in \{0,1\}$ is defined as:

$$D^{(L,A)} = \begin{cases} 1 & \left|\mathrm{Coff}_{J0}^{(L,A)}\right| \geq \left|\mathrm{Coff}_{J0}^{(L,B)}\right| \\ 0 & \text{otherwise} \end{cases} \tag{2}$$

where $D^{(L,A)}$ and $D^{(L,B)} = 1 - D^{(L,A)}$ are used in equation (7) to obtain the coefficients of low frequency coefficients for fused image. This method were used in CCT-Max proposed by (Chen and Li, 2005). However, it cannot obtain fused approximation of high quality for medical image.

Method 2: Dual tree complex contourlet transform based on PCA (DT-CCT-PCA)
The principal component analysis PCA can be used as a weighted precision measure to determine which pixel or region is important for fused. Dual tree complex contourlet transform based on PCA is implemented as described in (Al-Azzawi *et al.*, 2009; Al-Azzawi and Abdullah, 2010). PCA is also called the Karhunen-Loève transform or the Hotelling transform. It involves a mathematical procedure that transforms a number of correlated variables into a number of uncorrelated variables called principal components. It is also used to reduce dimensionality in a dataset while retaining those characteristics of the dataset that contribute most to its variance. It computes a compact and optimal description of the data set. PCA has been employed in previous researches (Huaixin, 2007; Zheng *et al.*, 2005) as fusion rules. The fusion rule for low frequency component in contourlet domain is implemented as:

$$D^{(L,A)} = \frac{i}{i+j} \quad \text{and} \quad D^{(L,B)} = \frac{j}{i+j} \tag{3}$$

where i and j are the elements of the principal eigenvector, which are computed by analyzing the original input image A and B for corresponding image coefficients. $D^{(L,A)}$ and $D^{(L,B)}$ are the normalized weights. Thus the fused image has the same energy distribution as the original input images.

Method 3: Dual tree complex contourlet transform based on PCA and Local energy (DT-CCT-PCA/LE).
In this method, PCA and local energy weighted selection are incorporated as the fusion rules in contourlet domain. First, calculate the local energy $E^{(A \text{ or } B)}{}_{Low}(x,y)$ of low frequency component in contourlet domain centering at the current coefficient $\mathrm{Coff}_{J0}^{(L,A \text{ or } B)}$ (Nunez *et al.*, 1999; Pudney *et al.*, 1995), which is defined as:

$$E^{(A \text{ or } B)}{}_{Low}(x,y)_{J0} = \sum_m \sum_n \mathrm{Coff}_{J0}^{(L,A \text{ or } B)}(x+m,y+n)^2 . W(m,n) \tag{4}$$

where W is a template of size 3 × 3 and satisfy the normalization rule.

$$W = \frac{1}{9}\begin{bmatrix} 1 & 1 & 1 \\ 1 & 1 & 1 \\ 1 & 1 & 1 \end{bmatrix} \quad \text{and} \quad \sum_m \sum_n W(m,n) = 1 \tag{5}$$

The normalized weight $D^{(L,A \text{ or } B)} \in \{0,1\}$ is defined as:

$$\begin{cases} \left. \begin{array}{l} D^{(L,A)} = \begin{cases} 1 & \left|E^{(A)}{}_{Low}(x,y)_{J0}\right| \geq \left|E^{(B)}{}_{Low}(x,y)_{J0}\right| \\ 0 & \text{otherwise} \end{cases} \\ D^{(L,B)} = 1 - D^{(L,B)} \end{array} \right\} & \text{for } E^{(A \text{ or } B)}{}_{Low}(x,y)_{J0} \geq \partial \\ \left. \begin{array}{l} D^{(L,A)} = i/(i+j) \\ D^{(L,B)} = j/(i+j) \end{array} \right\} & \text{for } E^{(A \text{ or } B)}{}_{Low}(x,y)_{J0} < \partial \end{cases} \tag{6}$$

where i and j are the elements of the principal eigenvector, which are computed by analyzing the original input image A and B for corresponding image coefficients. ∂ is threshold defined by user. $D^{(L,A)}$ and $D^{(L,B)}$ are the normalized weights. The coefficients of low frequency components for fused image F is shown below:

$$\text{Coff}_{j0}^{(L,F)} = \text{Coff}_{j0}^{(L,A)}.\, D^{(L,A)} + \text{Coff}_{j0}^{(L,B)}.\, D^{(L,B)} \tag{7}$$

3.2.2 Fusion rules for high frequency coefficients

High frequency coefficients generally correspond to sharper brightness in the image. The most commonly used selection principle is the local energy scheme to pick out the salient features of an image, e.g. edges and boundaries. The local energy (Yang *et al.*, 2008; Morrone and Owens, 1987) $E^{(A)}{}_{High}(x,y)$ and $E^{(B)}{}_{High}(x,y)$ is defined as:

$$E^{(A\ or\ B)}{}_{High}(x,y)_{J,l} = \sum_m \sum_n \text{Coff}_{J,l}^{(H,A\ or\ B)}(x+m,y+n)^2 .W(m,n) \tag{8}$$

where W is a template defined in equation (5). Larger value of local energy $E^{(A\ or\ B)}{}_{High}(x,y)$ means there is more high frequency information. Weights $D^{(H,A)}$ and $D^{(H,B)}$ needs to be calculated as:

$$D^{(H,A)} = \begin{Bmatrix} 1 \ \text{ for } E^{(A)}{}_{High}(x,y) \geq E^{(B)}{}_{High}(x,y) \\ 0 \ \text{ for } E^{(A)}{}_{High}(x,y) < E^{(B)}{}_{High}(x,y) \end{Bmatrix} \text{ and } D^{(H,B)} = 1 - D^{(H,A)} \tag{9}$$

The coefficients of high frequency coefficients for fused image F is defined as:

$$\text{Coff}_{J,l}^{(H,F)} = \text{Coff}_{J,l}^{(H,A)}.\, D^{(H,A)} + \text{Coff}_{J,l}^{(H,B)}.\, D^{(H,B)} \tag{10}$$

The multiresolution coefficients with large local energy values are considered as sharp brightness changes or salient features in the corresponding source image, such as the edges, lines, contours and object boundaries. So, the fused high frequency components in contourlet domain preserve all the salient features in source images and introduce as less artifacts or inconsistency as possible. Therefore, the fusion result will contain all high resolution form original image.

4. Objective evaluation of image fusion

Objective evaluations of fused images are important in comparing the performance of different image fusion algorithms (Petrovic and Xydeas, 2005a; Petrovic and Xydeas, 2005b; Ruiz *et al.*, 2002; Yinghua *et al.*, 2007; Youzhi and Zheng, 2009). Objective evaluation methods are needed to compare "good" or "bad" fused images. So far, only a limited number of relatively application dependent objective image fusion performance metrics has been published in the literature (Petrovic and Xydeas, 2005b; Piella, 2003; Wang and Bovik,

2002; Yang *et al.*, 2008; Rockinger and Fechner, 1998). Many image quality evaluations in the literature use an ideal fused image as a reference for comparison with the image fusion results (Yinghua *et al.*, 2007; Li *et al.*, 1995). Rockinger and Fechner, (1998) proposed metrics based on mutual information for image sequence and still image fusion performance.

The root mean squared error and peak signal to noise ratio-based metrics were widely used for these comparisons. The gradient representation metric of (Petrovic and Xydeas, 2005b) is based on the idea of measuring localized preservation of input gradient information in the fused image. An image quality index based on the structural metric proposed by (Wang and Bovik, 2002) was improved for image fusion assessment by (Piella and Heijmans, 2003) into a pixel by pixel or region by region method, giving weighted averages of the similarities between the fused image and each of the source images.

A reliable method for choosing an optimal fusion algorithm for each particular application however, largely remains an open issue. A number of objective comparison metrics have been investigated:

Image Quality Index (IQI), is easy to calculate and applicable to various image processing application (Wang and Bovik, 2002; Piella and Heijmans, 2003). The dynamic range of IQI is [-1, 1]. The best value 1 is achieved if and only if $F = R$, where F is fused image and R is reference image. IQI is defined as:

$$\mathrm{IQI} = \frac{\sigma_{FR}}{\sigma_F \sigma_R} \cdot \frac{2\overline{F}\overline{R}}{\left(\overline{F}\right)^2 + \left(\overline{R}\right)^2} \cdot \frac{2\sigma_F \sigma_R}{\sigma_F^2 + \sigma_R^2} \tag{11}$$

where :

$$\overline{g} = \frac{1}{Z}\sum_{i=1}^{Z} g_i,\ \sigma_{FR} = \frac{1}{Z-1}\sum_{i=1}^{Z}(F_i - \overline{F})(R_i - \overline{R}) \text{ and } \sigma_g^2 = \frac{1}{Z-1}\sum_{i=1}^{Z}(g_i - \overline{g})^2,$$

$$g = F \text{ or } R \text{ and } Z = N \times M \quad \text{(size of the image)}.$$

Coefficient Correlation (CC), can show similarity in the small structures between the original and reconstructed images (Roche *et al.*, 1998). Higher value of correlation means that more information is preserved. Coefficient correlation in the space domain is defined by:

$$d = \text{image } A \text{ or image } B.$$

$$\mathrm{CC}(F,d) = \frac{\sum_{i=0}^{M-1}\sum_{j=0}^{N-1}\left(F(i,j) - \overline{F}\right)\left(d(i,j) - \overline{d}\right)}{\sqrt{\sum_{i=0}^{M-1}\sum_{j=0}^{N-1}\left(F(i,j) - \overline{F}\right)^2 \sum_{i=0}^{M-1}\sum_{j=0}^{N-1}\left(d(i,j) - \overline{d}\right)^2}} \tag{12}$$

where $\overline{F}$ and $\overline{d}$ are the mean value of the corresponding data set.

Overall Cross Entropy (OCE), is used to measure the difference between the two source images and the fused image. Small value corresponds to good fusion result obtained (Yang *et al.*, 2008). The OCE calculation is as follows:

$$\text{OCE}(A,B;F)=\frac{CE(A,F)+CE(B,F)}{2} \tag{13}$$

where $CE(A,F)$ and $CE(B,F)$ are the cross entropy of the source image and fused image respectively , given by following:

$$CE(d,F)=\sum_{i=0}^{L-1} p_d(i)log_2\frac{p_d(i)}{p_f(i)} \tag{14}$$

where d = A or B is the input multimodality medical images, F is the fused image result, p_f, p_d are the normalized histogram of the fused image and source image respectively, and L is the maximum gray level for a pixel in the image, usually L is set to 255.

Root Mean Square Error (RMSE), is found between the reference image R and the fused image F, (Zheng *et al.*, 2005), defined as:

$$\text{RMSE}=\left(\frac{1}{c}\right)\sum_k\sqrt{\frac{\sum_{x=1}^{N}\sum_{y=1}^{M}\left(R_k(x,y)-F_k(x,y)\right)^2}{M\times N}} \tag{15}$$

where c=3 and k=R,G,B for color image and c=1 for gray image. The smaller the value of the RMSE means a better performance of the fusion algorithm.

5. Experimental results for image fusion

In this section, we present some experimental results obtained with presented fusion methods.

5.1 Robust image fusion using Dual Tree Complex Contourlet Transform (DT-CCT-PCA and DT-CCT-PCA/LE)

To test proposed method, thirty five groups of human brain images were selected, includes a CT and a MRI images. The corresponding pixels of two input images have been perfectly co-aligned. All images have the same size of 512×512 pixels, with 256-level grayscale. The proposed medical fusion algorithm, traditional complex contourlet and DT-CWT are applied to these image sets. In our experiment an image is decomposed into 2-levels using biorthogonal Daubechies 9-7 wavelet, (Lina and Gagnon, 1995; Mallat, 1999).

Each subband at each level is fed to the DFB stage with 8-directions at the finest level. In the DFB stage, the 23-45 biorthogonal quincunx filters were used designed by (See-May *et al.*, 1995) and modulate them to obtain the biorthogonal fan filters. DT-CWT is available in Matlab wavelet software (Selesnick *et al.*, 2003).

In addition, image quality index (IQI), root mean square error (RMSE), correlation coefficient (CC) and overall cross entropy (OCE) are used to evaluate the fusion performance (objective evaluation). Experiment results were conducted to compare the proposed methods DT-CCT-PCA and DT-CCT-PCA/LE with complex contourlet transform based on maximum amplitudes (CCT-max) (Chen and Li, 2005) and dual tree complex wavelet transform (DT-DWT) (Hill *et al.*, 2002). Figure 4, it shows the original multimodality image dataset 1 and 2.

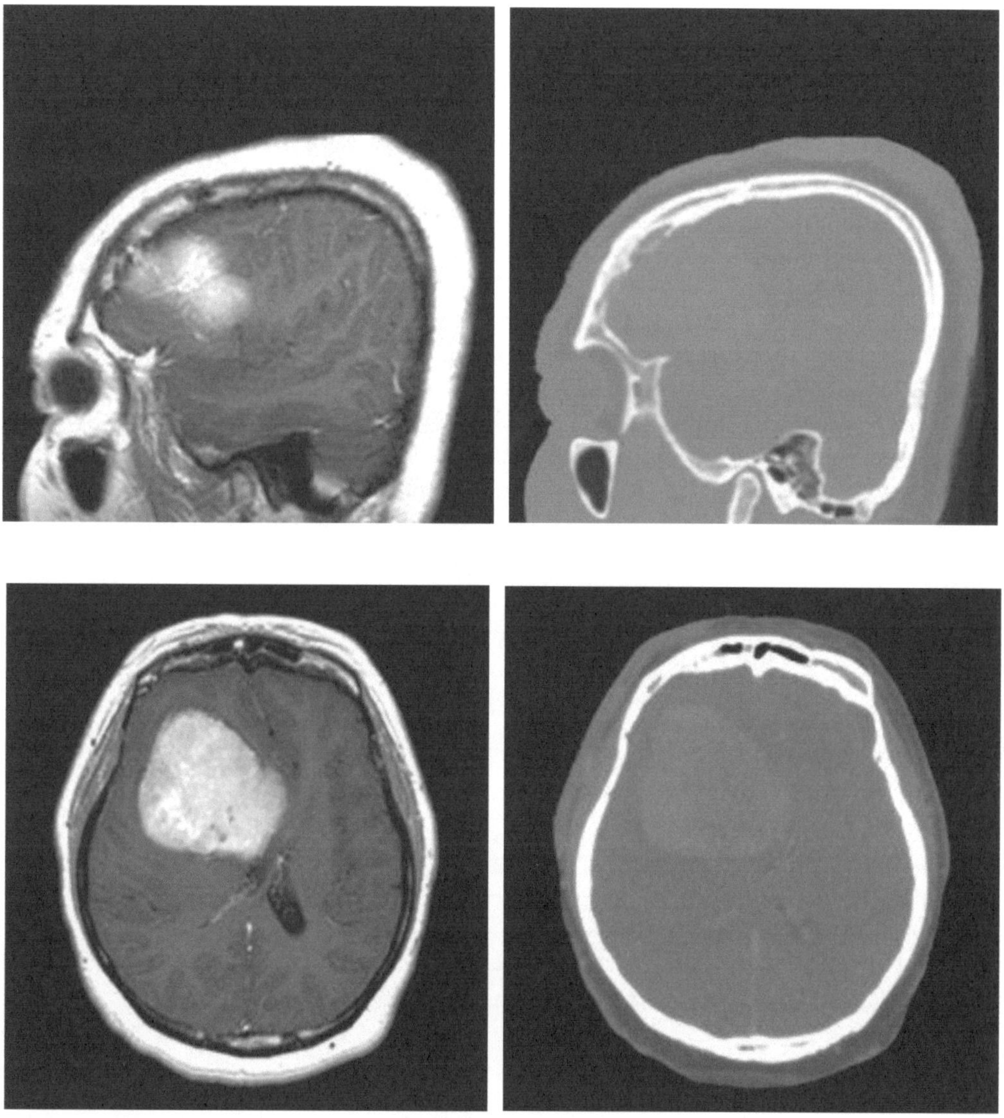

MRI CT

Fig. 4. Original multimodality image dataset 1 and 2.

The evaluation results in Table 1 and the complete data sets show that:

1. From indicators, the IQI and CC are the best with the proposed methods, higher value of correlation or IQI, means that more information is preserved. The OCE and RMSE of the new methods are least in the two sets. It is shown that, the proposed method gives the best fusion results in the two fused images.

2. For the two image sets, the corresponding fused image results are given in Figure 5. DT-CCT-PCA performs better than previous method. However, the best image fusion result is obtained by applying the proposed DT-CCT-PCA/LE fusion algorithm.
3. It is evident to see from the Table 1 and the complete data sets that the resulting image from DT-CCT-PCA/LE based fusion has better spectral quality than the other methods, in terms of the higher values of correlation coefficient and root mean square error. The highest value of correlation coefficient 0.9929 in this case indicates that most geometric details are enhanced in the image fused by DT-CCT-PCA/LE transform. As it could be seen from the preceding experimental results, DT-CCT-PCA/LE based fusion approach is the optimum and most well-suited fusion MRI-CT application, in terms of the spectral and spatial quality.
4. Fusion scheme based the novel weighted PCA/LE rule can get better fusion image. As shown in Table 1 and the complete data sets, for DT-CCT-PCA/LE the RMSE and OCE are both lower than that of traditional based methods, lowest values of RMSE and OCE are 0.1017, 0.4527 respectively. The lowest values of RMSE and OCE are 0.1683, 0.8726 respectively for CCT-max.
5. Experimental results demonstrate that the proposed method DT-CCT-PCA/LE outperforms the DT-CCT-PCA-based fusion approach and the traditional CCT-max-based approaches and including the DT-CWT-based in terms of both visual quality and objective evaluation.

Data	Evaluation	DT-CWT	CCT-max	DT-CCT-PCA	DT-CCT-PCA/LE
Data set 1	IQI	0.2581	0.2513	0.3236	0.4250
	RMSE	0.1683	0.1683	0.1442	0.1017
	CC	0.9482	0.9482	0.9523	0.9641
	OCE	0.8726	0.8726	0.8683	0.8531
Data set 2	IQI	0.3340	0.3523	0.4171	0.3843
	RMSE	0.2179	0.2180	0.1480	0.2281
	CC	0.9750	0,9750	0,9853	0.9929
	OCE	1.0865	1.0863	0.9911	0.4527

Table 1. Results of Quality Measures for Various Fusion Schemes.

6. Conclusion

A new approach for multimodal image fusion using dual-tree complex contourlet transform (DT-CCT) based on PCA and combined (PCA and local energy) are proposed. The method is based on PCA, local energy and dual tree complex contourlet transform. We can see from Figure 5 that the feature and detailed information presented in section 3.2.1 method 3 is much richer than other fused images. The image contents like tissues are clearly enhanced. Other useful information like brain boundaries and shape are almost perfectly. The dual tree complex contourlet transform produces images with improved contours and textures, while the property of shift invariance is retained. It enhances the reliability of conventional approaches considerably and thereby their acceptability by practitioners in a clinical environment.

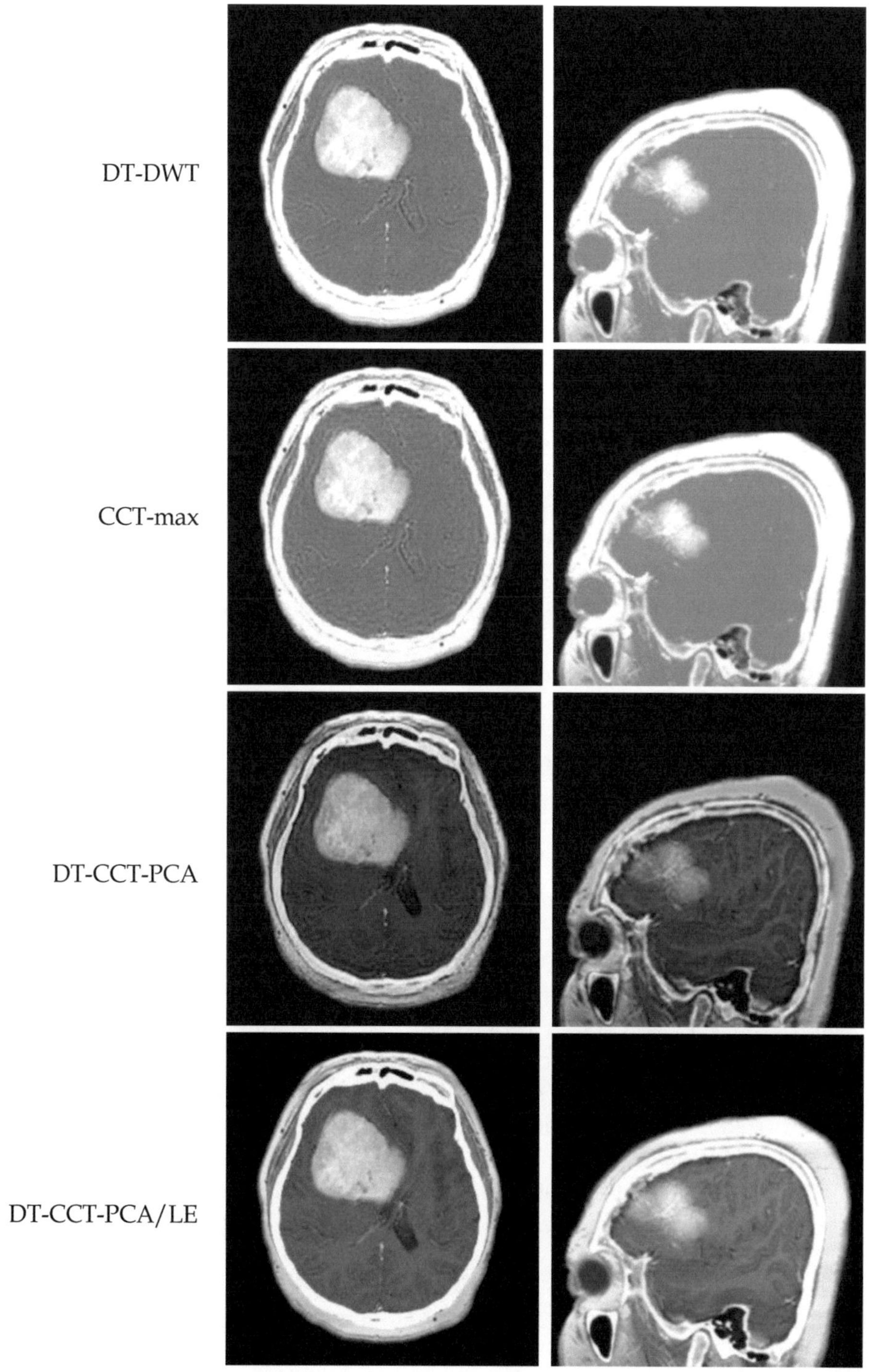

Fig. 5. Fusion results on test original multimodality image dataset 1 and 2 using DT-CWT, traditional CCT-max and proposed methods.

The methods present a new development in the fusion of MRI and CT images, which is based on the DT-CCT. Visual and objective evaluation comparisons demonstrated that the fusion results (Figure 5) of the new method contain more detail information, while information distortion is very small. It enhances the reliability of conventional approaches considerably and thereby their acceptability by practitioners in a clinical environment.

7. Acknowledgment

Authors of this chapter sincerely would like to thank Hospital Universiti Sains Malaysia (HUSM) for provided all medical images.

8. References

Aguilar, M. & New, J. R. (2002). Fusion of multi-modality volumetric medical imagery, *In Proceedings of the Fifth International Conference on Information Fusion*, 2, pp. 1206-1212, ISBN 0-9721844-1-4, Annapolis, MD, 2002.

Al-Azzawi, N., Sakim, H. A. M., Abdullah, W. A. K. W. & Ibrahim, H. (2009). Medical image fusion scheme using complex contourlet transform based on PCA, *Annual International Conference of the IEEE Engineering in Medicine and Biology Society, EMBC 2009*, pp. 5813-5816, ISBN 1557-170X, Hilton Minneapolis, Minnesota, USA, 2-6 September, 2009.

Al-Azzawi, N. A. & Abdullah, W. A. K. W. (2010). Improved CT-MR image fusion scheme using dual tree complex contourlet transform based on PCA. *International Journal of Information Acquisition*, Vol. 7, No.2, pp. 99-107, ISSN 0219-8789.

Ali, F. E., El-Dokany, I. M., Saad, A. A. & El-Samie, F. E. A. (2008). Curvelet fusion of MR and CT images. *Progress In Electromagnetics Research C*, Vol. 3, pp. 215-224, ISSN 1937-8718.

Anna, W., Wu, L., Li, D. & Chen, Y. (2007). Research on medical image fusion based on orthogonal wavelet packets transformation combined with 2v-SVM, *IEEE/ICME International Conference on Complex Medical Engineering*, pp. 670-675, ISBN 978-1-4244-1078-1, Beijing, 23-27 May, 2007.

Bamberger, R. H. & Smith, M. J. T. (1992). A filter bank for the directional decomposition of images: Theory and design. *IEEE Transactions on Signal Processing*, Vol. 40, No.4, pp. 882-893, ISSN 1053587X.

Baum, K., Helguera, M. & Krol, A. (2008). Fusion viewer: A new tool for fusion and visualization of multimodal medical data sets. *Journal of Digital Imaging*, Vol. 21, pp. 59-68, ISSN 0897-1889.

Burt, P. (1984). The pyramid as a structure for efficient computation, *Multiresolution Image Processing and Analysis, A. Rosenfeld, Ed. Springer-Verlag, Berlin*, pp. 6-35, ISBN 0387130063, 1984.

Byeungwoo, J. & Landgrebe, D. A. (1999). Decision fusion approach for multitemporal classification. *IEEE Transactions on Geoscience and Remote Sensing*, Vol. 37, No.3, pp. 1227-1233, ISSN 0196-2892.

Carroll, J., Ruskey, F. & Weston, M. (2007). Which n-venn diagrams can be drawn with convex k-gons? *Discrete and Computational Geometry*, Vol. 37, No.4, pp. 619-628, ISSN 0179-5376.

Chen, D. & Li, Q. (2005). The use of complex contourlet transform on fusion scheme. *proceedings of world academy of science, engineering and technology*, Vol. 7, pp. 342-347, ISSN 975-98458-6-5.

Cunha, A. L. D., Zhou, J. P. & Do, M. N. (2006). The nonsubsampled contourlet transform: theory, design, and applications. *IEEE Transactions on Image Processing*, Vol. 15, No.10, pp. 3089-3101, ISSN 1057-7149.

Daneshvar, S. & Ghassemian, H. (2007). Fusion of MRI and PET images using retina based multi-resolution transforms, *9th International Symposium on Signal Processing and its Applications, ISSPA 2007*, pp. 1-4, ISBN 978-1-4244-0778-1, Sharjah, United arab emirates, 12-15 Febrary, 2007.

Ghassemian, H. (2001). A retina based multi-resolution image-fusion, *IEEE International Geoscience and Remote Sensing Symposium. IGARSS '01*, 2, pp. 709-711, ISBN 0-7803-7031-7, Sydney, NSW, 9-13 July, 2001.

Gonzalez, R. C. & Woods, R. E. (2002). *Digital image processing.* (Second Edition), Prentice Hall, ISBN 0201180758, Upper Saddle River, N.J.

Hill, P. R., Canagarajah, C. N. & Bull, D. R. (2002). Image fusion using complex wavelets, *Electronic Proceedings of 13th British Machine Vision Conference, BMVC 02*, pp. 487-496, ISBN 1 901725 19 7, Wales, 2-5 September, 2002.

Hong, Z., Lei, L. & Nan, L. (2007). A novel wavelet medical image fusion method, *International Conference on Multimedia and Ubiquitous Engineering, MUE '07*, pp. 548-553, ISBN 0-7695-2777-9, Seoul, 26-28 April, 2007.

Huaixin, C. (2007). A multiresolution image fusion based on principle component analysis, *Fourth International Conference on Image and Graphics, ICIG 2007*, pp. 737-741, ISBN 0-7695-2929-1, Sichuan, 22-24 August, 2007.

Kingsbury, N. (1999). Shift invariant properties of the dual-tree complex wavelet transform, *Proceedings IEEE International Conference on Acoustics, Speech, and Signal Processing, ICASSP '99*, 3, pp. 1221-1224, ISBN 0-7803-5041-3, Phoenix, AZ., 15-19 March, 1999.

Lai, S.-H. & Fang, M. (2000). A hierarchical neural network algorithm for robust and automatic windowing of MR images. *Artificial Intelligence in Medicine*, Vol. 19, No.2, pp. 97-119, ISSN 0933-3657.

Li, H., Manjunath, B. S. & Mitra, S. K. (1995). Multisensor image fusion using the wavelet transform. *Graphical Models and Image Processing*, Vol. 57, No.3, pp. 235-245, ISSN 1077-3169.

Lina, J.-M. & Gagnon, L. (1995). Image enhancement with symmetric Daubechies wavelets, *Wavelet Applications in Signal and Image Processing III. Part 1 (of 2)*,Society of Photo-Optical Instrumentation Engineers, 2569, pp. 196-207, ISBN 0277786X, San Diego, CA, USA, 12-14 July, 1995.

Mallat, S. (1999). *A wavelet tour of signal processing.* (Second Edition), Academic, ISBN 012466606X, San Diego, Calif.

Mandal, T., Jonathan Wu, Q. M. & Yuan, Y. (2009). Curvelet based face recognition via dimension reduction. *Signal Processing*, Vol. 89, No.12, pp. 2345-2353, ISSN 0165-1684.

Morrone, M. C. & Owens, R. A. (1987). Feature detection from local energy. *Pattern Recognition Letters*, Vol. 6, No.5, pp. 303-313, ISSN 0167-8655.

Nemec, S. F., Donat, M. A., Mehrain, S., Friedrich, K., Krestan, C., Matula, C., Imhof, H. & Czerny, C. (2007). CT-MR image data fusion for computer assisted navigated neurosurgery of temporal bone tumors. *European Journal of Radiology*, Vol. 62, No.2, pp. 192-198, ISSN 0720-048X.

Nunez, J., Otazu, X., Fors, O., Prades, A., Pala, V. & Arbiol, R. (1999). Multiresolution-based image fusion with additive wavelet decomposition. *IEEE Transactions on Geoscience and Remote Sensing*, Vol. 37, No.3, pp. 1204-1211, ISSN 0196-2892.

Pajares, G. & Manuel De La Cruz, J. (2004). A wavelet-based image fusion tutorial. *Pattern Recognition*, Vol. 37, No.9, pp. 1855-1872, ISSN 0031-3203.

Patias, P. (2002). Medical imaging challenges photogrammetry. *ISPRS Journal of Photogrammetry and Remote Sensing*, Vol. 56, No.5-6, pp. 295-310, ISSN 0924-2716.

Petrovic, V. & Xydeas, C. (2005a). Objective evaluation of signal-level image fusion performance. *Optical Engineering*, Vol. 14, No.8, pp. 1-8, ISSN 00913286.

Petrovic, V. & Xydeas, C. (2005b). Objective image fusion performance characterisation, *Tenth IEEE International Conference on Computer Vision, ICCV 2005*, 2, pp. 1866-1871, ISBN 1550-5499, Beijing, 17-21 October, 2005b.

Piella, G. (2003). A general framework for multiresolution image fusion: from pixels to regions. *Information Fusion*, Vol. 4, No.4, pp. 259-280, ISSN 1566-2535.

Piella, G. & Heijmans, H. (2003). A new quality metric for image fusion, *Proceedings International Conference on Image Processing, ICIP 2003*, 3, pp. 173-176, ISBN 1522-4880, Barcelona Catalonia, Spain, 14-17 September, 2003.

Pohl, C. & Van Genderen, J. L. (1998). Multisensor image fusion in remote sensing: concepts, methods and applications. *International Journal of Remote Sensing*, Vol. 19, No.5, pp. 823-854, ISSN 01431161.

Pudney, C., Kovesi, P. & Robbins, B. (1995). A 3D local energy surface detector for confocal microscope images, *Proceedings of the Third Australian and New Zealand Conference on Intelligent Information Systems, ANZIIS-95*, pp. 7-12, ISBN 0-86422-430-3, Perth, WA, Australia, 27 November, 1995.

Roche, A., Malandain, G., Pennec, X. & Ayache, N. (1998). The correlation ratio as a new similarity measure for multimodal image registration. *In:* WELLS, W. M., COLCHESTER, A. & DELP, S. (eds.) *Medical Image Computing and Computer-Assisted Interventation - MICCAI'98.* Springer Berlin Heidelberg, 1496, pp. 1115-1124, ISBN 978-3-540-65136-9.

Rockinger, O. (1996). Pixel-level fusion of image sequences using wavelet frames, *In Proceedings of the 16th Leeds Annual Statistical Research Workshop, LASR1996*,Leeds University Press, pp. 149-154, ISBN 0853161615, Leeds, England, July, 1996.

Rockinger, O. & Fechner, T. (1998). Pixel-Level Image Fusion: The Case of Image Sequences, *SPIE proceedings series, Signal processing, sensor fusion, and target recognition VII*, 3374, pp. 378-388, ISBN 0-8194-2823-X, Orlando FL , ETATS-UNIS, 1998.

Ruiz, V. G., Fernández, J. J., López, M. F. & García, I. (2002). Progressive image transmission in telemicroscopy: A quantitative approach for electron microscopy images of biological specimens. *Real-Time Imaging*, Vol. 8, No.6, pp. 519-544, ISSN 1077-2014.

See-May, P., Kim, C. W., Vaidyanathan, P. P. & Ansari, R. (1995). A new class of two-channel biorthogonal filter banks and wavelet bases. *IEEE Transactions on Signal Processing*, Vol. 43, No.3, pp. 649-665, ISSN 1053-587X.

Selesnick, I., Cai, S. & Li, K. (2003). *Matlab implementation of wavelet transforms.* January 2008. Available from: http://taco.poly.edu/WaveletSoftware/index.html.

Singh, R., Vatsa, M. & Noore, A. (2009). Multimodal medical image fusion using redundant discrete wavelet transform, *Seventh International Conference on Advances in Pattern Recognition, ICAPR '09*, pp. 232-235, ISBN 978-1-4244-3335-3, Kolkata, 4-6 February, 2009.

Toet, A. (1989). Image fusion by a ratio of low-pass pyramid. *Pattern Recognition Letters*, Vol. 9, No.4, pp. 245-253, ISSN 0167-8655.

Toet, A., Ruyven, L. V. & Velaton, J. (1989). Merging thermal and visual images by a contrast pyramid. *Optical Engineering*, Vol. 28, No.7, pp. 789-792, ISSN 0091-3286.

Wang, Z. & Bovik, A. C. (2002). A universal image quality index. *IEEE Signal Processing Letters*, Vol. 9, No.3, pp. 81-84, ISSN 10709908.

Yang, L., Guo, B. L. & Ni, W. (2008). Multimodality medical image fusion based on multiscale geometric analysis of contourlet transform. *Neurocomputing*, Vol. 72, No.1-3, pp. 203-211, ISSN 0925-2312.

Yinghua, L., Xue, F., Jingbo, Z., Rujuan, W., Kaiyuan, Z. & Jun, K. (2007). A multi-focus image fusion based on wavelet and region detection, *The International Conference on 'Computer as a Tool', EUROCON, 2007*, 3, pp. 294-298., ISBN 978-1-4244-0813-9, Warsaw, Poland, 9-12 September, 2007.

Yong, C., You, H. & Chaolong, Y. (2008). CT and MRI image fusion based on contourlet using a novel rule, *The 2nd International Conference on Bioinformatics and Biomedical Engineering, ICBBE 2008*, pp. 2064-2067, ISBN 978-1-4244-1747-6, Shanghai, 16-18 May, 2008.

Youzhi, Z. & Zheng, Q. (2009). Objective image fusion quality evaluation using structural similarity. *Tsinghua Science and Technology*, Vol. 14, No.6, pp. 703-709, ISSN 1007-0214.

Zhang, Q. & Guo, B.-L. (2009). Multifocus image fusion using the nonsubsampled contourlet transform. *Signal Processing*, Vol. 89, No.7, pp. 1334-1346, ISSN 0165-1684.

Zhang, Y. & Hong, G. (2005). An IHS and wavelet integrated approach to improve pan-sharpening visual quality of natural colour IKONOS and QuickBird images. *Information Fusion*, Vol. 6, No.3, pp. 225-234, ISSN 1566-2535.

Zheng, Y., Essock, E. A. & Hansen, B. C. (2005). Advanced discrete wavelet transform fusion algorithm and its optimization by using the metric of image quality index. *Optical Engineering*, Vol. 44, No.3, pp. 037003(1-12), ISSN 0091-3286.

Zheng, Y., Song, J. S., Zhou, W. M. & Wang, R. H. (2007). False color fusion for multi-band SAR images based on contourlet transform. *Acta Automatica Sinica*, Vol. 33, No.4, pp. 337-341, ISSN 1874-1029.

Zhongfei, Z., Jian, Y., Bajwa, S. & Gudas, T. (2003). "Automatic" multimodal medical image fusion, *Proceedings. 16th IEEE Symposium on Computer-Based Medical Systems*, pp. 42-49, ISBN 0-7695-1901-6, New York, NY, USA, 26-27 June, 2003.

7

Detecting Coronary Layers in IVUS Pictures Using Image Fusion Approach

Ahmad Ashoori, Behzad Moshiri and Seyed Kamaledin Setarehdan
Control and Intelligent Processing Centre of Excellence,
School of ECE, University of Tehran,
Tehran,
Iran

1. Introduction

Coronary artery disease is considered as the most important cause of death in most developed or semi-developed societies. It is known as a silent disease because it develops gradually without any serious symptoms and is recognized only after patient sudden death or serious infarction. The main cause of this type of disease is the plaque integration inside the coronary arteries. This obstructs blood circulation and cardiac muscles nutrition. Hence, finding methods for detecting vessels obstruction and curing it in time would be important to prevent complete obstruction. X-ray Angiography is one of the common methods to this end, which is an invasive method with a high risk due to X-ray radiations. In addition, this method is not strong enough to determine the quantity and the kind of the plaques (Fibrous Tissue, Necrotic Core classification, and/or Fibro-Fatty) (Agostoni et al., 2004).
One of the recent methods emerged for detecting vessels obstruction is Intra Vascular Ultra Sound (IVUS) imaging technique, which is based on inserting an ultrasound catheter inside a vessel and producing real-time cross-sectional images from the inner side of the vessel (Schoenhagen and Stillman, 2005). This semi-invasive method has not the X-ray harms and provides more accurate information from the vessel wall (Schoenhagen and White, 2003). In addition to its safety, IVUS is a reproducible method for imaging the vessel walls and determining the quantity of the vessel obstruction by the plaques. Fig. 1 shows a sample IVUS picture. IVUS imaging is carried out by inserting a catheter into a vessel, which travels through and reaches the artery. Since the area of this catheter is larger than the one of coronary vessels, it stops there and a fine probe (0.96- 1.17 mm long) emerges from it and penetrates to the end of the vessel. The probe is then pulled backward with a constant velocity and meanwhile IVUS frames are captured. Common frequency for imaging is 20-40 MHz. An increase in the frequency may improve the resolution; But due to energy absorption in tissues, quality of the images are low.
For medical usage of IVUS images, the borders of the inside and outside of a vessel and also plaque layers must be determined. This is usually done manually by a specialist, which is a time-consuming and error-prone procedure. Moreover, due to different noises such as motion artifact, ring-down, and speckle noise, automatic processing (Terzopoulos and Fleischer, 1988) of these images is one of the difficult problems in image processing. Lots of

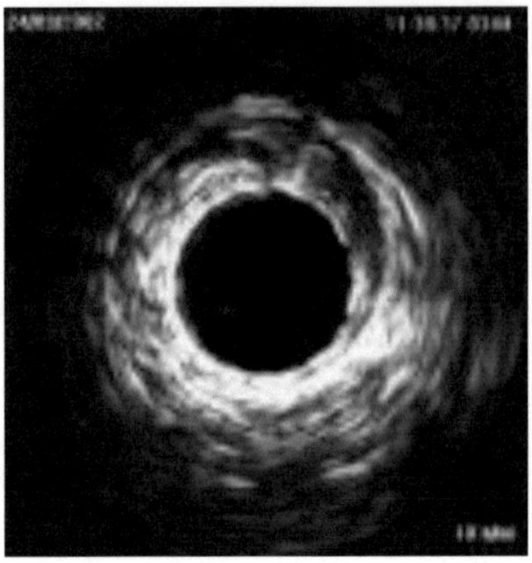

Fig. 1. A sample IVUS picture

efforts have been made to develop an accurate automated method for detection of the regions of interest in IVUS images (Sonka et al., 1995; Zhang et al., 1998; Takagi et al., 2000; Kovalski et al., 2000; Shekhar et al., 1999). Proposed methodologies usually take the advantage of characteristic appearance of arterial anatomy in two-dimensional IVUS images. Several segmentation methods have also been proposed. Some of earlier works on segmentation of IVUS images were based on heuristic graph searching algorithms using a cost function, in which a priori information of the expected pattern in IVUS frames was incorporated (Zhang et al., 1998; Takagi et al., 2000). A class of methods, based on expected similarity of the regions of interest in adjacent IVUS frames, takes into account that the sequence of frames constitutes a three-dimensional object. Under this perspective, active contour principles (Kovalski et al., 2000; Shekhar et al., 1999) could be used to extract the desired lumen and media–adventitia borders.

In this article, the IVUS images of NIOC hospital are to be processed. Section 2 discusses about the deformable models, which are going to be exploited to detect the coronary layers. According to low quality of these images, pre-processing actions including substituting catheter region with the average brightness of the whole image, wavelet transform and edge-preserving smoothing are performed in section 3. Section 4 discusses about detecting the borders applying deformable models (Terzopoulos and Fleischer, 1988), where distance-potential snake is used according to these images topology. The merit of this method comparing with the method presented in (Plissiti et al., 2004), which uses a neural network is its execution time. In section 4, using fuzzy integral operators for fusion in three levels including data-level (before pre-processing), feature-level (after pre-processing) and decision-level (after finding borders in each sample), the process explained in section 4.1 is done again in 4.2 and the results are compared with the previous one. Finally, in section 5, the good effect of image fusion on the IVUS frames of NIOC hospital dataset has been discussed.

2. IVUS image processing methods

Healthy arteries have three layers in IVUS images: 1) the inner layer, Intima; 2) the middle layer, Media; 3) the outer layer, Adventitia. The acoustic impedance difference between cell walls causes these layers to be displayed in these images. These layers' diameters in a healthy person are constant in a vessel from beginning to the end and any change is a symptom of disease.

As mentioned before, finding manually detecting of borders in IVUS images to be time consuming and error prone, lead to introduce automated methods for that. Common edge detection methods such as Sobel mask does not succeed in this task (Paul et al., 1996) (Fig. 2), since these images are perturbed with special noises such as ring down and speckle. Other methods based on first order derivative such as Laplacian or Prewitt mask do not succeed either (Zhu et al., 2002; Gil et al., 2000) (Fig. 3).

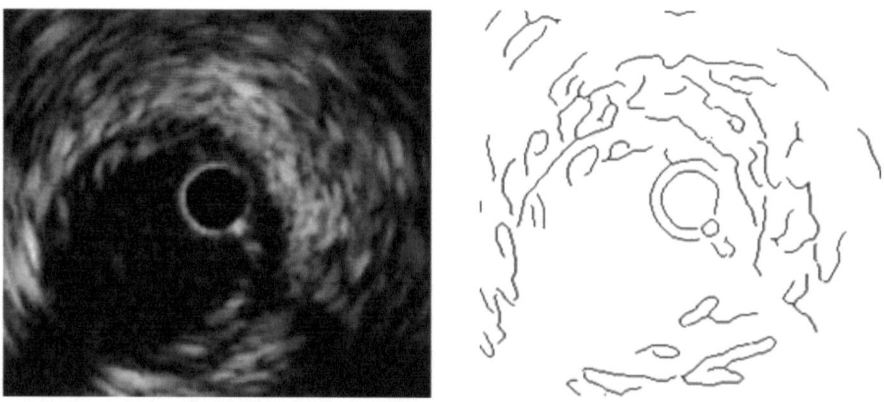

Fig. 2. The border detected by the Sobel mask

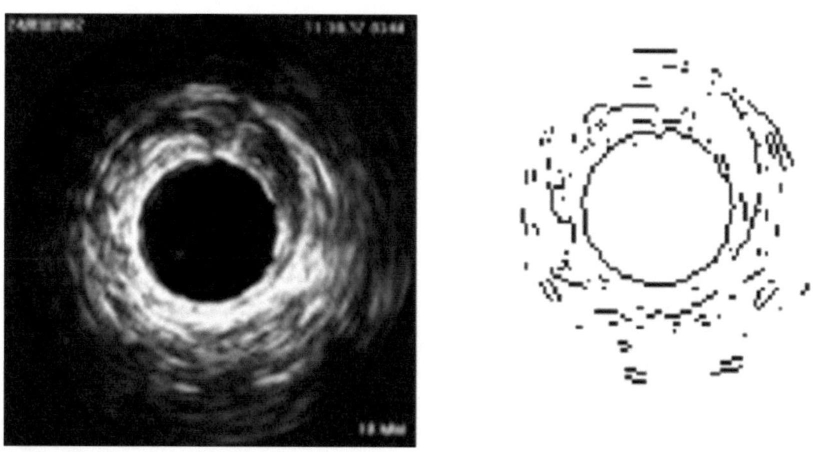

Fig. 3. The border detected by the Prewitt mask

2.1 Deformable models

Introduction of deformable models (active contours) by Kass et al. (Kass et al., 1987) led to extreme progress in edge detection. Active contours move under the influence of internal forces within the curve itself and external forces derived from image data. The internal and external forces are defined so that the active contour will conform to a boundary or other desired features within an image. They are widely used in many applications, including edge detection (Kass et al., 1987), segmentation (Leymarie and Levine, 1993; Durikovic et al., 1995), shape modeling (Terzopoulos and Fleischer, 1988; McInerney and Terzopoulos, 1995), and motion tracking (Terzopoulos and Szeliski, 1992).

There are two main categories of deformable models: parametric (also known as snakes) (Kass et al., 1987) and geometric (Caselles et al., 1993; Malladi et al., 1995). In this paper, we focus on snakes, which synthesize parametric curves within an image domain and allow them to move toward desired features, usually edges. Snakes are usually drawn toward the edges by potential forces, which are defined to be the negative gradient of apotential function. Some extra forces, such as pressure forces (Cohen, 1991), together with the potential forces comprise the external forces. There are also internal forces designed to hold the curve together (elasticity forces) and to keep it from bending too much (bending forces) (Xu and Price, 1997).

2.2 Parametric active contours (Snakes)

A traditional snake is a curve in the form of a rubber object that moves through an image to minimize the following energy function (Xu and Price, 1997):

$$E = \int_0^1 \frac{1}{2}[\alpha|x'(s)|^2 + \beta|x''(s)|^2] + E_{ext}(x(s))ds \tag{1}$$

In which, α is tension factor in order to control the elasticity energy and β is the rigidity factor in order to control the bending energy and *x(s)* denotes the curve. These two form the internal energy of the snake. The other term in Eq. (1) is external energy, which is obtained from image derivative. Having a gray-level image read in MATLAB software as *I(x,y)*, the common external energy functions can be described:

$$E_{ext}^{(1)}(x,y) = -|\nabla I(x,y)|^2 \tag{2}$$

$$E_{ext}^{(2)}(x,y) = -|\nabla[G_\sigma(x,y) * I(x,y)]|^2 \tag{3}$$

In which $G_\sigma(x,y)$ is a two dimensional Gaussian function with the standard deviation σ and ∇ is the gradient operator. Actually, there are more external energy functions that are mostly used for special images, which is not mentioned here. It is obvious from the Eq. (2) and Eq. (3) that the larger the σ is, the more dark the edges will be; but these large standard deviations are needed to increase capture range for the snake (Cohen, 1991; Leroy et al., 1996; Cohen and Cohen, 1993).

The snake, which is going to minimize *E* has to satisfy the Euler equation:

$$\alpha x''(s) - \beta x''''(s) - \nabla E_{ext} = 0 \tag{4}$$

The aforementioned equation can be rewritten as a force equation:

$$F_{\text{int}} + F_{ext}^{(p)} = 0 \tag{5}$$

In which $F_{\text{int}} = \alpha x''(s) - \beta x''''(s)$ and $F_{ext}^{(p)} = -\nabla E_{ext}$. The internal force opposes bending and extra elasticity, while the external force pushes snake to the desired edges. To solve Eq. (4), snake x has been considered to be dynamic with respect to time. Now, differentiating with respect to time gives:

$$x_t(s,t) = \alpha x''(s) - \beta x''''(s,t) - \nabla E_{ext} \tag{6}$$

In when the left term reaches zero Eq. (4) will be derived. A numerical solution for Eq. (6) can be found using discretizing the system and solving it iteratively.

2.3 Snakes' problems

There are two main problems dealing with parametric active contours. First, the initial contour must be near the correct border or the algorithm would not work efficiently. In Fig. 4.a an example of converging to a wrong border is provided. Some methods to solve this problem have been proposed including multi-resolution methods (Leroy et al., 1996), pressure forces (Cohen, 1991), distance potentials (Cohen and Cohen, 1993), whose main idea is to increase external forces capture range and drawing the contour to desired edges.

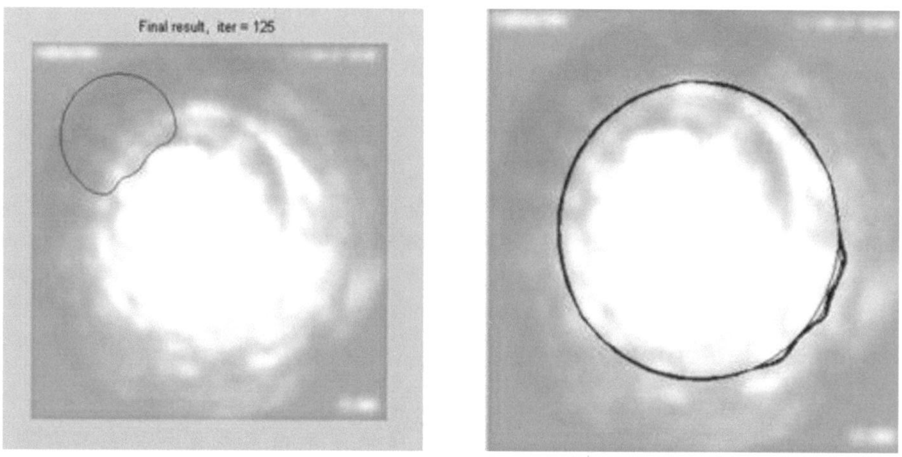

Fig. 4. a) left - Snake has converged to q wrong border. b) right - snake incapability of progressing to very concave edges

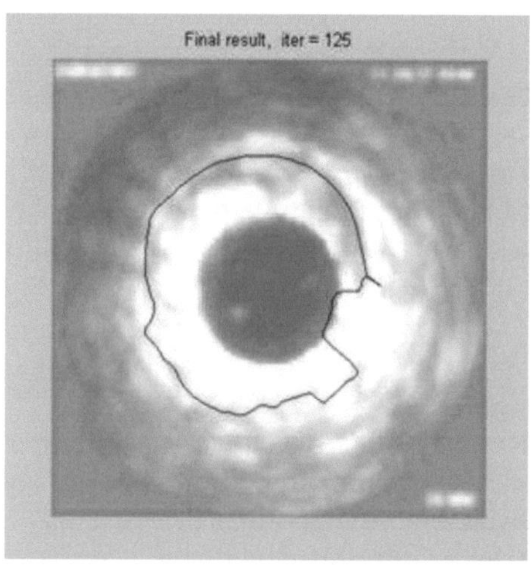

Fig. 5. The border detected by the distance potential snake algorithm applied on a raw image

The second problem is snake incapability of progressing to very concave edges (Davatzikos and Prince, 1995; Abrantes and Marques, 1996). Although some methods such as pressure forces (Cohen, 1991), control points (Davatzikos and Prince, 1995), directional attraction (Abrantes and Marques, 1996), and domain adaptivity (Davatzikos and Prince, 1994) have been emerged, but an acceptable solution has not been developed yet. However, these methods usually solve a problem, while creating another one. For instance, the multi-resolution methods solve the capture range problem, but the snake movement in points with different resolutions goes in trouble. Pressure forces also are very sensitive to the initial contour position. This problem is depicted in Fig. 4.b.
In this work, distance potential snake has been exploited to solve the aforementioned problems and its result is provided in Fig. 5, but still needs to be improved. Hence, before applying the snake (Kass et al., 1987) algorithm (which is active contour based on distance potentials) to the image, some pre-processing actions are performed first. The block diagram of the proposed algorithm for automatic coronary borders extraction is shown in Fig. 6. The blocks would be explained in the following section.

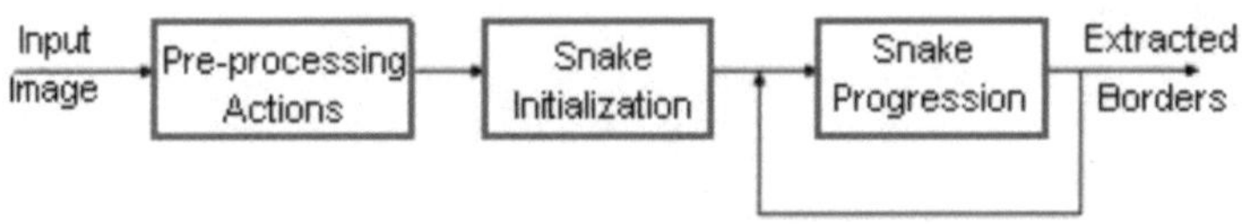

Fig. 6. Detection Algorithm Block Diagram

3. IVUS images pre-processing

Three phases of pre-processing are used in this part, which are a) detection of the catheter region and its substitution by mean value of darkness of the whole image, b) edge-preserving smoothing, and c) wavelet transform.

3.1 Catheter region substitution

The catheter region in the image has edges with very high darkness and is detected as a vessel edge when different deformable models are applied to the image. In this part, this region is detected and substituted with the average darkness of the whole image pixels. It is noticeable that detecting the catheter region is done using a method called region growing, which is going to be fully explained in the next part. This method is based on beginning from one arbitrary pixel of the image comparing the darkness of adjacent pixels to that pixel and this continues until the darkness differs very much. This difference is measured using a suitable threshold. The set of those pixels are considered as a segment, which is the catheter segment in this part.

3.2 Edge preserving smoothing

Most of applications tend to preserve the edges in smoothing procedure. To achieve this goal, some methods have been propounded, which are known as edge-preserving smoothing methods. The most famous algorithms of this family are averaging and median filtering, in which each pixel is substituted with the average or median of its neighbor pixels. Although they cancel the effect of salt and pepper noise very well, but they do not succeed to do so in parts of the image, which are smaller than half of the filter window.

In the method used in this article, the image is firstly segmented and then smoothed. In the smoothing process, the final value of each pixel in the smoothed image is mostly affected by the pixels with similar darkness to it and this makes the result image more useful for edge detection applications. Therefore, inter-region smoothing is avoided and intra-region smoothing is performed instead. Hence, segmentation must be performed first. An algorithm based on region growing (Xiaohan and Yla-Jaaski, 2000) is used for the segmentation. This algorithm is based on beginning from one point, selecting a suitable threshold, and comparing the neighbor pixels darkness with this threshold, which leads to the fact that whether this pixel is in that region or not. An algorithm for implementing the region growing is presented in (Xuan et al., 1995). Nevertheless, in different region growing algorithms a pixel is usually appended to a region if its darkness intensity is within a certain level from that region. This condition has not proven to be efficient in noisy images. Hence, this condition has been substituted with two other conditions here: a) in addition to comparing pixel intensity with the center pixel of a region, its intensity is also compared with that of the pixel neighbor to the center pixel as well. Assuming the independency of the noise in each pixel, if the probability of appending a wrong pixel to a region was p in common algorithms, it would reduce to p^2 here. Although this condition improves the known region algorithm performance, but it is a bit conservative and it makes the possibility of not appending a right point to a region more. So, another condition must also be taken into account: b) if the center pixel similarity to its neighbor pixel in one direction (i.e. up, down, left, or right) was more than its similarity to its neighbor of neighbor pixel in the same direction, then the neighbor pixel belongs to the center pixel region. Similarity of two pixels is defined as absolute value of their intensity difference.

After detecting a region, a pixel outside this region is chosen and this process is repeated until the whole image is segmented. When the segmentation is finished, a Gaussian filter is applied to (convolved with) each region according to its darkness.

3.3 Wavelet transform

Image analysis and processing using wavelet transform is one of the recent approaches in signal and image processing. Image processing using wavelet transform usually includes applying two-dimensional wavelet transform to the image, making suitable changes in the wavelet domain, and using inverse wavelet transform. In the third phase of the pre-processing part, wavelet transform is applied to the image in one level, which results the resolution decreased to half and hence, detecting the edges would be easier. The whole three phases done on a sample image is shown in Fig. 7.

4. Detecting coronary layers using deformable models

4.1 Detecting coronary layers in a single pre-processed IVUS picture

Once the image went through the pre-processing phase, it is ready to be used for applying deformable models to find the coronary layers. Here, detecting the internal layer i.e. intima-media has been focused; Nevertheless, the same algorithm could be applied to find the media-adventitia border as well. The snake initialization would be slightly different in that case.

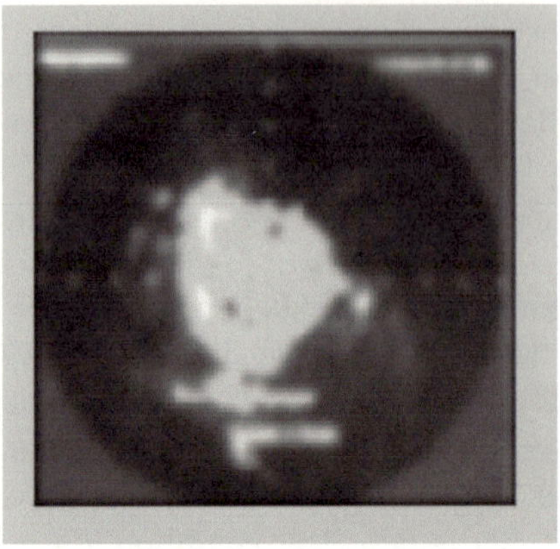

Fig. 7. Edge preserved smoothed picture of an IVUS image, in which the catheter region is substituted after applying one level wavelet transform.

Distance potential snake has been utilized according to the topology of this kind of images to find the borders. Somewhere a bit outsider of the detected catheter region has been considered as the initial state of the snake in order to overcome the drawbacks mentioned in section 2.3. This is an important advantage, which makes this method completely automatic while similar approaches need the initial contour to be made manually (Plissiti et al., 2004). The algorithm was implemented in MATLAB and the results on the pre-processed image (Fig. 7) are provided in Fig. 8.

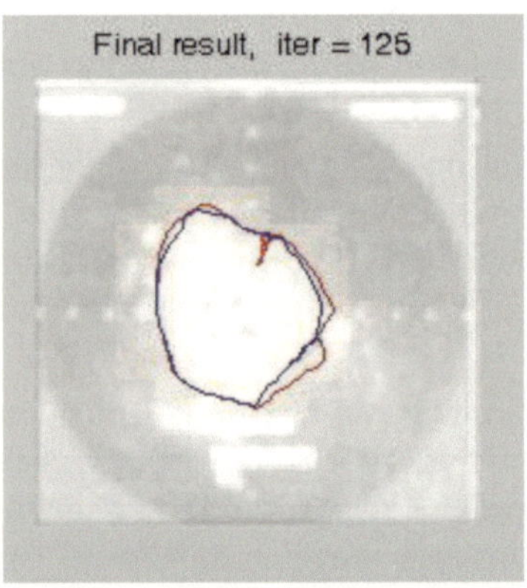

Fig. 8. Detected region as the internal border in one pre-processed image - Red border is detected by the algorithm and blue border is detected by a specialist

As can be seen in the picture, due to existence of ring-down noise in some parts of the image, the snake has moved neither to the inside nor to the outside in those regions.
It is also interesting that the sharp point observed in the picture is due to the speckle noise, which has affected the image in that area. The efficiency of this algorithm in detecting the true border on a single image is 88.42%.

4.2 Detecting coronary layers in fused IVUS pictures

Information fusion is used in many applications nowadays. In this paper, fusion of the images' information (Singh et al., 1996) with fuzzy approach is taken into action. Image fusion is used in several industrial and medical applications in order to get a more efficient image. Image fusion has the following advantages: a) Taking into account extra information (redundancy), increases the reliability; b) It improves the image capabilities as it keeps complementary information (Fig. 9).

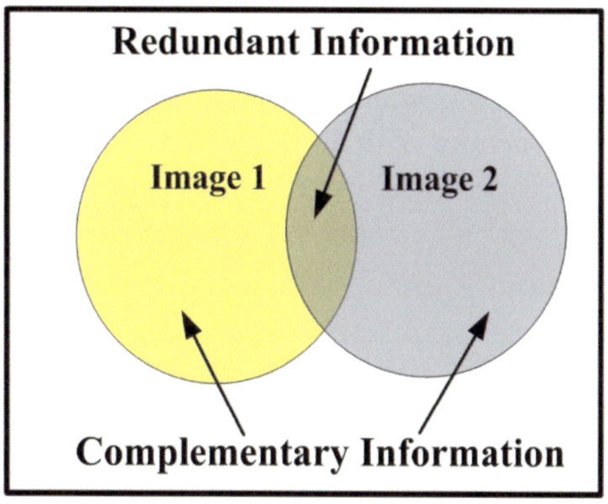

Fig. 9. Image fusion characteristics

Fuzzy approach to this context is very useful, when there is uncertainty and no mathematical relations. Each IVUS frame in a sequence of frames obtained from the same arterial segment can be considered quite similar to the previous one. In this paper, fusion of some IVUS sequential frames, having energy difference less than 10% of each, is exploited using fuzzy integral operators.

4.2.1 Fuzzy integral operators

Two great categories for fuzzy information fusion exist, which are Choquet and Sugeno fuzzy integral operators (Yager, 2004). These operators are based on the fuzzy measured data. It is translated as the gray-scale of any pixel in the image, which is a number between zero and one. The Choquet discrete fuzzy integral operator based on the mentioned fuzzy measures $a_1,...,a_n$, which belong to $[0,1]$ is described as:

$$C_\mu(a_1,a_2,...,a_n)=\sum_{i=1}^{n}(a_{(i)}-a_{(i-1)})\mu(A_{(i)}) \tag{7}$$

And the Sugeno discrete fuzzy integral operator based on the fuzzy measures $a_1,\ldots,a_n$, which belong to *[0,1]* is described as:
in which $a_{(0)}=0$ and $i=1,2,\ldots,n$ is a permutation of a_i s such that $a_{(1)}\leq a_{(2)}\leq\cdots\leq a_{(n)}$ and $A_{(i)}=\{x_{(1)},x_{(2)},\ldots,x_{(n)}\}$.

$$S_\mu(a_1,a_2,...,a_n)=\underset{i=1}{\overset{n}{Max}}(Min(a_{(i)},\mu(A_{(i)}))) \tag{8}$$

in which $a_{(0)}=0$ and $i=1,2,\ldots,n$ is a permutation of a_i s such that $a_{(1)}\leq a_{(2)}\leq\cdots\leq a_{(n)}$ and $A_{(i)}=\{x_{(1)},x_{(2)},\ldots,x_{(n)}\}$.

The Choquet integral is stable under positive linear transformations, while the Sugeno integral is stable under similar transformations with minimum and maximum replaced by product and sum respectively. This property makes the Sugeno integral more suitable for ordinal aggregation (where only the order of the elements is important) while the Choquet integral is suitable for cardinal aggregation (where the distance between the numbers has a meaning).
The generalized characteristics of these two integrals are remarkable. The Choquet integral is the generalized form of the ordered weighted average (OWA) operator, while the Sugeno integral generalizes the weighted minimum and the weighted maximum. The corresponding parameters to create a certain operator with these operators are shown in Tables 1, 2.

	Choquet Integral
Minimum	$\begin{cases}\mu(A)=1 & if\ A=C\\ \mu(A)=0 & otherwise\end{cases}$
Maximum	$\begin{cases}\mu(A)=0 & if\ A=\varphi\\ \mu(A)=1 & otherwise\end{cases}$
k-order statistics	$\begin{cases}\mu(A)=0 & if\ card(A)\leq n-k\\ \mu(A)=1 & otherwise\end{cases}$
Arithmetic mean	$\mu(A)=\dfrac{card(A)}{card(C)}$
Weighted mean	$\mu(A)=\sum_{x_i\in A}\left[\mu\{x_i\}\right]$ $and\ \ \mu\{x_i\}=w_i\ \ for\ all\ i$
OWA	$\mu(A)=\sum_{j=0}^{card(A)-1} w_{n-j}$

Table 1. Choquet integral special cases

	Sugeno Integral
Minimum	$\begin{cases}\mu(A)=1 & if\ A=C\\ \mu(A)=0 & otherwise\end{cases}$
Maximum	$\begin{cases}\mu(A)=0 & if\ A=\varphi\\ \mu(A)=1 & otherwise\end{cases}$
k-order statistics	$\begin{cases}\mu(A)=0 & if\ card(A)\leq n-k\\ \mu(A)=1 & otherwise\end{cases}$
Weighted minimum	$\mu(A)=1-\max_{x_i\in A}\left[\mu\{x_i\}\right]$ $and\ \ \mu\{x_i\}=w_i\ \ for\ all\ i$
Weighted maximum	$\mu(A)=\max_{x_i\in A}\left[\mu\{x_i\}\right]$ $and\ \ \mu\{x_i\}=w_i\ \ for\ all\ i$

Table 2. Sugeno integral special cases

The only problem using these integrals is the number of 2^n weights to be determined, for a simple n criteria aggregation. These weights are nothing, but the characterization of fuzzy measures. Some solutions have been proposed to reduce the number of these weights: An interesting approach was proposed by Grabisch in (Grabisch, 1996), in which he suggests to use k-additive fuzzy measures. The idea is to define measures that are multilinear of degree k, i.e. if $card(A) > k$ then $\mu(A) = 0$. This approach allows the model the strength of small coalitions and reduces the number of weights to $\sum_{i=1}^{k} C_n^i$ instead of 2^n.

Another approach, which is used here is to determine the weights by training on examples, in which at least $\frac{n!}{[(n/2)!]^2}$ training vector is needed.

However, the Choquet and Sugeno fuzzy integral operators have fundamental difference; Because the former is based on linear operators, while the latter is based on nonlinear *Max* and *Min* operators. The relationships between different aggregations and fuzzy integral operators are provided in Fig. 10.

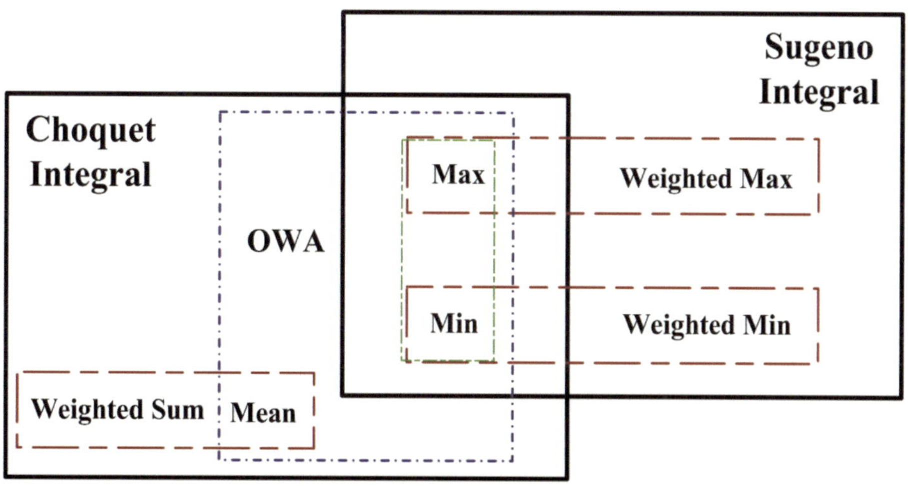

Fig. 10. The relationships between different aggregations and fuzzy integral operators

4.2.2 Applying the algorithm on fused frames

Information fusion can be performed in different levels. If this fusion is to be performed on data level, the samples of IVUS frames must be fused initially, then the pre-processing actions has to be performed and finally detecting the borders applying deformable models would be executed. If the fusion is to be performed on feature level, the pre-processing actions ought to be performed on each frame initially, the obtained images would be fused next, and the algorithm for detecting the borders would be executed finally. And if the fusion is intended to be performed on decision level, the pre-processing actions are to be performed on each frame initially; the borders are to be detected applying the algorithm to each frame next, and the result borders fused eventually. The images information fusion block diagram is provided in Fig. 11.

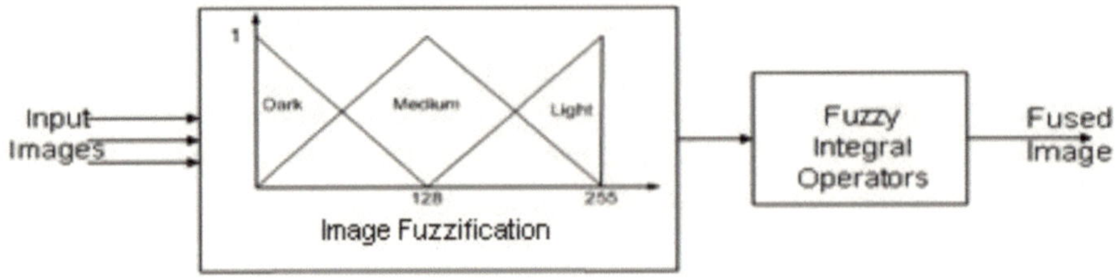

Fig. 11. Fuzzy image fusion block diagram

The results of the algorithm explained in the section 3 on fused frames would be studied in the following. Fig. 12 shows the border detected by the snake algorithm applied on the fused image using Sugeno operator in data level compared with the one detected by the specialist.

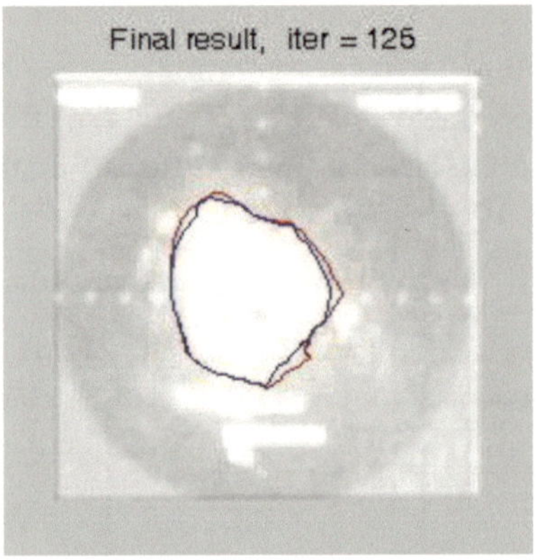

Fig. 12. The border detected by the snake algorithm applied on the fused image using Sugeno operator in data level- Red border is detected by the algorithm and blue one is detected by the specialist

The border detected by the snake algorithm applied on the fused image using Sugeno operator in feature and decision level compared with ones detected by the specialist are provided in the figures 13, 14 respectively.

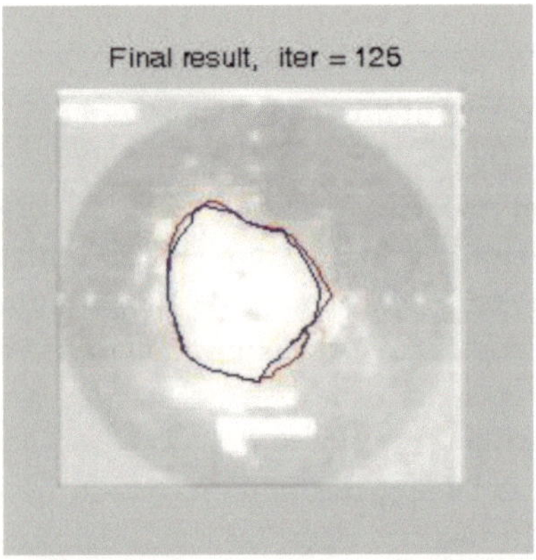

Fig. 13. The border detected by the snake algorithm applied on the fused image using Sugeno operator in feature level- Red border is detected by the algorithm and blue one is detected by the specialist

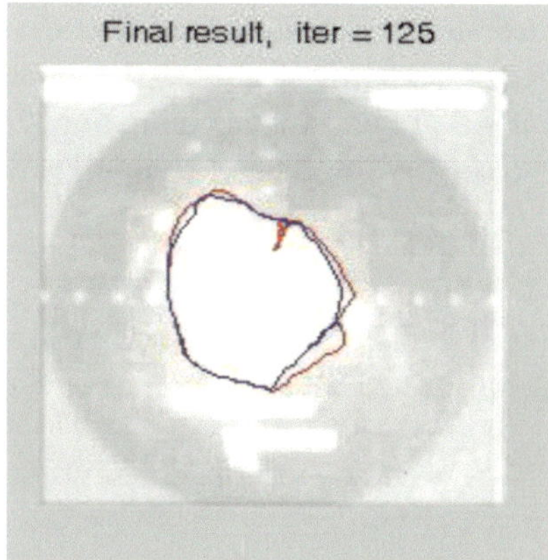

Fig. 14. The border detected by the snake algorithm applied on the fused image using Sugeno operator in decision level- Red border is detected by the algorithm and blue one is detected by the specialist

The higher level the fusion is performed, the more is affected the result by noise. This is due to the special noises of the images of this type (IVUS), which deviates the snake from the correct border and if an error occurs, its correction in higher levels is almost irreparable. Quantitative comparisons between fuzzy integral operators used in different levels of fusion, are shown in Table 3. The numbers in the table are the algorithm efficiency in finding the borders detected by the specialist.

	Fusion using Choquet fuzzy integral operator	Fusion using Sugeno fuzzy integral operator
Data Level Fusion	91.87%	93.125%
Feature Level Fusion	90.42%	91.58%
Decision Level Fusion	88.96%	89.11%

Table 3. Quantitative comparison between fuzzy integral operators used for fusion in different levels

5. Conclusion

In this article, taking into account the low quality of the IVUS images, edge-preserving smoothing and also wavelet transform were performed as pre-processing actions in order to improve the performance of detecting the coronary layers. Detecting the borders using deformable models was performed next; but due to the especial imaging noises of the IVUS pictures, fusion of these images verified efficient. Using fuzzy integral operators in three levels including data, feature and decision the images were fused, in which detecting borders in the fused images using Sugeno operator, and in data level was more successful than the others. This method has the advantage of being fully automated, without needing the initial contour to be manually assigned. The merit of this method comparing with similar methods is also its acceptable executing time, which is very important for curing patients.

6. Acknowledgment

The authors would like to thank the NIOC hospital for its support from this project. They especially thank Dr.Ghaziani because of her infinite endeavor for providing the dataset for this work.

7. References

Abrantes, A. J. & Marques, J. S. (1996). *A class of constrained clustering algorithms for object boundary extraction*, IEEE Trans. Image Processing, vol. 5, pp. 1507–1521

Agostoni, P.; Schaar, J. A. & Serruys, P. W. (2004). *The challenge of vulnerable plaque detection in the cardiac catheterization laboratory*, Kardiovaskuläre Medizin

Caselles, V.; Catte, F.; Coll, T. & Dibos, F. (1993). *A geometric model for active contours*, Numerische Mathematik, 66, 1–31

Cohen, L. D. (1991). *On active contour models and balloons*, CVGIP: Image Understanding, 53(2): 211–218

Cohen, L. D. & Cohen, I. (1993). *Finite-element methods for active contour models and balloons for 2-D and 3-D images*, IEEE Trans. Pattern Anal. Machine Intell., vol. 15, pp. 1131–1147

Davatzikos, C. & Prince, J. L. (1994). *Convexity analysis of active contour models*, in Proc. Conf. Information Science and Systems, pp. 581–587

Davatzikos, C. & Prince, J. L. (1995). *An active contour model for mapping the cortex*, IEEE Trans. Med. Imag., vol. 14, pp. 65–80

Durikovic, R.; Kaneda, K. & Yamashita, H. (1995). *Dynamic contour: A texture approach and contour operations*, Vis. Comput., vol. 11, pp. 277–289

Gil, D.; Radeva, P. & Saludes, J. (2000). *Segmentation of artery wall in coronary IVUS images: A Probabilistic Approach*, ICPR, pp.4352, 15th International Conference on Pattern Recognition (ICPR'00) - Volume 4

Grabisch, M. (1996). *k-additive fuzzy measures*, 6th International Conference on Information Processing and Management of Uncertainty in Knowledge-Based Systems (IPMU), Granada, Spain, July 1996

Kass, M.; Witkin, A. & Terzopoulos, D. (1987). *Snakes: Active contour models*. Int. J. Computer Vision, 1(4), pp. 321-331

Kovalski, G.; Beyar, R.; Shofti, R. & Azhari, H. (2000). *Three-dimensional automatic quantitative analysis of intravascular ultrasound images*, Ultrasound Med. Biol., vol. 26, No. 4, pp. 527-537

Leroy, B.; Herlin, I. & Cohen, L. D. (1996). *Multi-resolution algorithms for active contour models*, in 12th Int. Conf. Analysis and Optimization of Systems, pp. 58–65

Leymarie, F. & Levine, M. D. (1993). *Tracking deformable objects in the plane using an active contour model*, IEEE Trans. On Pattern Anal. Machine Intell., 15(6): 617–634

Malladi, R.; Sethian, J. A. & Vemuri, B. C. (1995). *Shape modeling with front propagation: A level set approach*, IEEE Trans. on Pattern Anal. Machine Intell., 17(2): 158–175

McInerney, T. & Terzopoulos, D. (1995). *A dynamic finite element surface model for segmentation and tracking in multidimensional medical images with application to cardiac 4D image analysis*, Comput. Med. Imag. Graph., vol. 19, pp. 69–83

Paul, J.; Brathwaite, A.; Chandran, K. B.; McPherson, D. D. & Dove, E. L. (1996). *Lumen Detection in Human IVUS Images using Region-Growing*, IEEE Computer in Cardiology

Plissiti, M. E.; Fotiadis, D. I.; Michalis, L. K. & Bozios, G. E. (2004). *An automated method for lumen and media-adventitia border detection in a sequence of IVUS frames*, IEEE Trans. On Information Tech. in Biomedicine, vol. 8, No. 2

Schoenhagen, J. P. & Stillman, A. E. MD, PhD (2005). *CT of the heart Principles, advances, clinical uses*, Cleveland Clinic Journal of Medicine Vol. 72, No. 2

Schoenhagen, P. & White, R. D. (2003). *Coronary imaging: Angiography shows the stenosis, but IVUS, CT, and MRI show the plaque*, Cleveland Clinic Journal of Medicine Vol. 70, No. 8

Terzopoulos, D. & Fleischer, K. (1988). *Deformable models*, Vis. Comput., vol. 4, pp. 306–331

Shekhar, R.; Cothren, R. M.; Vince, D. G.; Chandra, S.; Thomas, J. D. & Cornhill, J. F. (1999) *Three-dimensional segmentation of luminal and adventitial borders in serial intravascular ultrasound images*, Comput. Med. Imaging Graph, vol. 23, pp. 299-309

Singh, H.; Raj, J.; Kaur, G. & Meitzler, T. (2004). *Image Fusion Using Fuzzy Logic and Applications*, IEEE Trans. Image Processing, vol. 24, pp. 25–29

Sonka, M.; Zhang, X.; Siebes, M.; Bissing, M. S.; DeJong, S. C.; Collins, S. M. S. & McKay C. R. (1995). *Segmentation of Intravasular ultrasound images: A knowledge-based approach*, IEEE Trans. Med Imag., vol. 14, pp. 719-732

Takagi, A.; Hibi, K.; Zhang, X.; Teo, T. J.; Bonneau, H. N.; Yock, P. G. & Fitzgerald, P. J. (2000). *Automated contour detection for high-frequency intravascular ultrasound imaging: A technique with blood noise reduction for edge enhancement*, Ultrasound Med. Biol., vol. 26, No. 6, pp. 1033-1041

Terzopoulos, D. & Szeliski, R. (1992). *Tracking with Kalman snakes*, In A. Blake and A. Yuille, editors, Active Vision, Artificial Intelligence, pages 3-20. The MIT Press, Cambridge, Massachusetts

Xiaohan, Y. & Yla-Jaaski, J. (2000). *A new algorithm for image segmentation based on region growing and edge detection*, IEEE CH 336-4/91/2000

Xu, C. & Prince, L. (1997). *Gradient Vector Flow: A New External Force for Snakes*, IEEE Proc. Conf. on Comp. Vis. Patt. Recog. (CVPR'97), pp. 66-71

Xuan, J.; Adali, T. & Wang, Y. (1995). *Segmentation of magnetic resonance brain image: Integration region growing and edge detection*, in Proc. International Conference on Image Processing (ICIP'95), pp. 544-547

Yager, R. (2004). *Uncertainty Modeling and Decision Support*, Reliability Engineering and System Safety, pp. 341-354

Zhang, X.; McKay, C. R. & Sonka, M. (1998). *Tissue characterization in intravascular ultrasound images*, IEEE Trans. Med. Imag., vol. 17, pp. 889-898

Zhu, H.; Liang, Y. & Friedman, M. H. (2002). *IVUS image segmentation based on contrast*, Proc. SPIE 4684, 1727, DOI:10.1117/12.467143

8

Fusion of Multisource Images for Update of Urban GIS

D. Amarsaikhan[1] and M. Saandar[2]
[1]Institute of Informatics and RS, Mongolian Academy of Sciences,
[2]Monmap Engineering Company, Ltd,
Mongolia

1. Introduction

Image fusion is used for many purposes. Very often it is used to produce an image with an improved spatial resolution. The most common situation is represented by a pair of images where the first acquired by a multispectral sensor has a pixel size greater than the pixel size of the second image acquired by a panchromatic sensor. Combining these images, fusion produces a new multispectral image with a spatial resolution equal to the panchromatic one. In addition, image fusion introduces important distortion on the pixel spectra which in turn improve the information content of remote sensing (RS) images (Teggi *et al.* 2003). Over the years, different fusion methods have been developed for improving spatial and spectral resolutions of RS data sets. The techniques most encountered in the literature are the intensity-hue-saturation (IHS) transform, the Brovey transform, the principal components analysis (PCA) method, the Gram-Schmidt method, the local mean matching method, the local mean and variance matching method, the least square fusion method, the wavelet-based fusion method, the multiplicative and the Ehlers Fusion (Karathanassi *et al.* 2007, Ehlers *et al.* 2008). Most fusion applications use modified approaches or combinations of these methods.

In case of RS data sets, three different fusions such as fusion of optical data with optical data, fusion of microwave data with microwave data and fusion of optical and microwave data sets can be conducted. For several decades, fusion of multiresolution optical images has been successfully used for the improvement of information contents of images for visual interpretation as well as for the enhancement of land surface features. Many studies have been conducted on the improvement of spatial resolution of multispectral images by the use of the high frequencies of panchromatic images, while preserving the spectral information (Mascarenhas *et al.* 1996, Saraf 1999, Teoh *et al.* 2001, Teggi *et al.* 2003, Gonzalez *et al.* 2004, Colditz *et al.* 2006, Deng *et al.* 2008, Li and Leung 2009). A number of authors have attempted to successfully fuse the interferometric or multifrequency SAR images (Soh and Tsatsoulis 1999, Verbyla 2001, Baghdadi *et al.* 2002, Costa 2005, Palubinskas and Datcu 2008). Unlike the fusion of optical images, most fusions of the synthetic aperture radar (SAR) data sets have attempted to increase the spectral variety of the classes.

Over the years, the fusion of optical and SAR data sets has been widely used for different applications. It has been found that the images acquired at optical and microwave ranges of electro-magnetic spectrum provide unique information when they are integrated

(Amarsaikhan *et al.* 2007). Now image fusion based on the integration of multispectral optical and multifrequency microwave data sets is being efficiently used for interpretation, enhancement and analysis of different land surface features. As it is known, optical data contains information on the reflective and emissive characteristics of the Earth surface features, while the SAR data contains information on the surface roughness, texture and dielectric properties of natural and man-made objects. It is evident that a combined use of the optical and SAR images will have a number of advantages because a specific feature which is not seen on the passive sensor image might be seen on the microwave image and vice versa because of the complementary information provided by the two sources (Amarsaikhan *et al.* 2004, Amarsaikhan *et al.* 2007). Many authors have proposed and applied different techniques to combine optical and SAR images in order to enhance various features and they all judged that the results from the fused images were better than the results obtained from the individual images (Wang *et al.* 1995, Pohl and Van Genderen 1998, Ricchetti 2001, Herold and Haack 2002, Amarsaikhan and Douglas 2004, Westra *et al.* 2005, Ehlers *et al.* 2008, Saadi and Watanabe 2009, Zhang 2010). Although, many studies of image fusion have been conducted for derivation of new algorithms for the enhancement of different features, still little research has been done on the influence of image fusions on the automatic extraction of different thematic information within urban environment.

For many years, for the extraction of thematic information from multispectral RS images, different supervised and unsupervised classification methods have been applied (Storvik *et al.* 2005, Meher *et al.* 2007). Unlike the single-source data, data sets from multiple sources have proved to offer better potential for discriminating between different land cover types. Many authors have assessed the potential of multisource images for the classification of different land cover classes (Munechika *et al.* 1993, Serpico and Roli 1995, Benediktsson *et al.* 1997, Hegarat-Mascle *et al.* 2000, Amarsaikhan and Douglas 2004, Amarsaikhan *et al.* 2007). In RS applications, the most widely used multisource classification techniques are statistical methods, Dempster–Shafer theory of evidence, neural networks, decision tree classifier, and knowledge-based methods (Solberg *et al.* 1996, Franklin *et al.* 2002, Amarsaikhan *et al.* 2007).

The aim of this study is a) to investigate and evaluate different image fusion techniques for the enhancement of spectral variations of urban land surface features and b) to apply a knowledge-based classification method for the extraction of land cover information from the fused images in order to update urban geographical information system (GIS). The proposed image fusion includes two different approaches such as fusion of SAR data with SAR data (ie, SAR/SAR approach) and fusion of optical data with SAR data (ie, optical/SAR approach), while the knowledge-based method includes different rules based on the spectral and spatial thresholds. For the actual analysis, multisource satellite images with different spatial resolutions as well as some GIS data of the urban area in Mongolia have been used.

2. Test site and data sources

As a test site, Ulaanbaatar, the capital city of Mongolia has been selected. Ulaanbaatar is situated in the central part of Mongolia, on the Tuul River, at an average height of 1350m above sea level and currently has about 1 million inhabitants. The city is surrounded by the mountains which are spurs of the Khentii Mountain Ranges. Founded in 1639 as a small town named Urga, today it has prospered as the main political, economic, business, scientific and cultural centre of the country.

The city is extended from the west to the east about 30km and from the north to the south about 20km. However, the study area chosen for the present study covers mainly the central and western parts and is characterized by such classes as built-up area, ger (Mongolian national dwelling) area, green area, soil and water. Figure 1 shows ASTER image of the test site, and some examples of its land cover.

Fig. 1. 2008 ASTER image of the selected part of Ulaanbaatar (B1=B, B3=G, B2=R). 1-built-up area; 2-ger area; 3-green area; 4-soil; 5-water. The size of the displayed area is about 8.01kmx6.08km.

In the present study, for the enhancement of urban features, ASTER data of 23 September 2008, ERS-2 SAR data of 25 September 1997 and ALOS PALSAR data of 25 August 2006 have been used. Although ASTER has 14 multispectral bands acquired in visible, near infrared, middle infrared and thermal infrared ranges of electro-magnetic spectrum, in the current study, green (band 1), red (band 2) and near infrared (band 3) bands with a spatial resolution of 15m have been used. ERS-2 SAR is a European RS radar satellite which acquires VV polarized C-band data with a spatial resolution of 25m. ALOS PALSAR is a Japanese Earth observation satellite carrying a cloud-piercing L-band radar which is designed to acquire fully polarimtric images. In the present study, HH, VV and HV polarization intensity images of ALOS PALSAR have been used.

3. Co-registration of multisource images and speckle suppression of the SAR images

At the beginning, the ALOS PALSAR image was rectified to the coordinates of the ASTER image using 12 ground control points (GCPs) defined from a topograpic map of the study area. The GCPs have been selected on clearly delineated crossings of roads, streets and city building corners. For the transformation, a second-order transformation and nearest-neighbour resampling approach were applied and the related root mean square error (RMSE) was 0.94 pixel. Then, the ERS-2 SAR image was rectified and its coordinates were transformed to the coordinates of the rectified ALOS PALSAR image. In order to rectify the ERS-2 SAR image, 14 more regularly distributed GCPs were selected from different parts of the image. For the actual transformation, a second-order transformation was used. As a resampling technique, the nearest-neighbour resampling approach was applied and the related RMSE was 0.98 pixel.

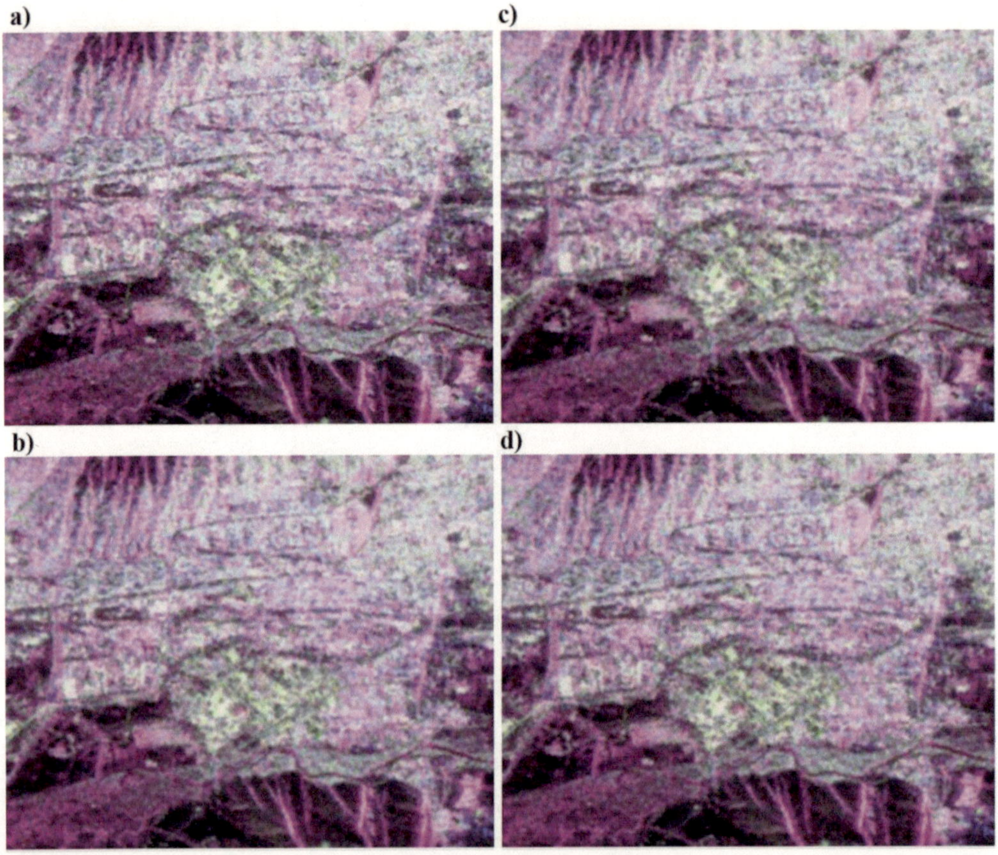

Fig. 2. The comparison of the ALOS PALSAR images, speckle suppressed by 3x3 size local region (a), lee-sigma (b), frost (c) and gammamap (d) filters.

As the microwave images have a granular appearance due to the speckle formed as a result of the coherent radiation used for radar systems; the reduction of the speckle is a very important step in further analysis. The analysis of the radar images must be based on the techniques that remove the speckle effects while considering the intrinsic texture of the image frame (Ulaby *et al.* 1986, Amarsaikhan and Douglas 2004, Serkan *et al.* 2008). In this study, four different speckle suppression techniques such as local region, lee-sigma, frost and gammamap filters (ERDAS 1999) of 3x3 and 5x5 sizes were applied to the ALOS PALSAR image and compared in terms of delineation of urban features and texture information. After visual inspection of each image, it was found that the 3x3 gammamap filter created the best image in terms of delineation of different features as well as preserving content of texture information. In the output images, speckle noise was reduced with very low degradation of the textural information. The comparison of the speckle suppressed images is shown in Figure 2.

4. Image fusion

The concept of image fusion refers to a process, which integrates different images from different sources to obtain more information, considering a minimum loss or distortion of the original data. In other words, the image fusion is the integration of different digital images in order to create a new image and obtain more information than can be separately derived from any of them (Pohl and Van Genderen 1998, Ricchetti 2001, Amarsaikhan *et al.* 2009a). In the case of the present study, for the urban areas, the radar images provide structural information about buildings and street alignment due to the double bounce effect, while the optical image provides the information about the spectral variations of different urban features. Moreover, the SAR images contain multitemporal changes of land surface features and provide some additional information about soil moisture condition due to dielectric properties of the soil. Over the years, different data fusion techniques have been developed and applied, individually and in combination, providing users and decision-makers with various levels of information. Generally, image fusion can be performed at pixel, feature and decision levels (Abidi and Gonzalez 1992, Pohl and Van Genderen 1998). In this study, data fusion has been performed at a pixel level and the following rather common and more complex techniques were compared: (a) multiplicative method, (b) Brovey transform, (c) the PCA, (d) Gram-Schmidt fusion, (f) wavelet-based fusion, (f) Elhers fusion. Each of these techniques is briefly discussed below.

Multiplicative Method: This is the most simple image fusion technique. It takes two digital images, for example, high resolution panchromatic and low resolution multispectral data, and multiplies them pixel by pixel to get a new image (Seetha *et al.* 2007). It can be formulated as follows:

$$\text{Red} = (\text{Low Resolution Band}_1 * \text{High Resolution Band}_1) \quad (1a)$$

$$\text{Green} = (\text{Low Resolution Band}_2 * \text{High Resolution Band}_2) \quad (1b)$$

$$\text{Blue} = (\text{Low Resolution Band}_3 * \text{High Resolution Band}_3) \quad (1c)$$

Brovey transform: This is a simple numerical method used to merge different digital data sets. The algorithm based on a Brovey transform uses a formula that normalises multispectral bands used for a red, green, blue colour display and multiplies the result by high resolution data to add the intensity or brightness component of the image (Vrabel 1996). The formulae used for the Brovey transform can be described as follows:

$$\text{Red} = \frac{\text{Band}_1}{\sum_{i=1}^{n} \text{Band}_n} * \text{High Resolution Band} \quad (2a)$$

$$\text{Green} = \frac{\text{Band}_2}{\sum_{i=1}^{n} \text{Band}_n} * \text{High Resolution Band} \quad (2b)$$

$$\text{Blue} = \frac{\text{Band}_3}{\sum_{i=1}^{n} \text{Band}_n} * \text{High Resolution Band} \quad (2c)$$

PCA: The most common understanding of the PCA is that it is a data compression technique used to reduce the dimensionality of the multidimensional datasets or bands (Richards and Jia, 1999). The bands of the PCA data are noncorrelated and are often more interpretable than the source data. The process is easily explained if we consider a two dimensional histogram which forms an ellipse. When the PCA is performed, the axes of the spectral space are rotated, changing the coordinates of each pixel in spectral space. The new axes are parallel to the axes of the ellipse. The length and direction of the widest transect of the ellipse are calculated using a matrix algebra. The transect, which corresponds to the major axis of the ellipse, is called the first principal component of the data. The direction of the first principal component is the first eigenvector, and its length is the first eigenvalue. A new axis of the spectral space is defined by this first principal component. The second principal component is the widest transect of the ellipse that is perpendicular to the first principal component. As such, the second principal component describes the largest amount of variance in the data that is not already described by the first principal component. In a two-dimensional case, the second principal component corresponds to the minor axis of the ellipse (ERDAS 1999).

In *n* dimensions, there are *n* principal components. Each successive principal component is the widest transect of the ellipse that is orthogonal to the previous components in the *n*-dimensional space, and accounts for a decreasing amount of the variation in the data which is not already accounted for by previous principal components. Although there are *n* output bands in a PCA, the first few bands account for a high proportion of the variance in the data. Sometimes, useful information can be gathered from the principal component bands with the least variances and these bands can show subtle details in the image that were obscured by higher contrast in the original image (ERDAS 1999).

To compute a principal components transformation, a linear transformation is performed on the data meaning that the coordinates of each pixel in spectral space are recomputed using a linear equation. The result of the transformation is that the axes in *n*-dimensional spectral space are shifted and rotated to be relative to the axes of the ellipse. To perform the linear transformation, the eigenvectors and eigenvalues of the *n* principal components must be derived from the covariance matrix, as shown below:

$$D = \begin{bmatrix} D_1 & \cdots & 0 \\ \vdots & \ddots & \vdots \\ 0 & \cdots & D_n \end{bmatrix} \quad (3)$$

$$E * Cov * E^T = D \quad (4)$$

Where:

E=matrix of eigenvectors

Cov=covariance matrix

^{T}=transposition function

D=diagonal matrix of eigenvalues in which all non-diagonal elements are zeros and D is computed so that its non-zero elements are ordered from greatest to least, so that $D_1 > D_2 > D_3 \ldots > D_n$.

Gram-Schmidt fusion method: Gram-Schmidt process is a procedure which takes a non-orthogonal set of linearly independent functions and constructs an orthogonal basis over an arbitrary interval with respect to an arbitrary weighting function. In other words, this method creates from the correlated components non- or less correlated components by applying orthogonalization process (Karathanassi *et al.* 2008).

In any inner product space, we can choose the basis to work. It often simplifies the calculations to work in an orthogonal basis. Let us suppose that K = $\{v_1, v_2,\ldots, v_n\}$ is an orthogonal basis for an inner product space V. Then it is a simple matter to express any vector $w \in V$ as a linear combination of the vectors in K:

$$\omega = \frac{\langle w,v_1\rangle}{\|v_1\|^2}v_1 + \frac{\langle w,v_2\rangle}{\|v_2\|^2}v_2 + \cdots + \frac{\langle w,v_n\rangle}{\|v_n\|^2}v_n \tag{5}$$

Given an arbitrary basis $\{u_1, u_2,\ldots, u_n\}$ for n-dimensional inner product space V, the Gram-Schmidt algorithm constructs an orthogonal $\{v_1, v_2,\ldots, v_n\}$ for V and the process can be described as follows:

$$v_1 = u_1 \tag{6a}$$

$$v_2 = u_2\text{-project}_{w1}\, u_2 = u_2 - \frac{\langle u_2,v_1\rangle}{\|v_1\|^2}v_1 \tag{6b}$$

$$v_3 = u_3\text{-project}_{w2}\, u_3 = u_3 - \frac{\langle u_3,v_1\rangle}{\|v_1\|^2}v_1 - \frac{\langle u_3,v_2\rangle}{\|v_2\|^2}v_2 \tag{6c}$$

$$v_4 = u_4\text{-project}_{w3}\, u_4 = u_4 - \frac{\langle u_4,v_1\rangle}{\|v_1\|^2}v_1 - \frac{\langle u_4,v_2\rangle}{\|v_2\|^2}v_2 - \frac{\langle u_4,v_3\rangle}{\|v_3\|^2}v_3 \tag{6d}$$

Where:
w1-space spanned by v_1
project$_{w1}$ u_2 is the orthogonal projection of u_2 on v_1
w2-space spanned by v_1 and v_2
w3-space spanned by v_1, v_2 and v_3.
This process continues up to v_n. The resulting orthogonal set $\{v_1, v_2,\ldots, v_n\}$ consists of n-linearly independent vectors in V and forms an orthogonal basis for V.
Generally, orthogonalization is important in diverse applications in mathematics and other applied sciences because it can often simplifiy calculations or computations by making it possible, for instance, to do the calculation in a recursive manner.
Wavelet-based fusion: The wavelet transform decomposes the signal based on elementary functions, that is the wavelets. By using this, an image is decomposed into a set of multi-resolution images with wavelet coefficients. For each level, the coefficients contain spatial differences between two successive resolution levels. The wavelet transform can be expressed as follows:

$$\mathrm{WT}(f)(a,b) = \frac{1}{\sqrt{a}}\int_{-\infty}^{+\infty} f(t)\varphi\left(\frac{t-b}{a}\right)dt \tag{7}$$

Where:
a-scale parameter
b-translation parameter.
Practical implementation of the wavelet transform requires discretisation of its translation and scale parameters. In general, a wavelet-based image fusion can be performed by either replacing some wavelet coefficients of the low-resolution image by the corresponding coefficients of the high-resolution image or by adding high resolution coefficients to the low-resolution data (Pajares and Cruz, 2004). In the present study, 'Wavelet Resolution Merge' tool of Erdas Imagine was used and the algorithm behind this tool uses biorthogonal transforms. Processing steps of the wavelet-based image fusion are as follows:

- Decompose a high resolution panchromatic image into a set of low resolution panchromatic images with wavelet coefficients for each level.
- Replace low resolution panchromatic images with multispectral bands at the same spatial resolution level.
- Perform a reverse wavelet transform to convert the decomposed and replaced panchromatic set back to the original panchromatic resolution level.

Elhers fusion: This is a fusion technique used for the spectral characteristics preservation of multitemporal and multi-sensor data sets. The fusion is based on an IHS transformation combined with filtering in the Fourier domain and the IHS transform is used for optimal colour separation. As the spectral characteristics of the multispectral bands are preserved during the fusion process, there is no dependency on the selection or order of bands for the IHS transform (Ehlers 2004).

The IHS method uses three positional parameters such as Intensity, Hue and Saturation. Intensity is the overall brightness of the scene and deviod of any colour content. Hue is the dominant wavelength of the light contributing to any color. Saturation indicates the purity of colour. In this method, the H and S components contain the spectral information, while the I component represents the spatial information (Pohl and Van Genderen 1998, Ricchetti 2001). The transformation from red, green, blue (RGB) colour space to IHS space is a nonlinear, lossless and reversible process. It is possible to vary each of the IHS components without affecting the others. It is performed by a rotation of axis from the first orthogonal RGB system to a new orthogonal IHS system. The equations describing the transformation to the IHS (Pellemans *et al.* 1993) can be written as follows:

$$\begin{Bmatrix} x \\ y \\ z \end{Bmatrix} = \begin{Bmatrix} \frac{1}{\sqrt{3}} & \frac{\sqrt{2}}{\sqrt{3}} & 0 \\ -\frac{\sqrt{2}}{\sqrt{3}} & \frac{1}{\sqrt{3}} & 0 \\ 0 & 0 & 1 \end{Bmatrix} \begin{Bmatrix} \frac{1}{\sqrt{2}} & 0 & \frac{1}{\sqrt{2}} \\ 0 & 1 & 0 \\ -\frac{1}{\sqrt{2}} & 0 & \frac{1}{\sqrt{2}} \end{Bmatrix} \begin{Bmatrix} R \\ G \\ B \end{Bmatrix} \tag{8}$$

$$\mathrm{I} = \frac{(\mathrm{x+y+z})}{\mathrm{I_m(H,S)}} \tag{9}$$

$$\mathrm{H} = \tan^{-1}\left[-\frac{\sqrt{\mathrm{z}}}{\sqrt{\mathrm{x}}}\right] \tag{10}$$

$$\mathrm{S} = \cos^{-1}\left[\frac{\sqrt{\mathrm{y}}}{\sqrt{\mathrm{x+y+z}}}\right] / \mathrm{K_m(H)} \tag{11}$$

Where:

$\mathrm{I_m(H,S)}$-maximum intensity permitted at a given H and co-latitude

$\mathrm{K_m(H)}$-maximum co-latitude permitted at a given H.

Unlike the standard approach, the Elhers fusion is extended to include more than 3 bands using multiple IHS transforms until the number of bands is fulfilled. A subsequent Fourier transform of the intensity component and the panchromatic image allows an adaptive filter design in the frequency domain.

By the use of the fast Fourier transform (FFT) techniques, the spatial components to be enhanced or suppressed can be directly accessed. The intensity spectrum is filtered with a low pass filter (LP) whereas the panchromatic spectrum is filtered with an inverse high pass filter (HP). After filtering, the images are transformed back into the spatial domain with an inverse FFT and added together to form a fused intensity component with the low-frequency information from the low resolution multispectral image and the high-frequency

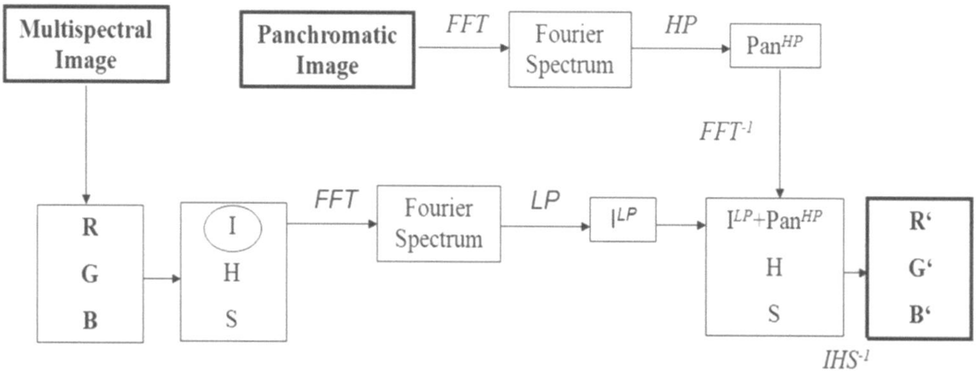

Fig. 3. Steps to implement the Elhers fusion.

information from the panchromatic image. This new intensity component and the original hue and saturation components of the multispectral image form a new IHS image. As the last step, an inverse IHS transformation produces a fused RGB image (Ehlers *et al.* 2008). This procedure can be illustrated as shown in Figure 3.

4.1 Comparison of the fusion methods using SAR/SAR approach

Generally, interpretation of microwave data is based on the backscatter properties of the surface features and most SAR image analyses are based on them. Below the backscatter characteristics of the available five classes have been described. In case of two urban classes (ie, built-up and ger areas), at both L-band and C-band frequencies the backscatter would contain information about street alignment, building size, density, roofing material, its orientation, vegetation and soil, that is it would contain all kinds of scattering. Roads and buildings can reflect a larger component of radiation if they are aligned at right angles to the incident radiation. Here, the intersection of a road and a building tends to act as a corner reflector. The amount of backscatter is very sensitive to street alignment. The areas of streets and buildings aligned at right angles to the incident radiation will have very bright appearance and non-aligned areas will have darker appearance in the resulting image. Volume and surface scattering will also play an important role in the response from urban areas. Therefore, these classes will have higher backscatter return resulting in bright appearances on the images.

In the study site, green area consists of some forest and vegetated surface. In the case of forest, at L-band frequency the wavelength will penetrate to the forest canopy and will cause volume scattering to be derived from multiple-path reflections among twigs, branches, trunks and ground, while at C-band frequency only volume scattering from the top layer can be expected, because the wavelength is too short to penetrate to the forest layer. The vegetated surface will act as mixtures of small bush, grass and soil and the backscatter will depend on the volume of either of them. Also plant geometry, density and water content are the main factors influencing the backscatter coming from the vegetation cover. As a result, green areas will have brighter appearance on the image. The backscatter of soil depends on the surface roughness, texture, existing surface patterns, moisture content, as well as wavelength and incident angle. The presence of water strongly affects the microwave emissivity and reflectivity of a soil layer. At low moisture levels there is a low increase in the dielectric constant. Above a critical amount, the dielectric constant rises rapidly. This increase occurs when moisture begins to operate in a free space and the capacity of a soil to hold and retain moisture is directly related to the texture and structure of the soil. As can be seen, soil will have brighter appearance if it is wet and dark appearance if it is dry. Water should have the lowest backscatter values and dark appearance at both frequencies because of its specular reflection that causes less reflection towards the radar antenna.

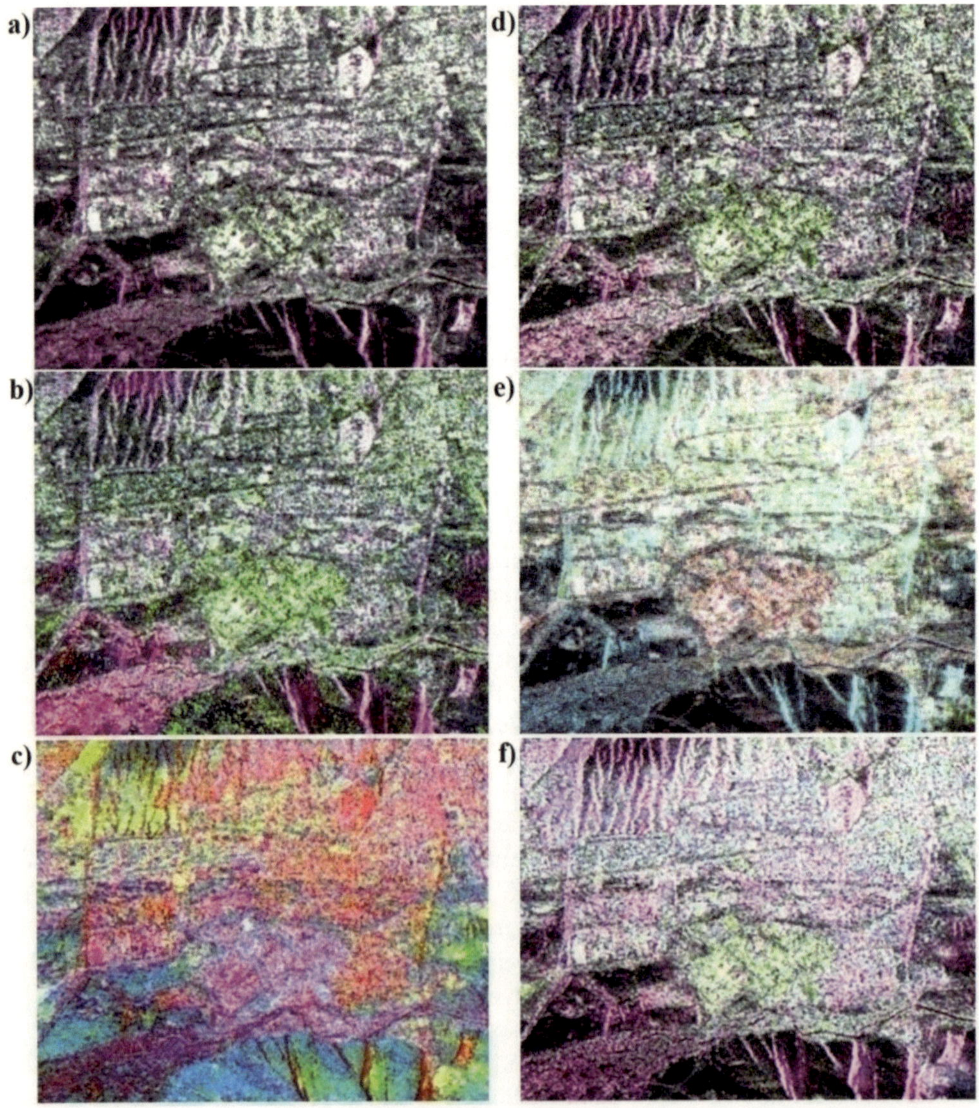

Fig. 4. Comparison of the fused images of ALOS PALSAR and ERS-2 SAR: (a) the image obtained by multiplicative method; (b) Brovey transformed image; (c) PC image (red=PC1, green=PC2; blue=PC3); (d) the image obtained by Gram-Schmidt fusion; (e) the image obtained by wavelet-based fusion; (f) the image obtained by Elhers fusion.

As can be seen from figure 4, the images created by the multiplicative method, Brovey transform and Gram-Schmidt fusion have very similar appearances. On these images, the built-up and ger areas have either similar (figure 4b) or mixed appearances (figure 4a, d). The green area has similar appearance as the built-up area. This means that the backscatter from double bounce effect in the built-up area has similar power as the volume and diffuse scattering from the green area. Moreover, it is seen that on all images (except the PC image), soil and water classes have dark appearances because of their specular reflection (though in some areas wet soil has increased brightness). As the original bands have been transformed to the new principle components, it is not easy to recognize the available classes on the image created by the PCA (figure 4c). On the PC image, the two urban classes, some roads aligned at right angles to the radar antenna as well as some areas affected by radar layover have magenta-reddish appearances, while other classes form different mixed classes. On the image created by the wavelet-based fusion (figure 4e), it is not possible to distinguish much detail. On this image, the two urban classes and green area as well as soil and water classes have similar appearances. Furthermore, it is seen that the image created by the Elhers fusion (figure 4f) looks similar to the image created by the Gram-Schmidt fusion, but has more light appearances. Overall, it is seen that the fused SAR images cannot properly distinguish the available spectral classes.

4.2 Comparison of the fusion methods using optical/SAR approach

Initially, the above mentioned fusion methods have been applied to such combinations as ASTER and HH, HV and VV polarization components of PALSAR as well as ASTER and ERS-2 SAR. Then, to obtain good colour images that can illustrate spectral and spatial variations of the classes of objects on the images, the fused images have been visually compared. In the case of the multiplicative method, the fused image of ASTER and PALSAR HH polarization (figure 5a) demonstrated a better result compared to other combinations, while in the case of Brovey transform the combination of ASTER and ERS-2 SAR (figure 5b) created a good image. On the image obtained by the multiplicative method, the built-up and ger areas have similar appearances, however, the green area, soil and water classes have total separations. Likewise, on the image obtained by the Brovey transform, the built-up and ger areas have similar appearances, whereas the green area and soil classes have total separations. Moreover, on this image, a part of the water class is mixed with other classes.

PCA has been applied to such combinations as ASTER and ERS-2 SAR, ASTER and PALSAR, and ASTER, PALSAR and ERS-2 SAR. When the results of the PCA were compared, the combination of ASTER, PALSAR and ERS-2 SAR demonstrated the best result than the other two combinations. The result of the final PCA is shown in table 1. As can be seen from table 1, PALSAR HH polarisation and ERS-2 SAR have very high negative loadings in PC1 and PC2. In these PCs, visible bands of ASTER also have moderate to high loadings.

This means that PC1 and PC2 contain the characteristics of both optical and SAR images. Although, PC3 contained 7.0% of the overall variance and had moderate to high loadings of ASTER band1, PALSAR HH polarisation and ERS-2 SAR, visual inspection revealed that it contained less information related to the selected classes. However, visual inspection of PC4 that contained 5.6% of the overall variance, in which VV polarisation of PALSAR has a high loading, revealed that this feature contained useful information related to the textural difference between the built-up and ger areas. The inspection of the last PCs indicated that they contained noise from the total data set. The image obtained by the PCA is shown in figure 5c. As can be seen from figure 5c, although the PC image could separate the two urban classes, in some parts of the image, it created a mixed class of green area and soil.

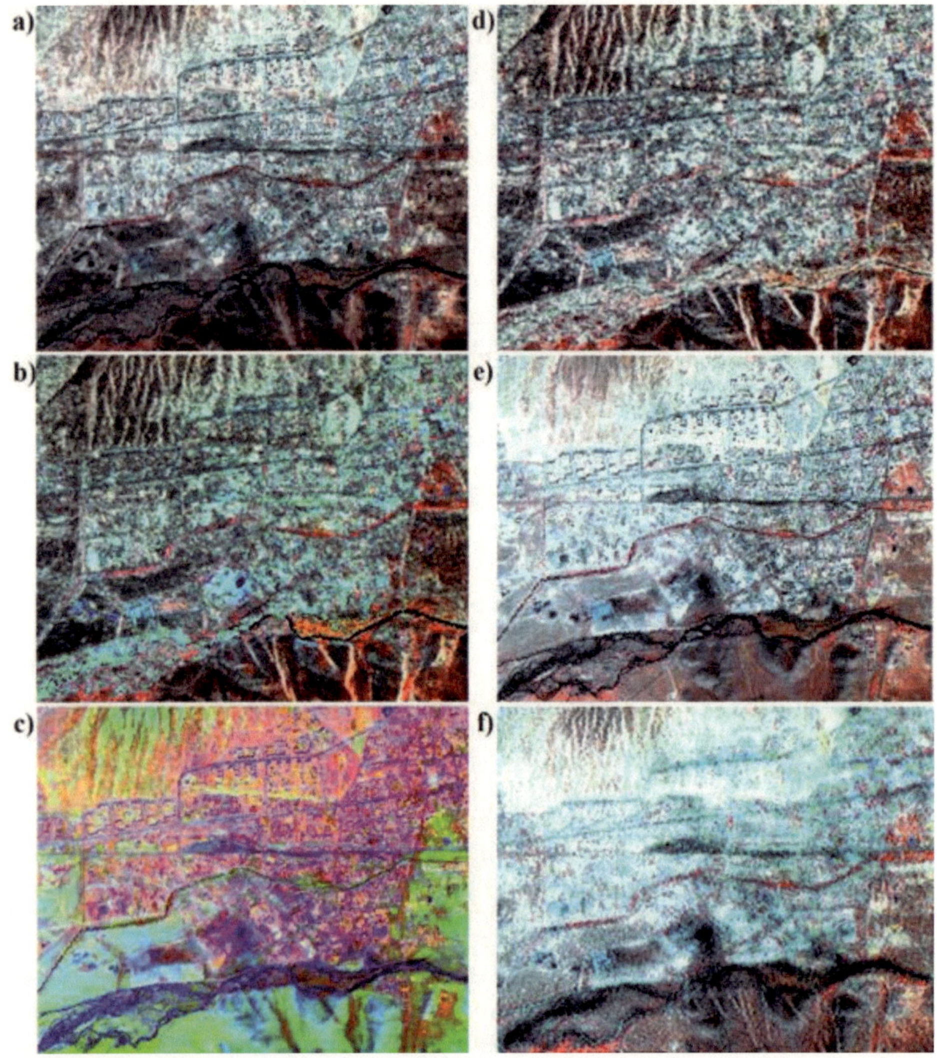

Fig. 5. Comparison of the fused optical and SAR images: (a) the image obtained by multiplicative method (ASTER and PALSAR-HH); (b) Brovey transformed image (ASTER and ERS-2 SAR); (c) PC image (red=PC1, green=PC2; blue=PC3); (d) the image obtained by Gram-Schmidt fusion (ASTER and ERS-2 SAR); (e) the image obtained by wavelet-based fusion (ASTER and ERS-2 SAR); (f) the image obtained by Elhers fusion (ASTER and PALSAR-VV).

In the case of the Gram-Schmidt fusion, the integrated image of ASTER and ERS-2 SAR (figure 5d) demonstrated a better result compared to other combinations. Although, the image contained some layover effects available on the ERS-2 image, looked very similar to the image obtained by the multiplicative method. In the case of the wavelet-based fusion, the fused image of ASTER and ERS-2 SAR (figure 5e) demonstrated a better result compared to other combinations, too. Also, this image looked better than any other images obtained by other fusion methods. On this image, all available five classes could be distinguished by their spectral properties. Moreover, it could be seen that some textural information has been added for differentiation between the classes: built-up area and ger area. In the case of the Elhers fusion, the integrated image of ASTER and PALSAR VV polarization (figure 5f) demonstrated a better result compared to other combinations. Although, this image had a blurred appearance due to speckle noise, still could very well separate green area, soil and water classes. Figure 5 shows the comparison of the images obtained by different fusion methods.

	PC1	PC2	PC3	PC4	PC5	PC6	PC7
ASTER band1	0.33	0.44	0.42	0.35	0.44	0.39	0.17
ASTER band2	0.50	0.37	0.34	-0.34	-0.38	-0.33	-0.32
ASTER band3	0.02	0.07	0.11	-0.09	-0.32	-0.19	0.91
PALSAR HH	-0.77	0.34	0.47	-0.14	0.06	-0.15	-0.08
PALSAR HV	0.14	-0.07	-0.06	-0.49	0.73	-0.40	0.13
PALSAR VV	0.02	-0.01	0.01	0.69	0.08	-0.71	-0.04
ERS-2 SAR	0.07	-0.73	0.67	0.01	-0.01	0.02	-0.01
Eigenvalues	8873.3	4896.7	1159.7	934.6	459.2	147.7	81.7
Variance (%)	53.6	29.6	7.0	5.6	2.8	0.89	0.51

Table 1. Principal component coefficients from ASTER, PALSAR and ERS-2 SAR images.

5. Evaluation of features and urban land cover classification

5.1 Evaluation of features using supervised classification

Initially, in order to define the sites for the training signature selection, from the multisensor images, two to four areas of interest (AOI) representing the selected five classes (built-up area, ger area, green area, soil and water) have been selected through thorough analysis using a polygon-based approach. The separability of the training signatures was firstly checked in feature space and then evaluated using transformed-divergence (TD) separability measure (table 2). The values of TD separability measure range from 0 to 2000 and indicate how well the selected pairs are statistically separate. The values greater than 1900 indicate that the pairs have good separability (ERDAS 1999, ENVI 1999). After the investigation, the samples that demonstrated the greatest separability were chosen to form the final signatures. The final signatures included 2669 pixels for built-up area, 592 pixels for ger area, 241 pixels for green area, 1984 pixels for soil and 123 pixels for water.

In general, urban areas are complex and diverse in nature and many features have similar spectral characteristics and it is not easy to separate them by the use of ordinary feature combinations. For the successful extraction of the urban land cover classes, reliable features derived from different sources should be used. In many cases, texture features derived from the occurrence and co-occurrence measures are used as additional reliable sources (Amarsaikhan *et al.* 2010). However, in the present study, the main objective was to evaluate the features obtained by the use of different fusion approaches. Therefore, for the classification the following feature combinations were used:

1. The features obtained by the use of the multiplicative method using SAR/SAR approach
2. The features obtained by the use of the multiplicative method using optical/SAR approach
3. The features obtained by the use of the Brovey transform using SAR/SAR approach
4. The features obtained by the use of the Brovey transform optical/SAR approach
5. The PC1, PC2 and PC3 of the PCA obtained using SAR/SAR approach
6. The PC1, PC2 and PC4 of the PCA obtained using optical/SAR approach
7. The features obtained by the use of the Gram-Schmidt fusion using SAR/SAR approach
8. The features obtained by the use of the Gram-Schmidt fusion using optical/SAR approach
9. The features obtained by the use of the wavelet-based fusion using SAR/SAR approach
10. The features obtained by the use of the wavelet-based fusion using optical/SAR approach
11. The features obtained by the use of the Elhers fusion using SAR/SAR approach
12. The features obtained by the use of the Elhers fusion using optical/SAR approach
13. The combined features of ASTER and PALSAR
14. The combined features of ASTER and ERS-2 SAR
15. The combined features of ASTER, PALSAR and ERS-2 SAR.

	Builtup area	Ger area	Green area	Soil	Water
Builtup area	0.000	787	1987	844	2000
Ger area	787	0.000	1999	1706	2000
Green area	1987	1999	0.000	1903	2000
Soil	844	1706	1903	0.000	2000
Water	2000	2000	2000	2000	0.000

Table 2. The separabilities measured by TD separability measure.

For the actual classification, a supervised statistical maximum likelihood classification (MLC) has been used assuming that the training samples have the Gaussian distribution (Richards and Xia 1999). The final classified images are shown in figure 6(1–15). As seen from figure 6(1–15), the classification results of the SAR/SAR approach give the worst results, because there are high overlaps among classes: built-up area, ger area, soil and green area. However, these overlaps decrease on other images for the classification of which SAR as well as optical bands have been used. As could be seen from the overall classification results (table 3), although the combined use of optical and microwave data sets produced a better result than the single source image, it is still very difficult to obtain a reliable land cover map by the use of the standard technique, specifically on decision boundaries of the statistically overlapping classes.

For the accuracy assessment of the classification results, the overall performance has been used. This approach creates a confusion matrix in which reference pixels are compared with the classified pixels and as a result an accuracy report is generated indicating the percentages of the overall accuracy (ERDAS 1999). As ground truth information, different AOIs containing 12578 purest pixels have been selected.

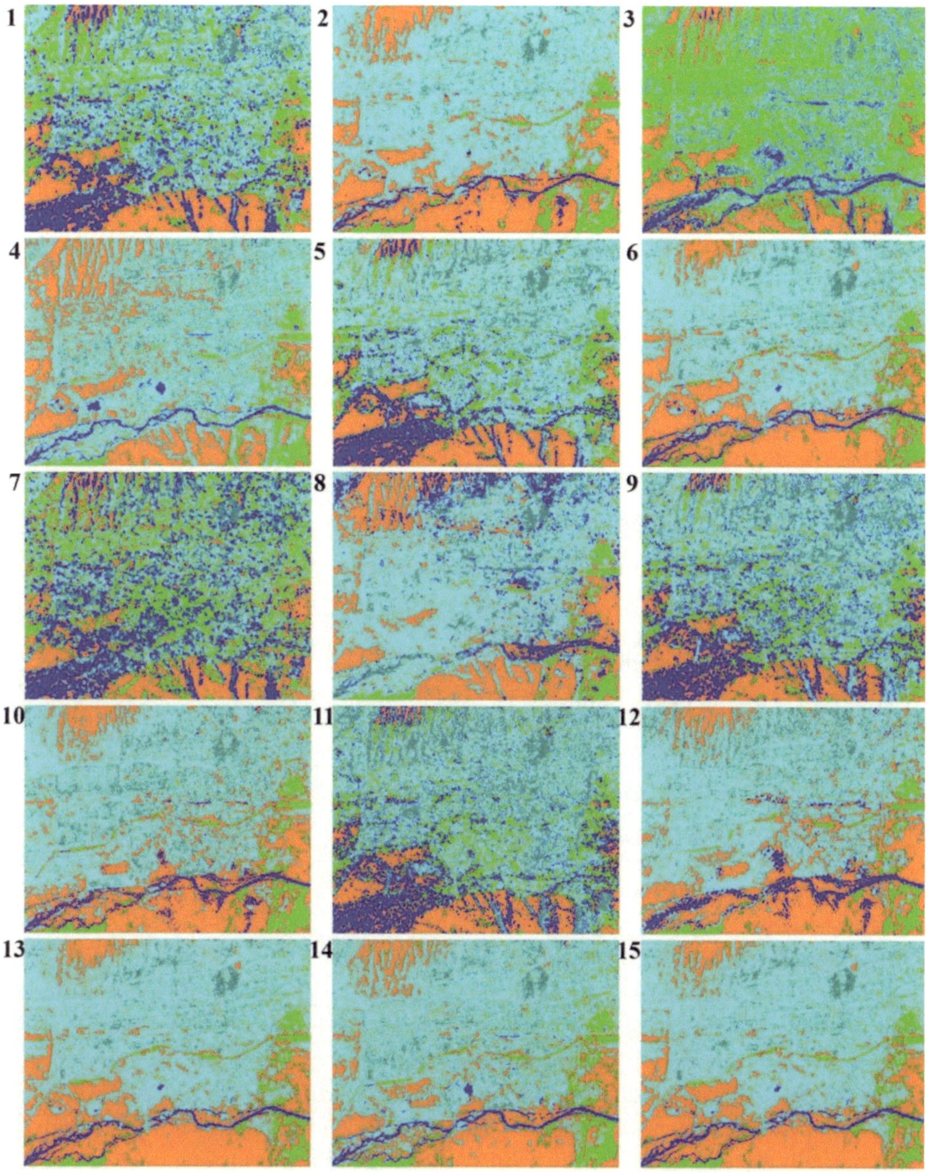

Fig. 6. Comparison of the MLC results for the selected classes (cyan-built-up area; dark cyan-ger area; green-green area; sienna-soil; blue-water). Classified images of: 1-multiplicative method using SAR/SAR approach, 2-multiplicative method using optical/SAR approach, 3-Brovey transform using SAR/SAR approach, 4-Brovey transform optical/SAR approach, 5-PCA using SAR/SAR approach, 6- PCA using optical/SAR approach, 7- Gram-Schmidt fusion using SAR/SAR approach, 8- Gram-Schmidt fusion using optical/SAR approach, 9- wavelet-based fusion using SAR/SAR approach, 10- wavelet-based fusion using optical/SAR approach, 11-Elhers fusion using SAR/SAR approach, 12- Elhers fusion using optical/SAR approach, 13- features of ASTER and PALSAR, 14- features of ASTER and ERS-2 SAR, 15-features of ASTER, PALSAR and ERS-2 SAR.

AOIs were selected on a principle that more pixels to be selected for the evaluation of the larger classes such as built-up area and ger area than the smaller classes such as green area and water. The overall classification accuracies for the selected classes are shown in table 3.

The bands (features) used for the MLC	Overall accuracy (%)
Multiplicative method using SAR/SAR approach	46.12
Multiplicative method using optical /SAR approach	78.17
Brovey transform using SAR/SAR approach	41.57
Brovey transform optical/SAR approach	74.34
PCA using SAR/SAR approach	71.83
PCA using optical/SAR approach	81.92
Gram-Schmidt fusion using SAR/SAR approach	40.86
Gram-Schmidt fusion using optical/SAR approach	74.08
Wavelet-based fusion using SAR/SAR approach	65.78
Wavelet-based fusion using optical/SAR approach	76.26
Elhers fusion using SAR/SAR approach	51.72
Elhers fusion using optical/SAR approach	60.08
ASTER and PALSAR	79.98
ASTER and ERS-2 SAR	78.43
ASTER, PALSAR and ERS-2 SAR	80.12

Table 3. The overall classification accuracy of the classified images.

5.2 Knowledge-based classification

In years past, knowledge-based techniques have been widely used for the classification of different RS images. The knowledge in image classification can be represented in different forms depending on the type of knowledge and necessity of its usage. The most commonly used techniques for knowledge representation are a rule-based approach and neural network classification (Amarsaikhan and Douglas 2004). In the present study, for separation of the statistically overlapping classes, a rule-based algorithm has been constructed. A rule-based approach uses a hierarchy of rules, or a decision tree describing the conditions under which a set of low-level primary objects becomes abstracted into a set of the high-level object classes. The primary objects contain the user-defined variables and include geographical objects represented in different structures, external programmes, scalars and spatial models (ERDAS 1999).

The constructed rule-based algorithm consists of 2 main hierarchies. In the upper hierarchy, on the basis of knowledge about reflecting and backscattering characteristics of the selected five classes, a set of rules which contains the initial image classification procedure based on a Mahalanobis distance rule and the constraints on spatial thresholds were constructed. The Mahalanobis distance decision rule can be written as follows:

$$MD_k=(x_i- m_k)^t V_k^{-1}(x_i- m_k) \quad (12)$$

Where:
x_i-vector representing the pixel
m_k-sample mean vector for class k
V_k-sample variance-covariance matrix of the given class.
It is clear that a spectral classifier will be ineffective if applied to the statistically overlapping classes such as built-up area and ger area because they have very similar spectral characteristics in both optical and microwave ranges. For such spectrally mixed classes, classification accuracies can be improved if the spatial properties of the classes of objects could be incorporated into the classification criteria. The spatial thresholds can be determined on the basis of historical thematic spatial data sets or from local knowledge about the site. In this study, the spatial thresholds were defined based on local knowledge about the test area.

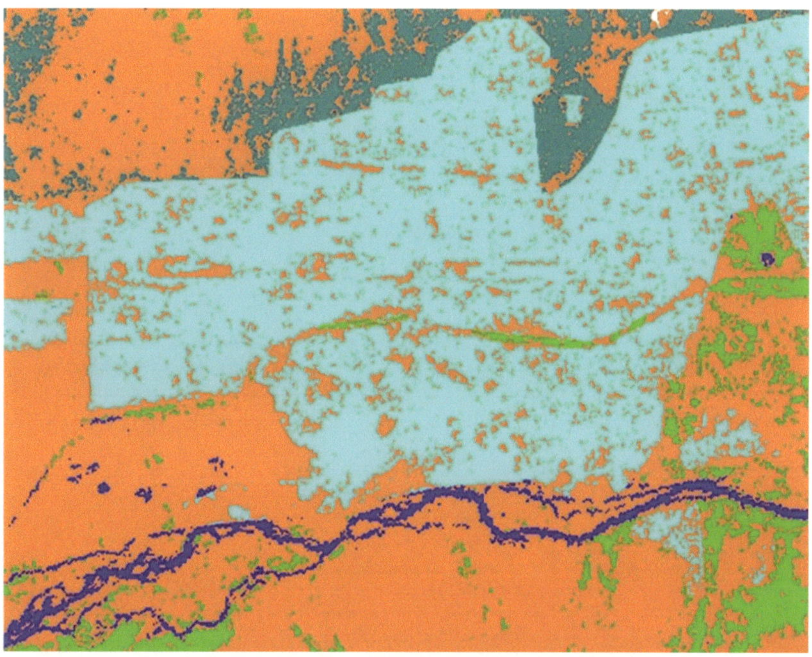

Fig. 7. Classification result obtained by the knowledge-based classification (cyan-built-up area; dark cyan-ger area; green-green area; sienna-soil; blue-water).

In the initial image classification, for separation of the statistically overlapping classes, only pixels falling outside of the spatial thresholds and the PC1, PC2 and PC4 of the PCA obtained using optical/SAR approach, were used. The pixels falling outside of the spatial thresholds were temporarily identified as unknown classes and further classified using the rules in which other spatial thresholds were used. As can be seen from the pre-classification analysis, there are different statistical overlaps among the classes, but significant overlaps exist among the classes: built-up area, ger area and soil. In the lower hierarchy of the rule-base, different rules for separation of these overlapping classes were constructed using spatial thresholds. The image classified by the constructed method is shown in Figure 7.

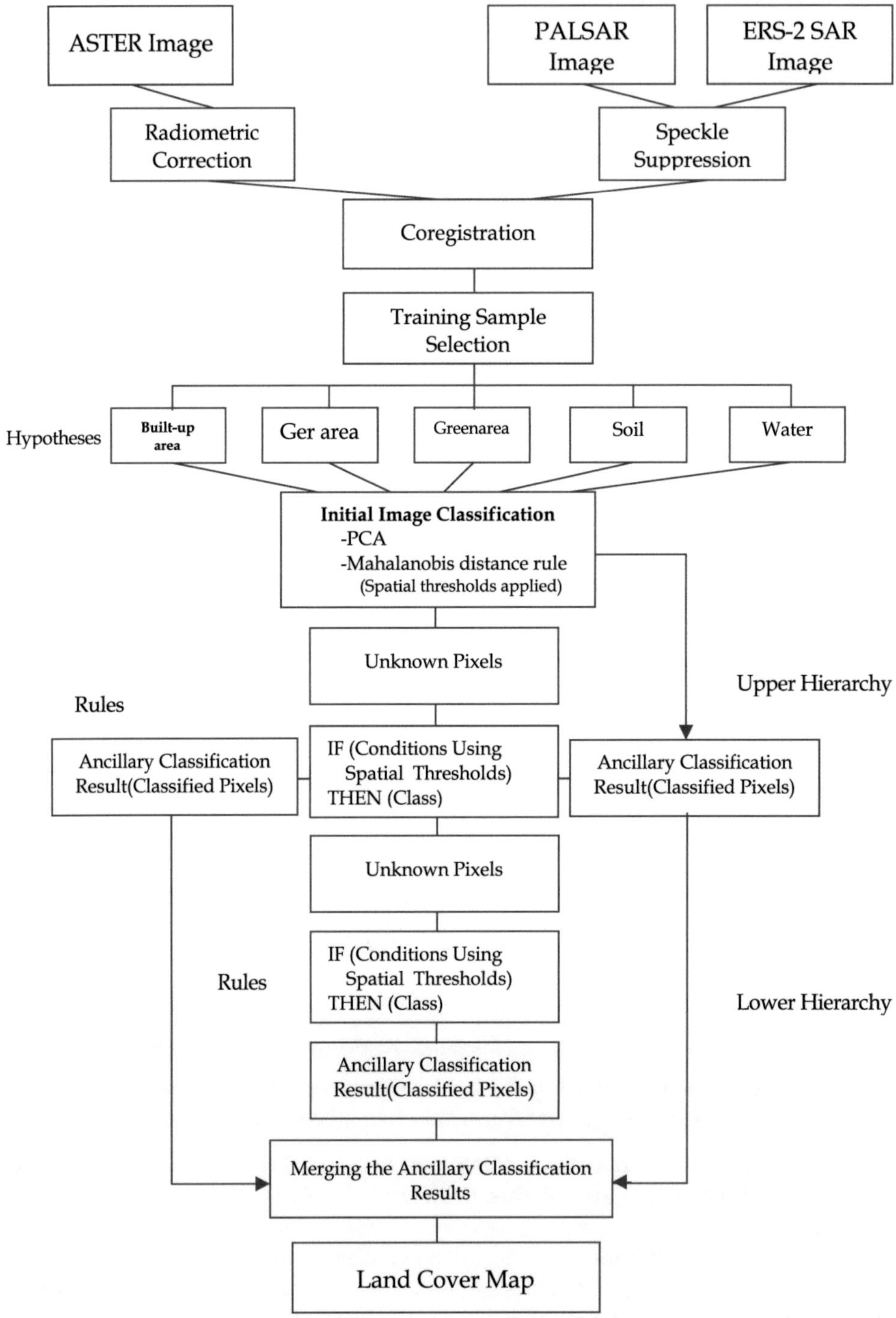

Fig. 8. The flowchart of the constructed knowledge-based classification.

For the accuracy assessment of the classification result, the overall performance has been used, taking the same number of sample points as in the previous classifications. The confusion matrix produced for the knowledge-based classification showed overall accuracy of 90.92%. In order to allow an evaluation of the class by class results, confusion matrices of the overall classification accuracies of the classified images using the knowledge-based classification and the best supervised classification (ASTER, PALSAR and ERS-2 SAR) are given in table 4a,b. As could be seen from figure 7 and table 4a,b, the result of the classification using the rule-based method is much better than result of the standard method. The flowchart of the constructed rule-based classification procedure is shown in Figure 8.

Classified data	Reference data				
	Builtup area	Ger area	Green area	Soil	Water
Builtup area	5212	0	0	267	0
Ger area	187	1305	0	77	0
Green area	18	0	911	61	0
Soil	297	98	126	3771	0
Water	0	0	0	11	237
Total	5714	1403	1037	4187	237
Overall accuracy=90.92% (11436/12578)					

a)

Classified data	Reference data				
	Builtup area	Ger area	Green area	Soil	Water
Builtup area	4902	407	18	980	28
Ger area	567	980	19	52	0
Green area	98	16	868	0	0
Soil	109	0	132	3136	17
Water	38	0	0	19	192
Total	5714	1403	1037	4187	237
Overall accuracy=80.12% (10078/12578)					

b)

Table 4. Comparison of the detailed overall classification accuracies of the classified images using the knowledge-based classification and supervised classification (ASTER, PALSAR and ERS-2 SAR).

6. Update of urban GIS

In general, a GIS can be considered as a spatial decision-making tool. For any decision-making, GIS systems use digital spatial information, for which various digitized data creation methods are used. The most commonly used method of data creation is the digitization, where hard copy maps or survey plans are transferred into digital formats through the use of special software programs and spatial-referencing capabilities. With the emergence of the modern ortho-rectified images acquired from both space and air platforms, heads-up digitizing is becoming the main approach through which positional data is extracted (Amarsaikhan and Ganzorig 2010). Compared to the traditional method of tracing, heads-up digitizing involves the tracing of spatial data directly on top of the acquired imagery. Thus, due to rapid development in science an technology, primary spatial data acquisition within a GIS is becoming more and more sophisticated.

The current GISs allow the users and decision-makers to view, understand, question, interpret, analyze and visualize data sets in many different ways. The power of GIS systems comes from the ability to relate different information in a spatial context and to reach a conclusion about this relationship. Most of the information we have about our world contains a spatial reference, placing that information at some point on the Earth's surface. For example, when information about urban commercial buildings is collected, it is important to know where the buildings are located. This can be done by applying a spatial reference system that uses a special coordinate system. Comparing that information with other information, such as the location of the main infrastructure, one can evaluate the market values of the buildings. In this case, a GIS helps in revealing important new information that leads to better decision-making.

Fig. 9. The digitized map, created from a topographic map of 1984 (cyan-built-up area; dark cyan-ger area; green-green area; sienna-soil; blue-water).

At present, GISs are being widely used for urban planning and management. For an efficient decision-making, one needs accurate and updated spatial information. In urban context, spatial information can be collected from a number of sources such as city planning maps, topographic maps, digital cartography, thematic maps, global positioning system, aerial photography and space RS. Of these, only RS can provide real-time information that can be used for the real-time spatial analysis. Over the past few years, RS techniques and technologies, including system capabilities have been significantly improved. Meanwhile, the costs for the primary RS data sets have drastically decreased (Amarsaikhan *et al.* 2009b). This means that it is possible to extract from RS images different thematic information in a cost-effective way and update different layers within a GIS.

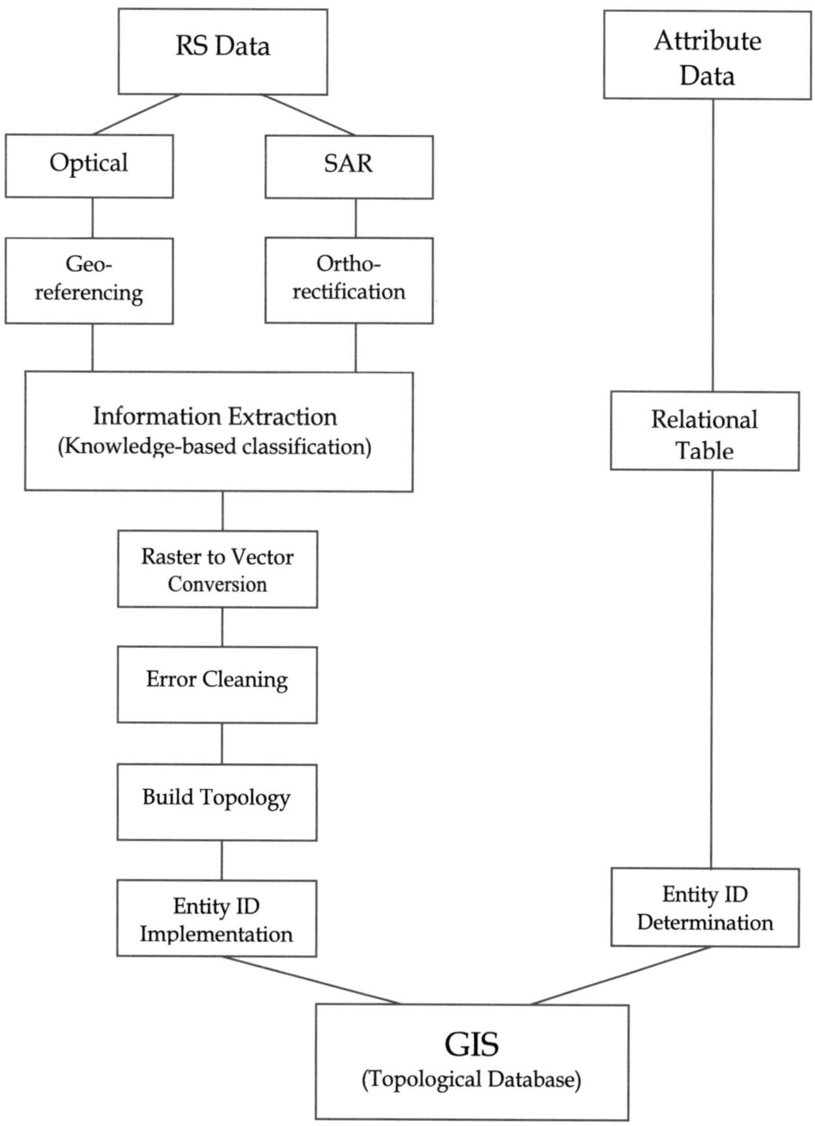

Fig. 10. A diagram for update of urban GIS via processing of multisource RS images.

In the present study, it is assumed that there is an operational urban GIS that stores historical thematic layers and there is a need to update a land cover layer. The current land cover layer was created using an existing topographic map of 1984 and for its digitizing ArcGIS system was used. The digitized map is shown in Figure 9. As the overall classification accuracy of the classified multisource images exceeds 90%, the result can be directly used to update the land cover layer of the operational GIS. For this end, a raster thematic map (i.e., classified image) extracted from the multisource RS data sets should be converted into a vector structure. After error cleaning and editing, the converted from raster to vector layer can be topologically structured and stored within the urban GIS. If one compares the land cover layers created from the topographic map and classified RS images, could see what changes had occurred. A diagram for update of a land cover layer of an urban GIS via processing of multisource RS images is shown in Figure 10.

7. Conclusions

The main purpose of the research was to compare the performances of different data fusion techniques for the enhancement of different surface features and evaluate the features obtained by the fusion techniques in terms of separation of urban land cover classes. For the data fusion, two different approaches such as fusion of SAR data with SAR data and fusion of optical data with SAR data were considered. As the fusion techniques, multiplicative method, Brovey transform, PCA, Gram-Schmidt fusion, wavelet-based fusion and Elhers fusion were applied. In the case of the SAR/SAR approach the fused SAR images could not properly distinguish the available spectral classes. In the case of the optical/SAR approach, although, fusion methods demonstrated different results, detailed analysis of each image revealed that the image obtained by the wavelet-based fusion gave a superior image in terms of the spatial and spectral separations among different urban features. For the classification of the fused images, statistical MLC and knowledge-based method were used and the results were compared. As could be seen from the classification results, the performance of the knowledge-based technique was much better than the performances of the standard method and output could be directly used to update urban GIS. Overall, the research indicated that multisource information can significantly improve the interpretation and classification of land cover classes and the knowledge-based method is a powerful tool in the production of a reliable land cover map.

8. References

Abidi, M.A., and Gonzalez, R.C. (1992). *Data Fusion in Robotics and Machine Intelligence* (New York: Academic Press).

Amarsaikhan, D., Ganzorig, M., Batbayar, G., Narangerel, D. and Tumentsetseg, S.H. (2004). An integrated approach of optical and SAR images for forest change study, *Asian Journal of Geoinformatics*, 3, pp.27–33.

Amarsaikhan, D., and Douglas, T. (2004). Data fusion and multisource data classification, *International Journal of Remote Sensing*, 17, pp.3529-3539.

Amarsaikhan, D., Ganzorig, M., Ache, P. and Blotevogel, H.H. (2007). The integrated use of Optical and InSAR data for urban land cover mapping, *International Journal of Remote Sensing*, 28, pp.1161-1171.

Amarsaikhan, D., Blotevogel, H.H., Ganzorig, M., and Moon, T.H. (2009a). Applications of remote sensing and geographic information systems for urban land-cover changes studies, *Geocarto International,_a multi-disciplinary journal of Remote Sensing and GIS*, 24, pp.257–271.

Amarsaikhan, D., Ganzorig, M., Blotevogel, H.H., Nergui, B. and Gantuya, R. (2009b). Integrated method to extract information from high and very high resolution RS images for urban planning, *Journal of Geography and Regional Planning*, 2(10), pp.258-267.

Amarsaikhan, D., Blotevogel, H.H., Van Genderen, J.L., Ganzorig, M., Gantuya, R. and Nergui, B. (2010). Fusing high resolution TerraSAR and Quickbird images for urban land cover study in Mongolia, *International Journal of Image and Data Fusion*, 1, pp.83-97.

Amarsaikhan, D. and Ganzorig, M. (2010). *Principles of GIS for Natural Resources Management, 2nd edn* (Ulaanbaatar: Academic Press).

Baghdadi, N., King, N., Bourguignon, A. and Remond, A. (2002). Potential of ERS and Radarsat data for surface roughness monitoring over bare agricultural fields: application to catchments in Northern France, *International Journal of Remote Sensing*, 23, pp.3427 - 3442.

Benediktsson, J.A., Sveinsson, J.R., Atkinson, P.M., and Tatnali, A. (1997). Feature extraction for multisource data classification with artificial neural networks, *International Journal of Remote Sensing*, 18, pp.727–740.

Cao, X., Chen, J., Imura, H. and Higashi, O. (2009). A SVM-based method to extract urban areas from DMSP-OLS and SPOT VGT data, *Remote Sensing of Environment*, 10, pp.2205-2209.

Colditz, R.R., Wehrmann, T., Bachmann, M., Steinnocher, K., Schmidt, M., Strunz, G. and Dech, S. (2006). Influence of image fusion approaches on classification accuracy: a case study, *International Journal of Remote Sensing*, 27, pp.3311 - 3335.

Costa, M. (2005). Estimate of net primary productivity of aquatic vegetation of the Amazon floodplain using Radarsat and JERS-1, *International Journal of Remote Sensing*, 26, pp.4527 - 4536.

Deng, J.S., Wang, K., Deng, K.D. and Qi, G.J. (2008). PCA-based land-use change detection and analysis using multitemporal and multisensor satellite data, *International Journal of Remote Sensing*, 29, pp.4823 - 4838.

Ehlers, M. (2004). Spectral characteristics preserving image fusion based on Fourier domain filtering. *Remote Sensing for Environmental Monitoring, GIS Applications, and Geology IV, Proceedings of SPIE*, pp.93–116.

Ehlers, M., Klonus, S. and Åstrand, P.J. (2008). Quality Assessment for multi-sensor multi-date image fusion, *CD-ROM Proceedings of ISPRS Congresses*, Beijing, China, July 3-11, 2008.

ENVI (1999). *User's Guide, Research Systems.*

Erbek, F.S., Zkan, C.O. and Taberner, M. (2004). Comparison of maximum likelihood classification method with supervised artificial neural network algorithms for land use activities, *International Journal of Remote Sensing*, 25, pp.1733–1748.

ERDAS (1999). *Field Guide, 5th edn* (Atlanta, Georgia: ERDAS, Inc.).

Franklin. S.E., Peddle, D.R., Dechka, J.A. and Stenhouse, G.B. (2002). Evidential reasoning with Landsat TM, DEM and GIS data for landcover classification in support of grizzly bear habitat mapping, *International Journal of Remote Sensing*, 23, pp.4633 - 4652.

Gonzalez, A.M., Saleta, J.L., Catalan, R.G. and Garcia, R. (2004). Fusion of multispectral and panchromatic images using improved IHS and PCA mergers based on wavelet decomposition, *IEEE Transactions Geoscience and Remote Sensing*, 6, pp.1291- 1299.

Hegarat-Mascle, S.L., Quesney, A., Vidal-Madjar, D., Taconet, O., Normand, M. and Loumagne, M. (2000). Land cover discrimination from mutitemporal ERS images and multispectral Landsat images: a study case in an agricultural area in France, *International Journal of Remote Sensing*, 21, pp.435–456.

Herold, N.D. and Haack, B.N. (2002). Fusion of Radar and Optical Data for Land Cover Mapping. *Geocarto International*, 17, pp.21 - 30.

Karathanassi, V., Kolokousis, P. and Ioannidou, S. (2007). A comparison study on fusion methods using evaluation indicators, *International Journal of Remote Sensing*, 28, pp.2309 - 2341.

Li, Z. and Leung, H. (2009). Fusion of multispectral and panchromatic images using a restoration-based method, *IEEE Transactions Geoscience and Remote Sensing*, 5, pp.1482-1491.

Mascarenha, N.D.A, Banon, G.J.F. and Candeias, A.L.B. (1996). Multispectral image data fusion under a Bayesian approach, *International Journal of Remote Sensing*, 17, pp.1457 - 1471.

Mather, P.M. (1999). *Computer Processing of Remotely-sensed Images: an Introduction, 2nd edn* (Chichester: John Wiley & Sons).

Meher, S.K., Shankar, B.U. and Ghosh, A. (2007). Wavelet-feature-based classifiers for multispectral remote-sensing images, *IEEE Transactions Geoscience and Remote Sensing*, 6, pp. 1881-1886.

Munechika, C.K., Warnick, J.S., Salvaggio, C., and Schott, J.R. (1993). Resolution enhancement of multispectral image data to improve classification accuracy, *Photogrammetric Engineering and Remote Sensing*, 59, pp.67–72.

Pajares, G. and Cruz, J.M. (2004). A wavelet-based image fusion, *Pattern Recognition*, pp. 1855-1872.

Palubinskas, G. and Datcu, M. (2008). Information fusion approach for the data classification: an example for ERS-1/2 InSAR data, *International Journal of Remote Sensing*, 29, pp.4689-4703.

Pellemans, A.H., Jordans, R.W. and Allewijn, R. (1993). Merging multispectral and panchromatic Spot images with respect to the radiometric properties of the sensor, *Photogrammetric Engineering and Remote Sensing*, 59, pp.81-87.

Pohl, C. and Van Genderen, J.L. (1998). Multisensor image fusion in remote sensing: concepts, methods and applications, *International Journal of Remote Sensing*, 19, pp.823–854.

Ricchetti, E. (2001). Visible-infrared and radar imagery fusion for geological application: a new approach using DEM and sun-illumination model, *International Journal of Remote Sensing*, 22, pp.2219–2230.

Richards, J. A. and Jia, S. (1999). *Remote Sensing Digital Image Analysis – An Introduction, 3rd edn* (Berlin: Springer-Verlag).

Saadi, N.M. and Watanabe, K. (2009). Assessing image processing techniques for geological mapping: a case study in Eljufra, Libya, *Geocarto International,* 24, pp.241 - 253.

Saraf, A. K. (1999). IRS-1C-LISS-III and PAN data fusion: an approach to improve remote sensing based mapping techniques, *International Journal of Remote Sensing,* 20, pp.90-96.

Seetha, M., Malleswari, B.L., Muralikrishna, I.V. and Deekshatulu, B.L. (2007). Image fusion - a performance assessment, *Journal of Geomatics,* 1, pp.33-39.

Serkan, M., Musaoglu, N., Kirkici, H. and Ormeci, C. (2008). Edge and fine detail preservation in SAR images through speckle reduction with an adaptive mean filter, *International Journal of Remote Sensing,* 29, pp.6727-6738.

Serpico, S. B., and Roli, F. (1995). Classification of multisensor remote sensing images by structural neural networks, *IEEE Transactions on Geoscience and Remote Sensing,* 33, pp.562–578.

Soh, L.K. and Tsatsoulis, C. (1999). Unsupervised segmentation of ERS and Radarsat sea ice images using multiresolution peak detection and aggregated population equalization, *International Journal of Remote Sensing,* 20, pp.3087-3109.

Solberg, A.H.S., Taxt, T. and Jain, A.K. (1996). A Markov random field model for classification of multisource satellite imagery, *IEEE Transactions on Geoscience and Remote Sensing,* 34, pp.100–112.

Storvik, G., Fjortoft, R. and Solberg, A.H.S. (2005). A bayesian approach to classification of multiresolution remote sensing data, *IEEE Transactions Geoscience and Remote Sensing,* 3, pp. 539- 547.

Teggi, S., Cecchi, R. and Serafini, R. (2003). TM and IRS-1C-PAN data fusion using multiresolution decomposition methods based on the 'a trous' algorithm, *International Journal of Remote Sensing,* 24, pp.1287-1301.

Teoh, C.C., Mansor, S.B., Mispan, M.R., Mohamed-Shariff, A.R. and Ahmad, N. (2001). Extraction of infrastructure details from fused image. *Geoscience and Remote Sensing Symposium, IGARSS '01. IEEE 2001 International,* 3 , July 9-13 2001, pp.1490 - 1492.

Verbyla, D.L. (2001). A test of detecting spring leaf flush within the Alaskan boreal forest using ERS-2 and Radarsat SAR data, *International Journal of Remote Sensing,* 22, pp.1159 - 1165.

Vrabel, J. (1996). Multispectral imagery band sharpening study, *Photogrammetric Engineering and Remote Sensing,* 62, pp.1075-1083.

Wang, Y., Koopmans, B. N., and Pohl, C. (1995). The 1995 flood in the Netherlands monitored from space – a multisensor approach, *International Journal of Remote Sensing,* 16, pp.2735–2739.

Westra, T., Mertens, K.C. and De Wulf, R.R. (2005). ENVISAT ASAR wide swath and SPOT-vegetation image fusion for wetland mapping: evaluation of different wavelet-based methods, *Geocarto International,* 20, pp.21 - 31.

Zhang, J. (2010). Multi-source remote sensing data fusion: status and trends, *International Journal of Image and Data Fusion*, 1, pp.5 – 24.

9

Image Fusion for Remote Sensing Applications

Leila Fonseca[1], Laercio Namikawa[1], Emiliano Castejon[1], Lino Carvalho[1], Carolina Pinho[1] and Aylton Pagamisse[2]
[1]*National Institute for Space Research, INPE*
[2]*São Paulo State University, Unesp*
Brazil

1. Introduction

Remote Sensing systems, particularly those deployed on satellites, provide a repetitive and consistent view of the Earth (Schowengerdt, 2007). To meet the needs of different remote sensing applications the systems offer a wide range of spatial, spectral, radiometric and temporal resolutions. Satellites usually take several images from frequency bands in the visual and non-visual range. Each monochrome image is referred to as a band and a collection of several bands of the same scene acquired by a sensor is called *multispectral image* (MS). A combination of three bands associated in a RGB (Red, Green, Blue) color system produce a color image.

The color information in a remote sensing image by using spectral band combinations for a given spatial resolution increases information content which is used in many remote sensing applications. Otherwise, different targets in a single band may appear similar which makes difficult to distinguish them. Different bands can be acquired by a single multispectral sensor or by multiple sensors operating at different frequencies. Complementary information about the same scene can be available in the following cases (Simone et al., 2002):

- Data recorded by different sensors;
- Data recorded by the same sensor operating in different spectral bands;
- Data recorded by the same sensor at different polarization;
- Data recorded by the same sensor located on platforms flying at different heights.

In general, sensors with high spectral resolution, characterized by capturing the radiance from different land covers in a large number of bands of the electromagnetic spectrum, do not have an optimal spatial resolution, that may be inadequate to a specific identification task despite of its good spectral resolution (González-Audícana, 2004). On a high spatial resolution panchromatic image (PAN), detailed geometric features can easily be recognized, while the multispectral images contain richer spectral information. The capabilities of the images can be enhanced if the advantages of both high spatial and spectral resolution can be integrated into one single image. The detailed features of such an integrated image thus can be easily recognized and will benefit many applications, such as urban and environmental studies (Shi et al., 2005).

With appropriate algorithms it is possible to combine multispectral and panchromatic bands and produce a synthetic image with their best characteristics. This process is known as multisensor merging, fusion, or sharpening (Pohl & Genderen, 1998; Zhang, 2004; Wald, 2002). It aims to integrate the spatial detail of a high-resolution panchromatic image (PAN) and the color information of a low-resolution multispectral (MS) image to produce a high-resolution MS image (hybrid product). The result of image fusion is a new image which is more suitable for human and machine perception or further image-processing tasks such as segmentation, feature extraction and object recognition.

The hybrid product should offer the highest possible spatial information content while still preserving good spectral information quality. It is known that the spatial detailed information of PAN image is mostly carried by its high-frequency components, while the spectral information of MS image is mostly carried by its low-frequency components. If the high-frequency components of the MS image are simply substituted by the high-frequency components of the panchromatic image, the spatial resolution is improved but with the loss of spectral information from the high-frequency components of MS image (Guo et al., 2010; Li et al. 2002; Zhou et al., 1998).

To produce hybrid images with good quality some aspects should be considered during the fusion process (Schowengerdt, 2007; Fonseca et al., 2008):

- The PAN and MS images should be acquired at nearby dates. Several changes may occur during the interval of acquisition time: variations in the vegetation depending on the season of the year, different lighting conditions, construction of buildings, or changes caused by natural catastrophes (e.g. earthquakes, floods and volcanic eruptions);
- The spectral range of PAN image should cover the spectral range of all multispectral bands involved in the fusion process to preserve the image color. This condition can avoid the color distortion in the fused image;
- The spectral band of the high resolution image should be as similar as possible to that of the replaced low resolution component in the fusion process;
- The high resolution image should be globally contrast matched to the replaced component to reduce residual radiometric artifacts;
- The PAN and MS images must be registered with a precision of less than 0.5 pixel, avoiding artifacts in the fused image.

Some of these factors are less important when the fused images are from regions of the spectrum with different remote sensing phenomenologies. For example, there is no reason to assume radiometric correlation between the images in the fusion of low-resolution thermal or radar images with multispectral visible imagery (Schowengerdt, 2007).

The merging process becomes more difficult in those cases where the ratio between the spatial resolutions of both images is greater than 4 due to the registration and resampling processes. Ling et al. (2008) showed that a spatial resolution ratio of 1:10 or higher is desired for optimal multisensor image fusion provided the input panchromatic image is not downsampled to a coarser resolution. Due to the synthetic pixels generated from resampling, the quality of the fused image decreases as the spatial resolution ratio decreases (e.g. from 1:10 to 1:30). In cases where the spatial resolution ratio is too small (e.g. 1:30), to obtain better spectral integrity of the fused image, one may downsample the input high-resolution panchromatic image to a slightly lower resolution before fusing it with the multispectral image.

Most image processing systems such as Environment for Visualizing Images - ENVI (Research System, 2011), SPRING (SPRING, 2011; Câmara et al., 1996) and ERDAS (ERDAS, 2011) have an image fusion module. Also, some image fusion algorithms have been

implemented using open software such as TerraLib, which is a Geographic Information Systems (GIS) classes and functions library available from the Internet as open source, allowing a collaborative environment and its use in the development of multiple GIS tools (TerraLib, 2011).
Based on the problems aforementioned, we present a brief review about fusion techniques and fusion evaluation methods, and also a discussion about the use of image fusion techniques in three remote sensing applications, which will be illustrated through case studies. Each case study presents results applied to real data and problems in remote sensing such as for inland water analysis, disaster and urban studies. Two of them use hybrid images generated from CBERS-2B images that are freely available on internet (INPE, 2011).
The chapter is organized in five sections: Section 2 briefly describes the most traditional fusion methods, Section 3 describes some techniques for fused image quality assessment, Section 4 presents three case studies that illustrate the application of image fusion in the remote sensing area, finally section 5 concludes the work.

2. Fusion methods

Ideally, image fusion techniques should allow combination of images with different spectral and spatial resolution keeping the radiometric information (Pohl and Genderen, 1998). Huge effort has been put in developing fusion methods that preserve the spectral information and increase detail information in the hybrid product produced by fusion process.
Methods based on IHS transform (Choi, 2006; Schetselaar, 1998; Silva et al., 2008; Tu et al., 2001a, 2001b, Tu et al., 2004; Tu et al., 2007) and Principal Components Analysis (PCA) (Chavez, 1989) probably are the most popular approaches used to enhance the spatial resolution of multispectral images with panchromatic images. However, both methods suffer from the problem that the radiometry on the spectral channels is modified after fusion. This is because the high-resolution panchromatic image usually has spectral characteristics different from both the intensity and the first principal components (Li et al., 2002). More recently, new techniques have been proposed such as those that combine wavelet transform with IHS model and PCA transform to manage the color and details information distortion in the fused image (Cao et al., 2003; González-Audícana et al., 2004; Simone et al., 2002).
Below, we present the basic theory of the fusion methods based on IHS, PCA, arithmetic operators, and Wavelet Transform (WT), which are the most traditional techniques used in remote sensing applications.

2.1 IHS color model

IHS method consists on transforming the R,G and B bands of the multispectral image into IHS components, replacing the intensity component by the panchromatic image, and performing the inverse transformation to obtain a high spatial resolution multispectral image (Schowengerdt, 2007; Carper et al., 1990).
The three multispectral bands, R, G and B, of a low resolution image are first transformed to the IHS color space as (Carper et al., 1990):

$$\begin{pmatrix} I \\ V_1 \\ V_2 \end{pmatrix} = \begin{pmatrix} \frac{1}{3} & \frac{1}{3} & \frac{1}{3} \\ \frac{1}{\sqrt{6}} & \frac{1}{\sqrt{6}} & -\frac{2}{\sqrt{6}} \\ \frac{1}{\sqrt{2}} & -\frac{1}{\sqrt{2}} & 0 \end{pmatrix} \begin{pmatrix} R \\ G \\ B \end{pmatrix} \tag{1}$$

$$H = tan^{-1}\left(\frac{V_2}{V_1}\right) \quad (2)$$

$$S = \sqrt{{V_1}^2 + {V_2}^2} \quad (3)$$

where I, H , S components are intensity, hue and saturation, and V_1 and V_2 are the intermediate variables. Fusion proceeds by replacing component I with the panchromatic high-resolution image information, after matching its radiometric information with the component I (Figure 1). The fused image, which has both rich spectral information and high spatial resolution, is then obtained by performing the inverse transformation from IHS back to the original RGB space as

$$\begin{pmatrix} R \\ G \\ B \end{pmatrix} = \begin{pmatrix} 1 & \frac{1}{\sqrt{6}} & \frac{1}{\sqrt{2}} \\ 1 & \frac{1}{\sqrt{6}} & -\frac{1}{2} \\ \frac{11}{\sqrt{2}} & -\frac{2}{\sqrt{6}} & 0 \end{pmatrix} \begin{pmatrix} I \\ V_1 \\ V_2 \end{pmatrix} \quad (4)$$

Although the IHS method has been widely used, the method cannot decompose an image into different frequencies in frequency space such as higher or lower frequency. Hence the IHS method cannot be used to enhance certain image characteristics (Shi et al., 2005). Besides, the color distortion of IHS technique is often significant. To reduce the color distortion, the PAN image is matched to the intensity component before the replacement or the hue and saturation components are stretching before the reverse transform. Ling et al. (2007) also propose a method that combines a standard IHS transform with FFT filtering of both the panchromatic image and the intensity component of the original multispectral image to reduce color distortion in the fused image.

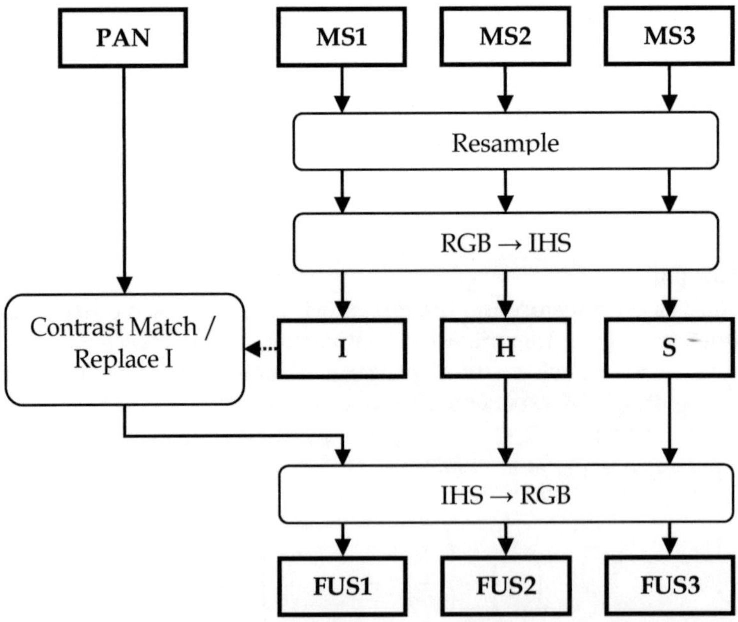

Fig. 1. Block scheme of the IHS fusion method.

2.2 Principal Components Analysis (PCA)

The fusion method based on PCA is very simple (Chavez & Kwakteng, 1989; Schowengerdt, 2007; Zhang, 1999). PCA is a general statistical technique that transforms multivariate data with correlated variables into one with uncorrelated variables. These new variables are obtained as linear combinations of the original variables. PCA has been widely used in image encoding, image data compression, image enhancement and image fusion. In the fusion process, PCA method generates uncorrelated images (PC1, PC2, …, PCn, where n is the number of input multispectral bands). The first principal component (PC1) is replaced with the panchromatic band, which has higher spatial resolution than the multispectral images. Afterwards, the inverse PCA transformation is applied to obtain the image in the RGB color model as shown in Figure 2.

In PCA image fusion, dominant spatial information and weak color information is often a problem (Zhang, 2002). The first principal component, which contains maximum variance, is replaced by PAN image. Such replacement maximizes the effect of panchromatic image in the fused product. One solution could be stretching the principal component to give a spherical distribution. Besides, the PCA approach is sensitive to the choice of area to be fused. Other problem is related to the fact that the first principal component can be also significantly different from the PAN image. If the grey values of the PAN image are adjusted to the grey values similar to PC1 component before the replacement, the color distortion is significantly reduced.

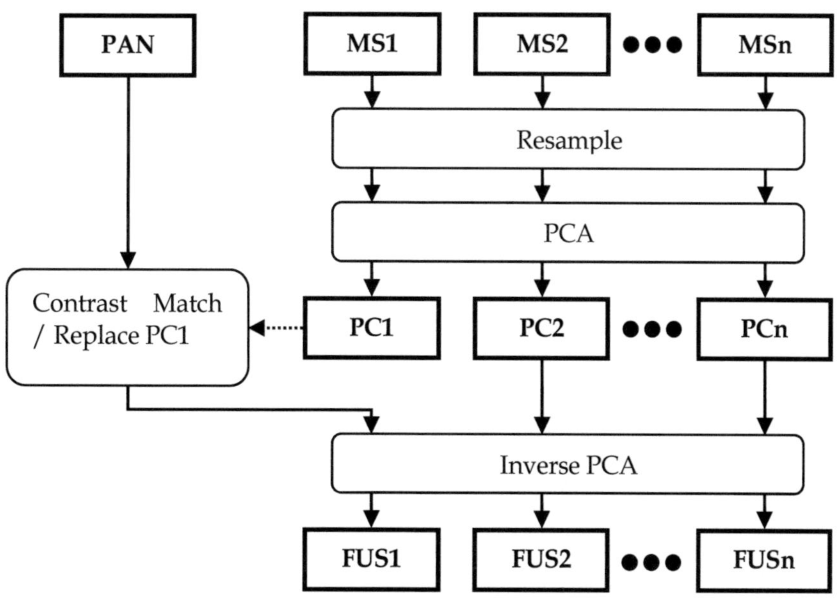

Fig. 2. Block scheme of the PCA fusion method.

2.3 Arithmetic combination

In accord to Zhang (2002), different arithmetic combinations such as Brovey Transform, Synthetic Variable Ratio (SVR) and Ratio Enhancement (RE) techniques have been employed for fusing multispectral and panchromatic images (Rahman & Csaplovics, 2007).

In the Brovey method, given the multispectral MS_i (i=1,2,3) and PAN images, the fused image FUS_i, for each band, is obtained as

$$FUS_i = \frac{MS_i}{\sum_{i=1}^{n} MS_i} \times PAN \qquad (5)$$

The Brovey Transform was developed to provide contrast in features such shadows, water and high reflectance areas. Consequently, the Brovey Transform should not be used if preserving the original scene radiometry is important. However, it is good to produce RGB images with a higher degree of contrast and visually appealing images (ERDAS, 2011).
Other arithmetic methods such as SVR and RE are similar and involve more computations for the simulated image (Chavez et al., 1991).

2.4 Wavelet Transform (WT)

In the fusion methods based on wavelet transform (Mallat, 1989), the images are decomposed into pyramid domain, in which coefficients are selected to be fused (Garguet-Duport et al., 1996). The two source images are first decomposed using wavelet transform. Wavelet coefficients from MS approximation subband and PAN detail subbands are then combined together, and the fused image is reconstructed by performing the inverse wavelet transform (Figure 3). Since the distribution of coefficients in the detail subbands have mean zero, the fusion result does not change the radiometry of the original multispectral image (Li et al., 2002). The simplest method is based on the selection of the higher value coefficients, but various other methods have been proposed in the literature (Amolins et al., 2007; Chen et al., 2005; Chibani & Houacine, 2000, 2003 ; Choi et al., 2005; Garzelli & Nencini, 2005; Ioannidou & Karathanassi, 2007; Li et al., 2002; Li et al., 2005; Lillo-Saavedra et al., 2005; Pajares & de la Cruz, 2004; Shi et al., 2005; Zhou et al., 1998).
The schemes used to decompose the images are based on decimated (Mallat, 1989) and undecimated algorithms (Lang et al., 1995, González-Audicana et al., 2005). In the decimated algorithm, the signal is down-sampled after each level of transformation. In the case of a two-dimensional image, down-sampling is performed by keeping one out of every two rows and columns, making the transformed image one quarter of the original size and half the original resolution (Amolins et al., 2007). In the lower level of decomposition, four images are produced, one approximation image and three detail images. The decimated algorithm is not shift-invariant, which means that it is sensitive to shifts of the input image. The decimation process also has a negative impact on the linear continuity of spatial features that do not have a horizontal or vertical orientation. These two factors tend to introduce artifacts when the algorithm is used in applications such as image fusion (Amolins et al., 2007).
On the other hand, the undecimated algorithm addresses the issue of shift-invariance. It does so by suppressing the down-sampling step of the decimated algorithm and instead up-sampling the filters by inserting zeros between the filter coefficients. The undecimated algorithm is redundant, meaning some detail information may be retained in adjacent levels of transformation. It also requires more space to store the results of each level of transformation and, although it is shift-invariant, it does not resolve the problem of feature orientation (González-Audícana et al., 2005 ; Garzelli & Nencini, 2005).
Most methods based on wavelet transform exploits the context dependency by thresholding the local correlation coefficient between the images to be merged, to avoid injection of spatial details that are not likely to occur in the high spatial image (Choi et al., 2005; Li et al.,

2005; Lillo-Saavedra & Gonzalo, 2006; Song et al., 2007; Ventura et al., 2002; Yang et al., 2007). These techniques seem to reduce the color distortion problem and to keep the statistical parameters invariable.

Zhou et al. (1998) compared a fusion method based on wavelet transform with IHS, PCA and Brovey transform to merge Landsat TM and SPOT panchromatic image. They conclude that with the wavelet merging method it is easy to control the trade-off between the spectral information from a low spatial-high spectral resolution sensor and the spatial structure from a high spatial-low spectral resolution sensor. They also showed that simultaneous best spectral and spatial quality can only be achieved with wavelet transform methods compared with the other approaches.The main drawback consists on the selection of the coefficients to be merged.

In accord to Zhang (2002), although the color distortion is reduced in the WT fusion methods, the colors seem not being smoothly integrated into the spatial features. Besides, some researchers have reported the loss of spectral content of small objects.

Pajares & de la Cruz (2004) conclude that when the images are smooth, without abrupt intensity changes, the wavelets work appropriately, improving the results of the classical methods. This has been verified with smooth images and also with medical images, where no significant changes are present. In this case, the type of images (remote sensing, medical) is irrelevant.

Other researchers have proposed alternative methods, which present some improvements, especially for holding spectral information, texture information, and contour information (Chai et al., 2010; Guo et al., 2010; Jing & Cheng, 2010; Miao et al., 2011; Yang & Jiao, 2008). Miao et al. (2011) stated that detail information can be easily caught when the images are decomposed by shearlet transform in any scale and any direction. Guo et al. (2010) proposed an approach based on Expectation Maximization (EM) and Covariance Intersection (CI) models for image fusion. The ideal MS and PAN images are estimated by EM along with the covariance matrices of the estimation error. Then, CI is applied to combine the two images

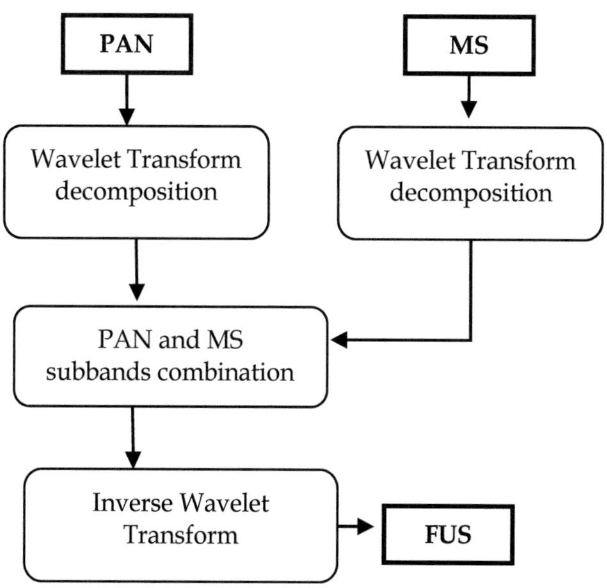

Fig. 3. Block scheme of the WT fusion method.

and provide a consistent estimate of the high-resolution MS image. Comparing with WT and PCA methods, the proposed EM–CI method preserves more significant spectral information at the cost of slightly lower improvement on spatial quality.

3. Methods for fused image quality assessment

Some researchers have evaluated different image fusion methods using different image quality measures (Alparone et al., 2004; Alparone et al., 2007; Amolins et al., 2007; Chavez et al., 1991; González-Audícana et al., 2005; Guo et al., 2010; Laporterie-Dejean et al., 2005; Marcelino et al., 2003; Nikolakopoulos, 2005; Wald, 2000; Wang & Bovik, 2002). Generally, the goodness of an image-fusion method can be evaluated by comparing the resulting merged image with a reference image, which is assumed to be ideal. This comparison can be based on spectral and spatial characteristics, and can be done both visually and quantitatively. Unfortunately, the reference image is not always available in practice, thus, it is necessary to simulate it or to perform a quantitative and blind evaluation of the fused images.

For assessing quality of an image after fusion, some aspects must be defined. These include, for instance, spatial and spectral resolution, quantity of information, visibility, contrast, or details of features of interest (Shi et al., 2005). Quality assessment is application dependant so that different applications may require different aspects of image quality.

Generally, image assessment methods can be divided into two classes: qualitative (or subjective) and quantitative (or objective) methods. Qualitative methods involve visual comparison between a reference image and the fused image whereas quantitative analysis involves quality indicators that measures spectral and spatial similarity between multispectral and fused images. Some of them will be briefly described below.

3.1 Qualitative analysis

This section is based on Shi et al. (2005). According to prior assessment criteria or individual experiences, personal judgment or even grades can be given to the quality of an image. The interpreter analyzes the tone, contrast, saturation, sharpness, and texture of the fused images. A final overall quality judgment can be obtained by, for example, a weighted mean based on the individual grades. This is the so called the mean opinion score (MOS) method (Wei et al., 1999). The qualitative method mainly includes absolute and the relative measures (Table 1). This method depends on the specialist's experiences or bias and some uncertainty is involved. Qualitative measures cannot be represented by rigorous mathematical models, and their technique is mainly visual (Shi at al., 2005).

Grade	Absolute measure	Relative measure
1	Excellent	The best in group
2	Good	Better than the average level in group
3	Fair	Average level in group
4	Poor	Lower than the average level
5	Very poor	The lowest in the group

Table 1. Objective method for image quality assessment (Shi et al., 2005)

3.2 Quantitative analysis

Some quality indicators include (a) average grey value, for representing intensity of an image, (b) standard deviation, information entropy, profile intensity curve for assessing details of fused images, and (c) bias and correlation coefficient for measuring distortion between the original image and fused image in terms of spectral information.

Let F_i and $R_i = (i = 1, \cdots, N)$ be the N bands of the fused and reference images, respectively. The following indicators are used to determine the difference in spectral information between each band of the merged and reference images (González-Audicana, 2004, Guo et al., 2010):

1. Correlation Coefficient (*CC*) between the reference and the merged image that should be close to 1 as possible;
2. Difference between the means of the reference and the merged images (*DM*), in radiance as well as its value relative to the mean of the original. The smaller these difference are, the better the spectral quality of the merged image. Thus, the difference value should be as close to 0 as possible;
3. Standard deviation of the difference image (*SSD*), relative to the mean of the reference image expressed in percentage. The lower its value, the better the spectral quality of the merged image.
4. Universal Image Quality Indicator - UIQI (Wang & Bovik, 2002):

$$UIQI = \frac{4\sigma_{F_iR_i} \cdot \mu_{F_i} \cdot \mu_{R_i}}{\left(\sigma_{F_i}^2 + \sigma_{R_i}^2\right)\left[\left(\mu_{F_i}\right)^2 + \left(\mu_{R_i}\right)^2\right]} \qquad (6)$$

   where $\sigma_{F_iR_i}$ is the covariance between the band of reference image and the band of fused image, μ and σ are the mean and standard deviation of the images. The higher UIQI index, the better spectral quality of the merged image. Wang & Bovik (2002) suggest the use of moving windows of different sizes to avoid errors due to index spatial dependence.

To estimate the global spectral quality of the merged image, one can use the following parameters:

1. The relative average spectral error index (RASE) characterizes the average performance of the method for all bands:

$$RASE = \frac{1}{\mu}\sqrt{\frac{1}{N}\sum_{i=1}^{N}\left(DM^2(R_i) + SSD^2(R_i)\right)} \qquad (7)$$

   where μ is the mean radiance of the N spectral bands (R_i) of the reference image. *DM* and *SSD* are defined above in the text.
2. Relative global dimensional synthesis error (ERGAS) (Wald, 2000):

$$ERGAS = 100\frac{h}{l}\sqrt{\frac{1}{N}\sum_{i=1}^{N}\left(\frac{DM^2(R_i) + SSD^2(R_i)}{\mu_i^2}\right)} \qquad (8)$$

   where h and l are the resolution of the high and low spatial resolution images, respectively, and μ_i is the mean radiance of each spectral band involved in the fusion process. *DM* and *SSD* are defined above in the text. The lower the values of RASE and ERGAS indexes, the higher the spectral quality of the merged images.

A good fusion method must allow the addition of a high degree of the spatial detail of the PAN image into the MS image. Visually the details information can be observed. However, the spatial quality of the merged images can be measured using the procedure proposed by Zhou et al. (1998):

- The PAN and merged images are filtered using the Laplacian Filter

$$\begin{vmatrix} -1 & -1 & -1 \\ -1 & 8 & -1 \\ -1 & -1 & -1 \end{vmatrix}$$

- Calculate the correlation between the filtered merged image and the filtered PAN image. The high correlation value indicates that the spatial information of the PAN image has been injected into the MS image in the fusion process.

Guo et al. (2010) use the average gradient index (AG) for spatial quality evaluation. AG describes the changing feature of image texture and the detailed information. Larger values of the AG index correspond to higher spatial resolution. The AG index of the fused images at each band can be computed by

$$AG = \frac{1}{KL}\sum_{m=1}^{K}\sum_{n=1}^{L}\sqrt{\frac{\left[\frac{\partial F(m,n)}{\delta m}\right]^2+\left[\frac{\partial F(m,n)}{\delta n}\right]^2}{2}} \quad (9)$$

where K and L are the number of lines and columns of the fused image F.

Other methods for assessing fusion quality have been proposed (Liu et al., 2008; Chen and Varshney, 2007; Zheng & Chin; 2009; Zheng et al., 2008; Chen & Blum, 2009; Wang et al., 2008). Liu et al. (2008) proposed two metrics based on a modified structural similarity measure (FSSIM) scheme and the local cross-correlation between the feature maps of the fused and input images. A similarity map with the fused image is generated for each input image. Then, the larger value at each location is retained for overall assessment. The second metric is implemented by computing the local cross-correlation between the phase congruency maps of the fused and input images. The index value is obtained by averaging the similarity or cross-correlation value in each predefined region. These metrics provide an objective quality measure in the absence of a reference image.

Chen & Varshney (2007) proposed a new quality metric for image fusion that does not require a reference image. It is based on local information given by a set of localized windows and by the difference in the frequency domain filtered by a contrast sensitivity function. The calculation is very simple and it is also applicable to different input modalities. The proposed metric is used to evaluate different fusion algorithms based on wavelet, averaging and Laplacian pyramid. The fusion performance is tested against several circumstances including: absence of noise, different window sizes, presence of additive Gaussian noise and for six sets of test images. In all tests, the fusion method based on wavelet transform outperformed the others.

Zheng & Chin (2009) have developed a structural similarity quality metric for image fusion which treats complementary and redundant regions in the original images. This objective quality evaluation also takes into account the amount of important information in the source images that can be transferred into the fused image. Comparisons with other standard objective quality metrics show that the proposed metric correlates well with subjective quality evaluation of the fused images, especially for input images where the complementary information and the redundant information can be well distinguished. They evaluate four image fusion methods based on arithmetic, PCA, and multi-resolution (MR) techniques using standard objective metrics. The results show that the current structural

similarity quality metric agrees with the subjective evaluation and three of the other standard structural metrics.
Chen & Blum (2009) propose a new perceptual image fusion quality assessment method motivated by human vision modeling. Generally, it is not possible to obtain an ideal image to be taken as a reference for fusion evaluation. Therefore, they measure the information present in the input images, which is transferred to the fused image to improve the fused image quality. For this, they filter the input images using a specified contrast sensitivity function; compute the local contrast; calculate the contrast preservation; generate a saliency map; and calculate the global quality measure.
Zhang (2008) has evaluated seven fusion quality metrics and the results showed that there was inconsistency between visual and quantitative image fusion quality analysis. Alparone et al. (2004) have got similar results. This inconsistency has proven that not all metrics produce reliable measurements for image fusion evaluation.

4. Applications for remote sensing imagery fusion

The availability of high spectral and spatial resolution images is desirable when undertaking identification studies in areas with complex morphological structure such as urban areas, heterogeneous forested areas or agricultural areas with a high degree of plot subsivision (González-Audicana et al., 2004). When this kind of images is not available one can produce images with higher spatial resolution using image fusion techniques.
Therefore, in this section we present three case studies in remote sensing applications to illustrate the use of fusion techniques for monitoring remaining forest, identifying landslide scars, and classifying intra-urban land cover. The first two applications use images acquired from CBERS-2B (CBERS, 2011) that are freely distributed on internet (INPE, 2011).

4.1 Monitoring of remaining forest using CBERS-2B images

An application that is still underused by the remote sensing community is the monitoring of remaining forest, which has an important role in ecological balance. However, traditional images of low and medium spatial resolution are not adequate for mapping forest fragments which occur along drainage channels and their boundaries.
Within this context, this study aims to evaluate a hybrid CBERS-2B image to map the remaining forest vegetation at Ibitinga, Brazil. This scene presents phytoplankton blooms on water areas and land use changes due to sugar cane plantation. CBERS-2B, launched in September 2007, has a high resolution panchromatic camera (HRC - High Resolution Camera), with spatial resolution of 2.7 m, a multispectral camera (CCD) with 20 meter spatial resolution, and a Wide Field Imager (WFI), with 260 m spatial resolution (CBERS, 2011).
To identify forest fragments we generate a hybrid product of 2.5 m spatial resolution from CCD and HRC images, acquired on 08/22/2008. The input images are shown in Figure 4. To evaluate the results from fused CBERS-2B images we used the Quickbird (QB) image of 09/01/2008, resampled to 2.5 m of spatial resolution. Table 2 presents the characteristics of HRC, CCD and QB sensors.
The CBERS-2B images are pre-processed using restoration (Fonseca et al., 1993), noise filtering and orthorectification procedures. Afterwards, the images are fused and classified

for mapping the remaining forest in the Ibitinga Resevoir. Figure 5 illustrates the hybrid CBERS-2B and QB images for purpose of comparison.

Characteristics	HRC-CBERS 2B	CCD – CBERS 2B	Quickbird
Multispectral bands (µm)	0.50 - 0,80 (Pan)	0.51 - 0.73 (Pan) 0.45 - 0.52 (Blue) 0.52 - 0.59 (Green) 0.63 - 0.69 (Red) 0.77 - 0.89 (IR)	0.45 – 0.90 (Pan) 0.45 – 0.52 (Blue) 0.52 – 0.60 (Green) 0.63 – 0.69(Red) 0.76 – 0.90 (IR)
Spatial Resolution	2.7 x 2.7 m	20 x 20 m	0.61 m (nadir) 2.44 m (nadir)
Swath width	27 km (nadir)	113 km (nadir)	16.5 km (nadir) 20.8 km (off- nadir)
Quantization	8 bits	8 bits	11 bits

Table 2. Data characteristics.

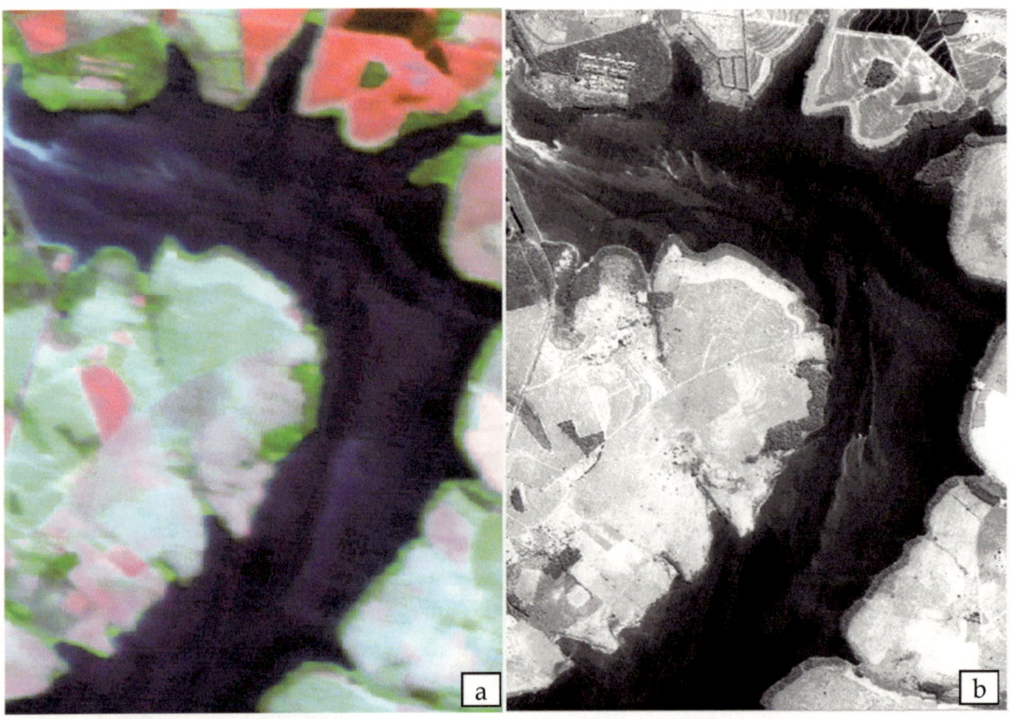

Fig. 4. CBERS-2B images: (a) filtered CCD image to reduce striping effects; (b) high resolution HRC image.

The hybrid product CBERS-2B and QB image are classified using maximum-likelihood method (SPRING, 2011). A total of 67 samples were selected: 33 for "Forest ", 12 for "bare soil" , 11 for "vegetation 1" and 11 samples for "vegetation 2". Theses classes were grouped to produce only two classes of interest ("forest" and "non-forest"), and the water body area was excluded in the thematic maps. In the thematic maps (Figure 6), green and beige colors represent forest and non-forest areas, respectively.

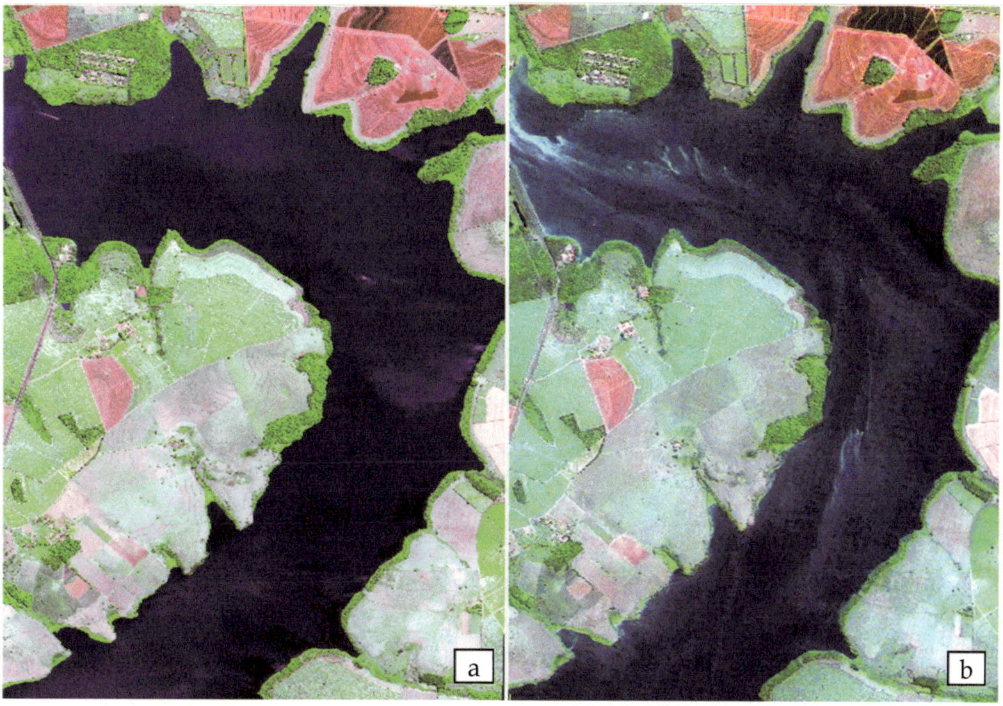

Fig. 5. Image Quickbird (a) and hybrid image produced by merging CBERS-2B CCD and HRC images (b), with 2.5 m spatial resolution.

Table 3 shows the overall accuracy and Kappa values for both classifications. The visual and quantitative analysis show that the results are quite similar. However, we observed that in some regions, the forest area was underestimated in the map produced by CBERS-2B product. The classification results differ mainly in the linear features and in the targets contours. Besides, the map obtained from the QB image shows isolated spots, particularly in areas of "high vegetation" (Figure 6a), not present in the map produced by CBERS-2B (Figure 6b).

Thematic maps	Overall accuracy	Kappa value
Hybrid CBERS-2B	0.93	0.83
QB	0.93	0.84

Table 3. Thematic map assessement.

Finally, the evaluation of hybrid products CBERS-2B for mapping of fragments of tree patches indicated that CBERS-2B images, after pre-processing and fusion processes, have potential for those applications in which QB images have been used.

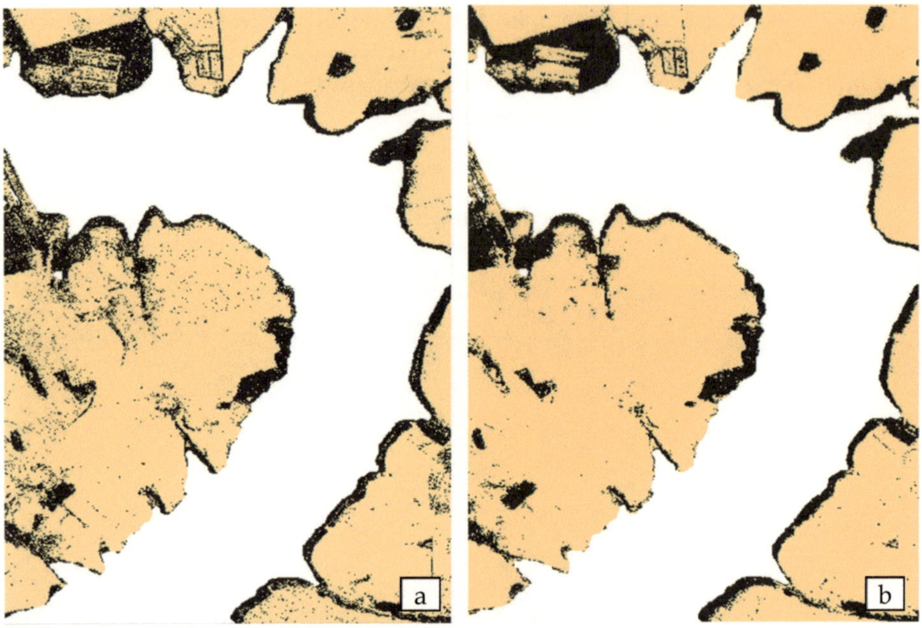

Fig. 6. Thematic maps produced for (a) QB image, and (b) CBERS-2B hybrid image. Forest and non-forest are represented by green and beige colours, respectively.

4.2 Image fusion techniques to identify landslide scars

Landslide is a fast mass movement responsible for the shape of montainous landscapes. These mass movements include a wide range of ground movement, such as rock falls, deep slopes and shallow debris flows. Although the action of gravity is the primary reason for the occurrence of this fenomenon, there are other contributing factors to start landslides such as lithology and structure, slope gradient and slope morphology, slope aspect, land-use type, etc (Dai & Lee, 2002).

The landslide mapping consists on the identification of erosion scars (loss of vegetation cover and soil horizons) on hillslope, using aerial photographies and and satellite images (Temesgen et al., 2001; Marcelino et al., 2003). Remote Sensing is a fundamental tool to detect, classify and monitor landslides because it allows one to obtain historical data series at a relatively low cost. Besides, various image processing techniques can be used to enhance the features and, thus, their identification is facilitated.

Considering this fact, we analyze two fusion methods for improving the interpretability of the CBERS-2B images to identify the scars of a landslide occurred in January, 2010, after heavy rains, which killed more than 20 people (BBC, 2010). The region covers an area of the Ilha Grande Island, Brazil (Figure 7). Hybrid images produced by image fusion techniques can be used to measure the extent of the landslide scar automatically or by a human interpreter.

The CCD and HRC images used in the methodology were acquired on February 21, 2010. The original CCD (RGB color composition: band 3 in red, band 4 in green and band 2 in blue) and HRC images are presented in Figure 8. We can observe the island Ilha Grande in the center of the image marked with a rectangle.The CCD images cover an area between longitude 44° 38´ west and longitude 43° 47´ west, and latitude 22° 42´ south and latitude 23° 50´ south; HRC image covers an area between longitude 44° 15´ west and longitude 44° 2´ west, and latitude 22° 57´ south and latitude 23° 14´ south.

Fig. 7. Landslide in Ilha Grande Brazil (BBC, 2010).

As the spatial resolution difference between CCD and HRC is large, firstly, we resample the CCD images to 10 meter spatial resolution by applying the restoration procedure (Fonseca et al., 1993). The restoration filter takes into account the spatial response of each sensor to resample and restore the image in a single processing step. Afterwards, the restored image (10 meter resolution) was resampled to 2.5 meters by a bilinear interpolation in order to match the pixel size of the HRC image.

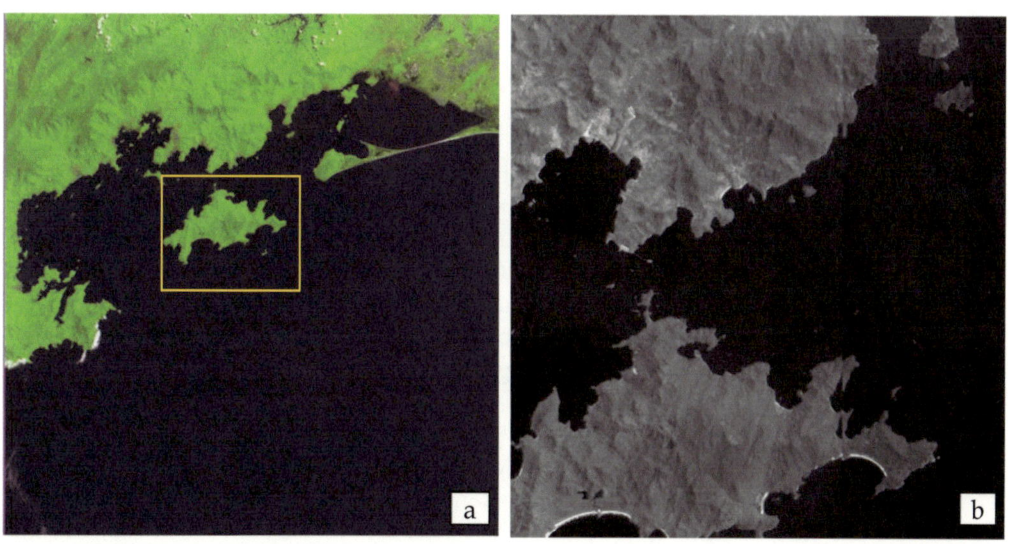

Fig. 8. CBERS-2B images acquired on February 21, 2010: (a) Color composition of CBERS-2B CCD images (b) HRC image.

The resampled CCD images and the HRC images were registered using control points and affine geometric transformation. Figure 9 presents a portion of the registered images, with the HRC image in gray levels and a strip of the corresponding region on the resampled CCD image, in order to demonstrate the quality of the registration procedure.

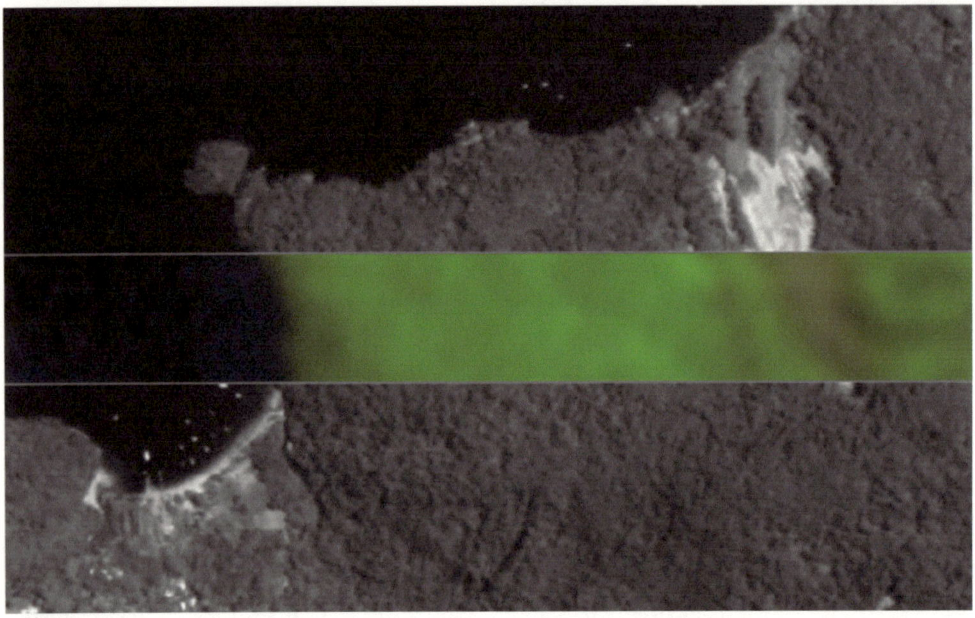

Fig. 9. CBERS-2B image registration: strip of CCD color image (R4G3B2) superimposed on HRC image.

Next, the registered CBERS-2B images were merged using IHS and PCA methods. A small portion around the landslide area of each original image and fused image was used in the fusion evaluation procedure. The original and fused images are displayed in Figure 10, with the landslide area shown on the right side images.

To evaluate the detail information injected into the hybrid image, we calculated the correlation between the original PAN image and the luminance component of the fused images. The fused images were converted from RGB to YIQ color space, where the Y luminance is calculated by the linear combination of the red, green, and blue components (Foley et al., 1993). Figure 11 shows the HRC and luminance images of the fused images.

The correlation values obtained for IHS and PCA fusion methods were 0.9982 and 0.9167, respectively. This indicates that fused image produced by IHS method is more similar to the PAN image in respect to the detail information. By visual analysis (Figure 11), we observe that the appearance of the luminance IHS image is quite similar to the PAN image.

To quantitatively evaluate the fusion results the UIQI metric (Wang & Bovik, 2002) was calculated for each band and their values are presented in Table 4. The values indicate that mean UIQI is almost the same for both methods PCA and IHS. Band 2 showed better result for PCA while UIQI values for Band 3 and Band 4 were higher for IHS than for PCA. Despite of these results, visually we observed significant color distortion in the landslide scar area in the IHS hybrid image. This indicates that PCA hybrid image is more adequate for analyzing the landslide in this case.

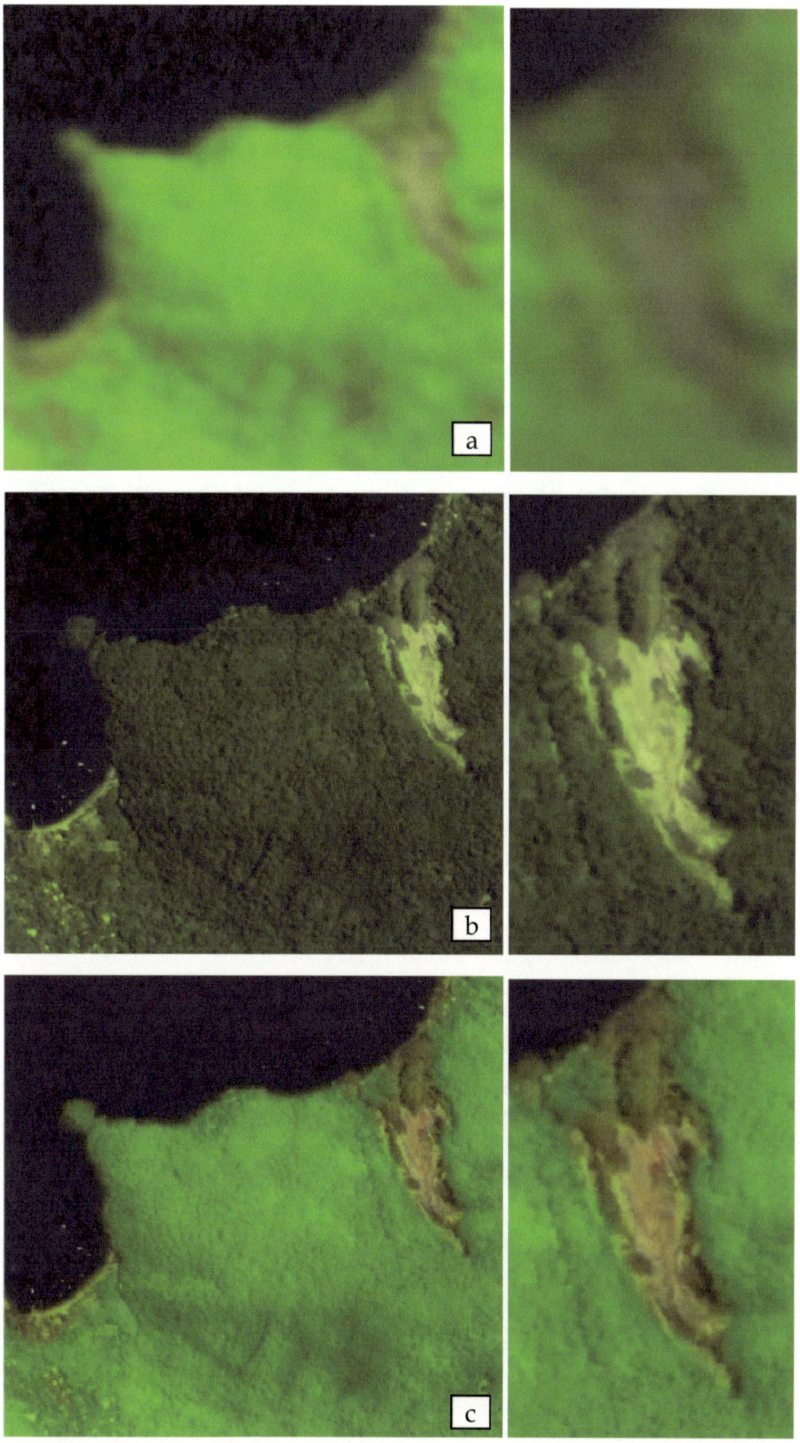

Fig. 10. Fused images: (a) original CCD image after restoration and resampling to 2.5 meter pixel size; (b) IHS fusion, and (c) PCA fusion.

	UIQI			Mean UIQI
Fusion	**Band 2**	**Band 3**	**Band 4**	
HSL	0.59	0.89	0.85	0.77
PCA	0.77	0.84	0.80	0.78

Table 4. UIQI index obtained for the fused images.

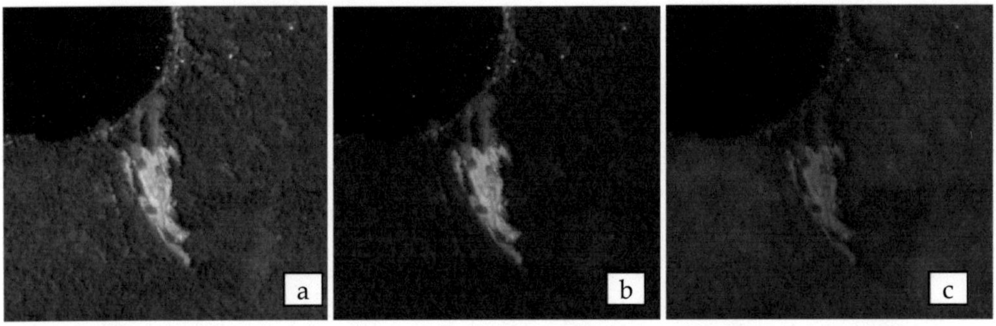

Fig. 11. HRC (a) and luminance images obtained from IHS (b) and PCA (c) fused images.

4.3 Intra-urban land cover classification from high-resolution images

Intra-urban land cover classification of high spatial resolution images provides a useful set of information for urban management and planning (Meinel et al., 2001). With this type of data, it is possible to generate information for many applications, such as analysis of urban micro-climate and urban greening maps amongst others. The usage of automatic methods to classify high spatial resolution images faces the challenge of processing images with wide intra- and inter-classes spectral variability.

This section presents a case study for intra-urban land cover classification of Quickbird imagery for the city of São José dos Campos - SP, southeast of Brazil, which is based on researches of Almeida et al. (2007) and Pinho et al. (2008). The total and urban areas of the São José dos Campos municipality cover about 1,099.60 and 298.99 square kilometers, respectively. The selected region is in the southern part of the urban area and contains a great variety of intra-urban land cover classes.

The QB images (Ortho-ready Standard 2A) used in this experiment consist of: a panchromatic image (0.6 m) and a multispectral image (2.4 m) with 4 bands (blue, green, red, and infrared) (Table 2). The images acquired on May 17, 2004 have an off-nadir incidence angle of 7.0º and a radiometric resolution of 11 bits. Figure 12 shows the panchromatic and multispectral images.

The hybrid images are segmented before the classification process. The segmentation approach selected is based on region growing and a multi-resolution procedure, in which the similarity measure depends on scale since segmentation parameters are weighted by the objects size (Baatz, 2000). The user defined four segmentation parameters: scale, weight for each spectral band, weight for color and shape, and weight for smoothness and compactness. Figure 13 shows segmentation results for three different scales of processing.

The fusion method used here is based on PCA since it has shown good results in urban analysis with high resolution images (Novack et al., 2008). The processing resulted in four images with spectral information similar to those of the original bands (blue, green, red and infrared) and spatial resolution equal to that of the panchromatic image (0.6 m). Figure 14 shows a small region of the panchromatic, multispectral, and fused images.

The classification phase was carried out using the decision tree method. The following attributes were selected in the training phase: brightness, hue channel mean, means of bands, belonging to super-object Block, maximum value in band 1, NDVI (Vegetation Index), ratio between bands 3 and 1, ratio between band 2 and the mean of all others, and difference mean for band 1. Figure 15 shows the original multispectral image and the resultant classification.

Fig. 12. Quickbird satellite scene acquired on 05/17/2004: (a) panchromatic image (0.6 m), and (b) multispectral image (2.4 m), (band 3 in red, band 2 in green and band 1 in blue).

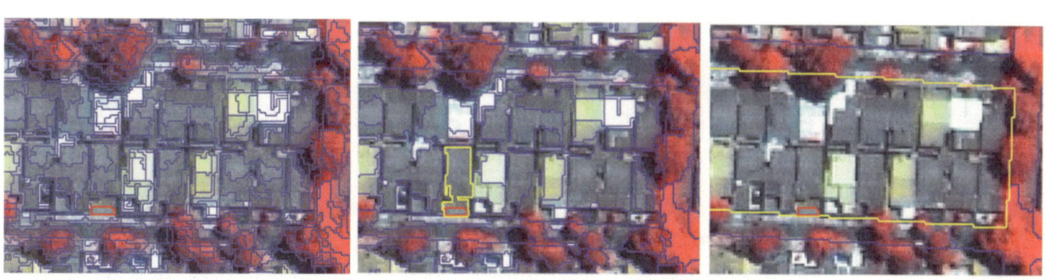

Fig. 13. Segmentation results for three different scales of processing.

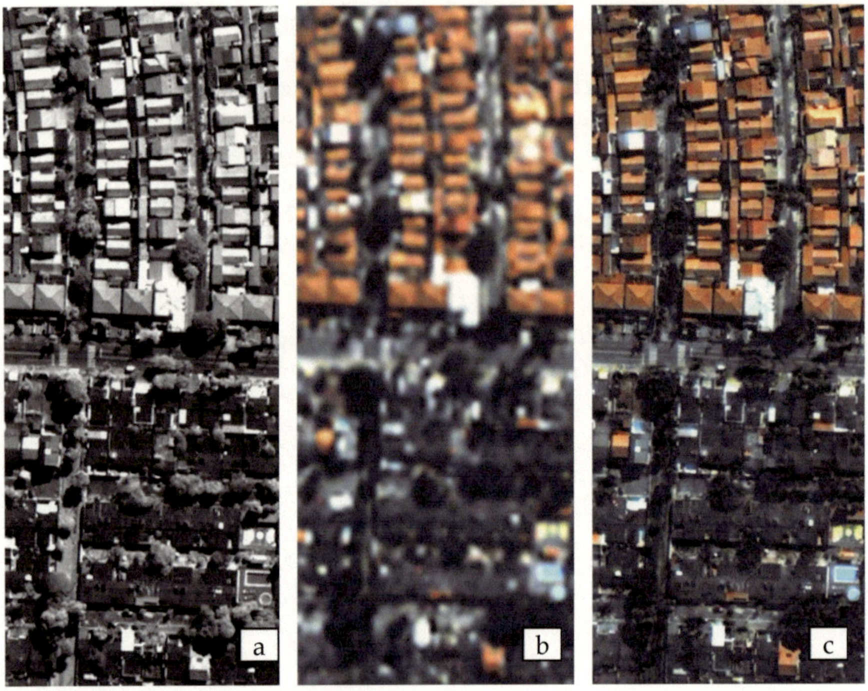

Fig. 14. A small region of the (a) panchromatic image (0.6 m), (b) multispectral image (2.4 m), and (c) fused image (0.6 m).

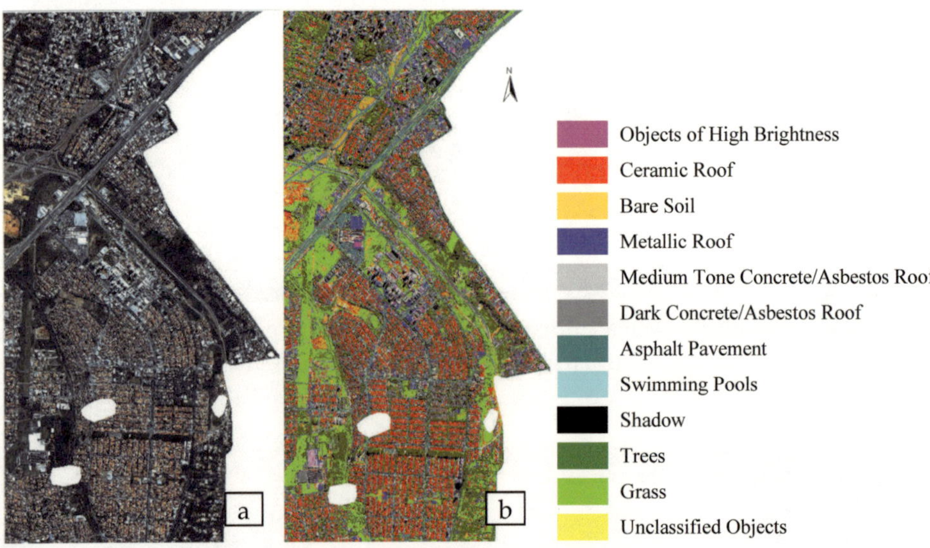

Fig. 15. Intra-urban classification: (a) original color image, and (b) thematic map.

The visual analysis of the classification indicates confusion between Ceramic Roof and Bare Soil classes while other classes are fairly well separated. Figure 16 illustrates the confusion between these classes in a small region. Quantitative classification accuracy assessment using error matrix indicates a good classification with Kappa value of 0.57. A conditional producer Kappa indicates lower values for Ceramic Roof and Bare Soil classes as expected from the visual analysis.

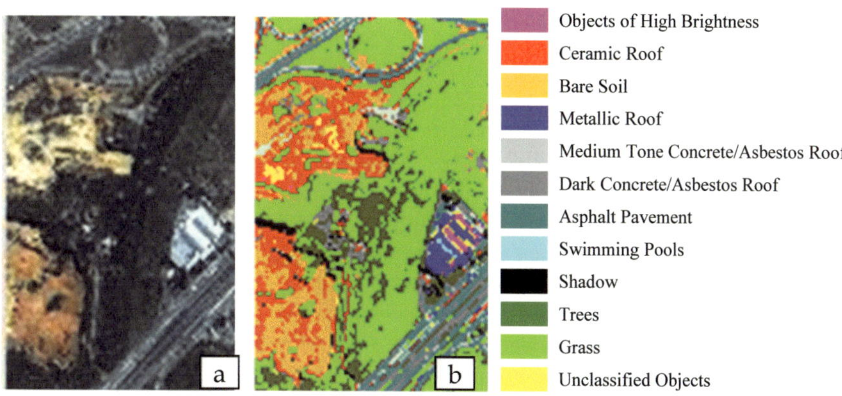

Fig. 16. Portion of the (a) true color image, and (b) thematic map showing the confusion between Ceramic Roof and Bare Soil classes.

5. Conclusion

Due to the advances in satellite technology, a great amount of image data has been available and has been widely used in different remote sensing applications. Thus, image data fusion has become a valuable tool in remote sensing to integrate the best characteristics of each sensor data involved in the processing.

To provide guidelines about the use of fusion techniques, we presented a brief review about fusion image techniques and fusion assessment methods that is illustrated with three case studies in remote sensing applications. Since there are a lot of fusion methods proposed in the literature only a few examples, mainly those applied for merging satellites images, were discussed in this work.

Indeed, there is not a unique method that is adequate for every data and application. The fusion quality often depends upon the user's experience, the fusion method, and upon the data set being fused. The objective of a fusion process is to generate a hybrid image with the highest possible spatial information content while still preserving good spectral information quality. Unfortunately, this task is not easy. One solution proposed in the literature is to combine different fusion methods in a single framework.

Despite the great number of fusion possibilities the most traditional methods such as PCA and IHS are still very used in remote sensing applications. This can be explained by the fact that most image processing systems have them implemented, and in many applications they have provided good results. Therefore, even if you have many fusion options it may be worth to test and evaluate some of them for the application of interest. Besides, the assistance of an interpreter in the fusion process is fundamental to guarantee the good quality of the final product

6. Acknowledgment

The authors would like to thank Imagem Soluções Inteligência Geográfica (www.img.com.br) for providing Quickbird images, and INPE for supporting our work.

7. References

Almeida, C.M., Souza, I.M.E., Alves, C.D., Pinho, C.M.D., Pereira, M.N. & Feitosa, R.Q. (2007) Multilevel Object-Oriented Classification of Quickbird Images for Urban Population Estimates. In: *15th ACM International Symposium on Advances in Geographic Information Systems* (ACM GIS 2007), 2007, Seattle.

Alparone, L., Aiazzi, B., Baronti, A., Garzelli, A. & Nencini, P.(2004). A Golbal Quality Measurement of Pan-Sharpened Multispectral Imagery. *IEEE Geoscience and Remote Sensing Letters*, Vol. 1, No. 4, (October 2004), pp. 313-317. ISSN 1545-598X

Alparone, L., Wald, L., Chanussot, J., Thomas, C., Gamba, P. & Bruce, L.M. (2007). Comparison of Pansharpening Algorithms Outcome of the 2006 GRS-S Data-Fusion Contest. *IEEE Transactions on Geoscience and Remote Sensing*, Vol.45, No.10, (October 2007), pp.3012-3021, ISSN 0196-2892

Amolins, K., Zhang, Y. & Dare, P.(2007). Wavelet based image fusion techniques - An introduction, review and comparison. *ISPRS Journal of Photogrammetry and Remote Sensing*, Vol.62, No.4, (September 2007), pp.249-263, ISSN 0924-2716

Baatz, A. (2000). Multiresolution Segmentation-an optimization approach for high quality multi-scale image segmentation. *Angewandte Geographische Informationsverarbeitung XII*, Wichmann-Verlag, Heidelberg, v. 12, p. 12-23.

BBC. (2010, January 2). Deaths from Brazil Ilha Grande resort mudslide reach 26. In : *BBC News*, February 25, 2011, Available from: news.bbc.co.uk/2/hi/8438096.stm

Cao, W., Li, B. & Zhang, Y. (2003). A remote sensing image fusion method based on PCA transform and wavelet packet transform. *Proceedings of the 2003 International Conference on Neural Networks and Signal Processing*, Vol.2, pp.976-981 , Toulouse, France, 2003.

Carper, W., Lillesand, T. & Kiefer, R. (1990). The use of intensity-hue-saturation transformations for merging spot panchromatic and multispectral image data. *Photogrammetric Engineering and Remote Sensing*, Vol.56, No.4, (April 1990), pp.459-467, ISSN 0099-1112

CBERS (2011). CBERS, China-Brazil Earth Resources Satellite . April 5, 2011, Available from: http://www.cbers.inpe.br

Chai, Y., Li, H.F. & Qu, J.F. (2010). Image fusion scheme using a novel dual-channel PCNN in lifting stationary wavelet domain. *Optics Communications*, Elsevier, v. 283, n. 19, pp. 3591–3602.

Chavez, P.S. & Kwakteng, A.Y. (1989). Extracting spectral contrast in Landsat Thematic Mapper image data using selective principal component analysis. *Photogrammetric Engineering and Remote Sensing*, Vol.55, No.3, (March 1989), pp.339-348, ISSN 0099-1112

Chavez, P.S., Sides, S.C. & Anderson, J.A. (1991). Comparison of three different methods to merge multiresolution and multispectral data: Landsat TM and SPOT panchromatic. *Photogrammetric Engineering and Remote Sensing*, Vol.57, No.3 (March 1991), pp.295-303, ISSN 0099-1112

Chen, T., Zhang, J. & Zhang, Y. (2005). Remote sensing image fusion based on ridgelet transform. *Proceedings of the IEEE International Geoscience and Remote Sensing Symposium*, Vol.2, 2005, pp.1150-1153.

Chen, H. & Varshney, P.K. (2007). A human perception inspired quality metric for image fusion based on regional information. *Information Fusion*, Vol.8, No.2,(April 2007), pp.193-207, ISSN 1566-2535

Chen, Y. & Blum. R.S. (2009). A new automated quality assessment algorithm for image fusion. *Image and Vision Computing*, Vol.27, No.10, pp.1421-1432, ISSN 0262-8856

Chibani, Y. & Houacine, A. (2000). On the use of the redundant wavelet transform for multisensor image fusion. *Procedings of the 7th IEEE International Conference on Electronics, Circuits and Systems*, Vol.1, pp.442-445.

Chibani, Y. & Houacine, A. (2003). Redundant versus orthogonal wavelet decomposition for multisensor image fusion. *Pattern Recognition*, Vol.36, No.4, pp.879-887, ISSN 0031-3203

Choi, M., Kim, R.Y., Nam, M.R. & Kim, H.O. (2005). Fusion of multispectral and panchromatic satellite images using the curvelet transform. *IEEE Geoscience and Remote Sensing Letters*, Vol.2, No.2, (April 2005), pp.136-140, ISSN 1545-598X

Choi, M. (2006). A new intensity-hue-saturation fusion approach to image fusion with a tradeoff parameter. *IEEE Transactions on Geoscience and Remote Sensing*, Vol.44, No.6, (June 2006), pp.1672-1682, ISSN 0196-2892

Câmara, G., Souza, R.C.M., Freitas, U.M. & Garrido, J. (1996). SPRING: Integrating remote sensing and GIS by object-oriented data modeling. *Computers & Graphics*, Vol.20, No.3, pp.395-403, ISSN 0097-8493

Dai, F.C. & Lee, C.F. (2002). Landslide characteristics and slope instability modeling using GIS, Lantau Island, Hong Kong. *Geomorphology*, Vol.42, No.3-4, pp.213-228, ISSN 0169-555X

ERDAS Inc. (2011). *ERDAS – The Earth to Business Company*, 2011, Available from: http://www.erdas.com/Resources/ERDASFieldGuide.aspx

Foley, J.D., van Dam, A., Feiner, S.K., Hughes, J.F. & Phillips, R.L. (1993). *Introduction to Computer Graphics*. Addison-Wesley, ISBN 0-20-160921-5, Reading, USA

Fonseca, L.M.G., Prasad, G.S.S.D. & Mascarenhas N.D.A. (1993). Combined interpolation-restoration of Landsat images through FIR filter design techniques. *International Journal of Remote Sensing*, 1366-5901, Vol.14, No.13, pp.2547-2561, ISSN 0143-1161

Fonseca, L.M.G., Costa, M.H.M., Korting, T.S., Castejon, E. & Silva, F.C. (2008). Multitemporal image registration based on multiresolution decomposition. *Revista Brasileira de Cartografia*, Vol.60, No.3, (October 2008), pp.271 - 286, ISSN 0560-4613

Garguet-Duport, B., Girel, J., Chassery, J.M. & Pautou, G. (1996). The use of multiresolution analysis and wavelets transform for merging SPOT panchromatic and multispectral image data. *Photogrammetric Engineering and Remote Sensing*, Vol.62, No.9, (September 1996), pp.1057-1066, ISSN 0099-1112

Garzelli, A. & Nencini, F. (2005). Interband structure modeling for pan-sharpening of very high-resolution multispectral images. *Information Fusion*, Vol.6, No.3, (September 2005), pp.213-224, ISSN 1566-2535

González-Audicana, M., Saleta, J., Catalan, R. & Garcia, R. (2004). Fusion of multispectral and panchromatic images using improved IHS and PCA mergers based on wavelet decomposition. *IEEE Transactions on Geoscience and Remote Sensing*, Vol.42, No.6, (June 2004), pp.1291-1299, ISSN 0196-2892

González-Audicana, M., Otazu X., Fors, O. & Seco A. (2005). Comparison between Mallat´s and the ´à trous´ discrete wavelet transform based algorithms for the fusion of multispectral and panchromatic images. *International Journal of Remote Sensing*, Vol.26, No.3, pp.595-614, ISSN 0143-1161

Guo, Q., Chen, S., Leung, H. & Liu, S. (2010). Covariance intersection based image fusion technique with application to pansharpening in remote sensing. *Information Sciences*, Vol.180, No.18, pp.3434-3443, ISSN 0020-0255

INPE (2011). INPE image Catalog. February 25, 2011, Available from: http://www.dgi.inpe.br/CDSR/

Ioannidou, S. & Karathanassi, V. (2007). Investigation of the Dual-Tree Complex and Shift-Invariant DiscreteWavelet Transforms on Quickbird Image Fusion. *IEEE Geoscience and Remote Sensing Letters*, Vol.4, No.4, (January 2007), pp.166-170, ISSN 1545-598X

Jing, L. & Cheng, Q. (2009). Two improvement schemes of PAN modulation fusion methods for spectral distortion minimization. *International Journal of Remote Sensing*, Taylor & Francis Group, Vol. 30, No. 8, pp. 2119–2131, ISSN 0143-1161

Laporterie-Dejean, F., de Boissezon, H., Flouzat, G. & Lefevre-Fonollosa, M.J. (2005). Thematic and statistical evaluations of five panchromatic/multispectral fusion methods on simulated PLEIADES-HR images. *Information Fusion*, Vol.6, No.3, (September 2005), pp.193-212, ISSN 1566-2535

Li, S., Kwok, J.T. & Wang, Y. (2002). Using the discrete wavelet frame transform to merge Landsat TM and SPOT panchromatic images. *Information Fusion*, Vol.3, pp.17-23, ISSN 1566-2535

Li, Z., Jing, Z., Yang, X. & Sun, S. (2005). Color transfer based remote sensing image fusion using non-separable wavelet frame transform. *Pattern Recognition Letters*, Vol.26, No.13, pp.2006-2014, ISSN 0167-8655

Lillo-Saavedra, M., Gonzalo, C., Arquero, A. & Martinez, E. (2005). Fusion of multispectral and panchromatic satellite sensor imagery based on tailored filtering in the Fourier domain. *International Journal of Remote Sensing*, Vol.26, No.6, pp.1263-1268, ISSN 0143-1161

Lillo-Saavedra, M. & Gonzalo, C. (2006). Spectral or spatial quality for fused satellite imagery: a trade-off solution using the wavelet à trous´ algorithm. *International Journal of Remote Sensing*, Vol.27, No.7, pp.1453-1464, ISSN 0143-1161

Ling, Y., Ehlers, M., Usery, E.L. & Madden, M. (2007). FFT-enhanced IHS transform method for fusing high-resolution satellite images. *ISPRS Journal of Photogrammetry and Remote Sensing*, Vol.61, No.6, (February 2007), pp.381-392, ISSN 0924-2716

Ling, Y., Ehlers, M., Usery, E.L. & Madden, M. (2008). Effects of spatial resolution ratio in image fusion. *International Journal of Remote Sensing*, Vol.29, No.7, pp.2157-2167, ISSN 0143-1161

Liu, Z., Forsyth, D.S. & Laganiere, R. (2008). A feature-based metric for the quantitative evaluation of pixel-level image fusion. *Computer Vision and Image Understanding*, Vol.109, No.1, (January 2008), pp.56-68, ISSN 1077-3142

Marcelino, E.V., Ventura, F.N., Formaggio, A.R., Fonseca, L.M.G. & Rosa, A.N.C.S. (2003). Evaluation of image fusion techniques for the identification of landslide scars using satellite data. *Geografia*, Vol.28, No.3, pp.431-445, ISSN 0100-7912

Meinel, G., Neubert, M. & Reder, J. (2001). The potential use of very high resolution satellite data for urban areas – First experiences with IKONOS data, their classification and application in urban planning and environmental monitoring. In: Jürgens, C. (ed.): *Remote sensing of urban areas*. Regensburger Geographische Schriften 35, pp. 196-205.

Miao, Q., Shi, C., Xu, P., Yang, M. & Shi, Y. (2011). A novel algorithm of image fusion using shearlets. *Optics Communications*, Elsevier, Vol. 284, No.6, 2011, pp. 1540–1547.

Nikolakopoulos, K.G. (2005). Comparison of six fusion techniques for SPOT5 data. *Proceedings of the IEEE International Geoscience and Remote Sensing Symposium*, Vol.4, pp. 2811-2814.

Novack, T., Fonseca, L.M.G. & Kux, H.J. (2008). Quantitative comparison of segmentation results from ikonos images sharpened by different fusion and interpolation techniques In: *GEOBIA - Geo-Object Based Image Analysis Conference*, 2008, Calgary, 2008, GEOBIA - Geo-Object Based Image Analysis Conference, Calgary.

Pajares, G. & de la Cruz, J.M. (2004). A wavelet-based image fusion tutorial. *Pattern Recognition*, Vol.37, No.9, pp.1855-1872, ISSN 0031-3203

Pinho, C.M.D., Silva, F.C., Fonseca, L.M.G. & Monteiro, A.M.V. (2008). Urban Land Cover Classification from High-Resolution Images Using the C4.5 Algorithm. In: *XXI Congress of the International Society for Photogrammetry and Remote Sensing*, 2008, Beijing, Vol. XXXVII. Part B7, pp. 695-699.

Pohl, C. & Genderen, J.L.V. (1998). Multisensor image fusion in remote sensing: concepts, methods and applications. *International Journal of Remote Sensing*, Vol.19, No.5, pp.823-854, ISSN 0143-1161

Rahman, M.M. & Csaplovics, E.(2007). Examination of image fusion using synthetic variable ratio (SVR) technique, *International Journal of Remote Sensing*, 28: 15, pp. 3413-3424, ISSN 0143-1161

Research System, Inc. (2011). ENVI - Environment for Visualizing Images. In : *ENVI - Environment for Visualizing Images*, February 25, 2011, Available from: www.ittvis.com/ENVI

Schetselaar, E. M. (1998). Fusion by the IHS transform: should we use cylindrical or spherical coordinates? *International Journal of Remote Sensing*, Vol.19, No.4, pp.759-765, ISSN 0143-1161

Schowengerdt, R.A. (2007). *Remote Sensing: Models and Methods for Image Processing* (3rd. edition), Academic Press, ISBN 0-12-369407-8, San Diego, USA

Shi, W., Zhu, C., Tian, Y, & Nichol, J. (2005). Wavelet-based image fusion and quality assessment. *International Journal of Applied Earth Observation and Geoinformation*, Vol.6, pp.241-251

Li, S., Kwok, J.T & Wang, Y. (2002) Using the discrete wavelet frame transform to merge Landsat TM and SPOT panchromatic images. *Information Fusion* Vol. 3, Issue 1, March 2002, pp. 17-23.

Silva, F.C., Dutra, L.V., Fonseca, L.M.G. & Korting, T.S. (2007). Urban Remote Sensing Image Enhancement Using a Generalized IHS Fusion Technique. *Procedings of the Symposium on Radio Wave Propagation and Remote Sensing*, Rio de Janeiro, Brazil, 2007.

Simone, G., Farina, A., Morabito, F.C., serpico, S.B. & Bruzzone, L. (2002). Image fusion techniques for remote sensing applications. *Information fusion*, No.3, 2002, pp.3-15.

Song, H., Yu, S., Song, L. & Yang, X. (2007). Fusion of multispectral and panchromatic satellite images based on contourlet transform and local average gradient. *Optical Engineering*, Vol.46, No.2, (February 2007), 020502. doi:10.1117/1.2437125

SPRING. (2011). Georeferencing Information Processing System (SPRING). In : *SPRING, Georeferencing Information Processing System*, March 25, 2011, Available from www.dpi.inpe.br/spring/english/index.html

Temesgen, B., Mohammed, M.U. & Korme, T. (2001). Natural hazard assessment using GIS and remote sensing methods, with particular reference to the landslide in the Wondogenet area, Ethiopia. *Physics and Chemistry of the Earth, Part C*, Vol.26, No.9, pp.665-675.

TerraLib. (2011). GIS Classes and Functions libraries (TerraLib). In : *TerraLib. GIS Classes and Functions libraries*, February 25, 2011, Available from www.dpi.inpe.br/terralib

Tu, T.M., Su, S.C., Shyu, H.C. & Huang, P.S. (2001a). A new look at IHS-like image fusion methods. *Information Fusion*, Vol.2, No.3, pp.177-186, ISSN 1566-2535

Tu, T.M., Su, S.C., Shyu, H.C. & Huang, P.S. (2001b). Efficient intensity-hue-saturation-based image fusion with saturation compensation. *Optical Engineering*, Vol.40, No.5, 720 (2001); doi:10.1117/1.1355956

Tu, T.M., Huang, P.S., Hung, C.L. & Chang, C.P. (2004). A fast intensity-hue-saturation fusion technique with spectral adjustment for IKONOS imagery. *IEEE Geoscience and Remote Sensing Letters*, Vol.1, No.4, (October 2004), pp.309-312, ISSN 1545-598X

Tu, T.M., Cheng, W.C., Chang, C.P., Huang, P.S. & Chang, J.C. (2007). Best tradeoff for high-resolution image fusion to preserve spatial details and minimize color distortion. *IEEE Geoscience and Remote Sensing Letters*, Vol.4, No.2, (April 2007), pp.302-306, ISSN 1545-598X

Ventura, F.N., Fonseca, L.M.G. & Santa Rosa, A.N.C. (2002). Remotely sensed image fusion using the wavelet transform. *Proceedings of the International Symposium on Remote Sensing of Environment (ISRSE)*, Buenos Aires, 8-12, April, 2002, 4p.

Wald, L. (2000). Quality of high resolution synthesized images: is there a simple criterion. *Proceedings of the International Conference on Fusion of Earth Data*, pp.26-28.

Wald, L. (2002). *Data fusion: Definitions and Architectures - Fusion of Images of Diferent Spatial Resolutions*, Ecole des Mines de Paris, ISBN 2-911762-38-X, Paris, France

Wang, Q., Shen, Y. & Jin, J. (2008). Performance evaluation of image fusion techniques, In: *Image Fusion*, T. Stathaki, (Ed), Academic Press, ISBN 978-0-12-372529-5, Oxford, UK

Wang, Z. & Bovik, A.C. A universal image quality index. *IEEE Signal Processing Letters*, Vol.9, No.3, (March 2002), pp.81-84, ISSN 1070-9908

Wei, Z.G., Yuan, J.H. & Cai, Y.L., (1999). A picture quality evaluation method based on human perception. *Acta Electronica Sinica*, Vol.27, No.4, pp.79-82, ISSN 0372-2112

Yang, X.H., Jing, J.L., Liu, G., Hua, L.Z. & Ma, D.W. (2007). Fusion of multi-spectral and panchromatic images using fuzzy rule. *Communications in Nonlinear Science and Numerical Simulation*, Vol.12, No.7, pp.1334-1350.

Yang, X.H. & Jiao,L.C. (2008). Fusion Algorithm for Remote Sensing Images Based on Nonsubsampled Contourlet Transform. *Acta Automatica Sinica*, Elsevier, Vol. 34, No. 3, 2008, pp. 274-282.

Zhang, Y. (1999). A new merging method and its spectral and spatial effects. *International Journal of Remote Sensing*, Vol.20, No.10, pp.2003-2014, ISSN 0143-1161

Zhang, Y. (2002). Problems in the fusion of commercial high-resolution satellite, Landsat 7 images, and initial solutions. *Procedings of the Symposium on Geospatial Theory, Processing and Applications*, Vol. 34, Part 4, Ottawa, Canada, 2002.

Zhang, Y. (2004). Understanding image fusion. *Photogrammetric Engineering and Remote Sensing*, Vol.70, No.6, (June 2004), pp.657-661, ISSN 0099-1112

Zhang, Y. (2008). Methods for image fusion quality assessment- a review, comparison and analysis. *The International Archives of the Photogrammetry, Remote Sensing and Spatial Information Sciences*. Vol. XXXVII. Part B7. Beijing 2008, pp. 1101-1109.

Zheng, Y. & Qin, Z. (2009). Objective Image Fusion Quality Evaluation Using Structural Similarity. *Tsinghua Science & Technology*, Vol.14, No.6, (December 2009), pp.703-709, ISSN 1007-0214

Zhou, J., Civco, D.L. & Silander, J.A. (1998). A wavelet transform method to merge Landsat TM and SPOT panchromatic data. *International Journal of Remote Sensing*, Vol.19, No.4, pp.743-757, ISSN 0143-1161

10

Multitechnique Fusion of Imaging Data for Heterogeneous Materials

Kateryna Artyushkova, Jeffrey Fenton, Jabari Farrar and Julia E. Fulghum
University of New Mexico
USA

1. Introduction

Complete characterization of a complex multicomponent heterogeneous material requires information not only on the surface or bulk chemical components, but also on stereometric features such as size, distance, and heterogeneity in three-dimensional space. Probing vertical structures is equally important for nanocomposite materials with surface segregation, overlayers, concentration gradients or multiple layers. Such complexity of heterogeneous materials makes it difficult to uniquely distinguish between alternative morphologies using a single analytical method and routine data acquisition and analysis.

The combination of sputtering capabilities and high lateral resolution in images led to the wide spread use of three-dimensional imaging studies using Time-of-flight Secondary Ion Mass Spectrometry (TOF-SIMS). (Wucher et al., 2007; Delcorte, 2008; Jones et al., 2008; Rafati et al., 2008) Main drawback of this approach is limited quantitative information. X-ray Photoelectron Spectroscopy (XPS) has benefits of being quantitative and offers very similar capabilities in combining ion sputtering and imaging, and there have been a handful number of studies using this approach. (Gao et al., 2003; Artyushkova, 2010) Disadvantage of combining sputtering and imaging is its destructive nature and possibility of induced modification that may introduce artifacts within images.

XPS has the advantage of being one of the only surface analysis techniques that provides readily interpretable, surface-specific, chemical information, which is a core analytical method of choice in obtaining surface chemical composition. (Briggs & Grant, 2003) The development of commercial imaging XPS instrumentation has occurred in parallel with imaging developments in other spectroscopic techniques. Improved spatial resolution and decreased analysis time make it possible to correlate XPS analysis with a host of other imaging techniques which have comparable fields of view, but different information content from different depth levels. There is now some field of view (FOV) overlap between XPS and a variety of techniques, including Atomic Force Microscopy (AFM), imaging FTIR, confocal microscopy (CM), SIMS and Secondary Electron Microscopy (SEM). The overlapping FOVs for the techniques listed in Table 1 make correlative data analyses and a fusion of multiple analytical perspectives achievable and valuable for obtaining quantitative structural information in three dimensions.

Imaging using confocal microscopy provides three-dimensional, high-resolution, non-destructive imaging of sample features. (Fellers & Davidso; Pawley, 2006) Scanning permits many slices to be imaged and high resolution, three-dimensional volumes may be created for a variety of specimens in a non-destructive fashion. Topographic and phase imaging AFM may be used for obtaining topographical and chemical information from surface/air interface of materials. (Behrend et al., 1999; Garcia et al., 1999; Garcia & Perez, 2002) By using relatively large scanned areas, the AFM images can be correlated with XPS and CM.

Technique	**XPS**	**CM**	**AFM**
sampling depth	< 10 nm	<30 micron	topography
analysis area, spectra	15µm diam - 300x700µm	NA	NA
spatial resolution in images	2-15µm	0.2µm	Atomic
field of view (image)	200x200µm - 700 x700µm	variable	Up to 100 x100µm
optical microscope, availability	yes	yes	Yes
multidimensional data	yes (spectra-from-images)	yes	No
compatible with Matlab and ENVI	yes	yes	Yes
sample type and maximum size limitations	solid, insulators are OK <1 x 1'	optically transparent	solid, "smooth"
destructive	generally no	no	No
info-elemental	yes	no	No
info-chemical	yes	phase distribution	possible phase contrast
ease of quantification	yes	NA	NA
variable depth of analysis	yes	yes (depth res'n - 50-500 nm)	No

Table 1. Properties of analytical techniques of choice for image fusion

In recent years, a lot of research has been directed towards visualization of scientific data from various sophisticated, but unique visualization perspectives. (Adriaensens et al., 2000; Varshney, 2000; Peri, 2001; Viergever et al., 2001; Mahler, 2004; Artyushkova & Fulghum, 2005; Matsushita et al., 2007; Baum et al., 2008; Macii et al., 2008; Rieder et al., 2008; Ropinski et al., 2009; Artyushkova, 2010) This includes problem of visualizing data from multiple modalities (multimodal) and visualizing data by combining perspectives within the same modality (unimodal). In multimodal visualization image data from different sensors that use different physical principles are combined to form a new image that contains more interpretable information that could be gained using the original information.

Category of benefit	General Benefit	Example
Extended spatial coverage	One method can look where another cannot	Confocal - depth slicing; XPS - surface 10 nm, AFM - the very surface
Different types of information	Different properties samples - better understanding of chemistry	Multiple methods
Increased confidence	One or more methods can confirm the same observation	Multiple methods

Table 2. Benefits of technique fusion

Data fusion is concerned will the problem of how to combine data from multiple sensors to perform inferences that may not be possible from a single method alone. Benefits of technique fusion are shown in Table 2. Combining data acquired from the same area on a sample by different techniques should reveal more information than would be obtained if each data type was processed separately. Fusing imaging data from XPS, CM and AFM will be discussed in the current chapter for the purpose of obtaining fused volume representing quantitative structural morphological information from multicomponent heterogeneous systems, such as polymer blends. For such direct correlative studies, a variety of issues must be addressed. The techniques sampling properties, including sampling depth, field of view, spatial resolution and image information content must be considered in designing experiments that result in the acquisition of data from the same area. Correlating the data requires area marking, image matching, feature selection, image alignment, image registration and, finally, image fusion.

2. Experimental

2.1 Material preparation

Poly (vinyl chloride) (PVC), poly (methyl methacrylate) (PMMA) were used as received from Scientific Polymer Products, Inc. Fluorescein-labeled poly(styrene) (PS*) (excitation λ= 494 nm, emission λ = 518 nm) and poly(butadiene) (PB, MW = 233.0 kDa) were obtained from Polysciences, Inc. MEH-PPV (Poly(2-methoxy-5-(2′-ethyl-hexyloxyl)-p-phenylene vinylene of 1000kDa was used as received from from H.W. Sands Corporation.

For PVC/PMMA blends, films were prepared by combining the PMMA and PVC in a 2% w/v solution in HPLC-grade tetrahydrofuran. 0.2 wt% Rhodamine dye is added. The solutions of 50/50 mixtures were allowed to sit for at least 24 h and deposited on Teflon® watch glasses using pipettes. Films were allowed to air dry for 24-48 h before peeling and analysis of both air- and substrate- side.

For PS*/PB and PS*/PMMA blends, as received materials were used in a 2% (w/v) solution in HPLC grade toluene. Solutions containing a 50/50 mixture of the two polymers were allowed to sit for 24h before being solvent cast onto silicon wafers.

10/90 PMMA/PPV blend was made from 2% (w/v) solutions of PMMA and MEH-PPV dissolved in toluene and deposited onto a cleaned glass slides.

2.2 XPS analysis

The XPS spectra and images were acquired on a Kratos AXIS Ultra photoelectron spectrometer using a monochromatic Al Kα source operating at 300W. The base pressure was $2x10^{-10}$ torr, and operating pressure was $2x10^{-9}$ torr. Charge compensation was accomplished using low energy electrons. Standard operating conditions for good charge compensation are -3.1 V bias voltage, -1.0 V filament voltage and filament current of 2.1 A. For all samples medium magnification images of 350x 350 microns in size were acquired.

For PVC/PMMA sample, O 1s, Cl 2p and C 1s images were acquired for 3 minutes each at pass energy (PE) of 80 eV. High resolution C 1s 55 micron spectra were acquired from bright and dark areas selected within Cl 2p images for 6 minutes at PE 20 eV.

For PS*/PMMA sample, 7 images were acquired at following binding energies (BEs): 5 type of C (288.5, 286.1, 283.7 ,282.3, 281.7) and 2 types of (531, 529.3) for 3 minutes and 80 eV PE. Small area O 1s and C 1s 55 micron spectra were acquired from 4 areas within images for 6 minutes each at 20 eV PE.

For PPV/PMMA sample, 6 images were acquired at following BEs: 4 types of C (286.5, 285.8, 282,8, 281.5) and 2 types of O (530.4, 528.8). Small area O 1s and C 1s 55 micron spectra were acquired from 4 areas within images for 6 minutes each at 20 eV PE.

For PS*/PB blend, an images-to-spectra dataset was acquired. In this experiment, images are acquired as a function of binding energy (BE) across the range of interest, in this case the C 1s peak, from 289 eV to 279 eV with a 0.2 eV step. This corresponds to a binding energy range from 291 eV to 281 eV after charge correction. Pass energy of 80 eV and acquisition time of 2 minutes per image was employed.

2.3 Confocal analysis

Confocal images were obtained with Zeiss LSM 510 confocal laser-scanning microscope. For PVC/PMMA blend with rhodamine dye Helium Neon laser (543nm excitation wavelength) was used. For PS* containing blends and PPV/PMMA blends argon-ion laser with an excitation wavelength of 488nm in the single channel mode. 20x dry and 60x oil objectives were used at iris diameter of 1.4. Depth series at 0.5-2 micron step were acquired depending on the objective used.

2.4 AFM analysis

AFM images were obtained on a Digital Instruments Multimode NanoScope IIIa scanning probe microscope. Height and phase images were recorded simultaneously under ambient conditions in tapping mode. Commercial Si3N4 cantilevers with force constants of 2.5-8.5 N/m, and resonance frequencies between 120-190 kHz were used.

2.5 Software

GUI (Graphical User Interface) for Image processing and fusion was written in house in Matlab. (The MathWorks) The GUI included all the necessary steps for image fusion, such as multivariate image analysis, image preprocessing using variety of filters, resizing, cropping, rotating, image registration using MI, concentration mapping, image morphing and visualization using rendered volumes. The image PCA routine in the PLS_Toolbox 5.2(Eigenvector Research) in MATLAB was used to extract principal component images and loadings. Rigid registration (translation and rotation) using MI was utilized using in-house-written routine in Matlab using MI function by Dennis Lucero. Morphing algorithm of Beier and Neely was implemented using Dean Krusienski's routine.

3. Results and discussion

In attempt to completely understand structure and chemistry of heterogeneous multicomponent materials using direct correlative multitechnique analysis, several steps have to be undertaken: the same area on the sample has to be analyzed by multiple analytical methods of choice, spectra and images acquired have to be processed and analyzed, and resulted information has to be fused to provide a final image representative of the 3D sample structure.

The heterogeneity in chemistry of the sample must be reflected in all of the analytical methods chosen for the analysis with understanding that each analytical imaging method has different mechanism of generating contrast. Chemical sensitivity of XPS offers great advantage for this purpose, however in some cases more elaborate experimental schemes might be needed for distinguishing between similar polymers in multicomponent polymeric samples or for increasing signal to noise ratio. Several ways to generate a fluorescent signal in CM can be thought of, the first being addition of the dye into the mixture with assumption that it will partition preferentially in one of the mixture constituents, the second is the use of fluorescently tagged polymers and the third, use of natively fluorescent polymers.

The next important consideration is different sampling depth of the technique. This being a main advantage of using multitechnique characterization, serves as somewhat limiting factor in terms of sample preparation requirements imposed by each method and types of data that can be obtained. Vertical heterogeneity may result in concentration gradients and/or surface segregation, while lateral heterogeneity may result in topographical heterogeneity. The AFM method is the most sensitive to the topography of the surface, and there is a limit of topographical height difference that instrument can handle. Large features of phase-separation, which can be easily detected in XPS and other methods and can be beneficial for registration purposes, can increase topographical heterogeneity to the point that AFM images of reasonably large size will be impossible to obtain. The next method of surface sensitivity is XPS, which is sampling top 8-10 nm of the surface. For some of the polymeric systems, big differences in macroscopic parameters of the constituents, can cause significant surface segregation, where within the bulk of the sample, there will be phase separation of the mixture and as the consequence, it will be reflected in CM images, while the top surface may be a homogeneous layer of one of the polymer resulting in featureless XPS images.

AFM is a limiting technique in the physical size of the images that can be acquired. The larger the heterogeneity of the sample, the smaller image size can be acquired. It is clear, that all other methods that can handle larger FOV's will be reduced to the AFM area of analysis.

Three types of polymer blends were designed for the purpose of demonstrating different approaches of image fusion. The first is 50/50 PVC/PMMA blend where the Rhodamine dye has been added to provide the fluorescent contrast for confocal microscopy. This blend represents the well-characterized system, as our and other groups extensively characterized it previously. Enough knowledge about the morphology of this blend allows us to consider it as test system, as it is well known how the composition changes laterally and vertically. In this blend, however, there is a problem of not 100% exclusive preferential dissolution of dye in one of the blend constituents. Another type of blend are mixture of fluorescin-labled PS (PS*) with PMMA, PB and PVC, i.e. PS*/PMMA, PS*/PB and PS*/PVC. The problem of partial dissolution of dye in both polymers is solved by this approach, as fluorescence is coming exclusively from the labeled polymer making confocal data interpretation less ambiguous. And the third blend used in this report is a mixture of natively fluorescent polymer, MEH-PPV with PMMA. This represents another way of solving ambiguities of confocal data interpretation. Throughout the discussion we will use examples from all three types of polymer blends.

Following steps required to be done prior to image fusion will be discussed now:

1. Area marking
2. Image acquisition
3. Pixel-to-feature conversion
4. Image registration of feature-level images: -resizing, preprocessing, AIR using MI
5. Registration of original data on pixel level

3.1 Area marking

The task of marking an area on the sample so that it can be easily located within each analytical method of choice and, at the same time, don't introduce damage or artifacts to the sample have been approached through a variety of means. The simplest approach is to mark sample areas with a felt pen, but this becomes difficult when the analysis area approaches the dimensions of the pen tip. Optical features on the sample provide internal marks, but may not always be present. TEM grids have also been used to locate areas, but the height differential between the grid and the sample is frequently greater than the vertical range of the AFM scanner, not allowing imaging the grid within FOV of the image.

An alternative method for marking an analysis area is AFM lithography, which allows the outline of the analysis area to be drawn using contact mode AFM. (Sugimura & Nakagiri, 1997; Cleveland et al., 1998; Ngunjiri & Garno, 2008; Lu et al., 2009) The tip is scanned under load forces that are experimentally determined to remove sample from the surface. We've successfully used AFM tip to introduce marking lines for several samples of varying morphologies (patterned and polymer blends). (Artyushkova et al., 2009)

Figure 1 shows optical image of the sample with a grid and two sets of vertical lines drawn by AFM tip. Grid helps to locate an area in confocal and XPS analysis, especially when lines are not observable in chemical images, which sometimes might be the case.

Fig. 1. Optical image of the sample with grid and sets of lines

3.2 Image acquisition

After the lines have been drawn, the AFM images between lines are acquired. The exact distance from left top line is measured to the location of a center of AFM images. This knowledge is very useful in checking the output results from image registration as will be discussed further. Figure 2 shows height and phase images acquired from PS*/PMMA sample.

Marks introduced by AFM tip can be easily located in all other instruments using optical cameras. Confocal image from the same sample is shown in Figure 2. The high intensity corresponds to fluorescent PS-enriched phase of the blend. The lines marked by AFM are readily visible. From the distance between the top of the line to the center of AFM images, one can register AFM image within confocal image. As discussed below, results of automatic image registration can be evaluated based on this knowledge.

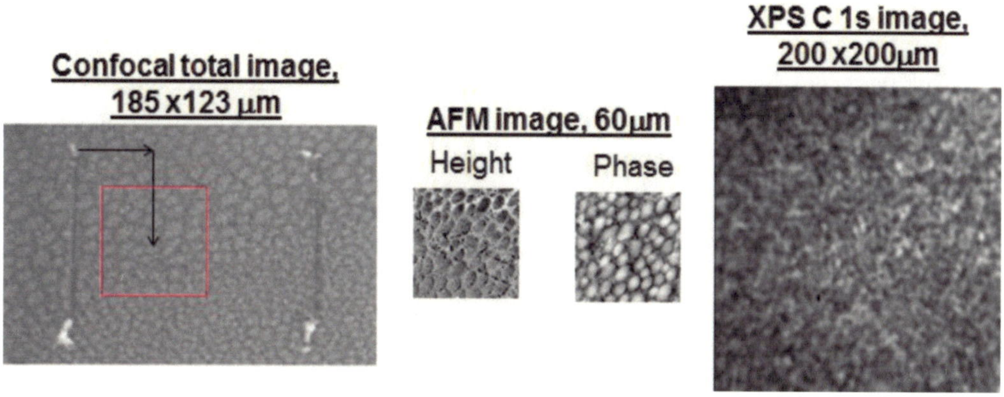

Fig. 2. Confocal, AFM and XPS images from marked area on PS*/PB sample. Lines are visible in CM but not in XPS chemical images

When the sample is transferred for the analysis into XPS spectrometer, the optical camera is used to locate the analysis area. The lines marked are readily visible in optical images. Chemical images are then acquired from the matched area. Figure 2 shows an XPS C 1s image acquired at BE of the main peak - 285 eV after charge correction. Lines are not visible, but having an optical image as reference, one can be certain that this XPS image is acquired from exactly the same area as AFM and confocal images.

3.3 Feature selection

Multisensor fusion can take place at the pixel, feature or symbol level of representation. (Varshney, 2000; Peri, 2001; Mahler, 2004; Macii et al., 2008) In pixel-level fusion, a new image is formed through the combination of multiple original images to increase information content associated with each pixel. Pixel-level fusion is recommended for images with similar exterior orientation, similar spatial, temporal and spectral resolution, and capturing similar physical phenomena. When images record information from very different chemical or physical phenomena, if they are collected from different platforms, or have significantly different sensor geometry, preference should be given to the feature-level fusion, where original images are converted to the images representative of the features, i.e. segmented images, for example.

In case of multitechnique fusion using XPS, AFM and confocal microscopy, images are acquired from different platforms sampling different physical and chemical properties. Moreover, multiple images per each technique are available, so they have to be converted to the feature images representing particular chemical component or phase. Depth array is acquired in CM. Several elemental and chemical XPS images are usually acquired. Often images-2-spectra data are acquired XPS, which consist of 50-70 images within the binding energy range of element of interest with small binding energy step. Two AFM images are usually acquired, one being representative of the height and another of the phase image. These multidimensional multivariate images may be converted to a single image representing features of interest for feature-based data fusion.

Image segmentation, classification or Multivariate Image Analysis (MIA) are among the methods capable to extract feature information from multivariate images. The goal of MIA methods is to extract the most significant information from an image data set, while reducing the dimensionality of the data. Principal Component Analysis (PCA) transforms multivariate images into a number of score images. (Artyushkova & Fulghum, 2001; Artyushkova & Fulghum, 2004) The first principal component accounts for as much of the variability in the data as possible, and each succeeding component accounts for a decreasing amount of the remaining variability. The objective of PCA is to identify images which are globally correlated or anti-correlated. This information is displayed as loadings of the different images, and the pixels responsible for the correlations can then be displayed in component score images. PCA is a method of choice for feature selection due its simplicity, uniqueness of solution and speed.

Data from PPV/PMMA blend are used as an example of using PCA as feature-selection method from both XPS and CM domains. This is an example of the sample, where large clearly-observed features in optical and chemical XPS and CM images allow for easy analysis area identification and matching. 6 chemical photoelectron images are acquired at BE's corresponding to two types of oxygen and four types of carbon. Principal component analysis of these 6 images results in 3 principal components. Figure 3 shows score images and loadings for these components. The 1st PC has high contribution from all photoelectron

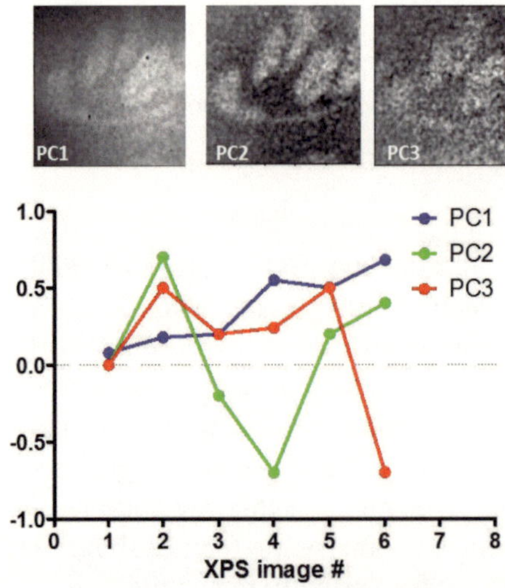

Fig. 3. PCA analysis applied to series of 6 XPS chemical images from PPV/PMMA blend

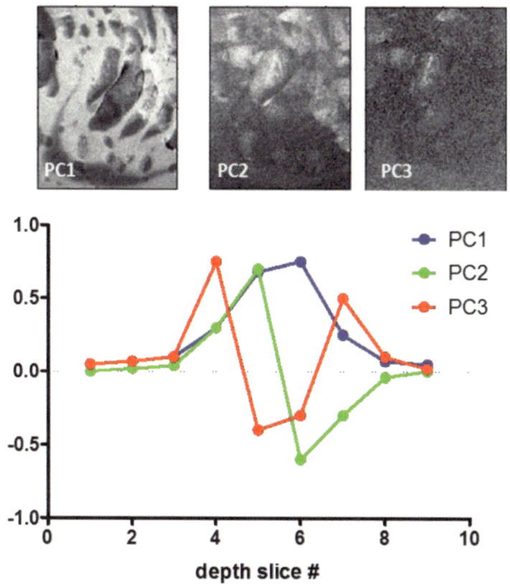

Fig. 4. PCA analysis applied to series of confocal depth images

images and results in intense and most homogeneous distribution. It has been shown that the 1st component is a representative of mixture of topographical and inelastic background. (Artyushkova and Fulghum 2004) The 2nd component image is more heterogeneous with loading having high positive contribution due to images #2, 5 and 6 and negative contribution due to image #4. Images 2, 5 and 6 are correspond to the BE where the highest contribution is from PMMA, while image 4 is a representative of PPV. So, PC score image 2 can be considered as being representative of PMMA-enriched phase of the blend and it will be used as a feature-representation of XPS domain.

For feature selection from confocal microscopy imaging data, PCA was applied to 9 confocal images acquired from the same area with 2 micron vertical step (Figure 4). Application of PCA to XPS imaging data allows identification of spatial distribution of chemical phases present in the sample and as the consequence one of the PC scores can be used as feature image representing one of the phases. PCA analysis of confocal depth series serves different purpose than that of XPS data. Each original confocal image within depth series represents PPV-enriched phase at different depth. PCA remove noise and provides confocal image representative of the PPV enriched phases with improved signal-to-noise. Alternatively, one can select most intense and contrast image from the depth array as a feature-representative of confocal data. The 5th and 6th images have a highest contribution into the 1st PC, so either PC score image 1 or original image 5 or 6 can be used as feature-representation of confocal data.

AFM topography and phase images contain very different type of information about the samples morphology; therefore either one or both of them can be used directly for image fusion.

3.4 Image registration

After the images representative of a particular chemical phase have been selected for each technique, they must be registered, or brought to the same spatial grounds.

The first step is bringing them to the same scale in pixel-to-micron ratio. The original scale of images is very different. XPS images are always acquired at 256x256 pixels. The smallest size is 200x200 micron. The pixel-to-micron ratio for XPS data is 1.28. AFM data are always acquired at 512x512 pixels size. The size of the AFM image acquired for all the samples is usually less than 100 microns. For 60x60 microns size image, the pixel-to-micron ratio is 8.53 for AFM data. The size of confocal image can be varied and it is usually less than 200 microns. For an analysis area of 123x185 micron image acquired at 512x768 pixels has the pixel-to-micron ratio of 4.15. As the loss of data is not desirable, it is not practical shrinking AFM and confocal data to match the size of XPS images. At the same time, if one would increase the size of XPS image to match the size of, let's say, AFM image, it will result in unreasonably large (1700x1700 pixels) size leading to excessively time- and computer-consuming image registration. Therefore, in each individual case of matching sizes of images in terms of their pixel-to-micron ratio, compromise should be found. For example, if confocal image is decreased in two times to a size of 256x384 pixels, the size of AFM image that matches the pixel-to-micron ratio of confocal is 124x124 pixels, while that for XPS becomes 416x416 pixels. These are reasonable sizes of images to process further.

The next step is spatial transformation of images to bring them to the same spatial coordinates. From the way the sample is positioned with respect to the detectors in all three instruments, only translation and rotation must be involved in spatial transformation, which is an example of rigid linear transformation. Manual registration may involve setting up ground control points (GCPs), i.e. points whose coordinates are known for both reference and target images. Manually selected GCPs are used for calculating linear rigid spatial transformation. This approach requires distinct features observable in all images, which is not always the case (see XPS image in Figure 2). It is also subjective to human errors. Alternative approach is automatic image registration (AIR) which iteratively adjusts spatial transformation parameters (rotation and translation) so as to maximize some similarity measure computed between the transformed target image and the corresponding reference image. (Black et al., 1996; Viergever et al., 2001; Zitova & Flusser, 2003; Bentoutou et al., 2005; DelMarco et al., 2007; Liu et al., 2008) There is a variety of automatic intensity based measures, which do not require the definition of GCPs or features.

The criterion of maximization of mutual information (MI) has proven to be a breakthrough in the field of image registration. It is a leading method in multimodal registration. (Maes et al., 1997; Chen et al., 2003; Maes et al., 2003; Bentoutou et al., 2005; Luan et al., 2008)The MI, originating from information theory, is a measure of a degree of grey level dependency between two images. The mutual information I of two images 1 and 2 is defined in terms of the entropies $H(1)$ and $H(2)$ of the images and their joint entropy $H(1,2)$, as follows:

$$I(1,2)=H(1)+H(2)-H(1,2) \tag{1}$$

Entropy is a measure of uncertainty; of how well it is possible to predict the grey value of an arbitrary pixel in an image given the probability density distribution function of the grey values. An image containing a large number of different grey values has a high entropy value. If two images are misregistered, the sharpness of the peaks in the joint histogram will decrease. From the definition of mutual information the registration of images depends on maximization of their mutual information.

The strength of mutual information is that generally it does not require preprocessing of the images. It is more suitable for multimodality image matching than other statistical measures, such as cross-correlation measures, which rely on an equivalence relation between the intensities of two images, whereas mutual information depends on the existence of a statistical distribution relation, hence posing less demands on the relation between the images' grey values.

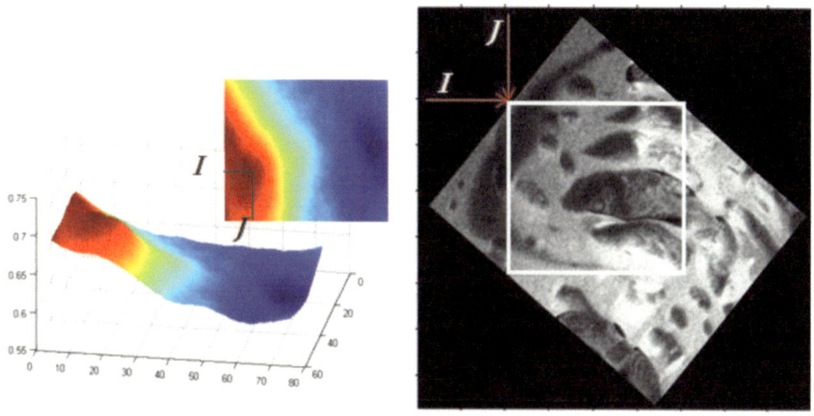

Fig. 5. Left - MI surface plot calculated for all values of shift in x and y for image rotated by angle Θ. i and j - coordinates of maximum of MI

MI is computed for window pairs from target and reference images and its maximum is searched. The maximum MI provides three parameters, i.e. angle of rotation Θ, and coordinates of i and j for maximum MI. i and j are the coordinates of the left corner of the rectangular area matching the size of target image that has to be cropped out from the rotated reference image by the angle Θ (see figure 5).

To facilitate AIR using MI of very different types of image pairs, various preprocessing routines may be utilized. Different lateral resolution may provide different levels of details in the same features captured by both techniques. Some smoothing filtering may be required to bring the images to be registered to similar details appearance. Sometimes image smoothing is not sufficient. In confocal image, for example, small bright features exist within the big dark feature. One way to simplify the images is to convert them to objects. In the analysis of the objects in images it is essential that we can distinguish between the objects of interest and the background. The techniques that are used to find the objects of interest are usually referred to as segmentation techniques - segmenting the foreground from background. Thresholding produces a segmentation that yields all the pixels that, in principle, belong to the object or objects of interest in an image. Figure 6b) shows thresholded images of original XPS and CM images representative of PVC-enriched phase in PVC/PS* blend in Figure 6a). The intensity distribution is simplified now so that there much fewer possible matches of best registration results. An alternative to this is to find those pixels that belong to the borders of the objects. Techniques that are directed to this goal are termed edge finding techniques. Example of edges extracted from XPS and confocal images is shown in Figure 6c).

Another parameter that should be paid attention to is phase inversion. Bright feature in one image can correspond to dark feature in another image. Image inversion might be necessary as preprocessing step.

Figure 7 shows registered XPS and confocal images for PS*/PVC blend in Figure 6. Large features in both images allow visual estimation of MI registration results as satisfactory.

Figure 8 shows registered images for PS*/PMMA sample. Original images for this blend are shown in Figure 2. AFM and confocal images were registered first. Features in both images are very similar, so the results can be visually estimated as satisfactory. The knowledge of position of the center of AFM images with respect to the line visible within the confocal image allows checking the accuracy of registration. XPS image does not have any distinct features in images to judge the registration results and there are no lines visible. XPS image was registered with AFM and with confocal separately and the fact that both pairs gave exactly the same translation and rotation parameters confirms that the image shown is indeed from exactly the same area as confocal and AFM.

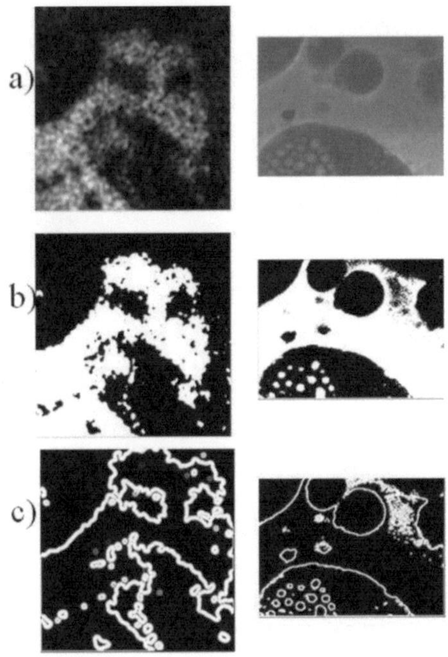

Fig. 6. Image preprocessing. XPS (left) and Confocal (right) images representative of PVC-enriched phase in PVC/PS* blend a) original images, b) thresholded and c) edges extracted.

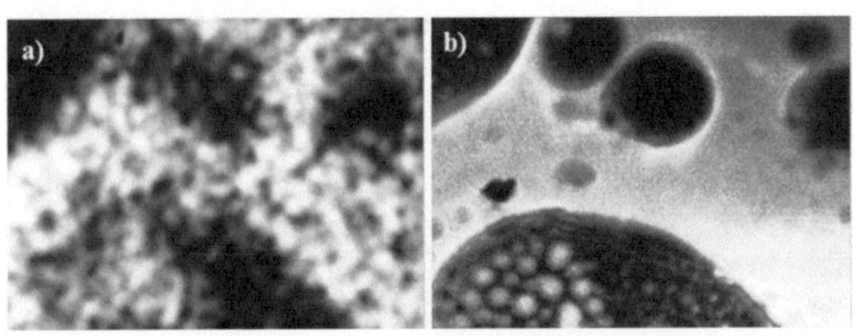

Fig. 7. Registered XPS (a) and Confocal (b) images for PVC/PS* blend

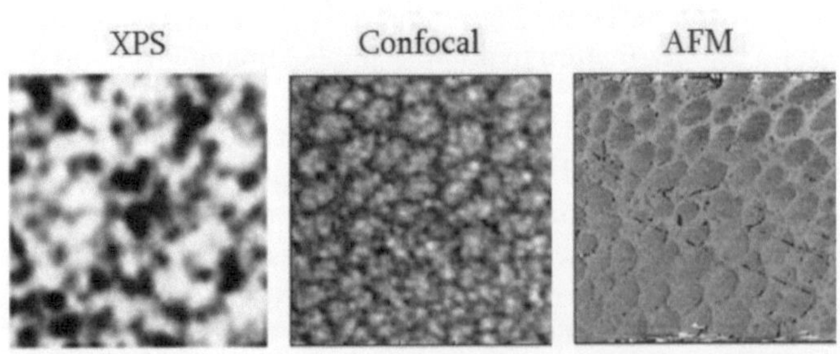

Fig. 8. Registered XPS, Confocal and AFM images for PS*/PMMA blend

3.5 Image fusion

Now that all the feature-level images are registered and therefore represent different types of chemical and physical information from exactly the same area, they can be fused. We will now discuss different examples of multitechnqiue image fusion.

3.5.1 Example 1. Confocal microscopy and XPS

Fusing confocal and XPS data provides a benefit of extended spatial coverage. CM provides information on how features change with depth, but the data are not quantitative, as intensity in confocal images represents fluorescence which is directly proportional to concentration of the fluorescent phase but exact or even approximate concentrations are unknown. XPS, on the other hand, is a quantitative method. Small area spectra from areas of interest within the images provide concentration of chemical phases. The 1st example of CM-XPS fusion involves use of quantitative information available from XPS top and, if possible, bottom, images to quantify confocal images and to build quantitative confocal volume, where each pixel represents a concentration of a particular chemical phase. The idea behind this fusion is presented in figure 9.

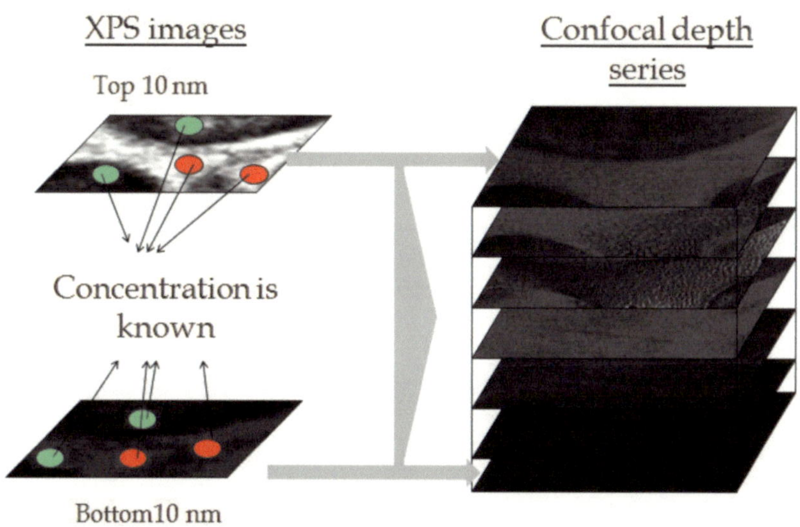

Fig. 9. Quantifying confocal depth series by using quantitative information from small area XPS spectra acquired from both sides of sample

Confocal array from PVC/PMMA blend has been quantified from quantitative chemical information provided by small area XPS spectroscopy. From XPS analysis of this blend it is discerned that the air side of the sample is heterogeneous and enriched in PMMA, while the substrate side is more homogeneous and enriched in PVC. The minimum and maximum concentration of PVC obtained from XPS small area spectra was used to map intensity in the top and bottom confocal images to 22/40 and 55/75, respectively. The intensities in intermediate confocal slices are then mapped by taking the weighted average between those numbers. Figure 10 plots max and min intensities in original and mapped confocal images as a function of depth. The resulted confocal volume representative of PVC enriched phase now can be displayed and analyzed as shown in Figure 11. Rendered volume allows us to see the exterior of the material from top and bottom side of the sample. Isosurfaces at three values of concentration, 30, 50 and 70 % PVC in the blend are displayed. It can be seen that air side is very heterogeneous with small islands with 30% of PVC in them. The 50/50 blend is located in the middle of the sample, while the bottom side is somewhat heterogeneous with higher PVC concentration.

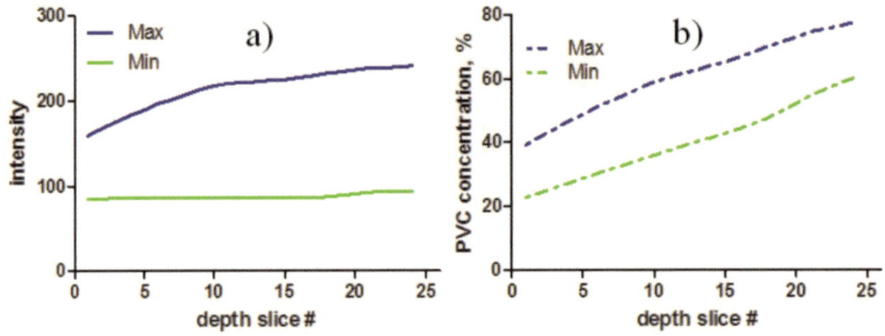

Fig. 10. Quantifying intensities in confocal images. Minimum and maximum values of intensity in a) original and b) quantified images.

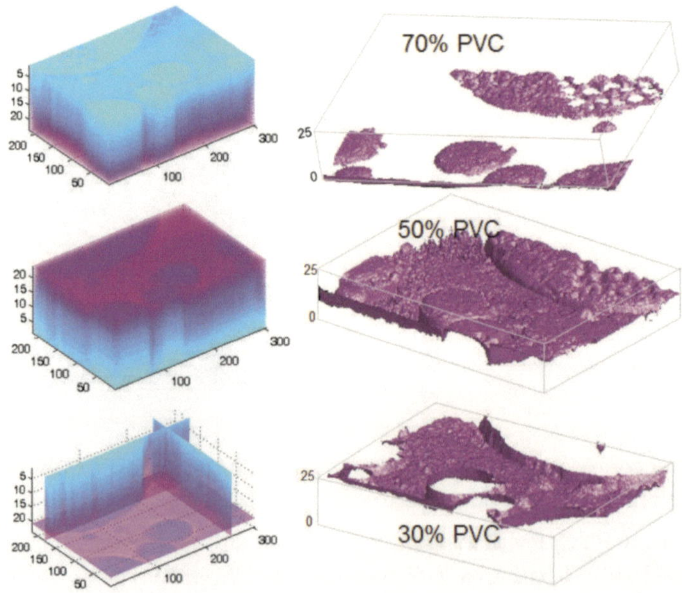

Fig. 11. Visualization of quantified confocal volume: Rendered volume – top (a) and bottom (b), three cross-sections, c), Isosurfaces of d)70% PVC, e) 50% PVC and f) 30% PVC

Another way to explore the quantitative confocal volume is to plot intensities within the regions of interest (ROIs) as a function of depth. These are plotted on Figure 12 for 4 ROI's selected of confocal image representing PVC concentration profiles. The concentration profiles within dark areas are more linear than in bright areas.

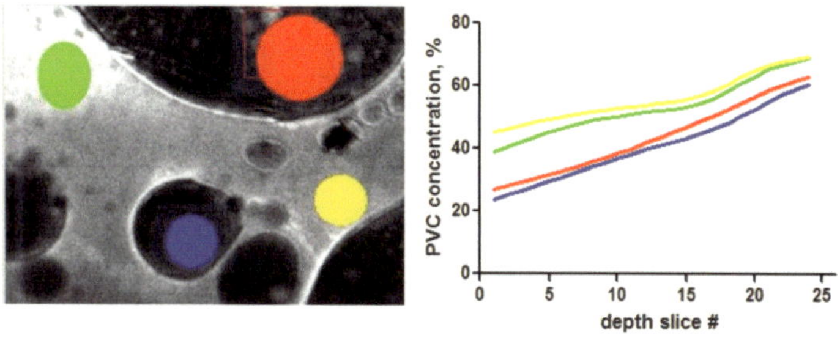

Fig. 12. Concentration depth profiles of PVC% in the blend from areas selected on confocal image

3.5.2 Example 2. Confocal microscopy and XPS

The very top surface determines most of the material's properties. Imaging and small area XPS represents an integral signal from total top 10 nm of the material. The top confocal image can be considered as an integrated image of top 1 micron thickness of the material. 3-D visualization of morphology from imaging data acquired from different depths from the same areas on the sample is a key factor for understanding 3-D structure. The idea behind the 2nd example of fusing CM and XPS images is visualization of changes in morphology and chemistry in the top 1 micron of the sample.

XPS and confocal images representative of PPV-enriched part of PPV/PMMA blend have been registered; images are shown in figure 13. The bright areas are enriched in PPV. The XPS image is then quantified using numbers obtained from small area spectroscopy, being 30% and 65% as lowest and highest concentration of PPV. Confocal image is quantified to approximately the same concentrations of PPV as in XPS image, i.e. 35% as lowest and 70% as largest PPV percentage. Approximately the same sample composition is expected for 1 micron depth. Small degree of concentration gradient is introduced by slight increase of concentration in both dark and bright parts of the image. The main focus of merging XPS and confocal images in this example is on morphological (shape) changes with depth.

The next step is merging these two quantitative images representing spatial distribution of PPV-enriched phase at two different depths into one display. This represents the problem of reconstructing a solid object from a series of parallel planar cross-sections. (Lin et al., 1989) To recreate a volume between quantitative images of polymer blends at different depths, additional slices have to be created in between pairs of images. Interpolation, which produces one or more intermediate images which smoothly and locally turn the 1st image into the 2nd one, is required. A linear interpolation, a simplest type, averages the intensities in two images. However in real heterogeneous samples, where surface segregation may exist, pixels belonging to the same feature in one slice do not necessarily connect to pixels exactly beneath them in the next slice. There are several ways to address this correspondence problem. An example of such approach is image morphing. The morphing is realized by coupling image warping (interpolation of shape) with color interpolation. Image warping applies 2D geometric transformations to the images to retain geometric alignment between their features, while color interpolation blends their color to produce in-between images. (Wolberg, 1998; Tal & Elber, 1999; Artyushkova & Fulghum, 2005; Penska et al., 2007) It begins with establishing correspondence between images with pairs of feature primitives, e.g., mesh nodes, line segments, curves, or points. A pairwise correspondence between two successive images is pre-computed and stored as a pair of morph maps. The feature correspondence is then used to compute mapping functions that define the spatial relationship between all points in both images. The warp function is used to interpolate the positions of the features across the morph sequence. Once both images have been warped into alignment for intermediate feature positions, ordinary color (intensity) interpolation generates in-between images.

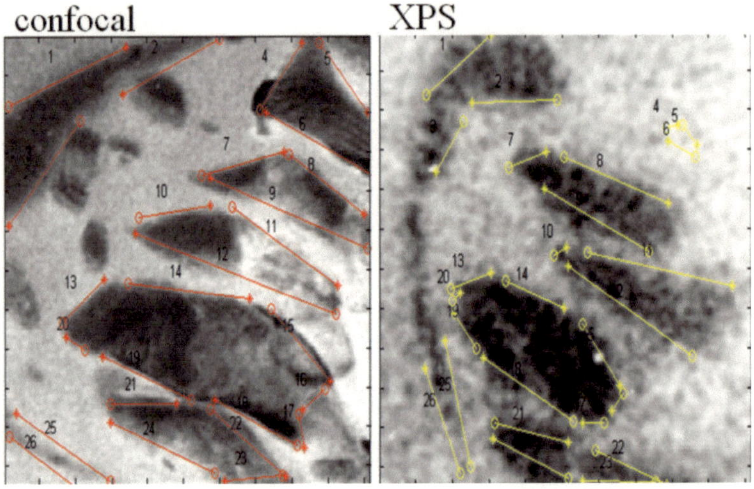

Fig. 13. 26 pairs of lines outlining features in both confocal (reference) and XPS (target) images are drawn for calculating warping function for image morphing

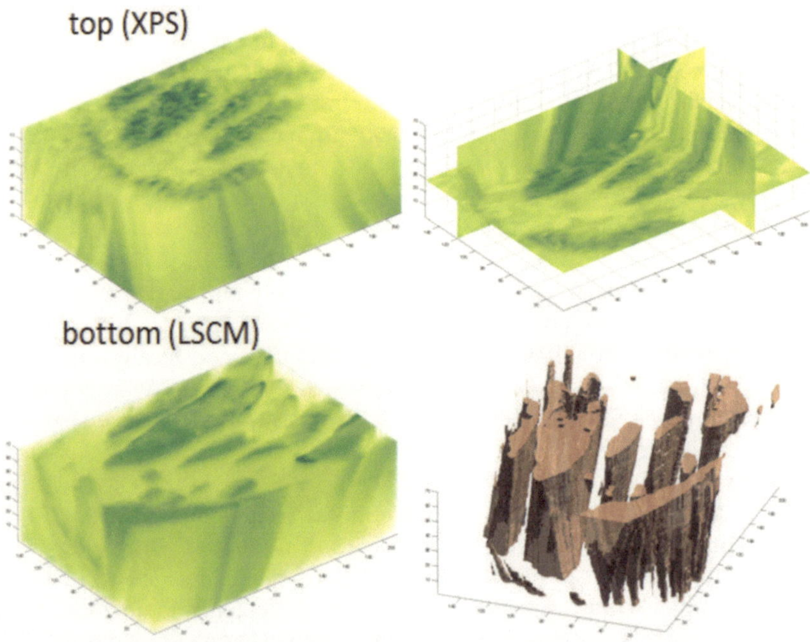

Fig. 14. Visualization of volume obtained through image fusion of XPS and confocal image. Rendered volumes from top (XPS) and bottom (confocal) are shown. Three cross-section and isosurface representing 50/50 PPV/PMMA blend are also shown

Lines are used as feature primitives in this image morphing algorithm. First the lines are drawn on the reference image so that they describe the shape of features the best. Then the corresponding lines are drawn on the target image to describe the same features. The more lines you draw the better the morphing results. The features for this blend change shape quite significantly so many lines have to be drawn for an accurate morphology description. The confocal image has more features to describe, so it is used as reference image. Then lines corresponding to the same exact feature in XPS images are drawn. The figure 13 shown both images with 26 pairs of lines defined. 20 images are reproduced between XPS and confocal image using the warping function calculated from pairs of lines.

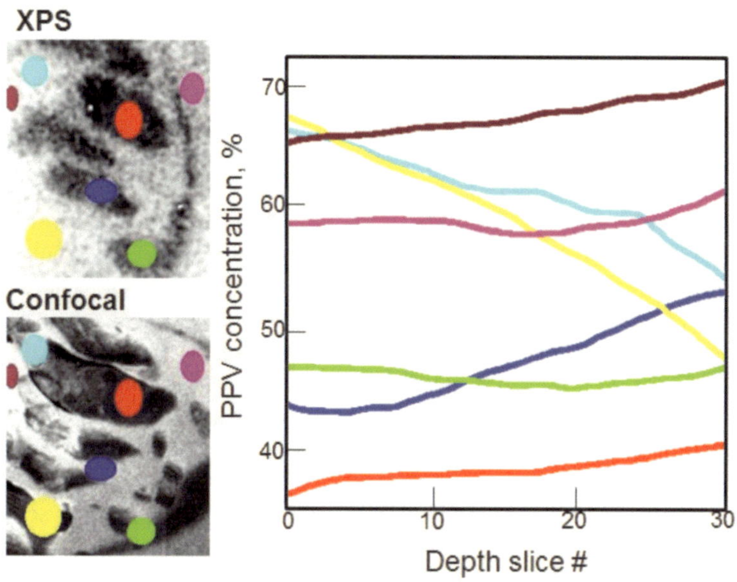

Fig. 15. Concentration depth profiles showing PPV% within 1 micron of depth from selected areas on XPS and Confocal image.

The visualized volume by rendering, isosurface (50/50 PPV/PMMA composition) and cross-sections are shown in Figure 14. Smooth transition in quite significant changes of morphological features is observed. The most important way to visualize the data is to plot profiles for regions of interest. As the volume represents the real chemical concentration of PPV, one can analyze the morphology this way. Regions of interest shown on XPS and confocal images together with concentration profiles (Figure 15), indicate several important observations. For some dark areas on XPS images (red and blue), the concentration increases a little bit towards dark areas in confocal images. For one of the areas (green), the concentration does not change. For few bright areas on XPS images (magenta, violet), the concentration also increases towards depth. For two other bright areas in XPS images, the concentration decreases with depth, so phase inversion is observed. One can really appreciate the quantitative level of morphological details fusion of XPS and confocal images provides.

3.5.3 Example 3. AFM and XPS

One can approach fusion of XPS and AFM images as the problem of combining images of drastically different resolutions, captured with different instruments and with different spectral characteristics into single image with the goal of facilitating interpretation and analysis. (Nunez et al., 1999; Pohl, 1999; Svab & Ostir, 2006; Ling et al., 2008; Rao et al., 2008; Artyushkova et al., 2009) For example, a typical tradeoff which often occurs in remote sensing is between spatial resolution and resolution in wavelength. It may be possible and desirable to combine a low resolution color image and a high resolution monochromatic image to produce a color image with high spatial resolution. Similarly, X-ray photoelectric spectroscopy (XPS) has very high resolution in spectral dimension (binding energy) but relatively low spatial resolution. In contrast, atomic force microscopy (AFM) images have significantly higher spatial resolution, but can be considered to be monochromatic, since they represent surface topography. The goal of this image fusion type is to improve the lateral resolution of XPS images using high lateral resolution AFM images.

The simplest approach to increasing the spatial resolution of a color image using a monochromatic image of higher spatial resolution is to convert from a red, green, blue (RGB) basis to intensity, hue, saturation (IHS) basis. (Pohl, 1999) While the RGB is a rectangular coordinate system, IHS is a cylindrical coordinate system. After converting the low resolution color image to IHS, the grey values of the monochromatic image are transformed using a simple linear greyscale transformation so that the smallest and largest values correspond to those in the low resolution intensity image. The low resolution intensity image is then replaced with the monochromatic image of higher resolution and the coordinate transformation is inverted, yielding a color image of higher resolution.

There are no RGB channels per se in photoelectron imaging. R, G and B channels expected to be spectrally independent. If one acquires a set of elemental and chemical XPS images, then three independent photoelectron images can be considered as RGB channels. In order for photoelectrons images to be spectrally independent, they have to represent different chemical compounds. For systems with more than two chemical species such as polymer blends which are used throughout this chapter, one can envision selecting three photoelectron chemically independent images as RGB channels, and applying RGB-to-IHS conversion algorithm for resolution merge with AFM image. In two-component systems, however, there are no three spectrally independent images. One image as representative of one of the component of the mixture is an inverse of a representative of another component. So, just a single XPS image (either an original photoelectron image or PC score) representing particular chemical phase present in the mixture is what is usually available in case of polymer blend samples. In this case single photoelectron image can be converted into RGB image by applying false-color mapping to a gray scale image. Concept behind RGB-2-IHS resolution merge for XPS and AFM images is shown in Figure 16. Low-spatial resolution XPS image representing particular chemical phase is color-mapped, this RGB image is converted to HIS components. Intensity component is then being replaced by high spatial-resolution AFM image and inverse transformation of IHS-2-RGB is done to obtain resolution merged image.

This procedure has been tested on XPS and AFM images acquired from PS*/PB blend. In this case images-to-spectra data set has been acquired within C 1s region as described in Experimental section. In order to extract one image representative of either PS* or PB-enriched phase of the blend, PCA was applied to images-to-spectra data set. The 1st PC is

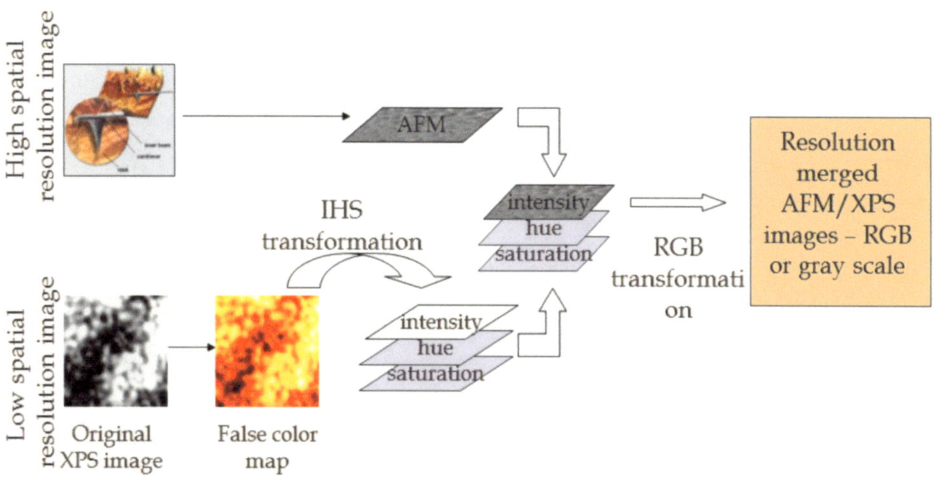

Fig. 16. Concept behind resolution-merging XPS and AFM images.

topographic and phase AFM images from the same area are shown in Figure 17 together with XPS false color-mapped PC score image. According to chemical composition of the blend obtained through small area XPS valence band (VB) spectra, this polymer blend is very homogeneous, i.e. PS*% is ranging from 75 to 85% in darkest and brightest areas within XPS images. The XPS image representative of PS*-enriched phase obtained through XPS shows large features that have slightly different composition but still it is detectable by XPS. AFM image accesses really different level of details due to much higher level of lateral resolution, showing small circular particle like features, while it is not able to detect such small chemical differences between large phase-separated areas. This shows how two techniques can be complimentary due to different sampling properties and different resolution scales. In order to represent this complementary information in one image, AFM and XPS images have been fused. For that, XPS image has been then color-mapped using hot as false color map in Matlab (figure 17). By performing RGB-2-IHS conversion and substituting value of I for AFM topography or phase image and performing IHS-2-RGB conversion, one obtains the resolution-merged images (figure 17). As one can see, in those images, small chemical heterogeneity from XPS images is preserved as color, while a great level of details is now available from AFM high spatial resolution images. One can consider fused images as either AFM images with added chemistry as color or better-quality XPS images. As discussed above, color does not mean a lot in case of XPS images, so one can convert fused images back to original grey color scheme and compare original XPS images to fused grey scale images. The same conclusions can be made from these images. Fusion with phase AFM images gives especially nice correlation that is might due to the fact that phase imaging reflects chemical information.

Another example of resolution-merging XPS and AFM images represent quite a different perspective of this approach. The original registered XPS (O 1s) and AFM images from PVC/PMMA blend are shown in Figure 18. As one can see, the bright features in O 1s image, i.e. PMMA-enriched phase, correspond to higher features in AFM images. Small area spectroscopy confirms that the surface is enriched in PMMA, as composition variation from dark to bright areas on the sample is between 60 to 90% PMMA concentration. The level of

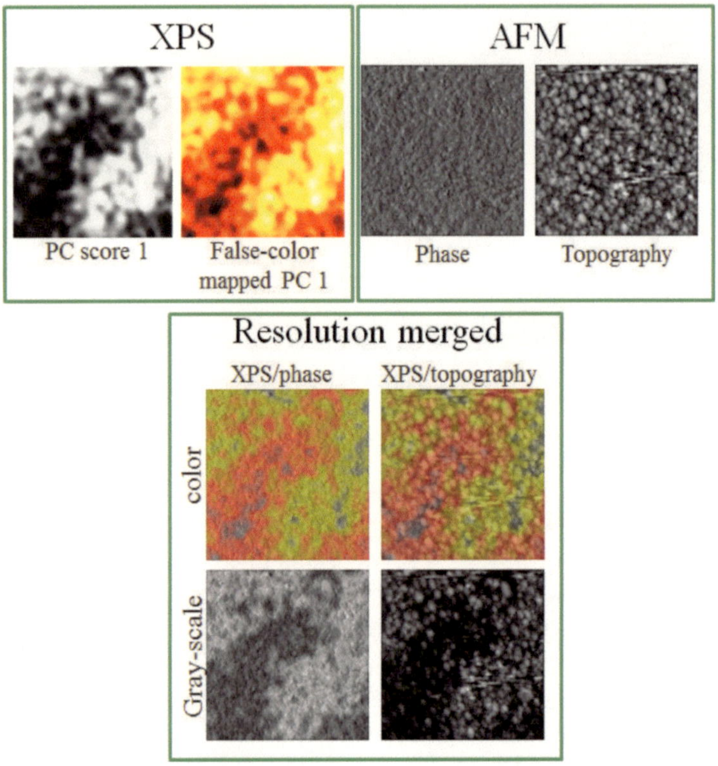

Fig. 17. Resolution-merge of XPS (PS* enriched phase) and AFM images for PS*/PB blend

details provided by both techniques is quite similar, which shows that there is no micro-separation of phases within large phase-separated features, but AFM images shows much better edge information and better resolution. The same procedure of RGB-2-IHS of false-colored PMMA-enriched phase XPS image with AFM image was performed. The merged image shown in Figure 18 does not show exact feature-to-feature correspondence, indicating that the chemical heterogeneity is not in direct correspondence to topography of the surface.

4. Conclusion

Fusing imaging data from XPS, CM and AFM is discussed in the current chapter for the purpose of obtaining fused data representing quantitative structural morphological information from multicomponent heterogeneous systems, such as polymer blends. Steps leading to image fusion discussed in details are area marking, area identification, image acquisition, feature selection, image alignment and image registration. Three examples of image fusion were discussed. In the first, confocal microscope depth series were quantified and visualized based on small area photoelectron spectroscopy acquired from exactly the same areas of polymer blends. In the second, image morphing between image acquired at 10 nm sampling depth by XPS and image acquired at ~1 micron depth by CM provided very detailed information on how morphology of polymer blend changes from the very top surface down into the bulk. And in the third, resolution merge between low spatial resolution XPS image and high spatial AFM image was tested for two types of polymer blend samples.

Combining data acquired from the same area on a sample by different analytical techniques reveals more information than would be obtained if each data type was processed individually.

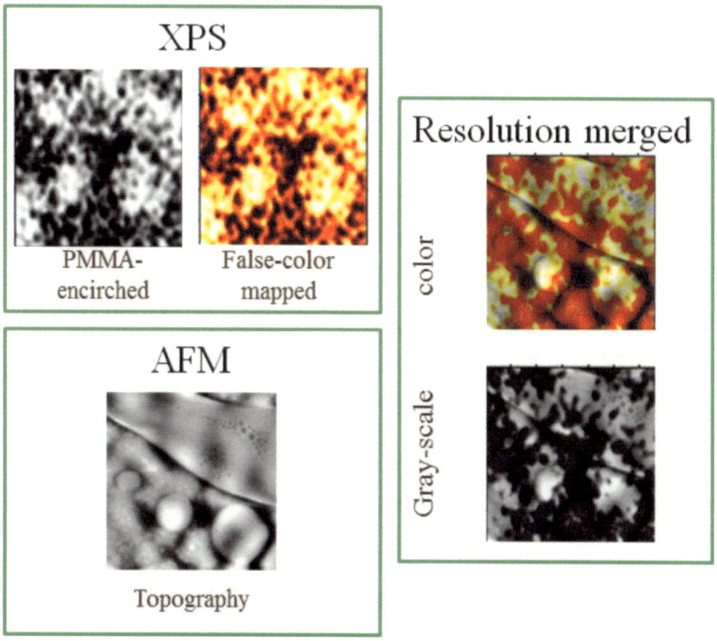

Fig. 18. Resolution-merge of XPS (PMMA enriched phase) and AFM images for PVC/PMMA blend

5. References

Adriaensens, P.; Storme, L.; Carleer, R.; Vanderzande,D.; Gelan, J.; Litvinov,V.M. & Marissen, R. (2000). Visualization of tensile stress induced material response at a crack tip in polymers under critical load by NMR imaging. *Macromolecules,* Vol.33, No.13, (June 2000), pp. 4836-4841, ISSN 0024-9297.

Artyushkova, K. (2010) Structure determination of nanocomposites through 3D imaging using laboratory XPS and multivariate analysis. *Journal of Electron Spectroscopy and Related Phenomena,* Vol.178, pp. 292-302, ISSN 0368-2048.

Artyushkova, K.; Farrar, J.O. & Fulghum, J.E. (2009) Data fusion of XPS and AFM images for chemical phase identification in polymer blends. *Surface and Interface Analysis,* Vol.41, No.2, (February 2009), pp. 119-126, ISSN 0142-2421.

Artyushkova, K. & Fulghum, J.E. (2001) Identification of chemical components in XPS spectra and images using multivariate statistical analysis methods. *Journal of Electron Spectroscopy and Related Phenomena,* Vol.121, No.1-3,(December 2001), pp. 33-55, ISSN 0368-2048.

Artyushkova, K. & Fulghum, J.E. (2004) Mathematical topographical correction of XPS images using multivariate statistical methods. *Surface and Interface Analysis*, Vol.36, No.9, (September 2004), pp. 1304-1313, ISSN 0142-2421.

Artyushkova, K. & Fulghum, J.E. (2005) Angle resolved imaging of polymer blend systems: From images to a 3D volume of material morphology. *Journal of Electron Spectroscopy and Related Phenomena,* Vol.149, No.1-3, (November 2005), pp. 51-60, ISSN 0368-2048.

Baum, K.G.; Helguera, M. & Krol, A. (2008) Fusion Viewer: A New Tool for Fusion and Visualization of Multimodal Medical Data Sets. *Journal of Digital Imaging,* Vol.21, (October 2008), pp. S59-S68, ISSN 0897-1189.

Behrend, O.P.; Odoni, L.; Loubet, J.L. & Burnham, N.A. (1999) Phase imaging: Deep or superficial? *Applied Physics Letters,* Vol.75, No.17, (August 1999), pp. 2551-2553, ISSN 0003-6951.

Bentoutou, Y.; Taleb, N.; Kpalma, K. & Ronsin, J. (2005) An automatic image registration for applications in remote sensing. *Ieee Transactions on Geoscience and Remote Sensing,* Vol.43, No.9, (September 2005), pp. 2127-2137, ISSN 0196-2892.

Black, K.J.; Videen, T.O. & Perlmutter, J.S. (1996) A metric for testing the accuracy of cross-modality image registration: Validation and application. *Journal of Computer Assisted Tomography,* Vol.20, No.5, (September 1996), pp. 855-861, ISSN 0368-8715.

Briggs, D. & Grant, J.T. editors (2003) Surface Analysis by Auger and X-Ray Photoelectron Spectroscopy: IM Publications, Chichester, UK.

Chen, H.M.; Arora, M.K. & Varshney, P.K. (2003) Mutual information-based image registration for remote sensing data. *International Journal of Remote Sensing,* Vol.24, No.18, (September 2003), pp. 3701-3706, ISSN 0143-1161.

Cleveland, J.P.; Anczykowski, B.; Schmid, A.E. & Elings, V.B. (1999) Energy dissipation in tapping-mode atomic force microscopy. *Applied Physics Letters,* Vol.75, No.20, (October 1999), pp. 2613-2615, ISSN 0003-6951.

Delcorte, A. (2008) On the road to high-resolution 3D molecular imaging. *Applied Surface Science,* Vol.255, No.4, (December 2008), pp. 954-958, ISSN 0169-4332.

DelMarco, S.P.; Tom, V. & Webb, H.F. (2007) A theory of automatic parameter selection for feature extraction with application to feature-based multisensor image registration. *Ieee Transactions on Image Processing,* Vol.16, No.11, (November 2007), pp. 2733-2742, ISSN 1057-7149.

Eigenvector Research, I. PLS_Toolbox 5.2

Fellers, T. J. & M. W. Davidso "Introduction to Confocal Microscopy." Available from http://www.olympusconfocal.com/theory/confocalintro.html.

Gao, J.X.; Liu. E; Butler, D.L. & Zeng, A.P. (2003) Compositional depth profile analysis of coatings on hard disks by X-ray photoelectron spectroscopy and imaging. *Surface & Coatings Technology,* Vol.176, No.1, (November 2003), pp. 93-102, ISSN 0257-8972.

Garcia, R. & Perez, R. (2002) Dynamic atomic force microscopy methods. *Surface Science Reports,* Vol.47, No.6-8, (September 2002), pp. 197-301, ISSN 0167-5729.

Garcia, R.; Tamayo, J. & San Paulo, A. (1999) Phase contrast and surface energy hysteresis in tapping mode scanning force microsopy. *Surface and Interface Analysis,* Vol.27, No.5-6, (May 1999), pp. 312-316, ISSN 0142-2421.

Jones, E.A.; Lockyer, N.P. & Vickerman, J.C. (2008) Depth profiling brain tissue sections with a 40 keV C-60(+) primary ion beam. *Analytical Chemistry,* Vol.80, No.6, (March 2008), p. 2125-2132, ISSN 0003-2700.

Lin, W.C.; Chen, S.Y. & Chen, C.T. (1989) A New Surface Interpolation Technique for Reconstructing 3d Objects from Serial Cross-Sections. *Computer Vision Graphics and Image Processing,* Vol.48, No.1, (October 1989), pp. 124-143, ISSN 0734-189X.

Ling, Y.; Ehlers, M.; Usery, E.L. & Madden, M. (2008) Effects of spatial resolution ratio in image fusion. *International Journal of Remote Sensing,* Vol.29, No.7, (April 2008), pp. 2157-2167, ISSN 0143-1161.

Liu, X.J.; Yang, J. & Shen, H.B. (2008) Automatic image registration by local descriptors in remote sensing. *Optical Engineering,* Vol. 47, No.8, (August 2008), pp. 087206, ISSN 0091-3286.

Lu, H.H.; Lin, C.W.; Hsiao, T.C.; Lee, C.K. & Hsu, S.M. (2009) Nanopatterning on Silicon Wafers Using AFM-Based Lithography-for Solar Cells. *Journal of Nanoscience and Nanotechnology,* Vol.9, No.3, (March 2009), pp. 1696-1700, ISSN 1533-4880.

Luan, H.X.; Qi, F.H.; Xue, Z.; Chen, L.Y. & Shen, D.G. (2008) Multimodality image registration by maximization of quantitative-qualitative measure of mutual information. *Pattern Recognition,* Vol.41, No.1, (January 2008), pp. 285-298, ISSN 0031-3203.

Macii, D.; Boni, A.; De Cecco, M. & Petri, D. (2008) Tutorial 14: Multisensor data fusion. *Ieee Instrumentation & Measurement Magazine,* Vol.11, No.3, (June 2008), pp. 24-33, ISSN 1094-6969.

Maes, F.; Collignon, A.; Vandermeulen, D.; Marchal, G. & Suetens, P. (1997) Multimodality image registration by maximization of mutual information. *Ieee Transactions on Medical Imaging,* Vol.16, No.2, (April 1997), pp. 187-198, ISSN 0278-0062.

Maes, F.; Vandermeulen, D. & Suetens, P. (2003) Medical image registration using mutual information. *Proceedings of the IEEE,* Vol.91, No.10, (October 2003), pp. 1699-1722, ISSN 0018-9219.

Mahler, R.P.S. (2004) "Statistics 101" for multisensor, multitarget data fusion. *IEEE Aerospace and Electronic Systems Magazine,* Vol.19, No.1, (January 2004), pp. 53-64, ISSN 0885-8985.

Matsushita, Y.; Sekiguchi, T.; Saito, K.; Kato, T.; Imai, T. & Fukushima, K. (2007) The characteristic fragment ions and visualization of cationic starches on pulp fiber using ToF-SIMS. *Surface and Interface Analysis,* Vol.39, No.6, (June 2007), pp. 501-505, ISSN 0142-2421.

Ngunjiri, J. & Garno, J.C. (2008) AFM-based lithography for nanoscale protein assays. *Analytical Chemistry,* Vol. 80, No.5, (March 2008), pp. 1361-1369, ISSN 0003-2700.

Nunez, J.; Otazu, X.; Fors, O.; Prades, A.; Pala, V. & Arbiol, R. (1999) Multiresolution-based image fusion with additive wavelet decomposition. *IEEE Transactions On Geoscience and Remote Sensing,* Vol.37, No.3, (May 1999), pp. 1204-1211, ISSN 0196-2982.

Pawley, J. editor (2006) Handbook of Biological Confocal Microscopy. Berlin: Springer.

Penska, K.; Folio, L. & Bunger, R. (2007) Medical applications of digital image morphing. *Journal of Digital Imaging,* Vol.20, No.3, (September 2007), pp. 279-283, ISSN 0897-1889.

Peri, J.S.J. (2001) Approaches to multisensor data fusion. *Johns Hopkins Apl Technical Digest,* Vol.22, No.4, (October-December 2001), pp. 624-633, ISSN 0270-5214.

Pohl, C. (1999) Tools and methods for fusion of images of different spatial resolution in *International Archives of Photogrammetry and Remote Sensing,* Vol. 32, W6, Spain: Valladolid.

Rafati, A.; Shard, A.G.; Alexander, M.R. & Davies, M.C. (2008) Characterisation of drug loaded polymer films using ToF-SIMS and XPS depth profiling. NMAET III & SSBII 10 meeting. Teddington, UK.

Rao, C.V.; Rao, K.M.M.; Reddy, P.S. & Pujar, G. (2008) A novel method for enhancement of radiometric resolution using image fusion. *International Journal of Applied Earth Observation and Geoinformation,* Vol.10, No.2, (June 2008), pp. 165-174, ISSN 0303-2434.

Rieder, C.; Ritter, F.; Raspe, M. & Peitgen, H.O. (2008) Interactive visualization of multimodal volume data for neurosurgical tumor treatment. *Computer Graphics Forum,* Vol.27, No.3, (May 2008), pp. 1055-1062, ISSN 0167-7055.

Ropinski, T.; Hermann, S.; Reich, R.; Schafers, M. & Hinrichs, K. (2009) Multimodal Vessel Visualization of Mouse Aorta PET/CT Scans. *IEEE Transactions on Visualization and Computer Graphics,* Vol. 15, No.6, (November-December 2009), pp. 1515-1522, ISSN 1077-2626.

Sugimura, H. & Nakagiri, N. (1997) AFM lithography in constant current mode. *Nanotechnology,* Vol.8, No.3A, (September 1997), pp. A15-A18, ISSN 0957-4484.

Svab, A. & Ostir, K. (2006) High-resolution image fusion: Methods to preserve spectral and spatial resolution. *Photogrammetric Engineering and Remote Sensing,* Vol.72, No.5, (May 2006), pp. 565-572, ISSN 0099-1112.

Tal, A. & Elber, G. (1999) Image morphing with feature preserving texture. *Computer Graphics Forum,* Vol.18, No.3, (December 1999), pp. C339-C348, ISSN 0167-7055.

The MathWorks, I. MatlabR2008a. Natick, Massachusetts.

Varshney, P.K. (2000) Multisensor data fusion. *Intelligent Problem Solving: Methodologies and Approaches, Proceedings,* Vol.1821,pp. 1-3, ISSN 0302-9743.

Viergever MA, Maintz JBA, Niessen WJ, Noordmans HJ, Pluim JPW, et al. (2001) Registration, segmentation, and visualization of multimodal brain images. Computerized Medical Imaging and Graphics 25: 147-151.

Wolberg, G. (1998) Image morphing: a survey. *Visual Computer,* Vol.14, No.8-9, pp. 360-372, ISSN 0178-2789.

Wucher, A.; Cheng, J. & Winograd, N. (2007) Protocols for three-dimensional molecular imaging using mass spectrometry. *Analytical Chemistry,* Vol.79, No.15, (August 2007), pp. 5529-5539, ISSN 0003-2700.

Zitova, B. & Flusser, J. (2003) Image registration methods: a survey. *Image and Vision Computing,* Vol.21, No.11, (October 2003), pp. 977-1000, ISSN 0262-8856.

11

A Directional-Edge-Based Face Detection Algorithm Adapted to the VLSI Image Recognition System

Yasufumi Suzuki[1] and Tadashi Shibata[2]
[1]*Department of Frontier Informatics, The University of Tokyo*
[2]*Department of Electrical Engineering and Information Systems, The University of Tokyo*
Japan

1. Introduction

There has been a considerable interest in the development of human-like image perception systems. Although a number of algorithms have been proposed so far, it is still a challenging task to achieve a human-like robustness in image perception under various circumstances. For robust image perception, the feature representation algorithm which extracts essential features from an image and represents them in a vector format is of critical importance. Since the discovery by Hubel and Wiesel (Hubel & Wiesel (1959)) in the study of visual cortex of animals, it is well known that the directional edge information in visual inputs plays an essential role in early visual processing. Namely, biological systems rely on the spatial relationship among edges in various directions for image perception. In this regard, local intensity gradients or directional edges have been widely used in computer vision and pattern recognition (Belongie et al. (2002); Dalai et al. (2005); Freeman & Roth (1995); Lowe (2004); Mikolajczyk & Schmid (2005); Shibata et al. (1999)). They are utilized in feature descriptors to represent object images in image and gesture recognition. The present work also relies on the edge information extracted from images.

A feature vector representation algorithm called Projected Principal-Edge Distribution (PPED for short) (Yagi & Shibata (2003)) has been developed to meet the demand of neural-associative-processor-based hardware recognition systems (Shibata (2002)). The original idea of PPED was first disclosed in 1999 (Shibata et al. (1999)) and developed in the work of Yagi & Shibata (2003). The robust nature of the PPED vector representation has been successfully demonstrated through its applications to hand-written pattern recognition and medical radiograph analysis (Yagi et al. (2000); Yagi & Shibata (2002)). The feature representation in PPED is based on the spatial distribution of four directional edges (horizontal, $+45°$, vertical, and $-45°$) extracted from an image, in which the local variance of pixel intensities is taken into account for edge detection. Since the processing is computationally very expensive, a dedicated VLSI chip has been developed which can generate PPED vectors at a rate of 10^6 vectors/sec (Yamasaki & Shibata (2007)). An architecture that enhances the throughput by a factor of about 30 was also developed (Nakagawa et al. (2009)). VLSI chips specialized for the associative processing (maximum likelihood search) have also been developed in both digital (Ogawa et al. (2002)) and analog (Yamasaki & Shibata (2003)) technologies aiming at real-time performances. The face detection algorithm in this article has been developed to explore a pattern matching algorithm specifically adapted to the psychologically-inspired VLSI brain model system, a hardware recognition system based on dedicated VLSI chips mimicking the processing in the mind (Shibata (2002; 2007)).

Humans have a specialized skill in face perception because it is directly related to our social life. However, it is still debated among psychologists whether the face perception is an ability specific to humans (Gauthier et al. (1999); Moscovitch et al. (1997)). A widely used technique to localize facial images in video sequences is to use the color information of faces as a clue (Hsu et al. (2002); McKenna et al. (1999)). The human perception of faces, however, does not rely on colors but on features as a clue. A number of face detection algorithms using facial features as a clue have been developed (Yang et al. (2002)) employing principal component analysis (Liu & Wechsler (2002)), neural networks (Feraud et al. (2001); Rowley et al. (1998a;b); Sung & Poggio (1998); Viola & Jones (2004)), support vector machines (Osuna et al. (1997)), and so forth. In these algorithms, however, a large amount of numerical computation is required in general. A fast search algorithm was proposed to apply the detector to real world applications (Feraud et al. (2001)). In Viola & Jones (2004), a real-time face detection system was developed by introducing "Integral Image" representation which is very efficient in computation, and face detection performance comparable to the best prior results was obtained (Rowley et al. (1998a); Sung & Poggio (1998)).

In this article, we focus on the face detection which localizes facial images in an input image without prior information about illumination, scales, numbers of faces, and so on. The PPED representation developed in the previous work (Yagi & Shibata (2003)) is not sufficient for face detection since certain essential information in facial images is lost during the dimensionality reduction in PPED vector formation, making it difficult to discriminate facial images from non-facial images. In order to solve the problem, other directional edge-based feature representations are proposed and the concept of a feature level image fusion called multiple-clue criterion has been introduced. Namely, several feature representations in addition to PPED are employed for template matching and the multiple clues derived from each of the feature representations are utilized for the classification to enhance the face detection performance. Furthermore, the robustness against scale variations and rotations of faces has also been achieved. The robustness of the proposed algorithm has been demonstrated using the CMU test set C (Rowley et al. (1998a)).

Face identification which identifies the localized face images as individuals is another important application of face perception. Developing both face detection and face identification systems realizes an automatic face recognition systems. In order to develop the face identification system, we have adapted the directional edge-based feature representations to a classification level image fusion with pseudo two-dimensional (2D) hidden Markov models (HMM). A dedicated VLSI hardware architecture for pseudo 2D HMM's has also been developed (Suzuki & Shibata (2007)), thus the real-time performance has been performed by combining of the dedicated VLSI chips for the feature generation and the pseudo 2D HMM's. The robustness against illumination variation was demonstrated in the face identification system using Yale face database B (Georghiades et al. (2001)).

The organization of the article is as in the following. Firstly, the directional edge-based feature representations utilized in the present work are described in Section 2. Then, the organization of face detection system and the concept of multiple-clue criterion are presented in Section 3. In Section 4, the proposed feature representations are also applied to multiple-angle-view face detection, which localizes not only frontal face but also posed faces and profiles. In Section 5, the proposed feature representations have been adapted to the hidden Markov model-based face identification system. Section 6 demonstrates the performance of the algorithm. Section 7 concludes the article.

2. Directional edge-based feature representation algorithm

The feature representations utilized in the present work are described in this section. They are based on the spatial distribution of directional edges extracted from an original image. As a region of interests (ROI) for generating a feature vector, we employ a fixed-size window of 64×64-pixel sites, which is compatible with the hardware organization of the VLSI vector generator chip (Yamasaki & Shibata (2007)). A 64-dimension feature vector is generated from the pixel intensities within the window.

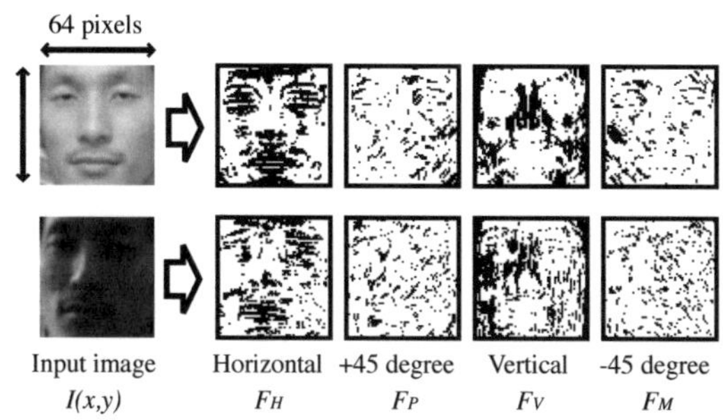

Fig. 1. Directional edge-based feature maps generated from bright and dark facial images. Since edges are detected taking local luminance variance into account, similar edge maps are obtained independent of the illumination condition.

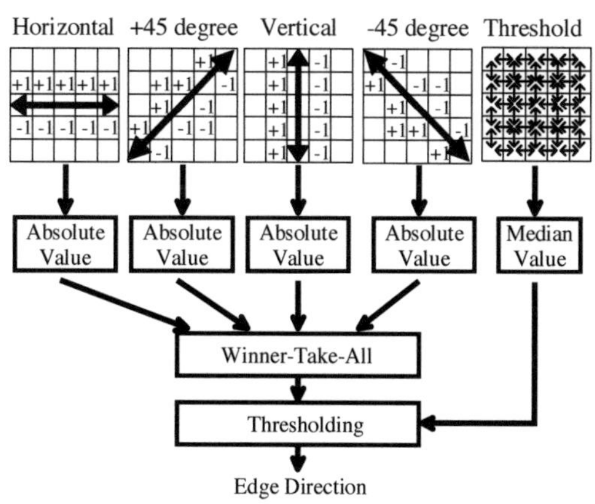

Fig. 2. Procedure of directional edge extraction.

2.1 Directional edge-based feature maps

The first step in forming feature vectors is the generation of four feature maps in which edges are extracted from a 64×64-pixel input image in four directions. Fig. 1 shows the relationship between an input image and four feature maps. Each feature map represents the distribution of edge flags corresponding to one of the four directions, i.e. horizontal, +45 degree, vertical, and -45 degree. These four directional-edge-based feature maps are regarded as representing the most fundamental features extracted from the original image

Horizontal (K_H)

0	0	0	0	0
1	1	1	1	1
0	0	0	0	0
-1	-1	-1	-1	-1
0	0	0	0	0

+45 degree (K_P)

0	0	0	1	0
0	1	1	0	-1
0	1	0	-1	0
1	0	-1	-1	0
0	-1	0	0	0

Vertical (K_V)

0	1	0	-1	0
0	1	0	-1	0
0	1	0	-1	0
0	1	0	-1	0
0	1	0	-1	0

-45 degree (K_M)

0	-1	0	0	0
1	0	-1	-1	0
0	1	0	-1	0
0	1	1	0	-1
0	0	0	1	0

Fig. 3. Filtering kernels utilized for extracting directional edges.

and all feature representations utilized in this work are derived from the feature maps. The procedure of feature-map generation is illustrated in Fig. 2. The input image is firstly subjected to pixel-by-pixel spatial filtering operations using kernels of 5×5-pixel size as in the following:

$$I_d(x,y) = \left| \sum_{i=-2}^{2} \sum_{j=-2}^{2} K_d(i,j) \cdot I(x+i, y+j) \right| \tag{1}$$

$$d \in \{H, P, V, M\}, \tag{2}$$

where $I(x,y)$ is the pixel intensity at the location (x,y), and $K_d(i,j)$ is the filtering kernel shown in Fig. 3. The kernel which gives the maximum value of $I_d(x,y)$ determines the direction of the edge at the pixel site. Namely, the preliminary edge flag $F_d^*(x,y)$ is determined as follows:

$$F_d^*(x,y) = \begin{cases} 1, & \text{if } I_d(x,y) = \max\limits_{d^* \in \{H,P,V,M\}} I_{d^*}(x,y) \\ 0, & \text{otherwise.} \end{cases} \tag{3}$$

This assigns one edge flag at every pixel site. In order to retain only edges of significance in feature maps, thresholding operation is introduced. The threshold value is determined by taking the local variance of luminance data into account. The intensity difference between two neighboring pixels in the horizontal direction $H_{nm}(x,y)$ and that in the vertical direction $V_{nm}(x,y)$ are obtained as

$$\begin{aligned} H_{nm}(x,y) &= |I(x+n+1, y+m) \\ &\quad - I(x+n, y+m)| \end{aligned} \tag{4}$$

$$\begin{aligned} V_{nm}(x,y) &= |I(x+m, y+n+1) \\ &\quad - I(x+m, y+n)| \end{aligned} \tag{5}$$

respectively, where $n = -2, -1, 0, 1$, and $m = -2, -1, 0, 1, 2$. The threshold value $TH(x,y)$ is calculated as

$$TH(x,y) = M_{ed}(x,y) \times 5, \tag{6}$$

where $M_{ed}(x,y)$ is the median of the 40 values of $H_{ij}(x,y)$ and $V_{ij}(x,y)$. For each direction $d \in \{H, P, V, M\}$, the directional edge map $F_d(x,y)$ is obtained as

$$F_d(x,y) = \begin{cases} F_d^*(x,y), & \text{if } I_d(x,y) > TH(x,y) \\ 0, & \text{otherwise.} \end{cases} \tag{7}$$

Thanks to such a thresholding operation, essential edges representing facial features are well extracted from both bright and dark facial images as shown in Fig. 1, thus making directional edge-based representations robust against illumination conditions.

2.2 Projected principal-edge distribution

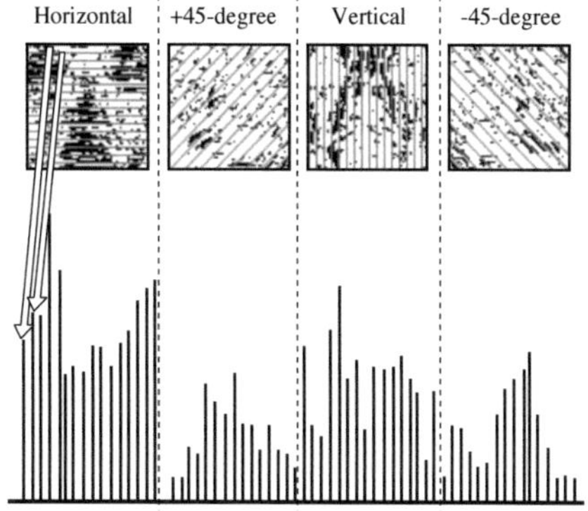

Fig. 4. Partitions of feature maps for vector generation based on projected principal-edge distribution (PPED).

Although the directional edge-based feature maps retain essential feature information in the original image, the amount of data is still massive and dimensionality reduction is essential for efficient processing of classification. Fig. 4 illustrates the procedure of feature-vector generation in the Projected Principal-Edge Distribution (PPED) (Yagi & Shibata (2003)). In the horizontal edge map, for example, edge flags in every four rows are accumulated and spatial distribution of edge flags are represented by a histogram. Similar procedures are applied to other three directions. Finally, a 64-dimension vector is formed by concatenating the four histograms. Details of the PPED feature representation are given in Yagi & Shibata (2003).

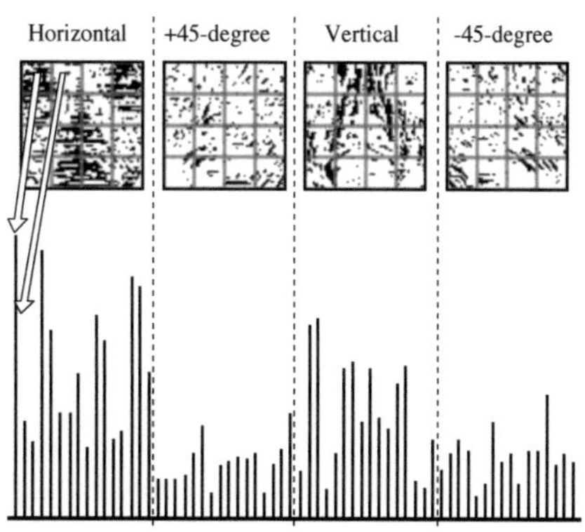

Fig. 5. Partitions of feature maps for vector generation based on averaged principal-edge distribution (APED).

2.3 Averaged principal-edge distribution

In the PPED feature representation, the information of edge distribution along the direction identical to the directional edge (e.g. the horizontal distribution of horizontal edge flags) is lost during the accumulation. In order to complement such loss in PPED vectors, other feature-vector generation schemes have been developed (Suzuki & Shibata (2004)). In the Averaged Principal-Edge Distribution scheme (which was originally named Cell Edge Distribution (CED) in Suzuki & Shibata (2004)), every feature map is divided into 4×4 cells each containing 16×16-pixel sites as shown in Fig. 5. The number of edge flags in each cell is counted and the number constitute a single element in the vector representation by the Averaged Principal-Edge Distribution (APED) scheme. From the four directional edge feature maps F_H, F_P, F_V, and F_M, four 16-dimension vectors are obtained as in the following:

$$\begin{aligned}
\mathbf{H}(a+4b) &= \sum_{i=0}^{15}\sum_{j=0}^{15} F_H(16a+i, 16b+j) \\
\mathbf{P}(a+4b) &= \sum_{i=0}^{15}\sum_{j=0}^{15} F_P(16a+i, 16b+j) \\
\mathbf{V}(a+4b) &= \sum_{i=0}^{15}\sum_{j=0}^{15} F_V(16a+i, 16b+j) \\
\mathbf{M}(a+4b) &= \sum_{i=0}^{15}\sum_{j=0}^{15} F_M(16a+i, 16b+j) \\
& a = 0,1,2,3, \; b = 0,1,2,3.
\end{aligned} \tag{8}$$

A 64-dimension feature vector $\mathbf{X}$ in the Averaged Principal-Edge Distribution scheme is obtained by concatenating these four vectors as

$$\mathbf{X} = [\mathbf{H}, \mathbf{P}, \mathbf{V}, \mathbf{M}]. \tag{9}$$

Two types of 64-dimension feature vectors, the PPED (Projected Principal-Edge Distribution) vector and the APED (Averaged Principal-Edge Distribution) vector, are utilized for face detection in the present work.

3. System organization of multiple-clue face detection

In this section, the organization of the face detection system developed in the present work is presented.

3.1 Overview of the system

In order to detect all faces in a target image, a window-scanning technique is employed for face detection as illustrated in Fig. 6. A partial image in the fixed-size window of 64×64 pixels is taken from the input image and a 64-dimension feature vector is generated according to the procedure described in Section 2. Then, the feature vector is matched with all template vectors of both face samples and non-face samples stored in the system and classified as a face or a non-face according to the category of the best-matched template vector. Namely, when the best-matched template is found in the group of face samples, the partial image is determined as a face. If the best-matched template is in the group of non-face samples, it is determined as a non-face. In this work, no threshold value is employed in the template matching. The template matching is carried out utilizing the Manhattan distance as the dissimilarity measure, which is given by

$$d(\mathbf{X}, \mathbf{T}) = \sum_{i=1}^{64} |\mathbf{X}(i) - \mathbf{T}(i)|, \tag{10}$$

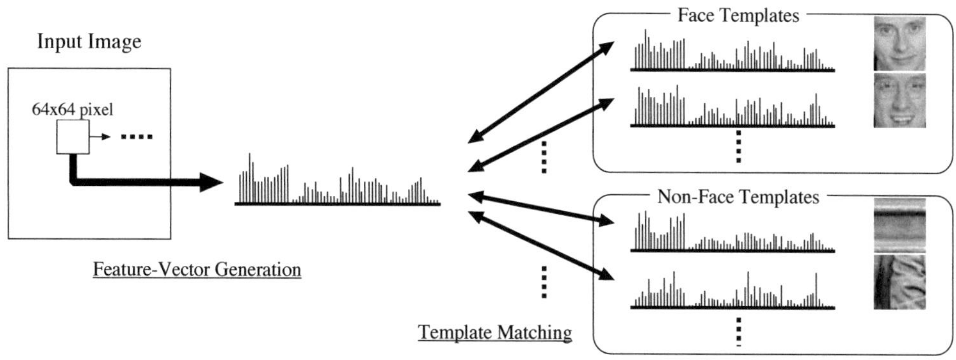

Fig. 6. A partial image in the fixed-size window of 64X64 pixels is taken from the input image and a 64-dimension feature vector is generated. Then, the feature vector is matched with all template vectors of both face samples and non-face samples and classified as a face or a non-face according to the category of the best-matched template vector. The window scans the entire image.

where **X** and **T** are a feature vector of the partial image and that of a template image, respectively. This classification is carried out by pixel-by-pixel scanning the entire image with the 64×64-pixel window.

3.2 Multiple-clue criterion

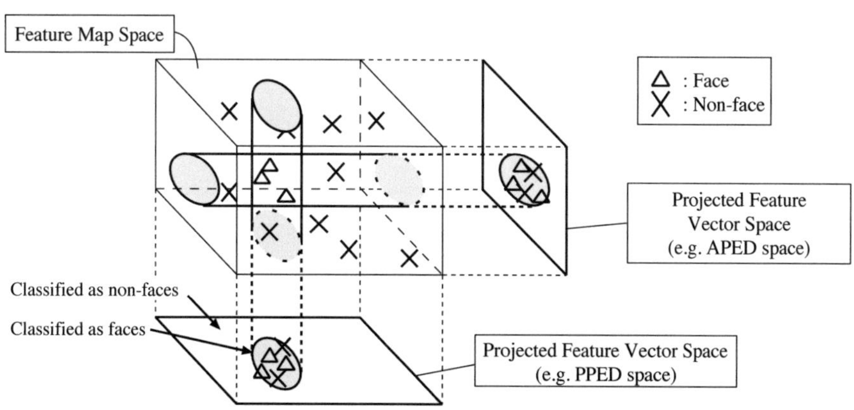

Fig. 7. Concept of multiple-clue criterion.

As we stated earlier, we assume that all essential feature information necessary to carry out correct classification is contained in the four directional edge-based feature maps. Then, the process of feature-vector generation is considered as the dimensionality reduction in the feature map space. In other words, the feature vectors are generated by projecting the data in the high-dimensional space of the four feature maps onto some lower-dimensional spaces as conceptually illustrated in Fig. 7. Then, we anticipate that some important features that separate faces from non-faces are certainly lost during the process of dimensionality reduction. This means, as illustrated in Fig. 7, the mixing of face samples ($\triangle$) and non-face samples ($\times$) necessarily occurs during the projection of sample points from the feature map space onto a reduced-dimension plane, e.g. the PPED space. However, if the sample points in

the feature map space are projected onto another plane, e.g. the APED space, the mixing of face and non-face samples would also occur, but the non-face samples mixed with face samples in the APED space would be different from the non-face samples mixed in the PPED space. Therefore, we can expect that true faces can be detected as sample points classified as faces in both PPED and APED spaces. This is the idea of multiple-clue criterion (Suzuki & Shibata (2004)). If the two low-dimensional spaces (PPED and APED in this example) are well separated from each other, a true face can be detected by taking logical AND of the detection results obtained using two types of vector representations.
In the principal components analysis (PCA), the dimensionality reduction is carried out by transforming the data to proper axes in order to maximize the variance of the data. Although the PCA is expected to retain essential feature information in the feature map space, it is not compatible with the VLSI hardware system. Therefore, in this work, we employed the multiple-clue criterion which is more compatible with the neural-associative processors.

3.3 Verification using fine-resolution feature representations

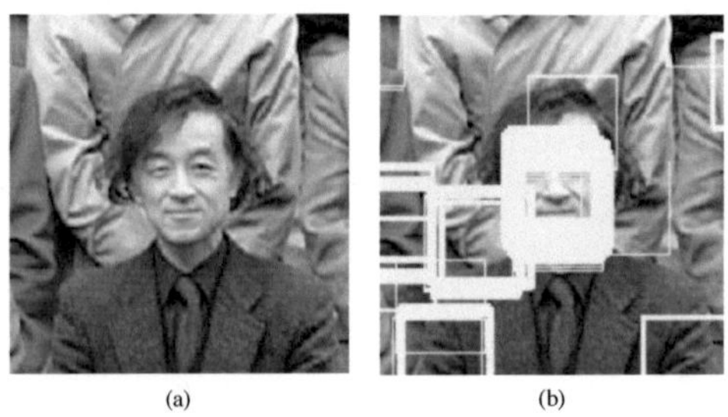

Fig. 8. Result of multiple-clue face detection from input image (a); many candidates are detected around a true face (b).

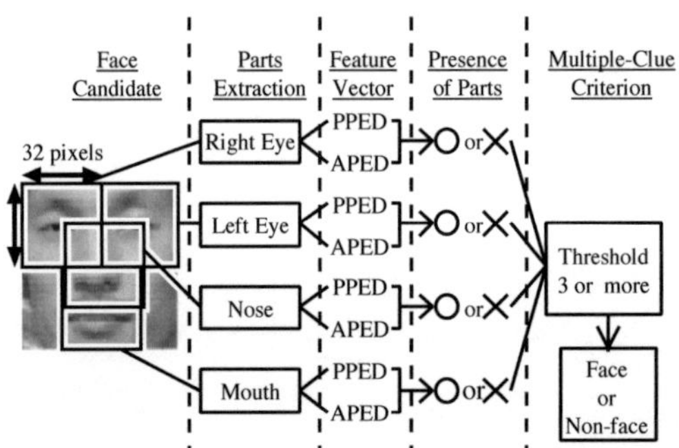

Fig. 9. Face verification by confirming existence of four facial parts by using finer edge information.

Due to the pixel-by-pixel scanning, multiple face candidates are detected around true faces as shown in Fig. 8(b). In order to merge the multiple detection results and determine the correct position of a face, we have utilized the image features extracted from a whole facial image. Confirming the presence of facial parts enhances the accuracy of the classification. Therefore, the face verification algorithm employing the feature vectors generated from local blocks with finer resolutions has been developed. In the verification algorithm, the presence of facial parts is confirmed by using finer edge information. If facial parts cannot be found, the candidate will be rejected. In the four directional feature maps, as shown in Fig. 1, a lot of edge flags are extracted around the areas of eyes and a mouth in the horizontal edge map and the area of a nose in the vertical edge map. In this work, these four facial parts are utilized in the face verification.

The procedure of the verification is as in the following. Four 32×32-pixel windows are taken from the left-top, the right-top, the center, and the bottom in the candidate window as illustrated in Fig. 9. They correspond to the locations of the right eye, the left eye, the nose and the mouth, respectively. Each 32×32-pixel window is converted to both PPED and APED vectors. In the face verification, finer edge information is utilized as compared to the original PPED and APED vectors representing whole facial features. Namely, the elements representing the horizontal or vertical edge histograms in the PPED representation, for instance, are produced by accumulating the number of edges within two columns or two rows, respectively, instead of four columns or four rows in the face detection. The elements in $\pm 45°$ histograms are also produced from reduced areas. Similarly, each element of the APED vector is generated as the number of edges in a 8×8-pixel cell instead of a 16×16-pixel cell. Template matching is carried out using the eight feature vectors generated from four facial parts with two options of PPED and APED vectors. The presence of each facial part is determined when both PPED and APED vectors match the respective template vectors. If three out of four parts are confirmed, the candidate is determined as a true face. This threshold value is determined by the experimental results discussed in Section 6 (Fig. 29).

3.4 Scale and rotation-invariant detection

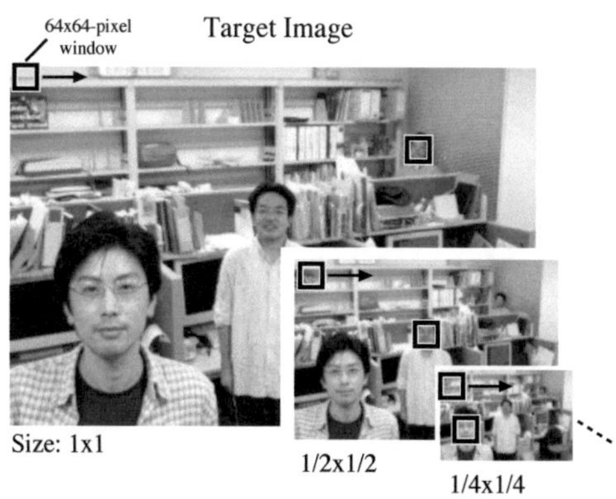

Fig. 10. Scale-invariant face detection is carried out using a fixed-size face detection window (64×64) which scans images with full-scale, 1/2, 1/4, and 1/8 scales.

Although we employed the fixed-size window, facial images may appear in various scales in the target image and not fit to the window. In order to accommodate our system to scale variations, the size of the input image is reduced by factors of 1, 1/2, 1/4, and 1/8 as illustrated in Fig. 10, and face detection is carried out for each scale. (Enlargement by factors of 1, 2, 4, ··· etc. is also possible.) Optional scaled samples are added to the set of face templates to cover the entire range between the original and 1/2 scaled images. Due to the robust nature of the directional edge-based representations, the face detection performance does not appreciably degrade for scale variations within ±15%. Since $(1 + 0.15 \times 2)^3 = 2.2$ is larger than 2, three types of scaled facial images are required to cover the scale range between 1 and 1/2. Therefore, facial images with reduced sizes of 80% and 60% are used in additional to the original images (see the results in Fig. 21).

Furthermore, facial images do not always appear upright. A similar interpolating scheme has been introduced to the system to accommodate the system to the rotated facial image detection. Namely, face detection is carried out for 90, 180, and 270 degree-rotated images in addition to the upright target image. Tilted face images within the angles between −45 and +45 degrees are added to the set of face template vectors to cover the entire 360 degrees rotation. Due to the symmetry of vector generation algorithm for 90-degree rotations in the PPED and APED vectors, the template vectors for 90, 180, and 270 degree-rotated images can be generated by just swapping elements in the original vector. The PPED and APED vectors have also tolerances for image rotation in a certain range. In this work, 0, ±18, and ±36-degree tilted face images are included as face templates for rotation invariant face segmentation (see Fig. 21(b)).

3.5 Noise reduction using Gaussian-blur filtering operation

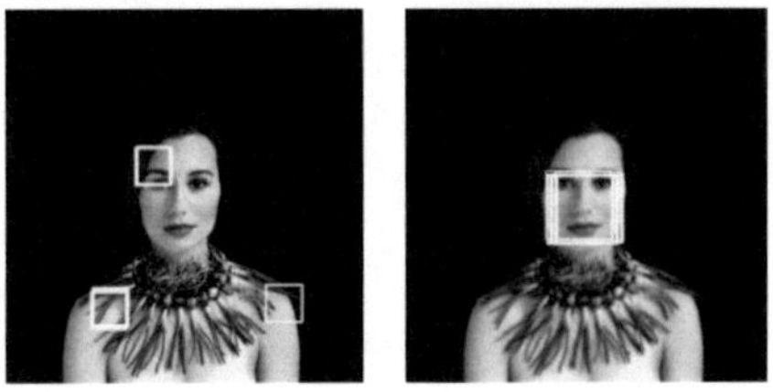

(a) (b)

Fig. 11. Face detection results from original image (a) and 5×5 Gaussian-blur filtered image (b).

Fig. 11(a) shows an example of face detection and verification result using an image in the CMU test set C (Rowley et al. (1998a)), which missed the true face. In this case, the target image is scanned from printed material, containing a lot of print noises. Such pattern noises degrade the performance of the system since the directional edge extraction is quite sensitive to them. In order to remove the noises, the target image is subjected to 5×5 Gaussian-blur filtering operation in advance. The detection result for the blurred image is show in Fig. 11(b). The true face is detected correctly without false positives. In our system, the face candidates are obtained by taking OR of the candidates from both the original and Gaussian blurred images.

4. Multi-view face detection

We have presented the frontal face detection system in Section 3. The system has been adapted to various scales and rotations of facial images. However, posed faces such as profiles cannot be detected since their appearance is different from frontal faces. The simple solution to this problem is to include posed faces into the template sets. Fig. 12 shows the directional edge-based feature maps generated from frontal face, half-way posed face, and profile images. Facial parts such as the eyes, the nose and the mouth can be easily recognized in the horizontal and vertical edge maps generated from frontal face images. However, it is difficult to identify the patterns of facial parts from the feature maps of the profile. The left-hand side of the feature map represents the rear half of the profile face, which varies a lot depending on the hairstyle of each person. Therefore, it degrades the performance of profile detection. Since the important facial parts are on the right-hand side of the feature map, the front side of the profile is utilized as a focus-of-attention (FOA) area for profile face detection. Fig. 13 illustrates the

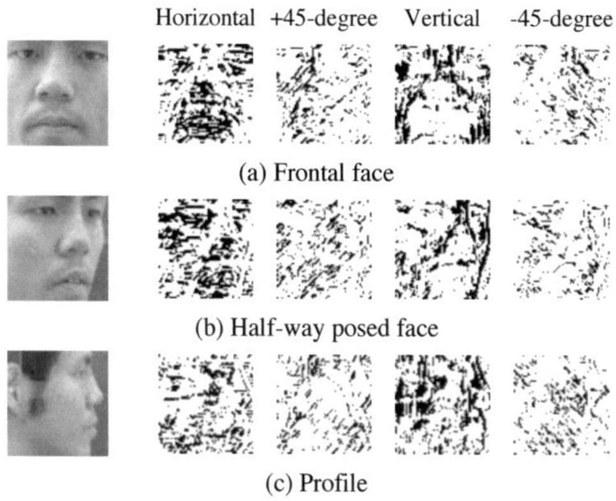

Fig. 12. Directional edge-based feature maps generated from frontal face (a), half-way posed face (b), and profile (c) images.

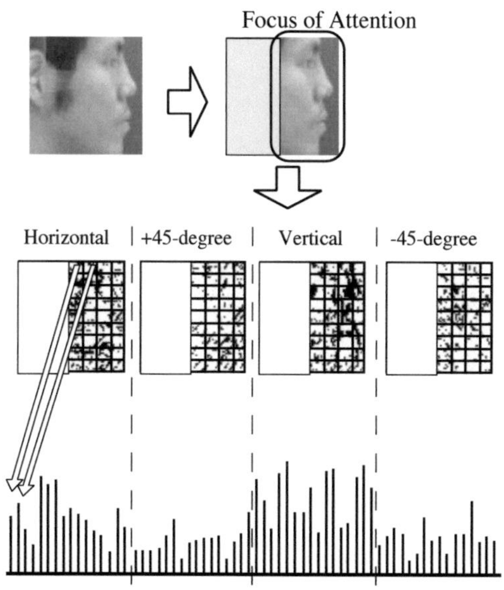

Fig. 13. Profile-specific feature-vector generation based on Averaged Principal-Edge Distribution from focus-of-attention (FOA) area.

profile-specific feature-vector generation from the focus-of-attention (FOA) area. The feature vectors are formed by similar procedures as in the APED vector generation. Namely, the FOA area is divided into 4×4 cells each of which contains 8×16-pixel sites, and each element of the 64-dimension vector represents the number of edge flags within the corresponding cell. In this system, the face verification algorithm described in Section 3.3 was not carried out.

5. Face identification employing pseudo two-dimensional hidden Markov models

In this section, we focused on a face identification system where the localized facial images, which are already detected and localized in the scene, are identified as individuals registered in the system. In order to realize a face identification system, a classification level image fusion with pseudo two-dimensional (2D) hidden Markov models (HMM) has been employed.

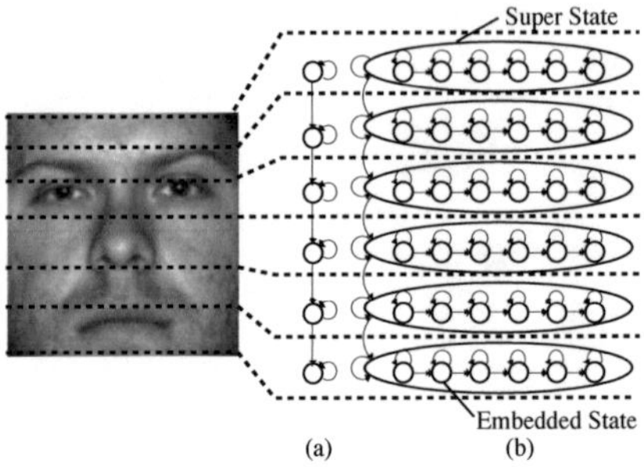

Fig. 14. 1D Hidden Markov Model (a) and pseudo-2D Hidden Markov Model (b).

HMM's are one of the statistical classifiers successfully applied to the speech recognition. The original form of HMM's is based on a simple one dimensional (1D) Markov chain. In order to process images as 2D data, pseudo-2D HMM's have been introduced (Kuo & Agazzi (1994)) and applied to face recognition (Nefian & Hayes (1998)). The pseudo-2D HMM consists of a set of super states which contain a 1D HMM within themselves. The pseudo-2D HMM is utilized for modeling facial images in a hierarchical manners as in the following. Several super states correspond to the vertical facial features, such as forehead, eyes, nose, and mouth as illustrated in Fig. 14 (b). Each state within the super state is utilized for modeling the horizontal sequence of the localized feature. The pseudo-2D HMM-based face identification has often utilized the coefficients of 2D discrete cosine transform (DCT) for feature representation (Eickeler et al. (2000); Nefian & Hayes (1999)). However, the representation is sensitive to the change in illumination conditions. In order to develop an illumination-invariant system, the directional edge-based feature representation is employed for the pseudo-2D Hidden-Markov-Model-based face identification.

5.1 Feature representations

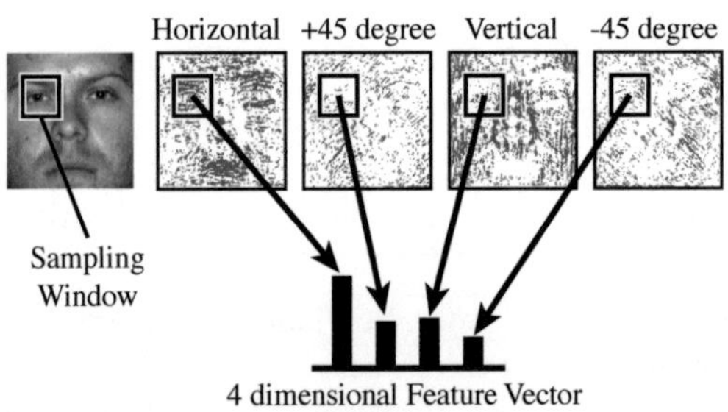

Fig. 15. Feature-vector-generation scheme from edge-based feature maps: each element represents the number of edge flags within sampling window.

The proposed feature representation vectors are generated from the edge-based feature maps described in Section 2.1 by counting the number of edge flags within the sampling window as illustrated in Fig. 15. Each element of the vector represents the number of edge flags within the window of the corresponding edge direction. Since four directional edges are available in the feature maps, four elements of the feature representation vector are generated from a sampling window. In order to represent the 2D structural information within the sampling window, another type of feature-vector-generation scheme illustrated in Fig. 16 was also employed. In this scheme, a larger size sampling window is employed and then divided into 2×2 cells. A 16-dimension feature vector is generated by counting the number of edge flags in each cell.

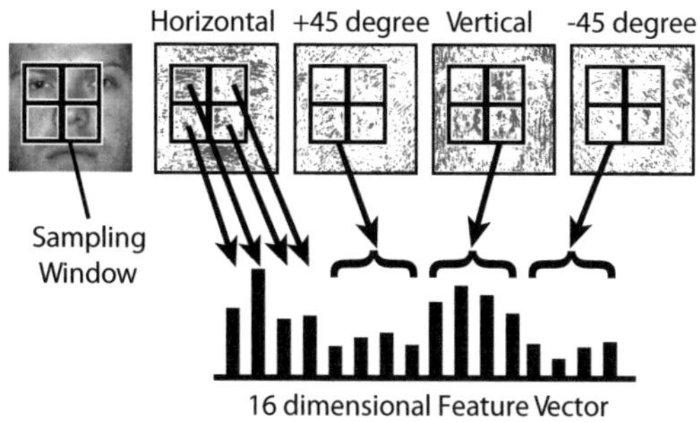

Fig. 16. Another feature-vector-generation scheme: four times larger size sampling window is divided into 2 × 2 cells and each element represents the number of edge flags within a cell.

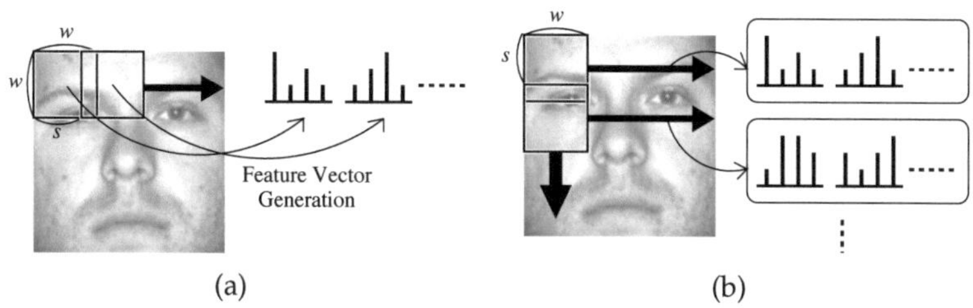

Fig. 17. Sampling window scans face image; horizontal scanning (a) and vertical scrolling (b).

The sequence of observation vectors is acquired as follows. The $w \times w$-pixel window scans the image from left to right and makes the sequence of feature vectors as illustrated in Fig. 17(a). For each sampling, the sampling window shifts s pixels to right. The horizontal scanning is repeated with the vertical pitch of s pixels from the top to bottom as shown in Fig. 17 (b). In this manner, a series of feature vectors is generated. These feature vectors are utilized as observation vectors for the pseudo-2D Hidden Markov Models on both training and identification stages.

5.2 Face identification using pseudo-2D HMM's

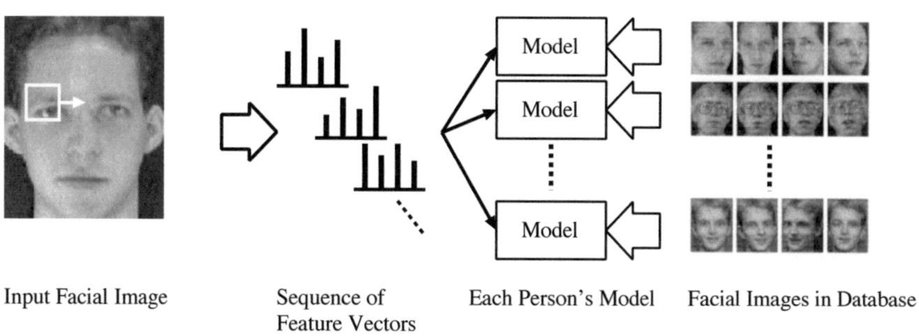

Fig. 18. Pseudo-2D HMM-based face identification system. A sequence of feature vectors is generated from the partial image in the scanning window, which is then matched with each person's HMM using the Viterbi algorithm. Then, the maximum-likelihood model yields the identity of the face.

The identification of the target facial image is carried out as in the following. The sequence of edge-based feature-vectors is classified by the pseudo-2D Hidden Markov Models. The 6×6-state left-right model illustrated in Fig. 14 (b) is utilized in this work. The model consists of six super states each of which contains an one-dimension Hidden Markov Model with six embedded states. The sum of three Gaussian mixtures is employed for the probability function of the embedded state. These parameters of the HMM are optimized by the experimental results on the AT&T face database (Samaria & Harter (1994)).

In the training, one HMM is generated for each person using the Baum-Welch algorithm. For avoiding false local minima, the common initial face model (Eickeler et al. (2000)) is utilized. Namely, the common initial face model is firstly trained on all faces in the training set. The face model for each person is obtained from the common model by refining it on the training faces of the person with the Baum-Welch algorithm. In the identification, the target facial image is evaluated by each face model using the Viterbi algorithm as illustrated in Fig. 18. The face model which gives the maximum probability determines the identity of the input image.

5.3 Dedicated VLSI architecture for pseudo-2D HMM classifier

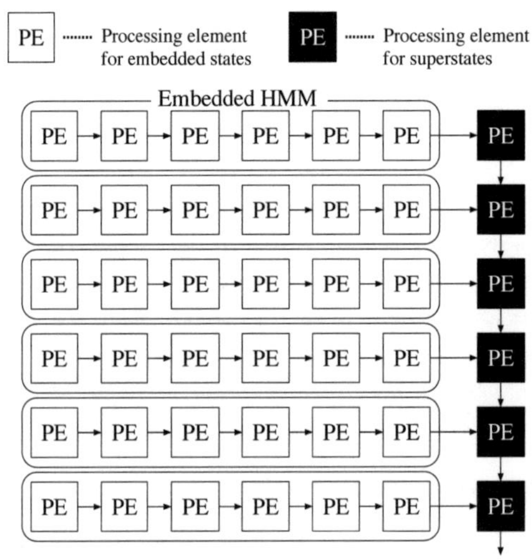

Fig. 19. Block diagram of pseudo-2D HMM VLSI processor. Each PE corresponds to an embedded state or a superstate in pseudo-2D HMM.

In order to realize the real-time face identification system, a dedicated VLSI hardware architecture for pseudo-2D HMM classifier has been developed. The proposed architecture consists of processing elements (PE's) each of which corresponds to an embedded state or a super state as illustrated in Fig. 19. The processing element for the embedded state is composed of the Viterbi decoder and the observation probability calculator which identifies the maximum-likelihood path among all possible state transitions within the HMM. The details of the proposed architecture are described in Suzuki & Shibata (2007).

The proposed architecture has been implemented in a field programmable gate array (FPGA). The processing time for identifying a 92×112 pixel grayscale facial image from 40 people was 4.42 ms at 100 MHz clock frequency. Therefore, the processor is capable of identifying more than 220 facial images in a second.

6. Experimental results and discussion

6.1 Frontal face detection

Fig. 20. Group photo in which 2,000 non-face images were randomly taken from the background scenery as non-face templates.

In this work, the upright frontal facial images of 300 Japanese people from HOIP facial image database were utilized as face templates in the experiment of frontal face detection. As the non-face templates, 2,000 non-face images which were randomly taken from the background scenery of only a group photo shown in Fig. 20 were employed. Updating of the non-face templates by feeding back the results of false positives, or other sorts of maintenance were not conducted in this work. The same non face templates were used throughout the experiments. The performance of the face detection system has been evaluated on the CMU test set (Rowley et al. (1998a)).

The system was evaluated by using two types of measures which are detection rates and false positive rates. They were defined as in the followings. Because of the pixel-by-pixel scanning, multiple windows of the detection results are overlapped as shown in Fig. 8(b). If two windows were overlapped in area more than 50% each other, they were merged into one window. Only when the merged window covered the entire face including the eyes, the nose, and the mouth, we determined that the face was detected correctly. The detection rate is the number of faces detected against faces in the test images. The false positive rate is the number of false detections against all 64×64-pixel windows examined in the evaluation. The system decides whether an image within the window is a face or not at each pixel site independently. Therefore, the false positive rate described above is employed for the evaluation.

6.1.1 Optimization for scale-invariant detection

As described in Section 3.4, it is required to append the optional scaled samples to the set of face templates to cover the range between the original and 1/2 scaled images. In order to optimize the sets of templates for scale variations, face detection was carried out with the template vectors derived from different combinations of scaled face samples. Fig. 21(a) demonstrates the results of face detection rate. The template set of 100%+70%, for example, means that 70% scaled 300 face samples were appended to the original 300 face samples for the face templates of reduced scales. As illustrated in Fig. 21(a), when three types of scaled face samples (100%, 80%, and 60%) were utilized, over 99% detection rate was shown. Therefore, the three types of face samples (100%, 80%, and 60%) were utilized in the following experiments.

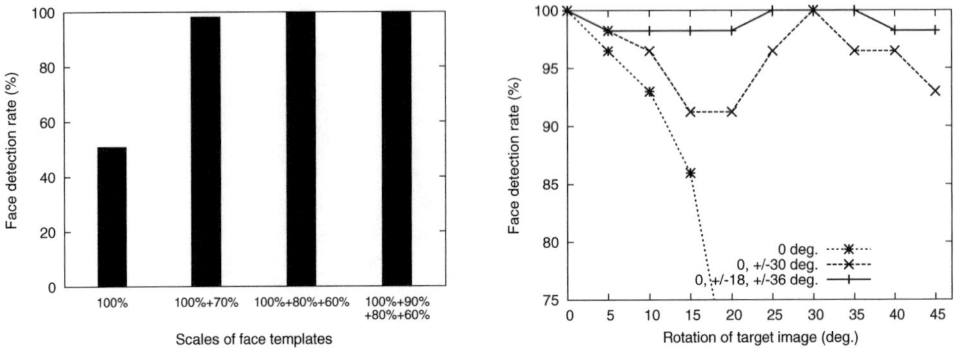

(a) (b)

Fig. 21. Face detection rates with template vectors derived from different combinations of scaled face samples (a); detection rates from rotated target images with template vectors derived from different combinations of tilted face samples.

6.1.2 Optimization for rotation-invariant detection

(a) (b)

Fig. 22. Results of scale and rotation-invariant face detection using images in Rowley et al. (1998b). Verification by facial parts were not carried out in the experiment.

As described in Section 3.4, it is required to prepare the tilted face samples as the face templates to cover the range between −45 and +45 degrees. To optimize the face template sets, face detection was carried out on rotated target images between 0 and +45 degrees using different combinations of tilted template vectors. The detection rates are presented in Fig. 21(b). Using only upright templates, namely only 0-degree template vectors, the detection rate falls rapidly at 10 degrees of tilting. Although the set of 0 and ±30-degree template vectors covers the range, the detection rate fluctuates depending on the tilt angle. The results obtained with the template set generated from 0, ±18, and ±36-degree tilted facial images show the detection rate over 95% all over the range. Fig. 22 demonstrates the results of scale and rotation-invariant face detection using images that contain difference size and angle of faces in the CMU rotation test set (Rowley et al. (1998b)).

6.1.3 Tests of face detection and verification

In order to eliminate false positives, face verification algorithm described in Section 3.3 was employed here. Here, if at least three facial parts were confirmed out of four parts, the

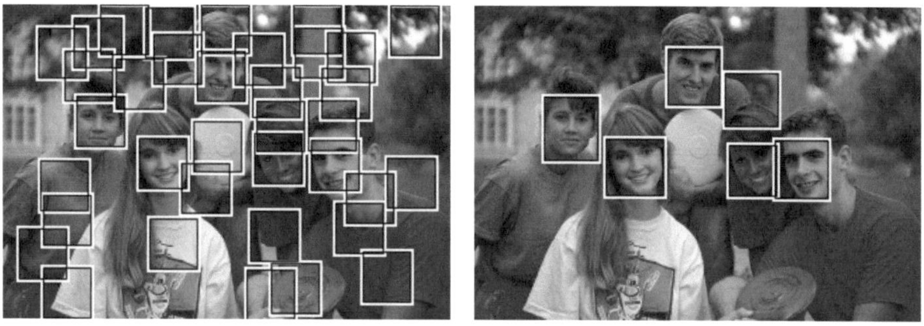

(a) (b)

Fig. 23. Result of face detection (a) and face verification (b).

(a) (b)

Fig. 24. Examples of face candidates which were detected in Fig. 23(a) but rejected by verification in Fig. 23(b); (a) and (b) are on top left and top right corner in original image, respectively.

(a) (b)

Fig. 25. Face detection results on line drawing face using original image (a) and 5×5 Gaussian-blur filtered image (b).

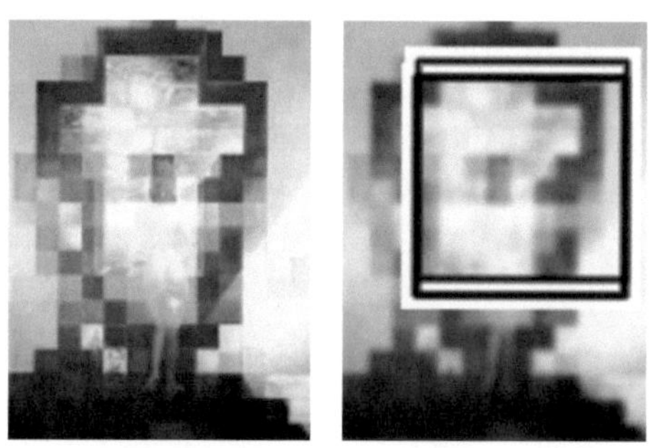

(a) (b)

Fig. 26. Results of face detection on Dali's "Gala Contemplating the Mediterranean Sea" from original image (a) and 5×5 Gaussian-blur image (b).

candidate was accepted as a true face. Fig. 23(a) demonstrates the result of face detection using a picture in the CMU test set B. All faces in the picture are detected. However, a lot of false positives occur. These detected faces were screened using the face verification algorithm and the result of verification is demonstrated in Fig. 23(b). All false positives except one were rejected by the verification without missing the true faces. Fig. 24 shows examples of false positives in face detection shown in Fig. 23. These candidates, which looks like faces at a glance by human perception, were rejected by verification algorithm since facial parts could not be confirmed.
As described in Section 3.5, the face candidates are obtained from both original and 5×5 Gaussian-blur filtered images. This Gaussian-blur operation makes another effect to face detection. A line drawing facial image shown in Fig. 25(a) was not detected from the original image but detected and verified from the blurred one as illustrated in Fig. 25(b). Fig. 26 demonstrates the face verification results for the drawing by Salvador Dali, "Gala Contemplating the Mediterranean Sea" which is also called "Lincoln in Dalivision". Although no faces are detected from the original image in a reduced size shown in Fig. 26(a), Lincoln is detected and verified correctly in the blurred image as illustrated in Fig. 26(b).

6.2 Performance evaluation on CMU test set

In order to evaluate the performance of the system, the proposed algorithm has been evaluated on the CMU test set C which consists of 65 images containing 183 faces. Fig. 27 presents the detection rates and false positive rates using the PPED and APED feature representations. The detection rate is the number of faces detected correctly against all 183 faces in the test set. The false positive rate is the number of false detections against 80,146,631 which is the number of 64×64-pixel windows examined in this evaluation. Generally, there are trade-offs between the detection rates and the false positive rates, and the closer the data points approach the left-top corner, the better the performance is. When PPED vectors are utilized, 93% of faces are detected from the original images and 97% detection rate is achieved for 5×5-pixel Gaussian-blur filtered images. APED vectors show better performance than PPED, and 97% and 99% detection rates are obtained for the original and Gaussian blurred images, respectively. Only one facial image shown in Fig. 28 was not detected from either original or blurred images. This image is composed of black-and-white dots and the high frequency components in the image were not removed by the Gaussian-blur filter, which contributed edge flags to the feature maps. When the image was subjected to Gaussian-blur filtering operation one more time, however, the face was detected. On the other hand, the false positive rates are about 0.01 (1%) and a huge number of false positives occur. Fig. 27 also shows the detection results using the multiple-clue criterion using both PPED and APED, which are 88% and 95% for the original and Gaussian-blur filtered images, respectively. Although the face detection rate is a little degraded as compared to the case using only PPED vectors or APED vectors, the false positive rate is improved. In order to improve the detection rate, we merged the detection results from both the original images and Gaussian blurred images. This OR operation achieves 95% detection rate when the multiple-clue criterion is employed as shown in Fig. 27.
In order to further reduce the number of false positives, the face verification algorithm explained in Section 3.3 was introduced and the number of facial parts to confirm in the face verification algorithm was varied. The face detection rates for the verification algorithm in which the existence of no less than one, two, three, and four facial parts out of four parts are given in Fig. 29. If all of four facial parts are required for verification, the detection rate is degraded to about 50% while the number of false positive is drastically reduced. From

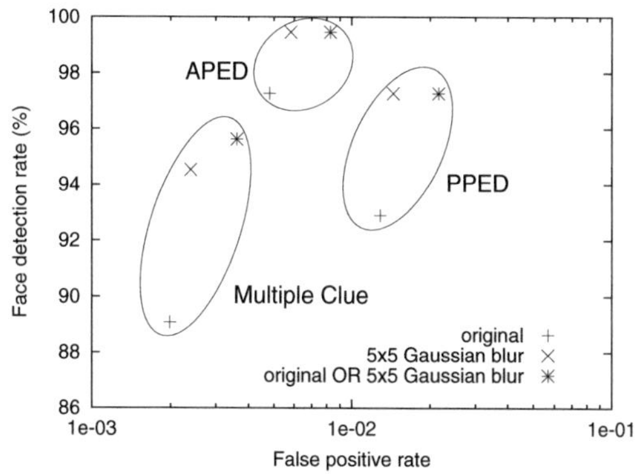

Fig. 27. Detection rates and false positive rates using PPED, APED, and multiple-clue criterion of them.

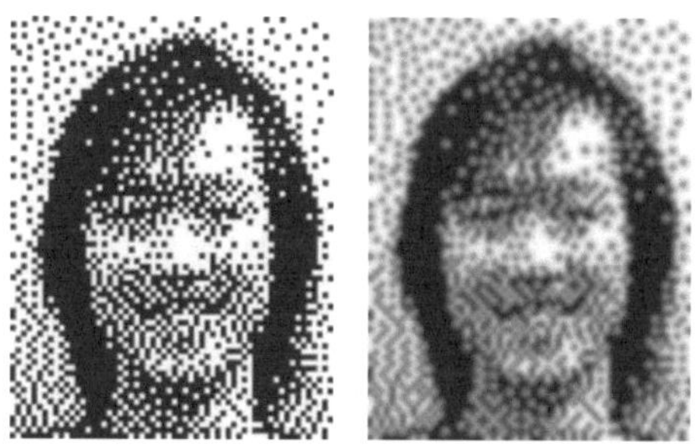

(a) (b)

Fig. 28. Facial image could not be detected using APED feature vector from either original image (a) or blur image (b).

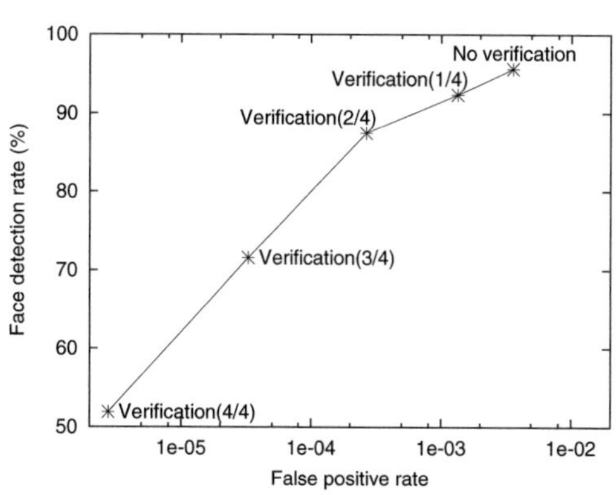

Fig. 29. Detection rates and false positive rates using face verification.

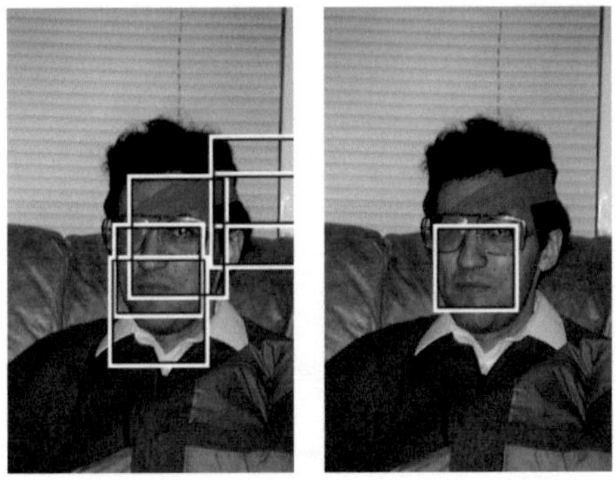

(a) (b)

Fig. 30. Results of face detection (a) and verification (b) from facial image whose right eye is occluded.

these results, we adopted three or more facial parts as the threshold for verification. Fig. 30 illustrates the result of detection and verification on an occluded face. In this case, the right eye failed to be confirmed but the other parts were validated and the true face was correctly verified.

As demonstrated in Fig 29, there are trade-offs between the detection rates and the false positive rates, thus the system yielding less false positives demonstrates the better performance at the same face detection rate. In the face detection system employing two facial parts for the threshold value in face verification, for instance, the detection rate using the CMU test set C was 87.4% while 689 false positives occured. When the system was evaluated on all images in the CMU test set A, B, and C, the detection rate was degraded to 71.5% while 1,055 false positives occured. The systems developed by Viola & Jones (2004) and by Rowley et al. (1998a) achieved the higher detection rate (81.1% and 83.2%) with 10 false positives, respectively. These results indicate that the performance of our system is not comparable to other systems. In the learning, Viola and Jones employed the AdaBoost algorithm which increases the effective number of non-face templates. Rowley et al. updated the non face-templates by feeding back the results of false positives. These techniques have not been studies in this work yet. Introducing such techniques to the learning algorithm of false positives would improve the performance of our system in reducing the false positive detection rate, which would be the subject of future study.

The present face detection algorithm has been developed as a typical pattern matching algorithm specifically tuned for the VLSI brain mimicking system under intensive development (Shibata (2002; 2007)). Therefore, it involves a lot of computationally demanding operations. However, they are very efficiently processed using dedicated VLSI chips developed for the system. For instance, the directional-edge based vector generation from every pixel site in a VGA-size image is carried out at a rate of 6.1 frames/s (Yamasaki & Shibata (2007)). Further enhancement in the processing speed by a factor of 30 has been achieved by an advancement in the chip architecture (Nakagawa et al. (2009)). In order to accelerate the scale-invariant detection, a CMOS image sensor chip capable of performing multiple-scale filtering processing for a 64×64-pixel image has been developed and operation at a 680 frames/s was demonstrated (Takahashi et al. (2009)). Therefore, the processing in the present algorithm is all very efficiently conducted in the VLSI brain mimicking system. However, regarding the recognition performance, the present results are not sufficient when compared to those of advanced software systems. If the false positive rate is defined as the number of false detections against all the detection results, our results are in the range of several 10%, which are far inferior to the results in Rowley et al. (1998a) and Viola & Jones (2004). PPED-based face detection was also studied using a support vector machine (SVM) as a classifier instead of the simple nearest-neighbor search method employed in this work, which showed much better results. In this regard, the basic VLSI circuits for SVM have also been developed for use in a certain kind of classification problems (Kang & Shibata (2009)).

6.3 Experiment on multi-view face detection

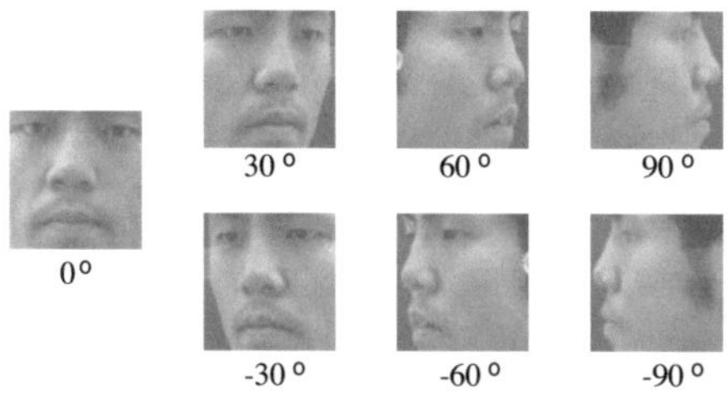

Fig. 31. Template images for multi-view face detection.

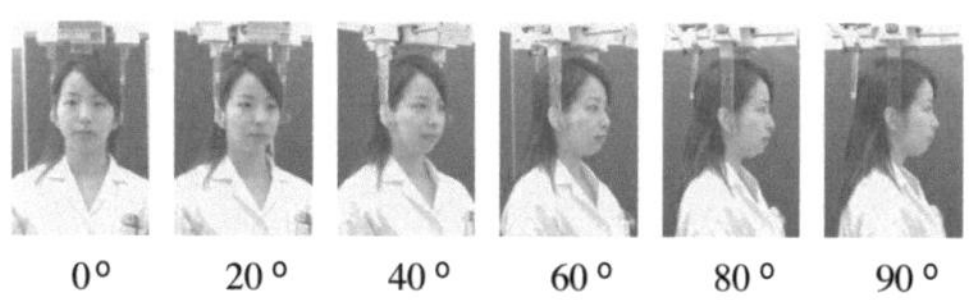

Fig. 32. Target images for multi-view face detection.

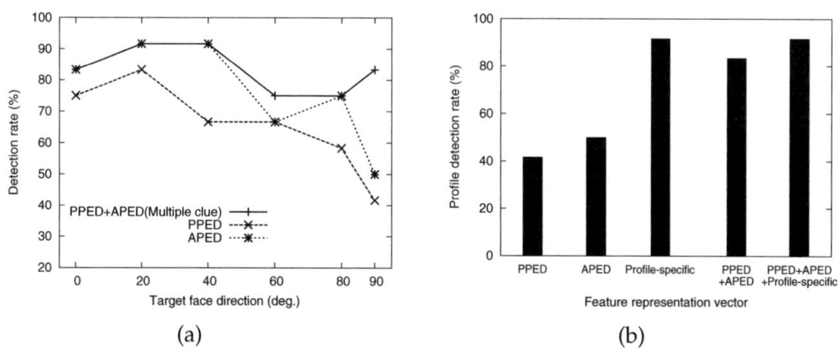

Fig. 33. Results of multi-view face detection rate (a); results of profile detection rate (b).

In order to evaluate the multi-view face detection, 130 face images of 13 people taken from 10 directions between the range of 0 to 90 degrees with an increment of 10 degrees were utilized. These sample images were prepared as a preliminary database to use in the multi-dimensional facial soft tissue analysis for the treatment planning in orthodontics. Four direction posed faces at 0, 30, 60, and 90 degrees were utilized as templates. In addition, −30, −60, and −90-degree direction faces were generated by taking the mirror images of original samples as shown in Fig. 31. Face detection was carried out on face images angled at 0, 20, 40, 60, 80, and 90 degrees for 13 people as shown in Fig. 32. The detection rate was evaluated by the cross validation. Namely, all face images except for one person were utilized as templates and the face detection was carried out for the face images of the person excluded from the templates. This procedure was repeated for all images in the database. In this experiments, based on the prior knowledge that only one face image is existing in the target image, the location where the feature vector gives the minimum distance to the best matched template was determined as a face. And the direction of the template which gives the minimum distance among the all templates determines the pose of the target face. Fig. 33(a) shows the detection rates of six direction faces using the PPED and APED feature vectors, respectively. Although almost over 80% detection rates are obtained in frontal and 20-degree faces for both feature vectors, the detection rates degrade to less than 60% in profile images. In order to improve the performance, the multiple-clue criterion have been utilized. Fig. 33(a) illustrates the correct detection rates using the multiple-clue criterion. The detection rates all of angled faces were improved and approximate 80% detection rates were obtained. Fig. 33(b) shows the detection rates of profile images for three types of feature vectors: the PPED, APED, and profile-specific APED as discussed in Section 4. In addition, the detection rates using the multiple clue derived from all three feature vectors are also shown in Fig. 33(b). Only about 50% of the target profile images were detected with the original feature vectors (PPED and APED). However, over 90% detection rate was obtained with the proposed profile-specific APED feature vector.

6.4 Experiment on face identification using pseudo-2D HMM's

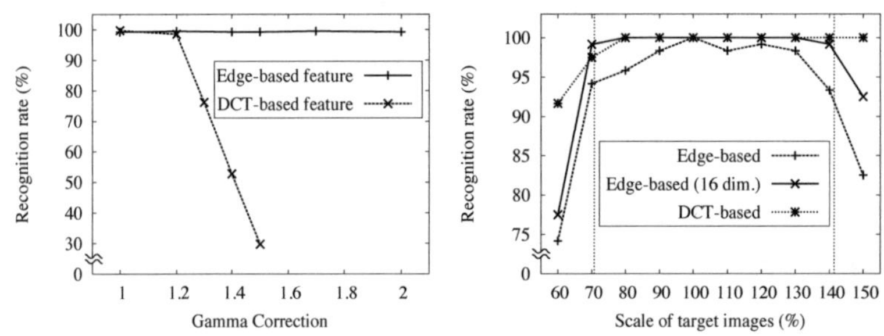

(a) (b)

Fig. 34. Recognition rate on AT&T database with different illumination conditions (a) and with different scales of target facial images (b).

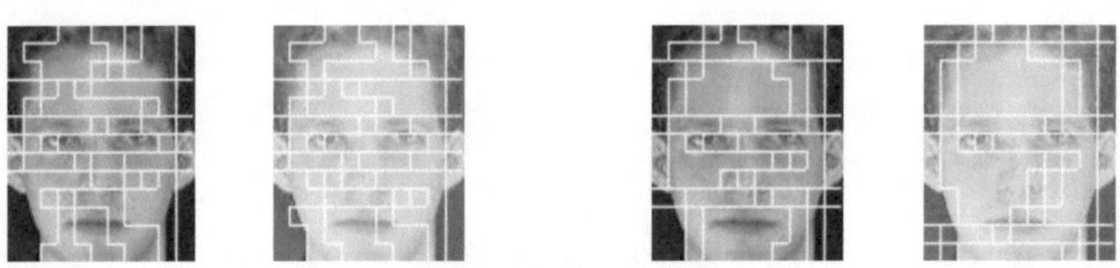

(a) (b)

Fig. 35. Viterbi segmentation of face images under different illumination conditions using edge-based feature vectors (a) and DCT-based feature vectors (b); each block corresponds to each state of pseudo-2D HMM.

In order to evaluate the performance of the proposed face identification system, the AT&T face database (Samaria & Harter (1994)) was used for both training and test sets. This database contains 10 different images for each of 40 people. These face images are taken at similar illumination conditions. As a preliminary evaluation of the robustness against illumination variations, various illumination conditions were emulated by the gamma correction. The recognition rate was evaluated by the cross validation. Namely, each person's model was trained on all face images except for one image and the classification was carried out for the image excluded in the training. This procedure was repeated for all images in the database.

The recognition rates on various illumination conditions employing the edge-based and the DCT-based feature representations are presented in Fig. 34(a). In this experiment, first nine coefficients of discrete cosine transform on the sampling window are utilized for the DCT-based feature vectors, and the four dimensional feature vector of Fig. 15 was used as the edge-based feature vectors. $w = 8$ and $s = 4$ were employed for both feature vectors as the parameters of window scanning. Figure 34(a) shows that the recognition rate of the DCT-based feature vectors falls rapidly at $\gamma = 1.3$ while the edge-based feature vectors performed over 99% recognition rate at the entire range. Figure 35 shows the results of the Viterbi segmentation on the two test images ($\gamma = 1.0$ and $\gamma = 2.0$). Each block separated by the white lines corresponds to each state of the pseudo-2D HMM illustrated in Fig. 14. The segmentation results using the edge-based features are almost the same independent of illumination conditions as shown in Fig. 35(a). On the other hand, Fig. 35(b) shows that the states to which the nose and the mouth belong do not match between the dark and bright images in case of the DCT-based feature vectors.

Figure 34(b) shows the recognition rate on the various size of the target faces. Although the recognition rate using the edge-based feature vectors (4 dimensions) is a little degraded as compared to that using the DCT-based ones, the recognition rate using the 16 dimensional edge-based feature vectors is almost same with that using the DCT-based ones. Over 99% recognition rate was obtained with the 16 dimensional edge-based vectors on the scale range between 70% ($\approx \frac{1}{\sqrt{2}}$) and 140% ($\approx \sqrt{2}$). The scale-invariant face detection system described in Section 3 is capable of enclosing facial images of any sizes in a frame in which the scale variation of the face image is limited within the range between $\frac{1}{\sqrt{2}}$ and $\sqrt{2}$. Therefore, it would be possible to build a scale-invariant face identification system using our already-developed face detection system as a preprocessing stage in the present identification system.

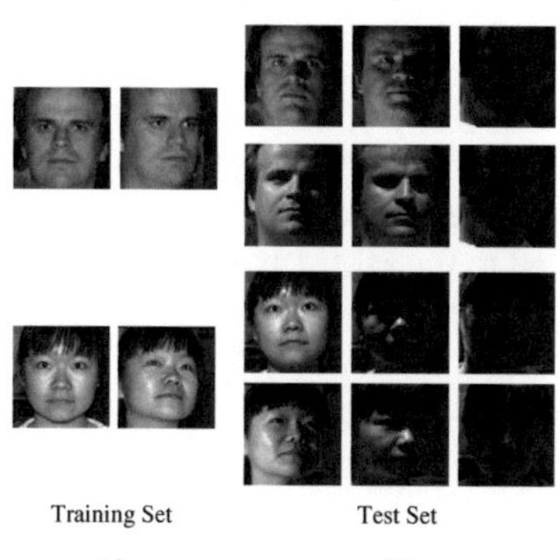

Fig. 36. Examples of facial images from Yale face database B used for training (a) and test (b).

The proposed system demonstrates a good performance. However, the results are obtained from the AT&T face database which consists of relatively simple images for identification. We also evaluated the performance on the Yale face database B (Georghiades et al. (2001)). The

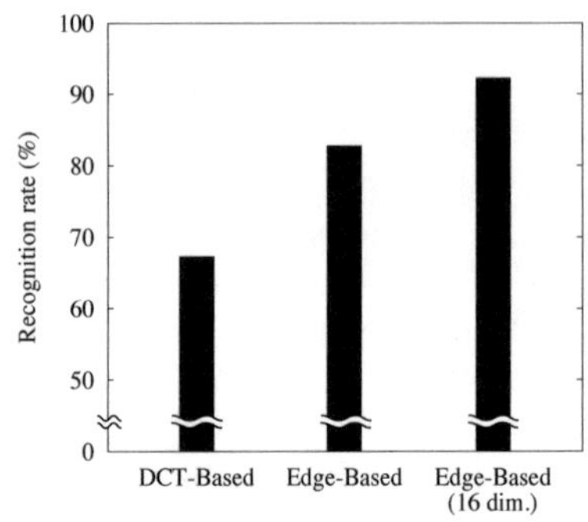

Fig. 37. Recognition rate on Yale face database B.

Yale face database B contains 5760 single light source images of 10 people each seen under 576 viewing conditions (9 poses × 64 illumination conditions). The face model of each person was learned from the nine poses with frontal illumination, and then the face identification is carried out for the images under various illumination conditions. Examples of facial images are shown in Fig. 36. Figure 37 illustrates the results of face identification. The recognition rate obtained with the proposed 16 dimensional edge-based feature vectors was 92% and better than that of the DCT-based feature vectors.

7. Summary

A face detection system has been developed aiming at exploring a pattern matching algorithm specifically adapted to the psychologically-inspired VLSI brain model system (Shibata (2002; 2007)). Namely, the computations involved in the algorithm are all very efficiently carried out by the dedicated VLSI chips developed for the system. Four directional edges are extracted from a 64×64-pixel image and two kinds of image feature vectors (PPED and APED) are generated by forming spatial distribution histograms from the edge maps. By the introduction of multiple-clue criterion using these two edge vectors, a face detection robust against scale variation and rotation has been developed. Although the total performance including the false positive rate has not yet reached those of advanced software systems, the algorithm has shown a lot of potentiality and issues for use in the VLSI hardware recognition system. The system has also been applied to the detection of posed faces and it has been shown that the performance for the profile face detection can be enhanced by generating edge-based vectors only from the region of focus-of-attention. Furthermore, the directional edge-based feature representations has been adapted to the HMM-based face identification system and the robust nature of the representations has been proven.

8. Acknowledgment

The authors would like to thank Daisuke Moriya at The University of Tokyo for his contribution to the work of posed face detection, and Prof. Kenji Takada and Dr. Masakazu Yagi at Osaka University for their support throughout the work.

9. References

Belongie, S., Malik, J. & Puzicha, J. (2002). Shape matching and object recognition using shape contexts, *IEEE Trans. Pattern Anal. Machine Intell.* 24(4): 509–522.

Dalai, N., Triggs, B., Rhone-Alps, I. & Montbonnot, F. (2005). Histograms of oriented gradients for human detection, *Proc. of Computer Vision and Pattern Recognition (CVPR 2005)*, Vol. 1, San Diego, CA.

Eickeler, S., Muller, S. & Rigoll, G. (2000). Recognition of JPEG compressed face images based on statistical methods, *Image and Vision Computing* 18: 279–287.

Feraud, R., Bernier, O. J., Viallet, J. E. & Collobert, M. (2001). Fast and accurate face detector based on neural networks, *IEEE Trans. Pattern Anal. Machine Intell.* 23(1): 42–53.

Freeman, W. & Roth, M. (1995). Orientation histograms for hand gesture recognition, *Proc. International Workshop on Automatic Face-and Gesture-Recognition*, Zurich, Switzerland, pp. 296–301.

Gauthier, I., Behrmann, M. & Tarr, M. (1999). Can face recognition really be dissociated from object recognition?, *Journal of Cognitive Neuroscience* 11(4): 349–370.

Georghiades, A., Belhumeur, P. & Kriegman, D. (2001). From few to many: Illumination cone models for face recognition under variable lighting and pose, *IEEE Trans. Pattern Anal. Machine Intell.* 23(6): 643–660.

Hsu, R. L., Abdel-Mottaleb, M. & Jain, A. K. (2002). Face detection in color images, *IEEE Trans. Pattern Anal. Machine Intell.* 24(5): 696–706.

Hubel, D. & Wiesel, T. (1959). Receptive fields of single neurons in the cat's striate cortex, *Journal of Physiology* 148(3): 574–591.

Kang, K. & Shibata, T. (2009). An on-chip-trainable Gaussian-kernel analog support vector machine, *Proc. IEEE Int. Symp. Circuits and Systems (ISCAS 2009)*, Taipei, Taiwan, pp. 2661–2664.

Kuo, S. & Agazzi, O. (1994). Keyword spotting in poorly printed documents using pseudo 2-D hidden Markov models, *IEEE Trans. Pattern Anal. Machine Intell.* 16(8): 842–848.

Liu, C. & Wechsler, H. (2002). Gabor feature base classification using the enhanced fisher linear discriminant model for face recognition, *IEEE Trans. Image Processing* 11(4): 467–476.

Lowe, D. G. (2004). Distinctive image features from scale-invariant keypoints, *International Journal of Computer Vision* 60(2): 91–110.

McKenna, S. J., Raja, Y. & Gong, S. (1999). Tracking colour objects using adaptive mixture models, *Image and Vision Computing* 17: 225–231.

Mikolajczyk, K. & Schmid, C. (2005). A performance evaluation of local descriptors, *IEEE Trans. Pattern Anal. Machine Intell.* 27(10): 1615–1630.

Moscovitch, M., Winocur, G. & Behrmann, M. (1997). What is special about face recognition? nineteen experiments on a person with visual object agnosia and dyslexia but normal face recogniton, *Journal of Cognitive Neuroscience* 9(5): 555–604.

Nakagawa, T., Fujita, K. & Shibata, T. (2009). A real-time image feature vector generator employing functional cache memory for edge flags, *Proc. IEEE Int. Symp. Circuits and Systems (ISCAS 2009)*, Taipei, Taiwan, pp. 3026–3029.

Nefian, A. & Hayes, M. (1998). Hidden Markov models for face recognition, *Proc. Int'l Conf. Accoustics, Speech and Signal Processing (ICASSP 1998)*, Vol. 5, pp. 2721–2724.

Nefian, A. & Hayes, M. (1999). An embedded HMM-based approach for face detection and recognition, *Proc. Int'l Conf. Accoustics, Speech and Signal Processing (ICASSP 1999)*, Vol. 6, pp. 3553–3556.

Ogawa, M., Ito, K. & Shibata, T. (2002). A general-purpose vector-quantization processor employing two-dimensional bit-propagating winner-take-all, *Digest of Technical Papers of 2002 Symposium on VLSI Circuits*, Honolulu, HI, pp. 244–247.

Osuna, E., Freund, R. & Girosi, F. (1997). Training support vector machines: an application to face detection, *Proc. IEEE International Conference on Computer Vision and Pattern Recognition 1997*, San Juan, Puerto Rico, pp. 130–136.

Rowley, H., Baluja, S. & Kanade, T. (1998a). Neural network-based face detection, *IEEE Trans. Pattern Anal. Machine Intell.* 20(1): 23–38.

Rowley, H., Baluja, S. & Kanade, T. (1998b). Rotation invariant neural network-based face detection, *Proc. IEEE International Conference on Computer Vision and Pattern Recognition 1998*, Santa Barbara, CA, pp. 38–44.

Samaria, F. & Harter, A. (1994). Parameterisation of a stochastic model for human face identification, *Proc. 2nd IEEE Workshop on Applications of Computer Vision*, Sarasota, FL, pp. 138–142.

Shibata, T. (2002). Intelligent signal processing based on a psychologically-inspired VLSI brain model, *IEICE Trans. Fundamentals* E85-A(3): 600–609.

Shibata, T. (2007). A VLSI brain system mimicking the processing in the mind, *Proc. COE Symp. Advanced Electronics for Future Generations*, Tokyo, Japan, pp. 183–191.

Shibata, T., Yagi, M. & Adachi, M. (1999). Soft-computing integrated circuits for intelligent information processing, *Proc. 2nd International Conference on Information Fusion*, Vol. 1, Sunnyvale, CA, pp. 648–656.

Sung, K. & Poggio, T. (1998). Example-based learning for view-based human face detection, *IEEE Trans. Pattern Anal. Machine Intell.* 20(1): 39–51.

Suzuki, Y. & Shibata, T. (2004). Multiple-clue face detection algorithm using edge-based feature vectors, *Proc. IEEE International Conference on Accoustic Conference on Acoustics, Speech, and Signal Processing (ICASSP 2004)*, Vol. 5, Montreal, Canada, pp. 737–740.

Suzuki, Y. & Shibata, T. (2007). A hardware architecture for pseudo-2d hidden-Markov-model-based face recognition systems employing Laplace distribution functions, *Japanese Journal of Applied Physics* 46(4B).

Takahashi, N., Fujita, K. & Shibata, T. (2009). A pixel-parallel self-similitude processing for multiple-resolution edge-filtering analog image sensors, *IEEE Trans. Circuits and Systems-I* 56(11): 2384–2392.

Viola, P. & Jones, M. J. (2004). Robust real-time face detection, *International Journal of Computer Vision* 57(2): 137–154.

Yagi, M., Adachi, M. & Shibata, T. (2000). A hardware-friendly soft-computing algorithm for image recognition, *Proc. European Signal Processing Conference (EUSIPCO 2000)*, Tampere, Finland, pp. 729–732.

Yagi, M. & Shibata, T. (2002). Human-perception-like image recognition system based on the associative processor architecture, *Proc. European Signal Processing Conference (EUSIPCO 2002)*, Toulouse, France, pp. 103–106.

Yagi, M. & Shibata, T. (2003). An image representation algorithm compatible with neural-associative-processor-based hardware recognition systems, *IEEE Trans. Neural Networks* 14(5): 1144–1161.

Yamasaki, H. & Shibata, T. (2007). A real-time image-feature-extraction and vector-generation VLSI employing arrayed-shift-register architecture, *IEEE J. Solid-State Circuits* 42(9): 2046–2053.

Yamasaki, T. & Shibata, T. (2003). Analog soft-pattern-matching classifier using floating-gate MOS technology, *IEEE Trans. Neural Networks* 14(5): 1257–1265.

Yang, M. H., Kriegman, D. J. & Ahuja, N. (2002). Detecting faces in images: a survey, *IEEE Trans. Pattern Anal. Machine Intell.* 24(1): 34–58.

12

Automatic Optical and Infrared Image Registration for Plant Water Stress Sensing

Weiping Yang[1], Zhilong Zhang[1], Xuezhi Wang[2], Bill Moran[2], Ashley Wheaton[3] and Nicola Cooley[3]
[1]School of Electronic Science & Engineering, National University of Defense Technology, Hunan, 410073,
[2]Melbourne Systems Laboratory, Faculty of Engineering, University of Melbourne, Vic, 3010,
[3]Melbourne School of Land and Environment, University of Melbourne, Vic 3010,
[1]China
[2,3]Australia

1. Introduction

In many countries around the world, about 70% of water resource will be used to for agriculture irrigation each year. Precisely control irrigation can significantly reduce the waste of irrigation water while increasing plant productivity. Automated sensing of plant water status via non-destructive, automatic techniques plays a central role in such irrigation control system development. Plant canopy temperature acts as a good indicator of the plant water status. When plants experience water stress, their temperature increases. A novel approach to irrigation scheduling and thus, potential water savings, is to monitor plant temperature and relate to the plants water status. To say further, if we want to know the plant water status, we need to know the canopy temperature at first. Recent research in agriculture indicates that plant water status may be monitored if the canopy temperature distribution of the plant is known (Jones, 1999a,b; Jones and Leinonen, 2003; Guilioni, et al., 2008; Grant, et al., 2007; Wheaton et al., 2007). Plant water status information can be obtained via the computation of the crop water stress index (CWSI) (Jones, 1999a). This index offers great potential to generate an automated irrigation control system where plant canopy temperature distribution is acquired via thermal imaging. Such a system is expected to be able to optimize irrigation water usage and the potential to maintain plant health in real time, thus increasing the productivity of limited water resources.
Typically, measurement data of the infrared (IR) thermography sensing system consists of a reference optical image and an IR image. The optical image is obtained by using a normal digital camera and is taken at the same location as the IR image to provide a true view of the IR image scene, one may identify the area of interest (e.g., plant leaves other than ground or sky) from the optical image. The optical image allows the underlying plant canopy of interest to be flawlessly identified. To quantify plant water stress, the value of CWSI is calculated based on the canopy temperature, and temperatures of a dry and wet reference surface. These temperatures can be estimated once the temperature distribution of the

canopy leaf area is obtained. Clearly, for automatic determination of plant canopy temperature, the detection of the overlap area between the pair of IR and optical images plays a central role in the plant canopy temperature acquisition in a program for the automatic controlled irrigation program. Preliminary results from recent work (Wang et al., 2010a,b) indicates that the accuracy of canopy temperature distribution estimation, for the evaluation of the plant water stress, strongly depends on the accuracy of optical and IR image fusion registration. But using nondestructive optical image sensing technique to obtain the canopy temperature is challenging. The first step is to automatically register the infrared image with the optical image, then extract the temperature of the interested regions, and finally can get the temperature estimation of the canopy. However, the exact canopy temperature can not be acquired only by using optical image or by using IR image. Thus image fusion registration between optical and IR image becomes vitally necessary.

Algorithms for image registration are numerous and widely available, for example, cross correlation (Tsai & Lin, 2003), mutual information(Roche, et al., 1998), correlation ratio(Klein，2007), and SIFT based methods(Chen & Tian, 2009). There are also some fast algorithms such as automatic registration approach based on point features(Yu, et al., 2008), automatic image registration algorithm with sub-pixel accuracy(Althof, et. al., 1997) and using importance sampling(Bhagalia, et al., 2009), etc. Image registration has been applied across a range of domains. For example, medical image registration to assisted clinical diagnosis, and remote sensing image fusion registration for multi-band images.

Although many effective image registration algorithms exist, in order to align images from different sources and formats, further algorithm refinement is required. The major difficulties which arise when intensive images are used for image registration are listed below:

- Images are taken by different sensors and possibly at different view angles and different times.
- At the overlap area the intensities of both images can be quite different. Therefore, approaches involving image intensity are unlikely to obtain satisfactory registration.
- Apart from some similarity in overall structure, it is difficult to identify consistent feature points from both images in some popular feature spaces via an automatic registration method, such as the scale invariant feature transformation (SIFT) method.

Image registration algorithms fundamentally fall into two main categories, i.e., area-based methods and feature-based methods. The SIFT method perhaps is the most representative approach in the feature-based automatic methods. The SIFT implementation is able to find distinctive points that are invariant to location, scale and rotation, and robust to affine transformations (changes in scale, rotation, shear, and position) and changes in illumination for images of the same source or of the same type of sensors. When this is the case, the algorithm is particularly effective. However, for our application the success rate of SIFT is less than 10%. Fig 1 demonstrates the SIFT based methods cannot get enough matching key points so the image registration process is not effective. The main reason is that the objects of interest are not rigid in this kind of image registration application.

Solutions based on area correlation techniques seem to be more applicable to the problem presented in Fig 1. Exception however, are those which use intensity (or color) dependent functions as similarity measures, such as the Fourier transformation type and mutual information type approaches.

(a) (b)

(c) (d)

Fig. 1. Results of SIFT based registration algorithm (no matching key-points) (a) 5906 keypoints found in optical image, (b) 447 keypoints found in IR image, (c) 5666 keypoints found in optical image, (d) 605 keypoints found in IR image

Instead of using cross correlation coefficient, Huttenlocher et al,(1993) used the Hausdorff distance as a similarity measure to register binary images that are the output of an edge detector(Huttenlocher, et al., 1993).. To deal with the problem of multimodality medical image registration, Maes et al, (1997) proposed a method which applies mutual information (MI) to measure the statistical dependence or information redundancy between the image intensities of corresponding pixels in both images. Using correlation ratio (CR) as the similarity measure, Roche et al, (1998) proposed a CR method which assumes the pixel-pair intensities between two registered images are functional dependent. These area-based methods were summarized in Lau et al., (2001).

A variety of image registration techniques and algorithms were tested in reference to their fast realization (Yang et al., 2009). Though the SIFT based methods have good effects in many applications, they are usually used to process rigid objects and same source image pairs registration. Here the main objects in the images are leaves which move over time, which can result in the same source images (IR & optical) containing different imaging characteristics.

Yang et al, (2009) suggested that because of the existing differences between optical and infrared images, an algorithm should edge the images at first, then use an image registration method to process the edge images. Because the standard cross correlation (NCC-- normalized cross correlation) method is slow, the variable resolution method based on

normalized cross correlation may be the best choice. Experiments show that the variable resolution normalized cross correlation method has not only the same good registration results, but also fast running speed, taking one fortieth the time compared to the standard cross correlation method (Yang et al, 2009). Among several image registration methods such as NMI(Normalized Mutual Information), CR(Correlation Ratio) and NCC, the variable resolution normalized cross correlation has the overall best performance.
Chapters are organized as follows:
Section 2 the algorithm is described and the flow diagram is given; Section 3 is the implementation of the above algorithm; The experimental results are presented in Section 4, followed by Section 5 Discussion and Section 6 Conclusion.

2. Variable resolution algorithm based on normalized cross correlation

By monitoring plant canopy temperature and the temperatures of wet and dry leaves, it is possible to estimate the underlying plant water stress status and therefore, intelligently control the related irrigation process. Fig. 2 illustrates a typical plant irrigation strategy, where the plant water status information acquired (inside the dotted box) plays a critical role in the optimization of plant productivity and water usage. As a key link of nondestructive plant water status monitoring processing, image registration method plays an important role. Via image registration from the optical and IR image pair, the plant canopy temperature can be acquired. Then by using expected maximum value method, the wet and dry leaf temperatures can be determined via image fusion between the optical and IR image (Wang et al, 2010a). Colour of canopy, and wet and dry leaves, plays an important role as green sunlit leave transpire most the plants water. Thus, the green leaf areas are correlated with their corresponding IR image data.

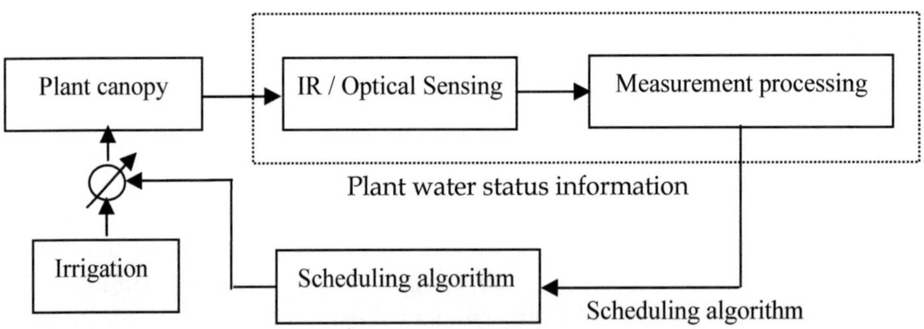

Fig. 2. Illustration of irrigation actuation via a plant based sensor

To register an IR image to a reference optical image, its location and rotation angle should be obtained. When the IR image is wholly overlapped by the reference optical image, it can be assumed that the space resolution of the two images is the same. A flow diagram of the variable resolution algorithm based on normalized cross correlation is shown in Fig 3.
Because the algorithm needs to calculate the correlation coefficient pixel by pixel, the normalized cross correlation (NCC) method is time expensive. In order to resolve the slow running speed, several methods can be tested, for example, the Sequential Similarity Detection Algorithm(SSDA), the Bit Plane Correlation Algorithm(BPCA), the Variable Resolution Correlation Algorithm(VRCA). Here, the Variable resolution correlation algorithm is used to accelerate it. The key steps in the variable resolution algorithm are: a)

reduce the image resolution, b) roughly register the lower resolution images, and c) register images more accurately at the possible positions in the full resolution images.
Suppose Im_O and Im_{IR} (image size is M×N) stands for the optical and IR image respectively, f is the image zoom factor, Im_{Ol} and Im_{IRl} (image size is Mh×Nh) stands for the lower resolution images, accordingly, Im_{Oe}, Im_{IRe}, Im_{Ole}, Im_{IRle} are the edged images of the corresponding images, then the generalize cross correlation can be expressed as:

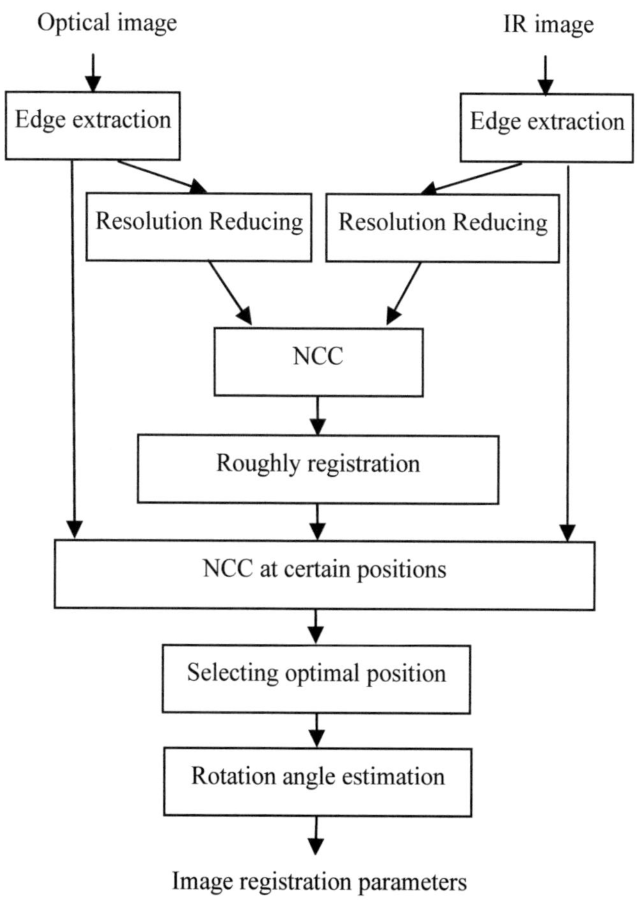

Fig. 3. Flow diagram of variable resolution algorithm based on NCC

$$\rho_l(u,v) = \frac{\sum_{i=0}^{Mh}\sum_{j=0}^{Nh}(\mathrm{Im}_{Oleu,v}(i,j) - \mathrm{Im}_{IRle}(i,j))}{\sigma_{Olu,v}\sigma_{IRl}} \tag{1}$$

$$\rho(k,l) = \frac{\sum_{i=0}^{M}\sum_{j=0}^{N}(\mathrm{Im}_{Oek,l}(i,j) - \mathrm{Im}_{IRe}(i,j))}{\sigma_{Ok,l}\sigma_{IR}} \tag{2}$$

where $\rho_l(u,v)$ is the cross correlation coefficient calculated from the lower resolution image pair Im_{Ole} and Im_{IRle}, (u,v) is the coordinate index of the optical image Im_{Ole}, $Im_{Oleu,v}$ is an image located in (u,v)th of the image Im_{Ole} and its size is the same as image Im_{IRle}, $\sigma_{Olu,v}$ and σ_{IRl} are the standard deviation of the corresponding images respectively; $\rho(k,l)$ is the cross correlation coefficient calculated from the raw resolution image pair Im_{Oe} and Im_{IRe}, (k,l) is the coordinate index of the optical image Im_{Oe}, $Im_{Oek,l}$ is an image located in (k,l)th of the image Im_{Oe} and its size is the same as image Im_{IRe}, $\sigma_{Ok,l}$ and σ_{IR} are the standard deviation of the corresponding images respectively.

In our case, f is set to 2, and the search strategy in the lower resolution layer is perform once rough image registration process for every 2x2pixels. The search strategy in the original resolution layer is to perform a pixel by pixel based image registration in the neighboring area of the rough registration position spanning 4 pixels for each direction.

3. Algorithm implementation of the variable resolution algorithm

(a) (b)

Fig. 4. One image pair (a) An optical image, (b) An IR image

The first stage of algorithm implementation is is edge extraction, which plays an important role in the image registration between different image sources. There are many methods on edge detection and extraction; such as Prewitt, Sobel, Robert operators and Canny algorithm, and so on. As the above mentioned, the infrared image is different with the reference optical image (see Fig 4, the resolution of the optical image is 2848*2136pixels, the resolution of the IR image is 320*240pixels), having a lower resolution, less details, and therefore it will need to reserve its edge information which are the common features in both Infrared and optical images (if they are in the same scene) while conducting the edge processing. Here the edge operation is based on the modified Sobel operators (There are four operators unlike the normal two operators with horizontal and vertical one) and they can be described as follows,

$$S_1 = \begin{bmatrix} 1 & 0 & -1 \\ 2 & 0 & -2 \\ 1 & 0 & -1 \end{bmatrix},\ S_2 = \begin{bmatrix} 1 & 2 & 1 \\ 0 & 0 & 0 \\ -1 & -2 & -1 \end{bmatrix} \tag{3a}$$

$$S_3 = \begin{bmatrix} 2 & 1 & 0 \\ 1 & 0 & -1 \\ 0 & -1 & -2 \end{bmatrix},\ S_4 = \begin{bmatrix} 0 & 1 & 2 \\ -1 & 0 & 1 \\ -2 & -1 & 0 \end{bmatrix} \tag{3b}$$

Using these four operators to convolute with the raw images, we can resolove

$$E_k(i,j) = \sum_{m=0}^{2}\sum_{n=0}^{2} \mathrm{Im}(i+m-1, j+n-1) * S_k(m,n) \qquad k=1,2,3,4 \tag{4}$$

$$E(i,j) = \max_k E_k(i,j) \tag{5}$$

Where $E(i,j)$ is the edge of the point (i,j) of image Im.

After edge detection, the edged image Im_{Oe} , Im_{IRe} , Im_{Ole} , Im_{IRle}, is processed using NCC algorithm to do the rough registration. On account of possible disturbing, we choose the some points with the former higher correlation coefficients marked as $\{(u_k, v_k)\}$.

The candidate points $\{(u_k, v_k)\}$ are obtained. The next step is to acquire accurate image registration is then performed in a small neighboring area in the full resolution images. Here we adopt a weighted coefficient c to ensure that the final point with the maximum correlation coefficient is the optimal one.

$$\rho_k = c\rho_l(u_k, v_k) + (1-c)\rho(u'_k, v'_k) \tag{6}$$

$$\rho_{k^*} = \max_k \rho_k \tag{7}$$

Where (u'_k, v'_k) is the point position in the full resolution image Im_{Oe} and $\rho(u'_k, v'_k)$ is the correlation coefficient of accurate image registration, $\rho_l(u_k, v_k)$ is the correlation coefficient of rough image registration. Through this step registration position (u'_{k^*}, v'_{k^*}) is obtained.

The final step is the estimation of rotation angle. In our case, the permitted rotation angle θ range is from -10°to 10°. The range is divided into 200 small angles. To each angle, its correlation coefficient is calculated, followed by an angle θ^* with the maximum correlation value.

4. Experiment results

The above algorithm was tested using many image pairs. As shown in Fig 5, all the results are successful with tolerable errors. In order to compare the algorithm run time, the experiment has been done using both the variable resolution algorithm and the standard NCC algorithm in an identical condition, and the results are shown in Table 1. Results illustrate that the variable resolution algorithm can achieve the same acceptable registration criteria as the standard NCC but with a fast speed, i.e., it requires less than one fortieth running time compared with the standard NCC algorithm. Because we do not know the true registration positions, need to compare them against the results of the manual registration. In order to verify the variable resolution method, the NMI and CR algorithms are tested concurrently. Results indicate that the NMI method almost has the same consistent results as that of the proposed algorithm, but the results of CR method are poor. Under the variable resolution technique, both NMI and CR methods require a higher computational load, for example, the run time of NMI algorithm is several times longer than the fast NCC one. If the calculated amount is disregarded, the NMI method may be the alternative method for this application.

	Number of Image pairs	Success number	Running time per pair (average)	Registration error (max, min, average)
Standard NCC	20	20	610s	(6,0,2.6)
Variable resolution algorithm	20	20	15s	(6,0,2.6)

Table 1. Experiment results of variable resolution algorithm based on NCC

Fig. 5. Image pairs and their registration results (a) Image pair 1(Optical(left),IR(right)), (b) Registration result of image pair 1(287,299,0.2), (c) Image pair 2(Optical(left),IR(right)), (d) Registration result of image pair 2(343,166,0)

In the NMI method the correlation matrix $R_{NMI}(u,v)$ is calculated by

$$R_{NMI}(u,v)=\frac{\sum_{i}(P_{uv}(i)\log P_{uv}(i)+P_{IR}(i)\log P_{IR}(i))}{\sum_{i,j}P_{OIRuv}(i,j)\log P_{OIRuv}(i,j)} \tag{8}$$

where $P_{OIRuv}(i,j)$ is the joint probability that the intensities of Im_{uv} and Im_{IR} are at levels i and j respectively. P_{uv} and P_{IR} are the marginal probability of the images Im_{uv} and Im_{IR}. Im_{uv} is the (u,v)th sub-image of optical image Im_O with the same size as the infrared image Im_{IR}. These probabilities can be computed from the normalized joint and marginal intensity histograms.
In the CR method the correlation matrix $R_{CR}(u,v)$ is calculated by

$$R_{CR}=1-\frac{1}{Var_{IR}}\sum_{i}Var_{uv}(i)P_{uv}(i) \tag{9}$$

where

$$Var_{IR}=\sum_{i}i^2P_{IR}^2(i)-\left(\sum_{i}iP_{IR}(i)\right)^2$$

and

$$Var_{uv}(i)=\frac{1}{P_{uv}(i)}\sum_{j}j^2P_{OIRuv}^2(i,j)-\left(\frac{1}{P_{uv}(i)}\sum_{j}jP_{OIRuv}(i,j)\right)^2$$

All summations in (8) and (9) are taken over image intensity space.

	Number of Image pairs	Success* number	Registration error (max, min, average)
Variable resolution algorithm	10	10	(6,0,2.6)
NMI algorithm	10	8	(9,0,2.7)
CR algorithm	10	0	Null

Table 2. Experiment results of several different algorithms
Remark: * stands for that a successful registration is whose position error is less than 10 pixels.

Fig. 6. Image pairs and their registration results using different algorithms (a) Image pair 1(Optical(left),IR(right)), (b) Registration result 1 of Variable resolution algorithm (299,120,0.8), (c) Registration result 1 of NMI algorithm (304,125,-0.5), (d) Registration result 1 of CR algorithm (318,257,0.5), (e) Image Pair 2(Optical(left),IR(right)), (f) Registration result 2 of Variable resolution algorithm (364,153,1.5), (g) Registration result 1 of NMI algorithm (362,157,1.0), (h) Registration result 1 of CR algorithm (283,93,3.9)

All of the tests are done in the condition of f = 2 and using Sobel operator to get the image edges. The contrasting experiments with the NMI (normalized mutual information) and CR(correlation ratio) algorithms have also been done(Fig 6, Table 2). From these figures and tables, we can see the variable resolution algorithm based on normalized cross correlation is the best choice. Fig 7 and Table 3 show that the variable resolution algorithm based on Sobel edge operators is a little inferior to Canny edge based algorithm, but it is a compromising solution with easier realization and higher running efficiency.

(a)

(b)

(c)

(d))

Fig. 7. Tests of variable resolution algorithm based on different edge extraction methods (a) Optical raw image(left) and infrared raw image(right), (b) Results of edge extraction using Canny algorithm(left) and registration result (266,254,-0.4), (c) Results of edge extraction using Roberts operators(left) and registration result (265,253,1.8), (d) Results of edge extraction using Sobel Operators(left) and registration result (265,256,1.1)

Edge extraction \ Type	Number of successful registration	Registration location error (maximum, minimum, average)
Sobel based edge	10	(6,0,2.8)
Canny edge extraction	10	(6,0,2.6)
Roberts based edge	10	(9,0,3.2)

Table 3. Image registration results based different edge extraction methods(10 image pairs)

5. Discussion

Our experiment results suggest that NMI and CR algorithms are unsuitable for image registration of different sources because these two methods are dependent on the intensity distributions of the images which is of different values in the input images, while the proposed algorithm considers the edge feature which is common to both images involved and is independent of the image intensities. The image registration methods base on SIFT are also unsuitable to our application because the common key points can rear. The important reason is that the key points are largely dependent on the image intensities.

With regard to computational efficiency, although the images are only zoomed out at 2 times, computational load is significantly reduced. The variable resolution algorithm can run about 40 times faster than the standard pixel by pixel cross correlation method without registration performance degradation.

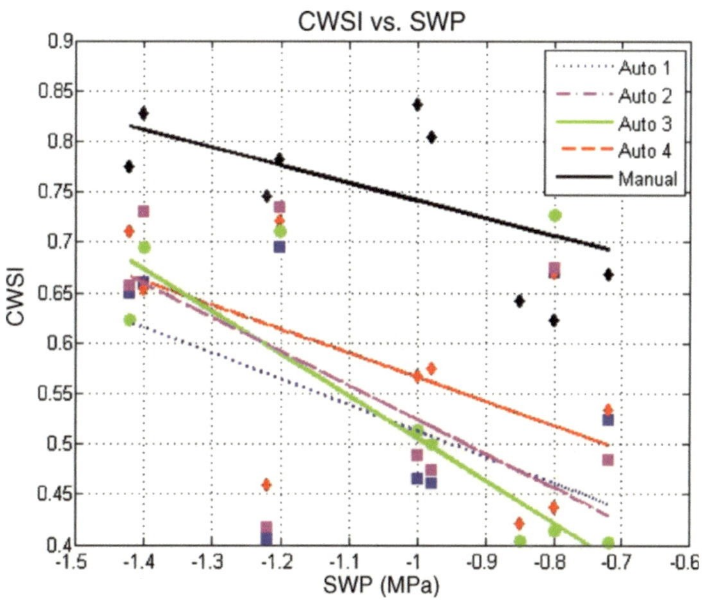

Fig. 8. Comparison of linear regression of CWSI calculated using different methods and conditions versus stem water potential (SWP)

As demonstrated in the experiment results, the rapid NCC algorithm implementation is able to achieve the same registration accuracy as the standard NCC implementation. Once an image pair is registered, the plant water status information can be estimated via the method in (Wang et. al. 2010a), where it is evidenced that the accuracy of the IR and optical image registration may have significant influence to the canopy temperature estimation. Fig 8 illustrates the experiment results presented in (Wang, et al., 2010a) which verifies that the trend of the computed CWSI is consistent with an alternative plant water stress indicator, the SWP data.

6. Conclusion

The chapter presented a fast realization algorithm of automatic optical and infrared image registration. It reduces the computation considerably by utilizing variable resolution algorithm without sacrificing registration performance. It can also be used in other applications. As we mentioned above, the image registration is only the first stage in the process to estimate the canopy temperature. We are developing methods to obtain more accurate registration and how to construct a algorithm suit to allow for more variation in the background images.

It is our aim to continue research in this field towards a decision support system to deliver real time automated irrigation control based on CWSI where the 'plant is the sensor'.

7. References

Jones, H.G. (1999a). Use of thermography for quantitative studies of spatial and temporal variation of stomatal conductance over leaf surfaces. Journal of Plant, Cell and Environment, Vol. 22, No.9, (September 1999), pp.1043–1055, ISSN 1365-3040.

Jones, H.G. (1999b). Use of infrared thermometry for estimation of stomatal conductance as a possible aid to irrigation scheduling. Journal of Agricultural and Forest Meteorology, Vol. 95 , No.3, (June 1999) , pp. 139-149, ISSN 1461-9563.

Jones, H.G., Leinonen, I. (2003). Thermal imaging for the study of plant water relations. Journal of Agricultural Meteorology, Vol.59, No.3, (September 2003), pp. 205–217, ISSN 0021-8588.

Guilioni, L.; Jones, H.G.; Leinonen, I.; Lhomme, J.P. (2008). On the relationships between stomatal resistance and leaf temperatures in thermography. Journal of Agricultural and Forest Meteorology, Vol.148 , No. 11, (October 2008), pp. 1908 - 1912, ISSN 1461-9563.

Grant, O.; Tronina1, L.; Jones, H. G.; Chaves, M. M. (2007). Exploring thermal imaging variables for the detection of stress responses in grapevine under different irrigation regimes. Journal of Experimental Botany, Vol.58, No.4, (March 2007), pp. 815–825, ISSN 0022-0957.

Wheaton, A.D., Cooley, N., Dunn, G., Goodwin, I., Needs, S. (2007). Evaluation of infrared thermography to determine the crop water status of Cabernet Sauvignon grapevines. Proceedings of The 13th Australian Wine Industry Technical Conference, Adelaide, 28 July – 2 August, 2007.

Wang, X.Z.; Yang, W.P.; Wheaton A.D.; Cooley, N.; Moran, B. (2010a). Automated canopy temperature estimation via infrared thermography: A first step towards automated plant water stress monitoring. Journal of Computers and Electronics in Agriculture, Vol. 73, No.1 , (July 2010), pp. 74-83, ISSN 0168-1699.

Wang, X.Z.; Yang, W.P.; Wheaton A.D.; Cooley, N.; Moran, B. (2010b). Efficient Registration of Optical and IR images for Automatic Plant Water Stress Assessment. Journal of Computers and Electronics in Agriculture, Vol. 74, No.2 , (November 2010), pp. 230-237, ISSN 0168-1699.

Tsai, D. M.; Lin, C. T. (2003). Fast normalized cross correlation for defect detection. Journal of Pattern Recognition Letters, Vol.24, No.15, (November 2003), pp. 2625–2631, ISSN 0167-8655.

Roche, A.; Malandain, G.; etc. (1998). The correlation ratio as a new similarity measure for multimodal image registration. Medical Image Computing and Computer Assisted Intervention - MICCAI'98, Vol.1496, pp1115-1124, Boston, USA, October, 1998.

Klein S.; Staring, M.; Pluim, J.P.W. (2007). Evaluation of Optimization Methods for Nonrigid Medical Image Registration Using Mutual Information and B-Splines. IEEE Transactions on Image Processing, Vol.16, No.12, (December 2007), pp.2879-2890, ISSN 1057-7149.

Chen, J.; Tian, J. (2009). Real-time multi-modal rigid registration based on a novel symmetric-SIFT descriptor. Progress in Natural Science, Vol.19, No.5, (May 2009), pp. 643–651, ISSN 1002-0071.

Yang, W.P.; Wang, X.Z.; etc. (2009). Automatic optical and IR image fusion for plant water stress analysis, Proceedings of The 12th International Conference on Information Fusion, pp. 1053-1059, Seattle, 6-9 July 2009.

Yu, L.; Zhang D.R.; Holden E.J. (2008). A fast and fully automatic registration approach based on point features for multi-source remote-sensing images. Journal of Computers & Geosciences , Vol.34, No.7, (July 2008), pp. 838–848, ISSN 0098-3004.

Althof, R. J.; Wind, M.G.J.; Dobbins, J.T. (1997). A Rapid and Automatic Image Registration Algorithm with Subpixel Accuracy, IEEE TRANS ON MEDICAL IMAGING, Vol.16, No.3, (June 1997), pp. 308-316, ISSN 0278-0062.

Bhagalia, R.; Fessler,J. A.; Kim,B. (2009). Accelerated nonrigid intensity-based image registration using importance sampling. IEEE TRANS ON MEDICAL IMAGING, Vol. 28, No.8, (August 2009), pp.1208-1216, ISSN 0278-0062.

Huttenlocher D. P.; Klanderman, G. A.; Rucklidge. W. J. (1993). Comparing images using the Hausdorff distance, IEEE Trans. on Pattern Analysis and Machine Intelligence, Vol. 15, No. 9, (September 1993), pp. 850–863, ISSN 0162-8828.

Maes, F.; Collignon, A.; Vandermeulen, D.; etc., (1997). Multimodality image registration by maximisation of mutual information", IEEE Trans. on Medical Imaging, Vol. 16, No.2,(April 1997), pp. 187–198, ISSN 0278-0062.

Lau, Y.H.; Braun, M.; Hutton, B. F. (2001). Non-rigid image registration using a median-filtered coarse-to-fine displacement field and a symmetric correlation ratio, Journal of Physics in Medicine and Biology, Vol. 46, No.4, (April 2001), pp. 1297-1319, ISSN 0031-9155.